Matt

TAKING SIDES

Clashing Views in

Cultural Anthropology

SECOND EDITION

Selected, Edited, and with Introductions by

Robert L. Welsch
Dartmouth College

and

Kirk M. Endicott
Dartmouth College

D0401312

McGraw-Hill/Contemporary Learning Series
A Division of The McGraw-Hill Companies

For Sarah and Karen

Photo Acknowledgment
Cover image: Kent Knudson/PhotoLink/Getty Images

Cover Acknowledgment
Maggie Lytle

Manufactured in the United States of America

Second Edition

123456789DOCDOC98765

Library of Congress Cataloging-in-Publication Data
Main entry under title:
Taking sides: clashing views in cultural anthropology/selected, edited, and with introductions by
Robert L. Welsch and Kirk M. Endicott.—2nd ed.
Includes bibliographical references and index.
1. Anthropology, cultural. 2. Ethnology. I. Welsch, Robert L., ed. II. Endicott, Kirk M., ed.
III. Series.
306
0-07-304396-6
ISSN: 1556-8911

Printed on Recycled Paper

Preface

Many courses and textbooks present cultural anthropology as a discipline that largely consists of well-established facts. In *Taking Sides: Clashing Views in Cultural Anthropology* we present the discipline in quite a different light. Here we focus on active controversies that remain unresolved. These issues represent the kind of arguments and debates that have characterized cultural anthropology for more than a century. They show the varied ways that cultural anthropologists approach the subject of their research and the kinds of anthropological evidence needed to bolster an academic argument.

Generally, we have chosen selections that express strongly worded positions on two sides of an issue. For most issues, several other reasonable positions are also possible, and we have suggested some of these in our introductions and postscripts that accompany each issue. And readers should note that these essays were not written specifically to address our framing of the issues, but were generally written for other purposes.

Taking Sides: Clashing Views in Cultural Anthropology is a tool to encourage and develop critical thinking about anthropological research questions, methods, and evidence. We have selected a range of readings and issues to illustrate the kinds of topics that cultural anthropologists study. Another goal of this volume is to provide opportunities for students to explore how cultural anthropologists frame and defend their interpretations of anthropological evidence. We have chosen issues that raise questions about research methods and the quality or reliability of different kinds of data. All of these complex matters go into shaping the positions that cultural anthropologists debate and defend in their writings. We hope that in discussing these issues students will find opportunities to explore how cultural anthropologists think about the pressing theoretical issues of the day.

Plan of the book This book is made up of 18 issues that deal with topics that have provoked starkly different positions by different cultural anthropologists. We have divided the volume into three parts reflecting three major concerns of the discipline: Theoretical Issues, Some Specific Issues in Cultural Anthropology, and Ethics in Cultural Anthropology. Each issue begins with an *introduction*, which sets the stage for the debate as argued in the YES and NO selections. Following these two selections is a *postscript* that makes some final observations and points the way to other questions related to the issue. In reading an issue and forming your own opinions, you should remember that there are often many alternative perspectives that are not represented in either the YES or NO selections. Most issues have reasonable positions that might appear to be intermediate between the two more extreme viewpoints represented here in the readings. There are also reasonable positions that lie totally outside the scope of the debate presented in these selections, and students should consider all of these possible positions. Each postscript also contains *suggestions for additional reading* that will help you find more resources to continue your study of any topic. Students researching any of these issues or related ones for a research paper will find these additional readings (as well as their bibliographies) a useful place to begin a more intensive analysis. At the end of the book we have also included a list of all the *contributors to this volume*, which will give you information on the anthropologists and other commentators whose views are debated here. An *On the Internet* page accompanies each part opener. This page gives you Internet site addresses (URLs) that are relevant to the issues discussed in that part of the book. Many of these sites contain links to related sites and bibliographies for further study.

Changes to this edition   This edition has been updated to reflect several current and ongoing controversies that can help undergraduates understand the breadth and range of research in cultural anthropology. Five issues are new to this edition "Should Anthropologists Abandon the Concept of Culture?" (Issue 3), "Is Ebonics (Black English) a Distinct Language from Standard English?" (Issue 5), "Does the Natural-Supernatural Distinction Exist in All Cultures?" (Issue 7), "Is Islam a Single Universal Tradition?" (Issue 13), and "Should Anthropologists and Linguists Be Concerned about Losing Endangered Languages?" (Issue 17). In addition, we have selected anew pair of readings to address "Did Napoleon Chagnon and Other Researchers Adversely Affect the Yanomami Indians of Venezuela?" (Issue 16) that bring out the most salient point of the controversy raised by Patrick Tierney's critique of napoleon Chagnon and his colleagues in *Darkness in El Dorado: How Scientists and Journalists Devaststed the Amazon* (W. W. Norton, 2000). We have also added a new reading by Robert L. Carneiro and reframed Issue 1 ("Should Anthropology Stop Trying to Model Itself on the Natural Sciences?"), and we have inserted a new reading on the issue about medical anthropology (Issue 14), "Do Some Illnesses Exist Only Among Members of a Particular Culture?" to make the arguments clearer to undergraduates.

A word to the instructor   An *Instructor's Manual With Test Questions* (multiple-choice and essay) is available for use with *Taking Sides*. Also available is a general guidebook, *Using Taking Sides in the Classroom*, which includes a discussion of techniques for integrating the pro-con format into an existing course. Instructors adopting this text also have access to an online version of *Using Taking Sides in the Classroom* as well as a correspondence service at http://www.mhcls.com/usingts/.

Taking Sides: Clashing Views in Cultural Anthropology is only one of many titles in the Taking Sides series. If you are interested in seeing the table of contents for any of the other titles, please visit the Taking Sides Web site at http://www.mhcls.com/takingsides/.

Acknowledgments   We received many helpful comments and suggestions from many friends and colleagues, including Kamyar Abdi, Hoyt Alverson, Colin Calloway, Elizabeth Carpenter, Brian Didier, Dale Eickelman, Rachel Flemming, Jana Fortier, Laura Garzon, Rosemary Gianno, Paul Goldstein,

Alberto Gomez, Robert Gordon, Allen Hockley, Judy Hunt, Peter Jenks, Sergei Kan, Steve Kangas, Kathryn Keith, Kenneth Korey, Christine Kray, Laura Litton, Lynn MacGillivray, Deborah Martin, Deborah Nichols, Ventura Perez, Lynn Rainville, Kevin Reinhart, John Edward Terrell, Robert Tonkinson, John Watanabe, and Lindsay Whaley. We also want to thank John Cocklin, Ridie Ghezzi, Lucinda Hall, Francis X. Oscadal, Cindy Shirkey, Reinhart Sonnenberg, and Amy Witzel, members of the Baker-Berry Library Reference Department at Dartmouth College, all of whom have helped track down many of the sources and background readings we have used in setting up these issues. We also want to thank our student research assistants Todd Rabkin Golden, Russell Herman, Adam Slutsky, Whitney Wilking, Rachel Yemini, and our Presidential Scholars/student research assistants Eric Goodman, Joseph Hanlon, Tate LeFevre, Nikolas Primack, and Lauren Weldon. Ted Knight and Juliana Gribbins at McGraw-Hill/Dushkin offered useful advice, patience, and suggestions. We also want to thank Nichole Altman of McGraw-Hill in Dubuque, Iowa for her help in making this new edition a reality. Finally, we wish to thank our wives, Sarah L. Welsch and Karen L. Endicott, for their support and encouragement during the preparation of this volume.

Robert L. Welsch
Dartmouth College

Kirk M. Endicott
Dartmouth College

Contents In Brief

Contents

Cultural anthropologist Clifford Geertz views anthropology as a science of interpretation, and he argues that anthropology should never model itself on the natural sciences. He believes that anthropology's goal should be to generate deeper interpretations of cultural phenomena, using what he calls "thick description," rather than attempting to prove or disprove scientific laws. Cultural anthropologist Robert Carneiro argues that anthropology has always been and should continue to be a science that attempts to explain sociocultural phenomena in terms of causes and effects rather than merely interpret them. He criticizes Geertz's cultural interpretations as arbitrary and immune to disconfirmation.

Social anthropologist Derek Freeman argues that Margaret Mead was wrong when she stated that Samoan adolescents had sexual freedom. He contends that Mead went to Samoa determined to prove anthropologist Franz Boas's cultural determinist agenda and states that Mead was so eager to believe in Samoan sexual freedom that she was consistently the victim of a hoax perpetrated by Samoan girls and young women who enjoyed tricking her. Cultural anthropologists Lowell D. Holmes and Ellen Rhoads Holmes contend that Margaret Mead had a very solid understanding of Samoan culture in general. During a restudy of Mead's research, they came to many of the same conclusions that Mead had reached about Samoan sexuality and adolescent experiences. Mead's description of Samoan culture exaggerates the amount of sexual freedom and the degree to which adolescence in Samoa is carefree but these differences, they argue, can be explained in terms of changes in Samoan culture since 1925 and in terms of Mead's relatively unsophisticated research methods as compared with field methods used today.

Cultural anthropologist Lila Abu-Lughod argues that the concept of culture exaggerates the distinctiveness, boundedness, homogeneity, coherence, and timelessness of a society's way of life. In her view, cultural descriptions also place the Western anthropologist in a position superior to the non-Western "other." She suggests that we use descriptions in terms of practices, discourses, connections, and the events of particular people's lives. Cultural anthropologist Christoph Brumann argues that the problems attributed to the culture concept are not inherent to the concept, but are a result of its being misused. He regards culture as a valuable concept for communication and one that is valid as long as we do not exaggerate the degree to which learned concepts, emotions, and practices are shared in a community.

Cultural anthropologist Roger M. Keesing argues that what native peoples in the Pacific now accept as "traditional culture" is largely an invented and idealized vision of their past. He contends that such fictional images emerge because native peoples are largely unfamiliar with what life was really like in pre-Western times and because such imagery distinguishes native communities from dominant Western culture. Hawaiian activist and scholar Haunani-Kay Trask asserts that Keesing's critique is fundamentally flawed because he only uses Western documents—and native peoples have oral traditions, genealogies, and other historical sources that are not reflected in Western historical documents. Anthropologists like Keesing, she maintains, are trying to hold on to their privileged position as experts in the face of growing numbers of educated native scholars.

Linguist Ernie Smith argues that the speech of many African-Americans is a separate language from English because its grammar is derived from the Niger-Congo languages of Africa. Although most of the vocabulary is borrowed from English, the pronunciations and sentence structures are changed to conform to Niger-Congo forms. Therefore, he says, schools should treat Ebonics-speaking students like other non-English-speaking minority students. Linguist John McWhorter counters that Black English is just one of many English dialects spoken in America that are mutually intelligible. He argues that the peculiar features of Black English are derived from the dialects of early settlers from Britain, not from African languages. Because African-American children are already familiar with standard English, he concludes, they do not need special language training.

Issue 6.   Are San Hunter-Gatherers Basically Pastoralists Who Have Lost Their Herds?   107

Archaeologists James R. Denbow and Edwin N. Wilmsen argue that the San of the Kalahari Desert in southern Africa have been involved in pastoralism, agriculture, and regional trade networks since at least A.D. 800. They imply that the San, who were hunting and gathering in the twentieth century, were descendants of pastoralists who lost their herds due to subjugation by outsiders, drought, and livestock disease. Cultural anthropologist Richard B. Lee counters that evidence from oral history, archaeology, and ethnohistory shows that the Ju/'hoansi group of San living in the isolated Nyae Nyae-Dobe area of the Kalahari Desert were autonomous hunter-gatherers until the twentieth century. Although they carried on some trade with outsiders before then, it had minimal impact on their culture.

Issue 7.   Does the Natural-Supernatural Distinction Exist in All Cultures?   129

Cultural anthropologist Roger Ivar Lohmann argues that a supernaturalistic worldview or cosmology is at the heart of virtually all religions. For him the supernatural is a concept that exists everywhere, although it is expressed differently in each society. For him, supernaturalism attributes volition to things that do not have it. He argues that the supernatural is also a part of Western people's daily experience in much the same ways that it is the experience of the Papua New Guineans with whom he worked. Lutheran pastor and anthropological researcher Frederick (Fritz) P. Lampe argues that "supernatural" is a problematic and inappropriate term like the term "primitive." If we accept the term "supernatural," it is all too easy to become ethnocentric and assume that anything supernatural is unreal, and therefore false. He considers a case at the University of Technology in Papua New Guinea to show how use of the term "supernatural" allows us to miss out on how Papua New Guineans actually understand the world in logical, rational, and naturalistic terms that Westerners would generally see as illogical, irrational, and supernaturalistic.

Adoptee and adoption rights advocate Betty Jean Lifton argues that there is a natural need for human beings to know where they came from. Adoption is not a natural human state, she asserts, and it is surrounded by a secrecy that leads to severe social and psychological consequences for adoptees, adoptive parents, and birth parents. Anthropologists John Terrell and Judith Modell, who are each the parent of an adopted child, contend that the "need" to know one's birth parents is an American (or Western European) cultural construct. They conclude that in other parts of the world, where there is less emphasis placed on biology, adoptees have none of the problems said to be associated with being adopted in America.

Cultural anthropologist Maria Lepowsky argues that among the Vanatinai people of Papua New Guinea, the sexes are basically equal, although minor areas of male advantage exist. Men and women both have personal autonomy; they both have similar access to material possessions, influence, and prestige; and the activities and qualities of males and females are valued equally. Sociologist Steven Goldberg contends that in all societies men occupy most high positions in hierarchical organizations and most high-status roles, and they dominate women in interpersonal relations. He states that this is because men's hormones cause them to compete more strongly than women for high status and dominance.

Iranian historian Parvin Paidar considers how the position of women suffered following the 1979 Iranian Revolution because of the imposition of Islamic law (*shari'a*), as interpreted by conservative male clerics. She contends that the Islamic Revolution marked a setback in the progressive modernist movements, which had improved women's rights during the secular regime of the Shah; new rights and opportunities have emerged since 1979 only in opposition to conservative interpretations of Islamic law. American anthropologist Erika Friedl asserts that men in Iran have consistently tried to suppress women's rights since the 1979 Iranian Revolution. Despite these efforts to repress them, women in all levels of society have access to many sources of power. In fact, argues Friedl, women have considerably more power available to them than either Western or Iranian stereotypes might suggest, even though they must work within Islamic law to obtain this power.

Anthropologist and sociobiologist Napoleon A. Chagnon argues that the high incidence of violence and warfare he observed among the Yanomami in the 1960s was directly related to man's inherent drive toward reproductive fitness (i.e., the innate biological drive to have as many offspring as possible). For Chagnon, the Yanomami provide an excellent test of this sociobiological principle because the Yanomami were virtually unaffected by Western colonial expansion and exhibited intense competition for wives. Anthropologist and cultural materialist R. Brian Ferguson counters that the high incidence of warfare and violence observed by Chagnon in the 1960s was a direct result of contact with Westerners at mission and government stations. Fighting arose in an effort to gain access to steel tools that were increasingly important to the community. Ferguson asserts that fighting is a direct result of colonial circumstances rather than biological drives.

Indian social researcher Sudhir Kakar analyzes the origins of ethnic conflict from a psychological perspective to argue that ethnic differences are deeply held distinctions that from time to time will inevitably erupt as ethnic conflicts. He maintains that anxiety arises from preconscious fears about cultural differences. In his view, no amount of education or politically correct behavior will eradicate these fears and anxieties about people of differing ethnic backgrounds. American sociologist Anthony Oberschall considers the ethnic conflicts that have recently emerged in Bosnia and contends that primordial ethnic attachments are insufficient to explain the sudden emergence of violence among Bosnian ethnic groups. He adopts a complex explanation for this violence, identifying circumstances in which fears and anxieties were manipulated by politicians for self-serving ends. It was only in the context of these manipulations that ethnic violence could have erupted, concludes Oberschall.

Historian Francis Robinson argues that Islam is a single, universal tradition, whose proper practices and beliefs can best be understood from the study of religious texts. Islam as practiced in many local communities in India may have numerous syncretic elements borrowed from Hinduism. But these syncretic elements should best be understood as errors in belief and practice that will eventually be weeded out from the single, authentic religious tradition. Indian sociologist Veena Das counters that the numerous syncretic traditions of Islam found in India and other countries represent important religious differences. Emphasis on textual analysis misses the point that religion as lived and practiced is fundamentally different in various local traditions. Such differences are not likely to disappear through continuing contact with religious leaders in Mecca or other Islamic centers because interpretation will always introduce religious innovation and variation.

Physician Sangun Suwanlert from Thailand asks whether or not one particular illness he observed in northern Thai villages, called *phii pob*, corresponds to Western diagnostic categories or is restricted to Thailand. After documenting how this condition does not fit standard psychiatric diagnoses, he concludes that *phii pob* is indeed a "culture-bound syndrome" that can only occur among people who share rural Thai cultural values and beliefs. Medical anthropologist Robert A. Hahn counters that the very idea of the so-called culture-bound syndrome is flawed. He contends that culture-bound syndromes are reductionist explanations for certain complex illness conditions—that is, explanations that reduce complex phenomena to a single variable. Hahn suggests that such conditions are like any illness condition; they are not so much peculiar diseases but distinctive local cultural expressions of much more common illness conditions that can be found in any culture.

Postmodernist anthropologist James Clifford argues that the very act of removing objects from their ethnographic contexts distorts the meaning of objects held in museums. He contends that whether these objects are displayed in art museums or anthropological   museums, exhibitions misrepresent ethnic communities by omitting important aspects of contemporary life, especially involvement with the colonial or Western world. Anthropologist Denis Dutton asserts that no exhibition can provide a complete context for ethnographic objects, but that does not mean that museum exhibitions are fundamentally flawed. Dutton suggests that postmodernists misunderstand traditional approaches to interpreting museum collections, and what they offer as a replacement actually minimizes what we can understand of ethnic communities from museum collections.

PART 3   ETHICS IN CULTURAL ANTHROPOLOGY   321

Anthropologist Terence Turner contends that journalist Patrick Tierney's book *Darkness in El Dorado* accurately depicts how anthropologist Napoleon Chagnon's research among the Yanomami Indians caused conflict between groups and how Chagnon's portrayal of the Yanomami as extremely violent aided gold miners trying to take over Yanomami land. Anthropologists Edward Hagen, Michael Price, and John Tooby counter that Tierney systematically distorts Chagnon's views on Yanomami violence and exaggerates the amount of disruption caused by Chagnon's activities compared to those of others such as missionaries and gold miners.

Linguist Ken Hale contends that the loss of endangered languages represents a major tragedy for humanity, because each language that goes extinct reduces the world's linguistic diversity. The pace of extinctions has increased over the past century, mostly because government policies routinely encourage language loss. While linguists have a responsibility for recording and documenting endangered languages, they also have a role to play in influencing government policies that can encourage retention of these minority languages. Linguist Peter Ladefoged accepts the fact that endangered languages are disappearing, but feels that the position taken by Ken Hale and his colleagues is unacceptably paternalistic. He contends that while it is a good thing to study linguistic diversity, the people who speak endangered languages have just as much right to participate in their nation's affairs as anyone else, even if it means their children will learn the metropolitan language, not the endangered language.

Professor of the history and philosophy of science Merrilee H. Salmon argues that clitoridectomy (female genital mutilation) violates the rights of the women on whom it is performed. She asserts that this operation is a way for men to control women and keep them unequal. Professor of anthropology Elliott P. Skinner accuses feminists who want to abolish clitoridectomy of being ethnocentric. He states that African women themselves want to participate in the practice, which functions like male initiation, transforming girls into adult women.

Introduction

Studying Cultural Anthropology

Robert L. Welsch
Kirk M. Endicott

Anthropology is the study of humanity in all its biological, social, cultural, and linguistic diversity. It is the broadest social science, encompassing four major subfields—cultural anthropology, prehistoric archaeology, biological anthropology, and anthropological linguistics—and several smaller ones. Cultural anthropology, the topic of this book, is the comparative study of human ways of life. Cultural anthropologists try to explain why these ways of life—cultures —take the form they do and what they mean to the people who follow them. Historically, cultural anthropologists have focused on small-scale non-Western societies, especially tribes and peasant communities, but nowadays they apply their methods and concepts to the study of groups in complex societies as well, such as occupational groups in the United States.

Several features of cultural anthropology distinguish it from other social sciences, like sociology and political science. One feature is the basic method of data collection—*ethnographic field work or participant observation.* Typically, cultural anthropologists live with the people they are studying for a year or more, learn their language, and participate in the daily life of the community as much as possible, thus enabling them to gain a personal understanding of the people and their world. Another feature is the cultural anthropologists' use of the concept of culture—which may be thought of as socially learned ways of acting, thinking, and feeling—both for describing specific ways of life and for analyzing and explaining particular practices and beliefs. Cultural anthropologists attempt to understand a wide variety of practices, ranging from child-rearing techniques to religious rituals, largely in terms of culture and cultural conditioning. Cultural anthropologists also try to understand a culture as a whole rather than focusing on only one or a few subsystems, such as a people's economy or religion. They are interested in how these subsystems fit together to form coherent—or sometimes discordant—wholes. Finally, cultural anthropologists use comparisons between different cultures to try to answer broad questions about similarities and differences in human behavior. They use cross-cultural comparison to look for patterns of association; for example, between certain religions and certain forms of government. Because cultural anthropologists study so many aspects of so many different cultures from so many different points of view, it may seem that no two anthropologists actually study the same things, yet they all are working toward a greater understanding of the cultural capabilities and productions of the human species.

Cultural anthropology as we know it today (called *social anthropology* in Great Britain) developed in the late nineteenth century out of European scholars' attempts to understand the radically different ways of life of the peoples outside Europe who were encountered by explorers, traders, missionaries, travelers, and colonial administrators. The standard explanatory concept at that time was *social evolution*, the idea that civilization as known in Europe was the culmination of a series of incremental changes from simpler beginnings. Scholars proposed hypothetical evolutionary sequences leading up to all the major components of European civilization. One of the more general schemes, that of the American anthropologist Lewis Henry Morgan, divided human history into the stages of "Savagery," "Barbarism," and "Civilization," the first two having three subdivisions, based mainly on advances in technology, such as the invention of pottery. All societies were thought to have followed the same evolutionary path, but those outside Europe and North America suffered from arrested development, getting stuck at some lower stage of development. The Australian Aborigines, for instance, were commonly seen as living examples of the lowest stage of social evolution ("Lower Savagery" for Morgan), one that Europeans had passed through thousands of years before. The slow progress of non-Europeans was attributed to their inferior intellectual endowment, a racist interpretation used by scholars and laypeople alike. Yet the notion that such peoples could overcome their inherent limitations with help from more talented Europeans was one of the justifications given for colonialism, the so-called *white man's burden* to civilize and Christianize the "backward" peoples outside Europe and North America. Most cultural anthropologists today vehemently reject the idea that any society is superior to any other, but notions of cultural evolution are still used in some theories of culture change.

The defining features of cultural anthropology—the idea of culture and the modern fieldwork method—developed along separate paths, only becoming firmly joined in the twentieth century. The first influential definition of culture in the anthropological sense was that of the British scholar E. B. Tylor. As he writes in *Primitive Culture* (J. Murray, 1871), "Culture or Civilization, taken in its wide ethnographic sense, is that complex whole which includes knowledge, belief, art, morals, law, custom, and any other capabilities and habits acquired by man as a member of society." Since then anthropologists, especially in North America, have repeatedly defined and redefined what they mean by culture. In a 1952 survey of the literature, Alfred Kroeber and Clyde Kluckhohn found 166 different definitions of culture in print, reflecting numerous different emphases and points of view (*Culture: A Critical Review of Concepts and Definitions*, Papers of the Peabody Museum of American Archaeology and Ethnology, vol. 47, no. 1 [Harvard University]). However, a few common threads run through the theorizing and debate about culture that went on during the first half of the twentieth century. Cultural anthropologists were trying to establish that culture was a thing in itself, a so-called *emergent phenomenon*, not something that could be reduced to the sum of the actions and ideas of the individuals making up a society and therefore not explainable in terms of individual psychology or biological instincts. Culture was thought of as having an existence of its own, apart from the individuals who happened to carry it at any given time; it needed to be explained in its own terms, with distinctively cultural theories. The founder of American academic anthropology, Franz Boas, considered each culture to be a unique tradition or way of life, the result of a particular history of innovations and borrowings from other cultures. However, subsequent generations of cultural anthropologists were not content to view cultures as merely the outcome of the accidents of history. They attempted to explain the forms cultures took in terms of environmental adaptation or other forces. Cultural anthropologists like Margaret Mead (see Issue 2, "Was Margaret Mead's Fieldwork on Samoan Adolescents Fundamentally Flawed?") debated whether biologically inherited instincts ("nature") or cultural conditioning ("nurture") was the predominant influence on human behavior, with most cultural anthropologists coming down strongly on the side of nurture. The debate about the importance of instinct versus culture in shaping behavior continues today. (See Issue 9, "Do Sexually Egalitarian Societies Exist?"; Issue 10, "Has the Islamic Revolution in Iran Subjugated Women?"; and Issue 16, "Did Napoleon Chagnon and Other Researchers Adversely Affect the Yanomami Indians of Venezuela?")

Today anthropologists still argue about how best to conceptualize culture and even about whether or not such a concept is needed and useful. (See Issue 3, which addresses this question directly.) Nevertheless, in practice most cultural anthropologists treat all enduring social groups, from clubs to whole nations, as having a set of typical practices, ideas, and feelings that can be discovered and described in the form of a cultural description. Those practices, ideas, and feelings are shared because they are part of an interconnected—though not entirely coherent—tradition, which is learned, internalized, valued, and followed by each new generation. Cultures can change due to the innovations of creative individuals, but they also have great inertia, giving them a recognizable identity over time. For example, American culture can be defined as the set of practices, ideas, and feelings shared by all Americans, regardless of their ancestry, due to their learning and participating in a common tradition. Such a view does not deny that there are many layers of subcultures within the common American culture (e.g., working-class Mexican American culture) or that cultures continuously change. Issue 4 addresses this topic by asking, "Do Native Peoples Today Invent Their Traditions?".

The anthropological fieldwork method arose through a series of innovations by American and British researchers. The social evolutionists had generally been content to use the reports of European travelers, missionaries, officials, and so on rather than gathering their own data. Needless to say, the quality and accuracy of those reports were highly variable. The first systematic research into the customs of non-European peoples in North America were the studies made by officials of the U.S. government's Bureau of Indian Affairs on Indian reservations in the late nineteenth century. Typically an official would stay at the administrator's house and interview elderly members of the tribe about how they lived before they were defeated and placed on reservations, a process jokingly called "kitchen-table anthropology." Boas carried out his own research among Eskimos and the Kwakiutl Indians of British Columbia. He made numerous trips to the Kwakiutl and employed an educated Kwakiutl man as a research assistant and correspondent. Boas emphasized the importance of face-to-face research to his graduate students.

The modern method of fieldwork, however, derives from the pioneering research of the Polish-born British anthropologist Bronislaw Malinowski in the Trobriand Islands, off the east coast of New Guinea, beginning in 1914. Malinowski began his studies in New Guinea in the typical fashion of the day—living with a white administrator, visiting villages during the day or interviewing informants "on the veranda" through interpreters. However, with the outbreak of World War I, the Australian governor of Papua limited the movements of Malinowski, technically an enemy alien since he was Polish, to the Trobriand Islands. Making a virtue of necessity, Malinowski moved into a village, learned the Trobriand language, and stayed for more than two years. His findings formed the basis for a series of important monographs on Trobriand culture. Because of the unprecedented depth and richness of information Malinowski was able to obtain, his procedure became the standard fieldwork method for British anthropologists. However, that method spread only slowly to the United States, finally becoming fully established in the 1960s. In part the question of whether or not Mead's 1924 research in Samoa was flawed (Issue 2) is a question of whether or not her Boasian method of research was inferior to the Malinowskian approach followed by her critic, Derek Freeman. Today, most data used by cultural anthropologists are ultimately derived from observations, informal conversations, and interviews carried out by a researcher living within a study community. The fieldwork methodology distinguishes most anthropological research from that of sociologists, psychologists, economists, and other social scientists.

The information fieldworkers collect does not speak for itself; cultural data must be interpreted. Interpretation begins with the creation of the research questions themselves, for this reflects what investigators consider important to find out and directs their observations and questions in the field. At each step of data collection and analysis, the investigators' theories and interests shape their understandings of other cultures. In their reports (called *ethnographic monographs*), anthropologists draw on theories to create and test hypotheses or to shape their interpretations. It is easy to see why cultural anthropologists can arrive at different conclusions, even when studying the same society.

Much explanation in cultural anthropology is based on comparison of cultural features in different societies. Some anthropologists explicitly make cross-cultural comparisons, using statistics to measure the significance of apparent correlations between such variables as child-rearing practices and typical adult personalities. Even anthropologists who concentrate on explaining or interpreting features of particular cultures use their knowledge of similar or different features in other societies as a basis for insights. By viewing cultures in a comparative framework, anthropologists become aware of what is "missing" in a particular culture—in other words, what is found in other similar cultures—as well as what is there. Comparison is fundamental to the anthropological perspective.

Recently, cultural anthropologists have begun asking questions about anthropologists and the culture of anthropology, specifically about possible biases in the ways anthropologists depict and represent other cultures through writing, films, and other media. This movement has been called *post-modern anthropology* or *critical anthropology*. Post-modernists ask, among other things: Do our theories and methods of representation inadvertently portray the people we study as exotic "Others," in exaggerated contrast with Western peoples? This is the question that lies behind Issue 15, "Do Museums Misrepresent Ethnic Communities Around the World?"

Theoretical orientations   In Part 1 of this volume we look at controversies concerning general theoretical orientations in cultural anthropology. The first issue considers whether cultural anthropology should stop trying to model itself on the natural sciences and view itself as an interpretive branch of the humanities. Although most cultural anthropologists consider themselves social scientists, much anthropological analysis comes from interpretations of cultural data rather than from the material basis of human societies. In this issue, interpretive anthropologist Clifford Geertz argues that anthropology should be about making informed interpretations about the societies in which anthropologists work. Unlike the natural sciences, the anthropologist is the instrument through which all understanding must emerge. Materialist anthropologist Robert Carneiro favors analysis that considers the observable material conditions of human life, not merely interpretations that are subject to anthropological misinterpretation. Issue 2 asks about the best ways for anthropologists to conduct fieldwork and make interpretaions about social and cultural life. By examining whether Margaret mead's research—and perhaps more importantly her interpretations—were fundamentally flawed, this issue gets at the heart of what fieldwork is all aobut and how anthropologists should use field data in making their interpretations. Issue 3 takes up problems with the concept of culture. It asks whether anthropologists should abandon the concept altogether—substituting new ideas—or preserve the concept of culture while ensuring that it is not used ina way that distorts reality. Issue 4 asks whether or not native peoples continually invent and reinvent their traditions. This debate between the late anthropologist Roger M. Keesing and Hawaiian activist Haunani-Kay Trask concerns who is best able to speak about native culture. Do anthropologists have a privileged view that allows them to see native custom and beliefs more accurately or do native peoples themselves have a better understanding of their own culture? Clearly native peoples understand the nuances of their culture better than most foreign anthropologists, but do anthropologists bring an objectivity that allows them to see things that native peoples miss?

Some specific issues in cultural anthropology   Part 2 considers a variety of controversies that are being debated in cultural anthropology today. Because of the great breadth of subject matter in cultural anthropology, most cultural anthropologists become specialists in one or a few topics or subfields of cultural anthropology. Major subfields include kinship and social organization, economic anthropology, political anthropology, anthropology of religion, ethnicity, gender and culture, language and culture, psychological anthropology, and medical anthropology. We have tried to include at least one issue that bears on each of these subfields.

Issue 5 asks whether black American English (often called Ebonics) is a distinct language or just a dialect of standard American English, which raises a question in linguistic anthropology that has major implications for the education of African Americans. Issue 6 ("Are San Hunter-Gatherers Basically Pastoralists Who Have Lost Their Herds?") focuses specifically on San social organization and economic system. It considers whether contemporary hunting and gathering peoples are products of modern conditions. Two issues deal directly with questions about the anthropology of religion. Issue 7 asks whether the difference between the natural and supernatural is a conceptual distinction that exists in all societies, and Issue 13 asks, "Is Islam a Single Universal Tradition?". Issue 8, "Is It Natural for Adopted Children to Want to Find Out About Their Birth Parents?" is a question about kinship that concerns one of the pressing issues of our time, comparing social life in America with societies in the Pacific. Both Issue 9, concerning sexually egalitarian societies, and Issue 10, which asks if the Islamic revolution in Iran has subjugated women, address questions about gender and society. And Issue 11 ("Are Yanomami Violence and Warfare Natural Human Efforts to Maximize Reproductive Fitness?") raises the questions of whether or not the violence observed by anthropologist Napoleon Chagnon among the Yanomami Indians of Venezuela is a natural drive inherent in men to maximize the number of sexual partners and thus maximize their biological offspring. Issue 12, "Is Ethnic Conflict Inevitable?" deals with Muslim-Hindu tension in India and ethnic tension in Bosnia specifically but raises questions about whether or not ethnic tension is universal. In Issue 14, we consider an issue in medical anthropology, asking whether or not there are some illnesses that exist only among people from particular cultures. Finally, Issue 15 is a question about the display of ethnographic objects in museums, asking whether museums misrepresent ethnic communities around the world.

This set of issues is by no means exhaustive, either in representing the kinds of questions currently debated by anthropologists or the range of subfields in cultural anthropology. Nevertheless, these issues illustrate how cultural anthropology can and has weighed in on several pressing social issues of the day.

Ethics in cultural anthropology   Part 3 looks at controversies concerning the ethics of research, a topic that has become increasingly important in contemporary anthropology. The American Anthropological Association has developed a Code of Ethics covering both research and teaching (see the American Anthropological Association Web site at http://www.aaanet.org). It recognizes that researchers sometimes have conflicting obligations to the people, host countries, the profession, and the public. One basic principle is that researchers should do nothing that could harm or distress the people they study.

Here we consider four specific examples of ethical questions that affect cultural anthropologists. Issue 16 asks whether Chagnon and his colleagues actually harmed the Yanomami people (also spelled Yanomamö) with whom they worked. This issue rose suddenly in September 2000, when most American anthropologists received e-mails about charges leveled against the researchers by investigative journalist Patrick Tierney. This issue is thus timely, and it is also very important to the discipline because so many undergraduates have read one of Chagnon's books about the Yanomami or seen one of the ethnographic films he produced with Timothy Asch. Issue 17 asks what, if any, role linguists and anthropologists should play in helping to preserve endangered languages, mostly in developing countries. Everyone agrees that the loss of the world's minor languages reduces natural linguistic diversity. Nevertheless, Ken Hale argues that those who study such languages have an obligation to shape government policies to help preserve them. Peter Ladefoged counters that scholars have a very different responsibility to the people who speak such languages, arguing that linguists and anthropologists are in no position to dictate what languages people should speak. Such efforts would actually harm the people whose languages they are trying to protect by keeping them from participating in the national economic and political development. Issue 16, "Should Anthropologists Work to Eliminate the Practice of Female Circumcision?" concerns whether or not anthropologists have an obligation to try to stop a traditional cultural practice that some see as at odds with international human rights. This is the practice of female circumcision, which some call female genital mutilation. Can anthropologists sit still while women in African and Middle Eastern countries are mutilated? Or do anthropologists have an obligation to help preserve traditional customs?

Some Basic Questions

On the surface, the issues presented in this book are very diverse. What has attracted us to the issues presented here is that each raises much broader questions that affect the entire discipline. In this section we briefly describe some of the basic questions lying behind specific issues.

Is Anthropology a Science or a Humanity?

Science is a set of ideas and methods intended to describe and explain phenomena in a naturalistic way, seeing individual things and events as the outcome of discoverable causes and as conforming to general laws. Anthropologists taking a scientific approach are concerned with developing broad theories about the processes that lead to observed patterns of variation in human biology, language, and culture. The humanities, on the other hand, are concerned with understanding people's cultural creations in terms of their meanings to their creators and the motivations behind their creation.

Cultural anthropologists are sharply divided over whether cultural anthropology should model itself on the natural sciences or on the humanities. Issue 11 explores how sociobiologists and their critics approach explanations for certain patterns in human behavior. Here Chagnon argues that anthropologists can use biologically based models from sociobiology to understand why native peoples behave the way they do. Anthropologist Brian Ferguson counters that Chagnon has misinterpreted his data, suggesting that Chagnon's own behavior during fieldwork created the native behaviors that he is trying to explain.

Is Biology or Culture More Important in Shaping Human Behavior?

Most anthropologists accept that both genetically transmitted behavioral tendencies (instincts) and cultural ideas and norms influence human behavior, thought, and emotion. However, anthropologists diverge widely over the amount of weight they assign to these two influences. *Biological determinists* believe that all human behavior is ultimately determined by the genes, and culture merely lends distinctive coloration to our genetically driven behaviors. At the other extreme, *cultural determinists* believe that any instincts humans may have are so weak and malleable that cultural learning easily overcomes them. The conflict between supporters of the two extreme views, called the *nature-nurture debate*, has been going on for many years and shows no sign of being resolved soon.

Several of the issues in this volume deal directly with the nature-nurture question, including Issue 9 concerning sexually egalitarian societies, Issue 11 concerning Yanomami violence and warfare, and Issue 14 concerning illnesses that may or may not exist only among members of a particular culture. In addition, Issue 2, about the Mead-Freeman controversy, concerns two diametrically opposed positions on whether adolescence is shaped more by biology or by culture.

Is the Local Development of Culture or Outside Influence More Important in Shaping Cultures?

In trying to explain the form a particular culture takes, different anthropologists place different amounts of emphasis on the local development of culture and on outside influence. Those who favor local development emphasize unique innovations and adaptations to the natural environment, while those favoring outside influences emphasize the borrowing of ideas from neighbors (*diffusion*) and changes forced upon a people by more powerful groups (*acculturation*). Most anthropologists recognize some influence from both sources, but some attribute overriding importance to one or the other.

Two issues in this volume are about the relative importance of local cultural development and external influences: Issue 6 concerning San hunter-gatherers, and Issue 12 concerning ethnic conflict.

Is a Feminist Perspective Needed in Anthropology?

Although female anthropologists—like Mead and Ruth Benedict—have been very influential in the development of anthropology, there was a bias in early anthropological studies toward emphasizing the social and political lives of men.

Over the past 30 years feminist anthropologists have argued that these male-biased accounts have overlooked much of what goes on in traditional societies because male anthropologists have been preoccupied with men's activities and the male point of view. Feminist anthropologists want ethnographers and theorists to give full weight to the activities and perspectives of women and to recognize that gender identities and values pervade all cultures.

Issue 8 concerning sexually egalitarian societies considers whether or not a feminist perspective is needed to recognize sexual equality. In a somewhat different way Issue 10 reassesses what a feminist anthropology might actually look like by presenting two opposed perspectives on what has happened to women's rights following the Iranian Revolution of 1979. Feminist anthropologists have also asserted that male bias affects anthropological methodologies as well. Issue 4 concerning Mead's fieldwork on Samoan adolescents hinges in part on different methods available to male and female researchers.

Some Theoretical Approaches

Cultural anthropologists draw on many theories of widely varying scope and type. We present brief summaries of a number of theoretical approaches used by authors in this book so that you will recognize and understand them when you see them. We have arranged these theories in a rough continuum from most scientific in approach to most humanistic.

Sociobiology   Sociobiology is a theory that attempts to use evolutionary principles to explain all behavior of animals, including humans. The best-known practitioner is biologist E. O. Wilson, whose book *Sociobiology: The New Synthesis* (Harvard University Press, 1975) sets out the basic concepts. Sociobiologists believe that human behavior is determined by inherited behavioral tendencies. The genes promoting behaviors that lead to survival and successful reproduction are favored by natural selection and thus tend to become more common in a population over the generations. For sociobiologists such behaviors as selfishness, altruism to close kin, violence, and certain patterns of marriage are evolutionarily and biologically determined. They see individual and cultural ideas as mere rationalizations of innate patterns of behavior. In their view, no culture will persist that goes against the "wisdom of the genes."

Cultural ecology   The theory of cultural ecology was developed by cultural anthropologist Julian Steward in the 1930s as a corrective to the overly simple schemes of cultural evolution. Emphasizing the process of adaptation to the physical environment, he postulated that societies in different environments would develop different practices, though the general trend was toward higher levels of complexity, a process he called *multilinear evolution.* His idea of adaptation, like natural selection, explained why some societies and practices succeeded and were perpetuated, while other less well-adapted ones died out.

Many archaeologists and cultural anthropologists use versions of cultural ecology to explain why certain practices exist in certain environments. Harris's widely-used theory of *cultural materialism* is a further development of cultural ecology. The basic idea behind all versions of cultural ecology is that societies must fulfill their material needs if they are to survive. Therefore those institutions involved with making a living must be well adapted to the environment, while others, like religions, are less constrained by the environment.

Culture history   Boas rejected the cultural evolution schemes of the nineteenth century, with their fixed stages of cultural development. He pointed out that all societies had unique histories, depending on local innovations and diffusion of ideas from neighboring societies. Also, change is not always toward greater complexity; civilizations crumble as well as rise. Boas advocated recording the particular events and influences that contributed to the makeup of each culture.

World system theory   The world system theory, which has gained great prominence in the social sciences in recent years, asserts that all societies, large and small, are—and long have been—integrated in a single worldwide political-economic system. This approach emphasizes the connections among societies, especially the influence of politically powerful societies over weak ones, as in colonialism, rather than local development of culture.

Cultural interpretation   Humanist anthropologists emphasize their role as interpreters, not explainers, of culture. They focus on the task of describing other cultures in ways that are intelligible to Western readers, making sense of customs that at first glance seem incomprehensible. The most prominent practitioner of cultural interpretation is Geertz, who coined the term *thick description* for this process. This approach is used especially for dealing with aspects of culture that are products of human imagination, like art and mythology, but even the institutions involved in physical survival, like families and economic processes, have dimensions of meaning that warrant interpretation.

Feminist anthropology   Feminist anthropology began in the 1970s as an approach meant to correct the lack of coverage of women and women's views in earlier anthropology. It has now developed into a thoroughgoing alternative approach to the study of culture and society. Its basic idea is that gender is a cultural construction affecting the roles and meanings of the sexes in particular societies. The aim of feminist anthropology is both to explain the position of women and to convey the meanings surrounding gender. Feminist anthropologists emphasize that all social relations have a gender dimension.

How Anthropologists Reach Conclusions

We have selected all of the articles for this edition of Taking Sides from previously published books, journals, and Web-journals. In assembling the readings for each issue, we have framed the issue in terms that seem timely and appropriate to the ways cultural anthropologists generally think about some of the important unresolved questions of the day. None of the articles in this volume were written specifically to answer the questions we have asked. Nor were any of these essays written to address the questions we have asked in the specific ways we have framed these issues. As much as possible, we have selected readings that offer a clear position on the issues as we have framed them, but students should be aware that not all of the readings were intended to answer the questions we have asked. Thus, sorting out what the original purpose of the essay was will be each student's first task in making sense of the controversies presented.

None of the issues considered in this volume have been resolved, and several are still the subject of heated, and at times, acrimonious debate. The most heated controversies typically arise from the most extreme points of view. When reading these selections students should bear in mind that only two positions are presented formally, although in the introductions and post-scripts we raise questions that should guide you to consider other positions as well. We encourage you to question all of the positions offered before coming to any conclusions of your own. Remember, for more than a century anthropology has prided itself on revealing how our own views of the world are culturally biased. Try to be aware of how your own background, upbringing, ethnicity, religion, likes, and dislikes affect your assessments of the arguments presented here.

In our own teaching we have often used controversial issues as a way to help students understand how anthropologists think about research questions. We have found that five questions often help students focus on the most important points in these selections:

Who is the author?

What are the author's assumptions?

What methods and data does an author use?

What are the author's conclusions?

How does the author reach his or her conclusions from the data?

For each issue we suggest that you consider what school of thought, what sort of training, and what sort of research experience each author has. We often find it useful to ask why this particular author finds the topic worth writing about. Does one or the other author seem to have any sort of bias? What assumptions does each author hold? Do both authors hold the same assumptions?

For any anthropological debate, we also find it useful to ask what methods or analytical strategies each author has used to reach the conclusions he or she presents. For some of the issues presented in this book, authors share many of the same assumptions and are generally working with the same evidence, but disagree as to how this evidence should be analyzed. Some authors disagree most profoundly on what kinds of data are most suitable for answering a particular research question. Some even disagree about what kinds of questions anthropologists should be asking.

Finally, we suggest that you consider how the author has come to his or her conclusions from the available data. Would different data make any difference? Would a different kind of evidence be more appropriate? Would different data likely lead to different conclusions? Would different ways of analyzing the data suggest other conclusions?

If you can answer most of these questions about any pair of selections, you will be thinking about these problems anthropologically and will understand how anthropologists approach controversial research questions. After weighing the various possible positions on an issue you will be able to form sound opinions of your own.

On the Internet . . .

Interpretive Anthropology

This Web site from the University of Alabama offers some useful background on Clifford Geertz, who is one of the leading proponents of an interpretive anthropology. This site gives some important quotations and brief summaries of Geertz's major publications and also offers links to other relevant Web sites.

`http://www.as.ua.edu/rel/aboutrelbiogeertz.html`

Cultural Materialism

The Cultural Materialism Web site, prepared by Dr. M. D. Murphy of the University of Alabama, features an explanation of cultural materialism, a summary of its history, and a list of pertinent scholars. This site offers links to other relevant Web sites.

`http://www.as.ua.edu/ant/Faculty/murphy/cultmat.htm`

Margaret Mead

This Web site on Margaret Mead was prepared in association with the centennial of her birth. It offers information on Mead's career as an anthropologist.

`http://www.interculturalstudies.org/Mead/index.html`

PART 1

Theoretical Issues

Cultural anthropologists study the cultures and societies of living communities. Like other social scientists, they try to find patterns in social behavior and often develop and test models about the human condition and the range of human possibilities. But many cultural anthropologists disagree on the extent to which cultural anthropology is a science or one of the humanities. Should anthropology model itself on the natural sciences, seeking causal explanations, or should we see our role as an interpretive one, promoting understanding only? But if anthropologists are interpreters of other cultures, what are the guidelines and limits that we should set for our interpretations? Cultural anthropology is also defined by its research methods, which typically consist of a year or more of fieldwork. Here we ask about the proper conduct of fieldwork and the interpretations that anthropologists can make from their observations and interviews in the field, by considering whether Margaret Mead, one of the most famous American anthropologists, has fundamentally overinterpreted her field research. Another new issue has recently arisen in the discipline, asking whether the culture concept is a useful concept for anthropology. But if we abandon the culture concept, what should replace it? We also ask about the nature of cultural traditions by considering whether native peoples invent their traditions. To this question, a native activist responds that anthropologists have overinterpreted their data and have not listened to native voices.

- Should Anthropology Stop Trying to Model Itself on the Natural Sciences?

- Was Margaret Mead's Fieldwork on Samoan Adolescents Fundamentally Flawed?

- Should Anthropologists Abandon the Concept of Culture?

- Do Native Peoples Today Invent Their Traditions?

ISSUE 1

Should Anthropology Stop Trying to Model Itself on the Natural Sciences?

YES: Clifford Geertz, from *The Interpretation of Cultures: Selected Essays* (Basic Books, 1973)

NO: Robert L. Carneiro, from "Godzilla Meets New Age Anthropology: Facing the Postmodernist Challenge to a Science of Culture," *Europaea* (1995)

ISSUE SUMMARY

YES: Cultural anthropologist Clifford Geertz views anthropology as a science of interpretation, and he argues that anthropology should never model itself on the natural sciences. He believes that anthropology's goal should be to generate deeper interpretations of cultural phenomena, using what he calls "thick description," rather than attempting to prove or disprove scientific laws.

NO: Cultural anthropologist Robert Carneiro argues that anthropology has always been and should continue to be a science that attempts to explain sociocultural phenomena in terms of causes and effects rather than merely interpret them. He criticizes Geertz's cultural interpretations as arbitrary and immune to disconfirmation.

For more than a century, anthropologists have viewed their discipline as a science of humankind or of culture. But anthropologists disagree about what being a science should mean. At issue is the question: Just what kind of science is anthropology?

Nineteenth- and early-twentieth-century anthropologists generally viewed anthropology as one of the natural sciences, and most early theorists—such as Edward Tylor, James Fraser, and Lewis Henry Morgan—saw anthropology as an extension of biology. Like biology, anthropology is a comparative discipline. Early anthropologists were also attracted to the theory of natural selection of naturalist Charles Darwin. But for anthropologists, evolution meant explaining how one social form or type of society developed into another.

In the 1920s, most anthropologists abandoned evolutionary models as speculative and racist (white Europeans were always pictured as occupying the most "advanced" stage of cultural evolution). After the Second World War, Leslie White proposed a unilineal evolutionary model, arguing that cultural evolution could be explained in terms of how much energy people could capture with their technology. Julian Steward proposed a multilinear model, suggesting that cultures could be explained as adaptations to particular environments (now the theory of cultural ecology, a model popular among many prehistoric archaeologists). In the 1960s, Marvin Harris combined cultural ecology and neo-Marxian ideas into a new paradigm he called "cultural materialism." Harris and Carneiro believe that anthropology's goal should be to explain the existence and characteristics of cultural features by means of verifiable laws, like those used in other scientific fields.

In the 1920s, some anthropologists became more interested in what people thought than in what they did. Their definitions of culture emphasized shared beliefs and feelings more than behaviors (see Issue 3). This trend developed with the modern method of ethnographic fieldwork, which requires researchers to immerse themselves for a year or more in another society to learn the local language and engage in "participant observation." In the words of Bronislaw Malinowski, one objective of fieldwork is to grasp the "native's point of view." Geertz's "interpretive anthropology" grew out of this interest in cultural differences in thought worlds.

Geertz believes that it is futile to seek scientific laws to explain human behavior. Instead, he argues that anthropologists should produce interpretations of cultures in the form of "thick descriptions" that reveal the cultural meanings of what they have observed, heard, and experienced in the field. Thus, for Geertz, anthropology should be a science of interpretation rather than explanation.

Carneiro responds that anthropology should try to *explain* sociocultural phenomena, not merely interpret what people think about them, just as natural scientists seek to explain the phenomena they study. He argues that human thought and behavior are part of the external world and that they are subject to laws of cause and effect like other natural phenomena. He rejects Geertz's form of cultural interpretation as art rather than science. He saves his strongest criticism for the "postmodern" anthropologists, who take Geertz's interpretive anthropology to the next step, even of denying that a single objective reality exists.

These selections pose several questions that lie at the heart of all sociocultural anthropology. Should anthropologists try to explain the existence and characteristics of sociocultural phenomena, or should they merely seek to translate and make sense of other people's cultural beliefs and practices? Must we choose between these alternatives, or is anthropology broad enough to hold both of these perspectives and others as well? More specifically, to what extent is social action like a text? How can we know what interpretation of a practice is the correct one?

Clifford Geertz  **YES**

Thick Description: Toward an Interpretive Theory of Culture

I

[Here I argue] for a narrowed, specialized, and, so I imagine, theoretically more powerful concept of culture to replace E. B. Tylor's famous "most complex whole," which, its originative power not denied, seems to me to have reached the point where it obscures a good deal more than it reveals.

The conceptual morass into which the Tylorean kind of *pot-au-feu* theorizing about culture can lead, is evident in what is still one of the better general introductions to anthropology, Clyde Kluckhohn's *Mirror for Man*. In some twenty-seven pages of his chapter on the concept, Kluckhohn managed to define culture in turn as: (1) "the total way of life of a people"; (2) "the social legacy the individual acquires from his group"; (3) "a way of thinking, feeling, and believing"; (4) "an abstraction from behavior"; (5) a theory on the part of the anthropologist about the way in which a group of people in fact behave; (6) a "storehouse of pooled learning"; (7) "a set of standardized orientations to recurrent problems"; (8) "learned behavior"; (9) a mechanism for the normative regulation of behavior; (10) "a set of techniques for adjusting both to the external environment and to other men"; (11) "a precipitate of history"; and turning, perhaps in desperation, to similes, as a map, as a sieve, and as a matrix. In the face of this sort of theoretical diffusion, even a somewhat constricted and not entirely standard concept of culture, which is at least internally coherent and, more important, which has a definable argument to make is (as, to be fair, Kluckhohn himself keenly realized) an improvement. Eclecticism is self-defeating not because there is only one direction in which it is useful to move, but because there are so many: it is necessary to choose.

The concept of culture I espouse . . . is essentially a semiotic one. Believing, with [German sociologist and political economist] Max Weber, that man is an animal suspended in webs of significance he himself has spun, I take culture to be those webs, and the analysis of it to be therefore not an experimental science in search of law but an interpretive one in search of meaning. It is explication I am after, construing social expressions on their surface enigmatical. But this pronouncement, a doctrine in a clause, demands itself some explication.

II

From Clifford Geertz, *The Interpretation of Cultures: Selected Essays by Clifford Geertz* (Basic Books, 1973). Copyright © 1973 by Basic Books, Inc. Reprinted by permission of Basic Books, a member of Perseus Books, LLC. Notes omitted.

... [I]f you want to understand what a science is, you should look in the first instance not at its theories or its findings, and certainly not at what its apologists say about it; you should look at what the practitioners of it do.

In anthropology, or anyway social anthropology, what the practitioners do is ethnography [the study of human cultures]. And it is in understanding what ethnography is, or more exactly *what doing ethnography is,* that a start can be made toward grasping what anthropological analysis amounts to as a form of knowledge. This, it must immediately be said, is not a matter of methods. From one point of view, that of the textbook, doing ethnography is establishing rapport, selecting informants, transcribing texts, taking genealogies, mapping fields, keeping a diary, and so on. But it is not these things, techniques and received procedures, that define the enterprise. What defines it is the kind of intellectual effort it is: an elaborate venture in, to borrow a notion from [British philosopher] Gilbert Ryle, "thick description."

Ryle's discussion of "thick description" appears in two recent essays of his (now reprinted in the second volume of his *Collected Papers*) addressed to the general question of what, as he puts it, *"Le Penseur"* is doing: "Thinking and Reflecting" and "The Thinking of Thoughts." Consider, he says, two boys rapidly contracting the eyelids of their right eyes. In one, this is an involuntary twitch; in the other, a conspiratorial signal to a friend. The two movements are, as movements, identical; from an I-am-a-camera, "phenomentalistic" observation of them alone, one could not tell which was twitch and which was wink, or indeed whether both or either was twitch or wink. Yet the difference, however unphotographable, between a twitch or wink is vast; as anyone unfortunate enough to have had the first taken for the second knows. The winker is communicating, and indeed communicating in a quite precise and special way: (1) deliberately, (2) to someone in particular, (3) to impart a particular message, (4) according to a socially established code, and (5) without cognizance of the rest of the company. As Ryle points out, the winker has now done two things, contracted his eyelids and winked, while the twitcher has done only one, contracted his eyelids. Contracting your eyelids on purpose when there exists a public code in which so doing counts as a conspiratorial signal *is* winking. That's all there is to it: a speck of behavior, a fleck of culture, and— *voilà!*—a gesture.

That, however, is just the beginning. Suppose, he continues, there is a third boy, who, "to give malicious amusement to his cronies," parodies the first boy's wink, as amateurish, clumsy, obvious, and so on. He, of course, does this in the same way the second boy winked and the first twitched: by contracting his right eyelids. Only this boy is neither winking nor twitching, he is parodying someone else's, as he takes it, laughable, attempt at winking. Here, too, a socially established code exists (he will "wink" laboriously, overobviously, perhaps adding a grimace—the usual artifices of the clown); and so also does a message. Only now it is not conspiracy but ridicule that is in the air. If the others think he is actually winking, his whole project misfires as completely, though with somewhat different results, as if they think he is twitching. One can go further: uncertain of his mimicking abilities, the would-be satirist may practice at home before the mirror, in which case he is not twitching, winking, or parodying, but rehearsing; though so far as what a camera, a radical behaviorist, or a believer in protocol sentences would record he is just rapidly contracting his right eyelids like all the others. Complexities are possible, if not practically without end, at least logically so. The original winker might, for example, actually have been fake-winking, say, to mislead outsiders into imagining there was a conspiracy afoot when there in fact was not, in which case our descriptions of what the parodist is parodying and the rehearser rehearsing of course shift accordingly. But the point is that between what Ryle calls the "thin description" of what the rehearser (parodist, winker, twitcher . . .) is doing ("rapidly contracting his right eyelids") and the "thick description" of what he is doing ("practicing a burlesque of a friend faking a wink to deceive an innocent into thinking a conspiracy is in motion") lies the object of ethnography: a stratified hierarchy of meaningful structures in terms of which twitches, winks, fake-winks, parodies, rehearsals of parodies are produced, perceived, and interpreted, and without which they would not (not even the zero-form twitches, which, *as a cultural category,* are as much non-winks as winks are nontwitches) in fact exist, no matter what anyone did or didn't do with his eyelids.

Like so many of the little stories Oxford philosophers like to make up for themselves, all this winking, fake-winking, burlesque-fake-winking, rehearsed burlesque-fake-winking, may seem a bit artificial.

. . . In finished anthropological writings, . . . this fact—that what we call our data are really our own constructions of other people's constructions of what they and their compatriots are up to—is obscured because most of what we need to comprehend a particular event, ritual, custom, idea, or whatever is insinuated as background information before the thing itself is directly examined. . . . There is nothing particularly wrong with this, and it is in any case inevitable. But it does lead to a view of anthropological research as rather more of an observational and rather less of an interpretive activity than it really is. Right down at the factual base, the hard rock, insofar as there is any, of the whole enterprise, we are already explicating: and worse, explicating explications. Winks upon winks upon winks.

. . . The point for now is only that ethnography is thick description. What the ethnographer is in fact faced with—except when (as, of course, he must do) he is pursuing the more automatized routines of data collection—is a multiplicity of complex conceptual structures, many of them superimposed upon or knotted into one another, which are at once strange, irregular, and inexplicit, and which he must contrive somehow first to grasp and then to render. And this is true at the most down-to-earth, jungle field work levels of his activity: interviewing informants, observing rituals, eliciting kin terms, tracing property lines, censusing households . . . writing his journal. Doing ethnography is like trying to read (in the sense of "construct a reading of") a manuscript—foreign, faded, full of ellipses, incoherencies, suspicious emendations, and tendentious commentaries, but written not in conventionalized graphs of sound but in transient examples of shaped behavior.

III

Culture, this acted document, thus is public, like a burlesqued wink or a mock sheep raid. Though ideational, it does not exist in someone's head; though unphysical, it is not an occult entity. The interminable, because unterminable, debate within anthropology as to whether culture is "subjective" or "objective," together with the mutual exchange of intellectual insults ("idealist!"—"materialist!"; "mentalist!"—"behaviorist!"; "impressionist!"—"positivist!") which accompanies it, is wholly misconceived. Once human behavior is seen as (most of the time; there *are* true twitches) symbolic action—action which, like phonation in speech, pigment in painting, line in writing, or sonance in music, signifies—the question as to whether culture is patterned conduct or a frame of mind, or even the two somehow mixed together, loses sense. The thing to ask about a burlesqued wink or a mock sheep raid is not what their ontological status is. It is the same as that of rocks on the one hand and dreams on the other—they are things of this world. The thing to ask is what their import is: what it is, ridicule or challenge, irony or anger, snobbery or pride, that, in their occurrence and through their agency, is getting said.

This may seem like an obvious truth, but there are a number of ways to obscure it. One is to imagine that culture is a self-contained "super-organic" reality with forces and purposes of its own; that is, to reify it. Another is to claim that it consists in the brute pattern of behavioral events we observe in fact to occur in some identifiable community or other; that is, to reduce it. But though both these confusions still exist, and doubtless will be always with us, the main source of theoretical muddlement in contemporary anthropology is a view which developed in reaction to them and is right now very widely held—namely, that, to quote [anthropologist] Ward Goodenough, perhaps its leading proponent, "culture [is located] in the minds and hearts of men."

Variously called ethnoscience, componential analysis, or cognitive anthropology (a terminological wavering which reflects a deeper uncertainty), this school of thought holds that culture is composed of psychological structures by means of which individuals or groups of individuals guide their behavior. "A society's culture," to quote Goodenough again, this time in a passage which has become the *locus classicus* of the whole movement, "consists of whatever it is one has to know or believe in order to operate in a manner acceptable to its members." And from this view of what culture is follows a view, equally assured, of what describing it is—the writing out of systematic rules, an ethnographic algorithm, which, if followed, would make it possible so to operate, to pass (physical appearance aside) for a native. In such a way, extreme subjectivism is married to extreme formalism, with the expected result: an explosion of debate as to whether particular analyses (which come in the form of taxonomies, paradigms, tables, trees, and other ingenuities) reflect what the natives "really" think or are merely clever simulations, logically equivalent but substantively different, of what they think.

As, on first glance, this approach may look close enough to the one being developed here to be mistaken for it, it is useful to be explicit as to what divides them. If, leaving our winks and sheep behind for the moment, we take, say, a

Beethoven quartet as an, admittedly rather special but, for these purposes, nicely illustrative, sample of culture, no one would, I think, identify it with its score, with the skills and knowledge needed to play it, with the understanding of it possessed by its performers or auditors, nor, to take care, *en passant,* of the reductionists and reifiers, with a particular performance of it or with some mysterious entity transcending material existence. The "no one" is perhaps too strong here, for there are always incorrigibles. But that a Beethoven quartet is a temporarily developed tonal structure, a coherent sequence of modeled sound—in a word, music—and not anybody's knowledge of or belief about anything, including how to play it, is a proposition to which most people are, upon reflection, likely to assent.

To play the violin it is necessary to possess certain habits, skills, knowledge, and talents, to be in the mood to play, and (as the old joke goes) to have a violin. But violin playing is neither the habits, skills, knowledge, and so on, nor the mood, nor (the notion believers in "material culture" apparently embrace) the violin. To make a trade pact in Morocco, you have to do certain things in certain ways (among others, cut, while chanting Quranic Arabic, the throat of a lamb before the assembled, undeformed, adult male members of your tribe) and to be possessed of certain psychological characteristics (among others, a desire for distant things). But a trade pact is neither the throat cutting nor the desire. . . .

Culture is public because meaning is. You can't wink (or burlesque one) without knowing what counts as winking or how, physically, to contract your eyelids, and you can't conduct a sheep raid (or mimic one) without knowing what it is to steal a sheep and how practically to go about it. But to draw from such truths the conclusion that knowing how to wink is winking and knowing how to steal a sheep is sheep raiding is to betray as deep a confusion as, taking thin descriptions for thick, to identify winking with eyelid contractions or sheep raiding with chasing woolly animals out of pastures. The cognitivist fallacy—that culture consists (to quote another spokesman for the movement, [anthropologist] Stephen Tyler) of "mental phenomena which can [he means "should"]—be analyzed by formal methods similar to those of mathematics and logic"—is as destructive of an effective use of the concept as are the behaviorist and idealist fallacies to which it is a misdrawn correction. Perhaps, as its errors are more sophisticated and its distortions subtler, it is even more so.

The generalized attack on privacy theories of meaning is, since early [Edmund] Husserl and late [Ludwig] Wittgenstein, so much a part of modern thought that it need not be developed once more here. What is necessary is to see to it that the news of it reaches anthropology; and in particular that it is made clear that to say that culture consists of socially established structures of meaning in terms of which people do such things as signal conspiracies and join them or perceive insults and answer them, is no more to say that it is a psychological phenomenon, a characteristic of someone's mind, personality, cognitive structure, or whatever, than to say that Tantrism, genetics, the progressive form of the verb, the classification of wines, the Common Law, or the notion of "a conditional curse" . . . is. What, in a place like Morocco, most prevents those of us who grew up winking other winks or attending other sheep from grasping what people are up to is not ignorance as to how cognition works . . . as a lack of familiarity with the imaginative universe within which their acts are signs. . . .

IV

. . . [T]he aim of anthropology is the enlargement of the universe of human discourse. That is not, of course, its only aim—instruction, amusement, practical counsel, moral advance, and the discovery of natural order in human behavior are others; nor is anthropology the only discipline which pursues it. But it is an aim to which a semiotic concept of culture is peculiarly well adapted. As interworked systems of construable signs (what, ignoring provincial usages, I would call symbols), culture is not a power, something to which social events, behaviors, institutions, or processes can be causally attributed; it is a context, something within which they can be intelligibly—that is, thickly— described. . . .

In short, anthropological writings are themselves interpretations, and second and third order ones to boot. (By definition, only a "native" makes first order ones: it's *his* culture.) They are, thus, fictions; fictions, in the sense that they are "something made," "something fashioned"—the original meaning of *fictiō* —not that they are false, unfactual, or merely "as if" thought experiments. . . .

V

Now, this proposition, that it is not in our interest to bleach human behavior of the very properties that interest us before we begin to examine it, has sometimes been escalated into a larger claim: namely, that as it is only those properties that interest us, we need not attend, save cursorily, to behavior at all. Culture is most effectively treated, the argument goes, purely as a symbolic system (the catch phrase is, "in its own terms"), by isolating its elements, specifying the internal relationships among those elements, and then characterizing the whole system in some general way— according to the core symbols around which it is organized, the underlying structures of which it is a surface expression, or the ideological principles upon which it is based. Though a distinct improvement over "learned behavior" and "mental phenomena" notions of what culture is, and the source of some of the most powerful theoretical ideas in contemporary anthropology, this hermetical approach to things seems to me to run the danger (and increasingly to have been overtaken by it) of locking cultural analysis away from its proper object, the informed logic of actual life. There is little profit in extricating a concept from the defects of psychologism only to plunge it immediately into those of schematicism.

Behavior must be attended to, and with some exactness, because it is through the flow of behavior—or, more precisely, social action—that cultural forms find articulation. They find it as well, of course, in various sorts of artifacts, and various states of consciousness; but these draw their meaning from the role they play (Wittgenstein would say their "use") in an ongoing pattern of life, not from any intrinsic relationships they bear to one another. . . .

A further implication of this is that coherence cannot be the major test of validity for a cultural description. Cultural systems must have a minimal degree of coherence, else we would not call them systems; and, by observation, they normally have a great deal more. But there is nothing so coherent as a paranoid's delusion or a swindler's story. The force of our interpretations cannot rest, as they are now so often made to do, on the tightness with which they hold together, or the assurance with which they are argued. Nothing has done more, I think, to discredit cultural analysis than the construction of impeccable depictions of formal order in whose actual existence nobody can quite believe.

If anthropological interpretation is constructing a reading of what happens, then to divorce it from what happens—from what, in this time or that place, specific people say, what they do, what is done to them, from the whole vast business of the world—is to divorce it from its applications and render it vacant. A good interpretation of anything—a poem, a person, a history, a ritual, an institution, a society—takes us into the heart of that of which it is the interpretation. When it does not do that, but leads us instead somewhere else—into an admiration of its own elegance, of its author's cleverness, or of the beauties of Euclidean order—it may have its intrinsic charms; but it is something else than what the task at hand—figuring out what all that rigamarole with the sheep is about—calls for. . . .

The ethnographer "inscribes" social discourse; *he writes it down.* In so doing, he turns it from a passing event, which exists only in its own moment of occurrence, into an account, which exists in its inscriptions and can be reconsulted. . . .

The situation is even more delicate, because, as already noted, what we inscribe (or try to) is not raw social discourse, to which, because, save very marginally or very specially, we are not actors, we do not have direct access, but only that small part of it which our informants can lead us into understanding. . . .

VI

So, there are three characteristics of ethnographic description: it is interpretive; what it is interpretive of is the flow of social discourse; and the interpreting involved consists in trying to rescue the "said" of such discourse from its perishing occasions and fix it in perusable terms. The *kula* is gone or altered; but, for better or worse, *The Argonauts of the Western Pacific* remains. But there is, in addition, a fourth characteristic of such description, at least as I practice it: it is microscopic.

This is not to say that there are no large-scale anthropological interpretations of whole societies, civilizations, world events, and so on. Indeed, it is such extension of our analyses to wider contexts that, along with their theoretical implications, recommends them to general attention and justifies our constructing them. . . .

It is merely to say that the anthropologist characteristically approaches such broader interpretations and more abstract analyses from the direction of exceedingly extended acquaintances with extremely small matters. He confronts the same grand realities that others—historians, economists, political scientists, sociologists—confront in more fateful settings: Power, Change, Faith, Oppression, Work, Passion, Authority, Beauty, Violence, Love, Prestige; but he confronts them in contexts obscure enough . . . to take the capital letters off them.

These all-too-human constancies, "those big words that make us all afraid," take a homely form in such homely contexts. But that is exactly the advantage. There are enough profundities in the world already.

Yet, the problem of how to get from a collection of ethnographic miniatures— . . . an assortment of remarks and anecdotes—to wall-sized culturescapes of the nation, the epoch, the continent, or the civilization is not so easily passed over with vague allusions to the virtues of concreteness and the down-to-earth mind. For a science born in Indian tribes, Pacific islands, and African lineages and subsequently seized with grander ambitions, this has come to be a major methodological problem, and for the most part a badly handled one. The models that anthropologists have themselves worked out to justify their moving from local truths to general visions have been, in fact, as responsible for undermining the effort as anything their critics—sociologists obsessed with sample sizes, psychologists with measures, or economists with aggregates—have been able to devise against them.

Of these, the two main ones have been: the Jonesville-is-the-USA "microcosmic" model; and the Easter-Island-is-a-testing-case "natural experiment" model. Either heaven in a grain of sand, or the farther shores of possibility.

The Jonesville-is-America writ small (or America-is-Jonesville writ large) fallacy is so obviously one that the only thing that needs explanation is how people have managed to believe it and expected others to believe it. The notion that one can find the essence of national societies, civilizations, great religions, or whatever summed up and simplified in so-called "typical" small towns and villages is palpable nonsense. What one finds in small towns and villages is (alas) small-town or village life. If localized, microscopic studies were really dependent for their greater relevance upon such a premise—that they captured the great world in the little—they wouldn't have any relevance.

But, of course, they are not. The locus of study is not the object of study. Anthropologists don't study villages (tribes, towns, neighborhoods . . .); they study *in* villages. You can study different things in different places, and some things—for example, what colonial domination does to established frames of moral expectation—you can best study in confined localities. But that doesn't make the place what it is you are studying. . . .

The "natural laboratory" notion has been equally pernicious, not only because the analogy is false—what kind of a laboratory is it where *none* of the parameters are manipulable?—but because it leads to a notion that the data derived from ethnographic studies are purer, or more fundamental, or more solid, or less conditioned (the most favored word is "elementary") than those derived from other sorts of social inquiry. The great natural variation of cultural forms is, of course, not only anthropology's great (and wasting) resource, but the ground of its deepest theoretical dilemma: how is such variation to be squared with the biological unity of the human species? But it is not, even metaphorically, experimental variation, because the context in which it occurs varies along with it, and it is not possible (though there are those who try) to isolate the y's from x's to write a proper function. . . .

The methodological problem which the microscopic nature of ethnography presents is both real and critical. But it is not to be resolved by regarding a remote locality as the world in a teacup or as the sociological equivalent of a cloud chamber. It is to be resolved—or, anyway, decently kept at bay—by realizing that social actions are comments on more than themselves; that where an interpretation comes from does not determine where it can be impelled to go. Small facts speak to large issues, winks to epistemology, or sheep raids to revolution, because they are made to.

VII

There is an Indian story—at least I heard it as an Indian story—about an Englishman who, having been told that the world rested on a platform which rested on the back of an elephant which rested in turn on the back of a turtle, asked (perhaps he was an ethnographer; it is the way they behave), what did the turtle rest on? Another turtle. And that turtle? "Ah, Sahib, after that it is turtles all the way down."

. . . Cultural analysis is intrinsically incomplete. And, worse than that, the more deeply it goes the less complete it is. It is a strange science whose most telling assertions are its most tremulously based, in which to get somewhere with the matter at hand is to intensify the suspicion, both your own and that of others, that you are not quite getting it right. But that, along with plaguing subtle people with obtuse questions, is what being an ethnographer is like.

There are a number of ways to escape this—turning culture into folklore and collecting it, turning it into traits and counting it, turning it into institutions and classifying it, turning it into structures and toying with it. But they *are* escapes. The fact is that to commit oneself to a semiotic concept of culture and an interpretive approach to the study of it is to commit oneself to a view of ethnographic assertion as, to borrow W. B. Gallie's by now famous phrase, "essentially contestable." Anthropology, or at least interpretive anthropology, is a science whose progress is marked less by a perfection of consensus than by a refinement of debate. What gets better is the precision with which we vex each other. . . .

My own position in the midst of all this has been to try to resist subjectivism on the one hand and cabbalism on the other, to try to keep the analysis of symbolic forms as closely tied as I could to concrete social events and occasions, the public world of common life, and to organize it in such a way that the connections between theoretical formulations and descriptive interpretations were unobscured by appeals to dark sciences. I have never been impressed by the argument that, as complete objectivity is impossible in these matters (as, of course, it is), one might as well let one's sentiments run loose. As [economist] Robert Solow has remarked, that is like saying that as a perfectly aseptic environment is impossible, one might as well conduct surgery in a sewer. Nor, on the other hand, have I been impressed with claims that structural linguistics, computer engineering, or some other advanced form of thought is going to enable us to understand men without knowing them. Nothing will discredit a semiotic approach to culture more quickly than allowing it to drift into a combination of intuitionism and alchemy, no matter how elegantly the intuitions are expressed or how modern the alchemy is made to look.

The danger that cultural analysis, in search of all-too-deep-lying turtles, will lose touch with the hard surfaces of life—with the political, economic, stratificatory realities within which men are everywhere contained—and with the biological and physical necessities on which those surfaces rest, is an everpresent one. The only defense against it, and against, thus, turning cultural analysis into a kind of socio-logical aestheticism, is to train such analysis on such realities and such necessities in the first place. It is thus that I have written about nationalism, about violence, about identity, about human nature, about legitimacy, about revolution, about eth-nicity, about urbanization, about status, about death, about time, and most of all about particular attempts by particular peoples to place these things in some sort of comprehensible, meaningful frame.

To look at the symbolic dimensions of social action—art, religion, ideology, science, law, morality, common sense—is not to turn away from the existential dilemmas of life for some empyrean realm of de-emotionalized forms; it is to plunge into the midst of them. The essential vocation of interpretive anthropology is not to answer our deepest questions, but to make available to us answers that others . . . have given, and thus to include them in the consultable record of what man has said.

NO ⬅

Godzilla Meets New Age Anthropology: Facing the Postmodernist Challenge to a Science of Culture

As we strive to understand nature, do we seek truth or solace?

Stephen Jay Gould

When I began working on the first incarnation of this paper, years ago, the greatest threat to a science of culture, it seemed to me, came from those anthropologists who considered themselves humanists. Today, though, the picture has changed radically. A much greater threat now comes from that large, amorphous host who march under the banner of postmodernism. Compared to the old-fashioned humanists, the threat they pose is as the Black Plague to the chicken pox. So it is against *them* that my major battle will be waged. By comparison, my engagement with traditional humanists will be but a preliminary skirmish.

Nonetheless, let me begin with the humanists, for, in their distaste for a science of culture, both humanists and postmodernists have much in common. If not genetically related, the two have at least sprouted from the same seedbed.

The antagonism between humanism and science is not only deep, but old. Almost two centuries ago the poet John Keats was provoked to cry "A Confusion on Newton!". Why? Because Newton had shown the rainbow to be caused by the refraction of light through raindrops, and *that*, for Keats, destroyed the wonder of it all. . . .

More recently, Joseph Wood Krutch has argued that "the experience of living is the thing which . . . has the greatest value, and . . . all the social sciences which tend to manipulate and regularize and unify human conduct result in a general lowering of the intensity of the experience . . . and . . . therefore, from my standpoint, they are bad."

Finally, E. E. Cummings expressed his contempt for science in this short verse:

> While you and I have lips and voices which,
> are for kissing and to sing with
> who cares if some oneeyed son of a bitch
> invents an instrument to measure spring with?

From *EUROPÉA*, 1995, I-1. Copyright © 1995 by EUROPÉA. Reprinted by permission. Notes omitted.

14

That scientists and humanists should be antagonists is thus nothing new or unusual. What *is* anomalous is that within something calling itself a science, there should be a large nucleus of persons who reject the ways of science and profess to practice anthropology as a humanity.

Since science vs. humanism is such a major issue, let us look at its philosophical basis. Part of this basis is the distinction between science and art, a distinction which Leslie White has expressed very nicely:

> Science is one of two basic ways of dealing with experience. The other is art. . . . The purpose of science and art is one: to render experience intelligible. . . . But although working toward the same goal, science and art approach it from opposite directions. Science deals with particulars in terms of universals: Uncle Tom disappears in the mass of Negro slaves. Art deals with universals in terms of particulars: the whole gamut of Negro slavery confronts us in the person of Uncle Tom. Art and science thus grasp a common experience, or reality, (but) by opposite poles.

White's distinction strikes me as valid. At bottom, humanists do look at the world as artists. But there is more to it than that. Humanists are not content merely to *contemplate* their subject; they also *celebrate* it. If you doubt this, just look inside the front cover of the *Anthropology and Humanism Quarterly*, a new journal published by our Association. There you will read that humanistic anthropology "celebrates" the fact that "human reality" is something that "we creative primates construct".

Now, celebration is all well and good, but it is not part of science. No physicist "celebrates" acceleration, and no chemist "celebrates" carbon tetrachloride. This is simply not a function of science. Our job, as scientists, is not to celebrate, but to *explain*, to *account for.* That's what makes us scientists. Let a poet enrapture himself over a lily, admiring the symmetry of its petals, the delicacy of its stamens, and let him sigh over the subtle fragrance of its nectar, but let him not try to pass himself off as a botanist! . . .

Let us not think, though, that by asserting that humanists do not do science, we are puncturing their balloon. You cannot puncture what was never inflated to begin with, and the fact is that the humanists in our ranks do not *claim* to be doing science. On the contrary, they cheerfully admit that they are *not*. But they aren't content with this. They go on to assert that *we* cannot do science, social science, either. Indeed, many of them claim that social science *cannot* be done.

Clifford Geertz, the leading literary humanist in anthropology, finds those of us who consider ourselves social scientists "ignorant and pretentious usurpers of the mission of the humanities". So the gauntlet has been thrown down. Well, if Geertz says there can't be a social science, why not? Only two possibilities exist: either we cannot do it because it is intrinsically undoable, or, if it is theoretically possible, we cannot do it because, in practice, it is too difficult.

Let us look at each possibility in turn. To begin with, why should a science of culture be inherently impossible? The answer is, only if the things and events it studies are not subject to cause and effect. So then we must ask, is human behavior subject to strict causality? Not if there is free will.

No one has put the matter more concisely than the 19th century British historian James Anthony Froude:

> When natural causes are liable to be set aside and neutralized by what is called volition, the word Science is out of place. If it is free to a man to choose what he will do or not do, there is no adequate science of him. . . .

This is not the place to attempt a formal refutation of free will. Instead, I would like to try to convince the humanists among you that determinism is not such a bad thing after all. In fact, I would argue that when you look at it deeply enough, free will turns out to be rather uncongenial to the artist. Let me present my case.

First, though, some background. Several years ago, to help us with an exhibit at the museum in which I work, we hired an artist from San Francisco. During the course of his work, I became well acquainted with him, and in one of our conversations, the subject of free will came up. As you might expect, he and I were on opposite sides of the fence on this issue. We argued about it, but neither of us made much headway in convincing the other. His work completed, the artist returned to San Francisco, but we continued to correspond. And in one of my letters, I presented an argument which I hoped might persuade him to abandon free will and embrace determinism. Here is what I wrote:

> *Dear ***,*
>
> *It is my contention that whenever an artist creates, he is never acting outside the stream of causation. What he engenders, no matter how novel, is never fortuitous. It is neither totally unforeseen nor unaccountable. It is, in fact, the product of lots of things swirling around in his psyche, conscious and unconscious. And—here's the kicker—I would argue that, from the artist's point of view, determinism, seen in this light, is better than free will! Genuine free will implies that, whatever you produce is entirely unconstrained by anything that went before. But if that were true, your creation would be completely out of your hands, entirely at the mercy of chance.*
>
> *And how could such a state of affairs possibly be satisfying to an artist? Isn't it much more congenial for you to think of your art as a summation and expression of everything that has gone into you, than for it to be unconnected and unrelated to you? Let's face it, free will—real free will—is completely depersonalizing and dehumanizing. It would work like a purely mechanical game of chance, in which you weren't even allowed to hold the dice. Surely the determinism I offer you, which puts you and your life experiences at the very heart of your artistic creation, should be much more congenial.*
>
> *Sincerely,*

Now, if free will is merely an illusion, if human behavior is indeed strictly determined, there is no reason why, in principle, there cannot be a science of human behavior, a science of culture. Some humanists may grudgingly concede this, but then raise another objection: Whatever the case may be in *principle*, they say, in *practice*, human behavior is simply too complex for any genuine regularities, let alone any laws, to be teased out of it.

But is complexity of behavior solely a problem for the anthropologist? Not at all. The phenomena of physics are intricate and complex too. Of the thousands of leaves on a tree, no two fall to earth exactly the same way. Yet physics was able to see past the unique and erratic behavior of each fluttering leaf, and to formulate a general law of falling bodies. Could it be, then, that the anthropological humanist has given up finding any underlying laws in human behavior because he has not looked for them hard enough? When he triumphantly proclaims the impossibility of formulating any cultural laws, could he merely be making a virtue out of his own shortcomings? Could this, then, be nothing more than a case of the tailless fox preaching taillessness?

Having thus warded off the humanists, we come now to the main event: the challenge to the science of culture posed by postmodern anthropology. Humanism was a straightforward, innocent adversary. Postmodernism is anything *but*. Sometimes it appears quite amorphous, but at other times it has the head of a hydra and the arms of a squid. Nor is this only my opinion. C. Richard King, a not unsympathetic observer of the movement, has said that postmodernism "lacks a single, unitary definition . . . It appears to be, at once, everything and nothing." . . .

[W]hatever else postmodernism might aspire to be, it is, at bottom, one more manifestation of the old, familiar prejudice against science. Thus, in her book, *Postmodernism and the Social Sciences*, Pauline Rosenau tells us that the postmodernist "questions the validity of modern science and the notion of objective knowledge". Moreover, postmodernism's headlong retreat from science goes further than humanism's ever did. Not only does it disdain science, it declares science to be dead.

Although postmodernism has challenged anthropology on all fronts, its main attack has been leveled at ethnography. To give the devil his due, postmodernists have had a valid point to make here. Ethnographers have traditionally tended to round things off, to smooth things up. Their monographs often present a single "authoritative" statement of a particular custom or belief, as if that were all there was to it. Yet anyone who has ever done fieldwork knows that informants' versions of a custom or belief often vary all over the map. Thus, presenting only one version *masks* the actual complexity. This foreshortening of reality, though, is not done to deceive. It is done for practical reasons. Were a monograph to include 16 different versions of every custom and belief, it might be more "real," but would also become so cumbersome and wearying as to vitiate the effort. So ethnographers generally round off their accounts to the first decimal place, so to speak, and present a kind of "official" version.

But what does this "official" version of a culture really represent?, ask the critics of traditional ethnography. Is it the opinion of one's best-liked informant? Or the most reliable one? Is it the response of one informant or of several? And if several, and if their range of responses has been "averaged," then what is this "average" that gets printed in the monograph—the mean, the median, or the mode?

Postmodern critics contend that ethnography should stress the many "voices" that may be raised in a primitive society. It is certainly true that there may well be many such "voices," even in a small native village, and that most of them usually remain unheard. That, in itself, is an objective fact, and deserves to be duly noted. But to *dwell* on the myriad voices of informants—indeed, to make a *career* out of it—seems to me to attenuate and trivialize the craft of ethnography.

Yet this has become a dominant theme in postmodern anthropology. With full-throated voice, postmodernists proclaim that there is not *one* reality, but *multiple* ones. The trouble is, though, that as realities are multiplied, they are also divided; as they become more numerous, they become correspondingly smaller. And, there being more and more of them, facts now count for less and less, and so reality becomes progressively diluted and rarified. And it is but a small step from this to saying that there is *no* reality at all! And once *that* assertion has been made, the wheels come off the wagon.

Let us look at this dissolution of reality a little more closely. Postmodern ethnography likes to call itself "dialogical". It puts a high premium on the *dialogue* that takes place between ethnographer and informant. James Clifford says that in the new ethnography "monophonic authority is questioned", and in its stead "dialogism and polyphony are recognized as modes of textual production". And Stephen Tyler, another leading voice in the movement, holds that postmodern ethnography "emphasizes the cooperative and collaborative nature of the ethnographic situation in contrast to the ideology of the transcendant observer". But Tyler goes a step further, claiming that the postmodern ethnographer "rejects the ideology of 'observer-observed', there being nothing observed and no one who is observer". If this is literally true, one is left to wonder, with Richard King, whether "an anthropology which dismisses the distinctions between self and other . . . is possible or even imaginable?".

Setting that question aside, we come to the matter of "truth". Consider the following dilemma. If "truth" is a statement about reality, but reality has already been bargained away, where does that leave truth? "In cultural studies", says Clifford, "we can no longer know the whole truth, or even claim to approach it". But if the search for truth, the traditional objective of science, is left lying in the dust, what happens to science itself? The answer is inescapable. If, as Clifford says, "Cultures are not scientific 'objects', the science of culture loses its subject matter, and with it, its identity and even its very existence. . . .

With ethnographic facts now having but a tenuous reality, they are being reassigned a place in the domain of literature, namely, fiction. Clifford puts his seal of approval on this change in the following words: "Ethnographic writings can properly be called fictions in the sense of 'something made or fashioned'. . . . But it is important to preserve the meaning not merely of making, but also of making up, of inventing things not actually real". So there we are, in the Land of Diggledy Dan.

Any serious study of literature naturally involves the use of *texts*. And texts have become a focus of postmodern ethnography. According to Geertz's oft-quoted remark, culture itself is "an ensemble of texts, themselves ensembles, which the anthropologist strains to read over the shoulder of those to whom they properly belong". So the new ethnographer's field notes become his texts, and he proceeds to deal with them accordingly.

Yet, the more texts are scrutinized, the more they seem to proliferate, spawning *subtexts*. Now, teasing subtexts from a main text is surely slippery business, but it's also a lot of fun. It's a game *any*one can play, and *every*one can win, because there are no rules. There is no correct interpretation, no right answer. Any answer is as good as any other. . . .

Another offshoot of literary ethnography is narrative. Its practitioners focus on *stories* rather than customs. These "stories" started out as biographies, the life histories of one's informants. But it wasn't long before biography turned into *auto*biography, and the subject of one's research became, not one's informants, but oneself. As James Clifford put it, "With the 'fieldwork account' the rhetoric of experienced objectivity yields to that of the autobiography and the ironic selfpor-trait. The ethnographer, a character in a fiction, is at center stage". . . .

Practiced with fervor, this form of postmodern ethnography becomes supremely self-centered. The ethnographer focuses, not on what he is observing, but on what he *feels* about what he is observing! He is, in effect, watching the patient, but taking his own pulse! Thus, he has become more important than his subject matter. Or rather, he has turned himself *into* his own subject matter. So, by sleight-of-hand, ethnography has become autobiography. . . .

Needless to say, all of this is the very antithesis of science. The corner-stone of science has always been the premise that there is a real world out there, independent of our individual existences. And it is *this* world that, as scientists—as *anthropologists*—we should be studying. If anyone still doggedly prefers to contemplate his own navel, fine. But let him call his contemplation by a different name than anthropology. . . .

I find it quite ironic that persons so concerned with "meaning" as postmodern ethnographers claim to be, should show so little regard for the process of *con-veying* meaning, namely, communication. Yet, "meaning" is certainly what they profess to be after. Listen to Clifford Geertz:

> Believing . . . that man is an animal suspended in webs of significance he himself has spun, I take culture to be those webs, and the analysis of it to be therefore not an empirical science in search of law but an interpretive one in search of meaning.

Beware of those "webs of significance"! From them we have much to fear. The new ethnographer, like a spider, draws forth from his spinaret, threads of infinite subtlety, and with them, creates his own webs which, like those of the spider, are not only delicate, but sticky. And in them, he entraps his prey, holding it fast while he sucks out its meaning. Then, perhaps, he will discard the eviscerated carcass, leaving it to the old-fashioned ethnographer to find whatever vestige of structure and substance may be left in it.

Confronted with a choice between substance and meaning, it is perfectly clear that Geertz will take meaning any day. For him, nothing is what it *is*. It is what it *means*. The famous Balinese cockfight, for example, becomes, at his hands—and here I quote Geertz directly—"image", "fiction", "a model", "a metaphor". So far does he give flight to his fancies in this regard that even his fellow postmodernist, Vincent Crapanzano, feels it necessary to bring him to heel. Thus, Crapanzano says sharply, "Cockfights are surely cockfights for the Balinese—and not images, fictions, models, and metaphors". Indeed, Geertz's rendition of Balinese cockfights so disturbs Crapanzano that he characterizes it as "constructions of constructions of constructions", a simple, bloody fight between two roosters transmogrified into Cloud Cuckooland! . . .

･❀･

In the frontal attack of postmodernism on anthropology, one major casualty has been . . . *ethnology.* So *fixated* are postmodernists at the level of ethnography, that they have failed to fulfill ethnography's traditional obligation to ethnology. From its earliest days, ethnography has always been the handmaiden of ethnology. It quarried and dressed the stones which ethnology then used to erect its larger stuctures. For it is here, in ethnology, that broad theories are built and generalizations crafted; where the major questions of anthropology are asked and answered. *Here* it is that we debate the origin of clans, the invention of agriculture, the function of crosscousin marriage, the role of age grades, the rise of chiefdoms, and the development of states. What have postmodernists contributed to the solution of these great problems? Nothing. Has anyone even *heard* of a postmodernist theory of the origin of the state? Alas, what will happen to such questions in an age of postmodern anthropology?

The new ethnographers are not, however, unaware that they're sidestepping these issues. George Marcus, for example, notes that "because of modern ethnography's commitment to social criticism, . . . it has rarely been directed to answering macrosociological questions about the causes of events or the constitution of major systems and processes". The new ethnographer, then, is like a mason so enamored of the peculiarities of each brick, that he turns them over in his hands, carefully studying them, but cannot bring himself to arrange them into some larger structure. He is a mason who has neglected to apply for his architect's license. And why not? Because he doubts that major edifices can ever be built anyway.

But it gets worse. Not only does the new ethnographer refuse to start building himself, he would deny the *ethnologist* a building permit too. He is not content to say what *he* can't do, he also tells us what *we* can't do. And why can't we? Because—among other things—the tools we choose to employ are defective. They are tools of our own devising—"hegemonic concepts"—rather than the simple adzes and digging sticks of our informants. And, Stephen Tyler tells us, "postmodern ethnography . . . seeks . . . to avoid grounding itself in the theoretical and commonsense categories of . . . Western tradition".

Were we to follow Tyler's injunction, though, we would be severely hamstrung. Consider this example. I regard the proportion of waking time that a society spends on subsistence to be of fundamental importance in determining the general level of its culture. Accordingly, I have tried to ascertain this figure for the Kuikuru of central Brazil during the course of my field work among them. However, not being a concept the Kuikuru themselves would be likely to think of, Tyler would rule such a calculation out of court as a "hegemonic Western category". Carried to this extreme, cultural relativism surely cuts us off at the knees. . . .

⊷❦⊶

As we noted earlier, postmodernists are rather ambivalent about truth. At times, they assert there is no such thing; but at other times they tell us there are a thousand different truths. Where on earth does that leave us?

Needless to say, one can define truth any way one feels like. If one wants to define it as that which it is impossible to attain, fine. That takes care of the matter, once and for all. But what *good* does that do? It merely evades an important issue. Here's what I suggest instead. Truth need not be regarded as some mystical, vaporous essence; a holy grail to be sought for but never found. Truth can simply be defined as an *agreement* or *correspondence* between a proposition and something in the external world. As such, it becomes quite possible to attain it. In fact, it is, and has always been, the stated goal of science.

Another notion I rebel against is that truth, if allowed to exist at all, is at best tenuous and protean, and that anyone's "truth" is just as valid as anyone else's. The implications of this view for an ethnographer working in the field are jolting, to say the least. It implies that he should be satisfied with whatever answer he gets to a question, and not try to ferret out the "truest" truth he can. . . .

Is this really where we want to be? Suppose, for example, that Napoleon Chagnon had accepted at face value the genealogies first given to him by the Yanomamö as being as good as any other, and let it go at that. By eschewing verification he would, according to Tyler, have been following good, postmodernist procedure. But he would also have been sorely deceived, because, as he found out months later, the Yanomamö had purposely and systematically lied to him. Now, can any postmodernist seriously hold that the spurious genealogies Chagnon first obtained were just as good, just as true, just as valid, as the ones he got later? . . .

⊷❦⊶

I have often been struck by the fact that there is no such thing as postmodern chemistry, or postmodern geology. Why not? To begin with, no serious science would be foolish enough to define itself out of existence. Nor could it afford to spend so much of its time dabbling in hairsplitting and pettifogging. No real science would devote itself so wholeheartedly to the inconsequential. To be sure, all the sciences have their many tiny facts, but these are gathered, not for their own sake, but to serve some larger purpose. And this purpose is to formulate a series of overarching propositions that seek to explain ever larger segments of nature. And are these aims not all we really need? . . .

So, what is to happen? What can we expect in the future? Despite my previous lamentations, I am not altogether worried; at least not in the long run. Why? Because I'm a firm believer in the principle of natural selection, and natural selection works on ideas just as it does on organisms. In the realm of ideas, as everywhere else, it's the payoff that counts. Ultimately, any intellectual movement will be judged by its results. If it produces nothing tangible, substantial, or enlightening, it will fall by the wayside, just as so many intellectual fads have before it. Thus I am ready to predict that postmodernism, like phrenology, prohibition, and free silver, will quietly fade away, and center stage will once more be occupied by less scintillating but more productive forms of inquiry. . . .

POSTSCRIPT

Should Anthropology Stop Trying to Model Itself on the Natural Sciences?

Cultural anthropology is often viewed as a big tent capable of embracing many diverse points of view, as the selections by Geertz and Carneiro suggest. Many anthropologists easily slip back and forth between humanistic and scientific approaches, depending on the type of problem they are trying to solve. For example, one might use an interpretive approach to analyze a religious ritual and a scientific approach to work out the effects of globalization on a people's economy. But true partisans of the two paradigms, such as Geertz and Carneiro, would point out that the approaches are based on fundamentally incompatible epistemologies, totally different conceptions of what knowledge is and how we can get at it.

Geertz believes that it is futile to seek natural laws of human thought and behavior and that any positivist, nomothetic anthropology leaves out what is most important to understand, namely, the meanings and significance of social action to the people themselves. To Geertz, the job of the anthropologist is to decipher the meanings of social behaviors as if they were manuscripts in an obscure foreign language. Elsewhere he says, "The culture of a people is an ensemble of texts, themselves ensembles, which the anthropologist strains to read over the shoulders of those to whom they properly belong" (*The Interpretation of Cultures*, Basic Books, 1973, p. 452). Carneiro, on the other hand, considers anthropology's job to be explaining why human ideas and actions take the form they do. He is committed to the notion that forms of culture have causes, some within the culture itself and others—like the natural environment—external to it. He is best known for creating the "circumscription theory" of the origin of the state, which suggests that state forms of social organization (social hierachy, centralized political systems, geographical boundaries, etc.) arise when the population of a society increases, but there are geographical or social barriers preventing the people from merely spreading out while retaining a less complex form of political organization. Such problems, he would argue, cannot be solved by humanistic approaches like interpretive anthropology.

While Geertz is an ardent champion of humanistic anthropology, he is not the harshest critic of anthropology as a law-based science. A number of so-called postmodern scholars—such as James Clifford, George Marcus, and Edward Tylor—have been much more vocal in their attacks on positivism in anthropology. They have urged anthropology to become a self-reflective social science, practicing what has been termed "critical theory." For these scholars, anthropologists should seek the implicit, underlying assumptions and motivations of the anthropologists who have produced what passes for anthropological knowledge. They have borrowed methods from literary criticism to "deconstruct" many classic ethnographic monographs, revealing the rhetorical techniques used by the authors to convince readers of the veracity of their accounts. Opponents have suggested that critical theorists are more concerned with studying the culture of anthropology than with understanding anthropology's traditional subject matter. Postmodernists have offered suggestions on how to improve the writing of ethnography, but do not offer any substitute for the kinds of explanations of sociocultural phenomena that natural science-minded anthropologists aim to produce.

Marvin Harris's cultural materialist approach, incorporating cultural evolution and environmental adaptation, is probably the most widely used scientific paradigm in anthropology. Carneiro uses this approach. Another scientific approach taken by some anthropologists (as well as biologists and psychologists) is "sociobiology." Sociobiologists argue that humans, like all animals, are genetically programmed to respond in certain ways, and cultural practices are just an external manifestation of inner biological drives. For an example of a sociobiological explanation, see the selection by Napoleon Chagnon in Issue 11.

Geertz's *The Interpretation of Cultures* (Basic Books, 1973), for which this selection was written, is the most coherent statement outlining the breadth and scope of an interpretive anthropology. It contains what is probably his best-known interpretive essay, "Deep Play: Notes on the Balinese Cockfight." Students should also consult his *Local Knowledge: Further Essays in Interpretive Anthropology* (Basic Books, 1983) and *Works and Lives: The Anthropologist as Author* (Stanford University Press, 1988). Michael Fisher's review essay "Interpretive Anthropology," *Reviews in Anthropology* (vol. 4, no. 4, 1977) offers a useful overview.

Important essays from a critical or postmodern perspective are contained in two edited volumes: George E. Marcus and Michael M.J. Fisher's *Anthropology as Cultural Critique: An Experimental Moment in the Human Sciences* (University of Chicago Press, 1986) and James Clifford and George E. Marcus's *Writing Culture: The Poetics and Politics of Anthropology* (University of California Press, 1986).

Recent books by Robert Carneiro include *The Muse of History and the Science of Culture* (Kluwer Academic/Plenum, 2000) and *Evolutionism in Cultural Anthropology: A Critical History* (Westview, 2003). A summary of his circumscription theory of state formation can be found in the article, "A Theory of the Origin of the State," *Science* (vol. 169, 1970). For an extended treatment of Harris's views, see his *Cultural Materialism: The Struggle for a Science of Culture* (Random House, 1979).

ISSUE 2

Was Margaret Mead's Fieldwork on Samoan Adolescents Fundamentally Flawed?

YES: Derek Freeman, from *Margaret Mead and Samoa: The Making and Unmaking of an Anthropological Myth* (Harvard University Press, 1983)

NO: Lowell D. Holmes and Ellen Rhoads Holmes, from *Samoan Village: Then and Now,* 2d ed. (Harcourt Brace Jovanovich College Publishers, 1992)

ISSUE SUMMARY

YES: Social anthropologist Derek Freeman argues that Margaret Mead was wrong when she stated that Samoan adolescents had sexual freedom. He contends that Mead went to Samoa determined to prove anthropologist Franz Boas's cultural determinist agenda and states that Mead was so eager to believe in Samoan sexual freedom that she was consistently the victim of a hoax perpetrated by Samoan girls and young women who enjoyed tricking her.

NO: Cultural anthropologists Lowell D. Holmes and Ellen Rhoads Holmes contend that Margaret Mead had a very solid understanding of Samoan culture in general. During a restudy of Mead's research, they came to many of the same conclusions that Mead had reached about Samoan sexuality and adolescent experiences. Mead's description of Samoan culture exaggerates the amount of sexual freedom and the degree to which adolescence in Samoa is carefree but these differences, they argue, can be explained in terms of changes in Samoan culture since 1925 and in terms of Mead's relatively unsophisticated research methods as compared with field methods used today.

In 1925 a student of anthropologist Franz Boas named Margaret Mead set off for a nine-month study of adolescent women in Samoa. At only 23 years old, Mead was just barely beyond adolescence herself. Concerned about Mead's safety in a remote and distant place, Boas arranged for her to stay with an American family. Here she could live in a European-style house and her physical safety would be ensured. For the next several months she studied the culture and lives of young Samoan women by visiting their village.

On her return to New York in 1925, she wrote up her dissertation for Boas, revising this volume for publication in 1928. She titled the book *Coming of Age in Samoa: A Psychological Study of Primitive Youth for Western Civilization.* Mead concluded that because Samoan culture was so much more relaxed about sexuality than Western culture, Samoan adolescents had a much more tranquil transition from childhood to adulthood than was observed in America and other Western countries. *Coming of Age in Samoa* was an immediate best-seller and it earned Mead renown as a scientist.

In 1983 Derek Freeman published his book entitled *Margaret Mead and Samoa: The Making and Unmaking of an Anthropological Myth* (Harvard University Press), an excerpt of which is provided as the Yes-side selection. Freeman argues that Mead was so eager to find support for her model that she blatantly biased her Samoan fieldwork findings and in effect falsified her data.

Freeman had worked in Western Samoa from 1940 to 1943, returning for further fieldwork from 1965 to 1967. During his research he found evidence that challenges some of Mead's published field data as well as a number of her conclusions regarding Samoan adolescence. He contends that his findings call into question Mead's entire project. He also contends that Mead's young Samoan informants perpetrated a hoax on her by making up stories about their promiscuity.

Freeman's selection is countered by a selection written by Lowell D. Holmes and Ellen Rhoads Holmes, who, in the 1950s, had conducted a restudy of the same community that Mead had visited. Holmes and Holmes had expressly intended to test the reliability and validity of Mead's findings. They conclude that while Mead's characterizations of Samoans are in some ways exaggerated, the characterizations are by no means fundamentally wrong.

These selections allow us to ask a number of questions about Mead's research: Did Mead unintentionally exaggerate her findings about sexual freedom? Or did she intentionally falsify her field data, specifically so that she could support Boas's model of cultural determinism? Could Mead's excesses be explained as the consequence of her being a youthful and inexperienced field researcher? Or can differences between Mead's findings and those of the selection authors be explained in other ways?

These selections raise a number of questions about the replicability of anthropological fieldwork, as well. Is it possible to conduct a systematic restudy of another anthropologist's field subjects? Can an anthropologist working in another village or on another island reliably challenge the findings of another anthropologist?

Derek Freeman  **YES**

Margaret Mead and Samoa

Preface

By far the most widely known of Margaret Mead's numerous books is *Coming of Age in Samoa,* based on fieldwork on which she embarked in 1925 at the instigation of Franz Boas, her professor at Columbia University. Boas had sent the 23-year-old Mead to Samoa to study adolescence, and she returned with a startling conclusion. Adolescence was known in America and Europe as a time of emotional stresses and conflicts. If, Mead argued, these problems were caused by the biological processes of maturation, then they would necessarily be found in all human societies. But in Samoa, she reported, life was easy and casual, and adolescence was the easiest and most pleasant time of life. Thus in anthropological terms, according to Mead, Samoa was a "negative instance"—and the existence of this one counterexample demonstrated that the disturbances associated with adolescence in the United States and elsewhere had cultural and not biological causes. In the controversy between the adherents of biological determinism and those of cultural determinism, a controversy that was at its height in the 1920s, Mead's negative instance appeared to be a triumphant outcome for believers in the sovereignty of culture.

When *Coming of Age in Samoa* was published in 1928 it attracted immense attention, and its apparently conclusive finding swiftly entered anthropological lore as a jewel of a case. Since that time Mead's finding has been recounted in scores of textbooks, and through the vast popularity of *Coming of Age in Samoa,* the best-selling of all anthropological books, it has influenced the thinking of millions of people throughout the world. It is with the critical examination of this very widely accepted conclusion that I am concerned [here].

Scientific knowledge, as Karl Popper has shown, is principally advanced through the conscious adoption of "the critical method of error elimination." In other words, within science, propositions and theories are systematically tested by attempts to refute them, and they remain acceptable only as long as they withstand these attempts at refutation. In Popper's view, "in so far as a scientific statement speaks about reality it must be falsifiable," and rational criticism entails the testing of any particular statement in terms of its correspondence with the facts. Mead's classing of Samoa as a negative instance obviously depends on the adequacy of the account of Samoan culture on which it is based. It is thus very much a scientific proposition, for it is fully open to testing against the relevant empirical evidence.

While the systematic testing of the conclusions of a science is always desirable, this testing is plainly imperative when serious doubts have been expressed about some particular finding. Students of Samoan culture have long voiced such doubts about Mead's findings of 1928. . . . I adduce detailed empirical evidence to demonstrate that Mead's account of Samoan culture and character is fundamentally in error. I would emphasize that I am not intent on constructing an alternative ethnography of Samoa. Rather, the evidence I shall present has the specific purpose of scientifically refuting the proposition that Samoa is a negative instance by demonstrating that the depictions on which Mead based this assertion are, in varying degree, mistaken.

In undertaking this refutation I shall limit my scrutiny to those sections of Mead's writings which have stemmed from, or refer to, her researches on Samoa. My concern, moreover, is with the scientific import of these actual researches and *not* with Margaret Mead personally, or with any aspect of her ideas or activities that lies beyond the ambit of her writings on Samoa. I would emphasize also that I hold in high regard many of the personal achievements of Margaret Mead, Franz Boas, and the other individuals certain of whose assertions and ideas I necessarily must question in the pages that follow.

. . . When I reached Western Samoa in April 1940, I was very much a cultural determinist. *Coming of Age in Samoa* had been unreservedly commended to me by [Ernest] Beaglehole, and my credence in Mead's findings was complete.

After two years of study, during which I came to know all the islands of Western Samoa, I could speak Samoan well enough to converse in the company of chiefs with the punctilio that Samoan etiquette demands, and the time had come to select a local polity for intensive investigation. My choice was Sa'anapu, a settlement of 400 inhabitants on the south coast of Upolu. On my first visit to Sa'anapu I had become friendly with Lauvi Vainu'u, a senior talking chief. . . . I was to become his adopted son. From that time onward I lived as one of the Lauvi family whenever I was in Sa'anapu.

In my early work I had, in my unquestioning acceptance of Mead's writings, tended to dismiss all evidence that ran counter to her findings. By the end of 1942, however, it had become apparent to me that much of what she had written about the inhabitants of Manu'a in eastern Samoa did not apply to the people of western Samoa. After I had been assured by Samoans who had lived in Manu'a that life there was essentially the same as in the western islands, I realized that I would have to make one of the objectives of my research the systematic testing of Mead's depiction of Samoan culture.

Soon after I returned to Sa'anapu its chiefs forgathered one morning at Lauvi's house to confer on me one of the chiefly titles of their polity. I was thus able to attend all *fono,* or chiefly assemblies, as of right, and I soon came to be accepted by the community at large. From this time onward I was in an exceptionally favorable position to pursue my researches into the realities of Samoan life.

By the time I left Samoa in November 1943 I knew that I would one day face the responsibility of writing a refutation of Mead's Samoan findings. This would involve much research into the history of early Samoa. This task I began in 1945 in the manuscript holdings of the Mitchell Library in Sydney and later continued in England, where I thoroughly studied the Samoan archives of the London Missionary Society.

During 1946–1948, while studying anthropology at the University of London, I wrote a dissertation on Samoan social organization. . . . There then came, however, the opportunity to spend some years among the Iban of Borneo. With this diversion, . . . the continuation of my Samoan researches was long delayed.

I finally returned to Western Samoa, accompanied by my wife and daughters, at the end of 1965. Sa'anapu, now linked Apia by road, was once again my center of research. The chiefs of Sa'anapu immediately recognized the title they had conferred on me in 1943, and I became once again an active member of the Sa'anapu *fono*. My family and I remained in Samoa for just over two years, making frequent visits elsewhere in the district to which Sa'anapu belongs, as also to numerous other parts of the archipelago, from Saua in the east to Falealupo in the west.

Many educated Samoans, especially those who had attended college in New Zealand, had become familiar with Mead's writings about their culture. A number of them entreated me, as an anthropologist, to correct her mistaken depiction of the Samoan ethos. Accordingly, early in 1966 I set about the systematic examination of the entire range of Mead's writings on Samoa, seeking to test her assertions by detailed investigation of the particulars of the behavior or custom to which they referred. . . .

[I]n 1967 organized a formal traveling party to [the island of] Ta'ū. We visitors were received as long-lost kinsmen, and in the company of chiefs from both Ta'ū and Sa'anapu I was able to review all those facets of Mead's depiction of Samoa which were then still at issue. In Ta'ū I also recorded the testimony of men and women who remembered the period to which Mead's writings refer. In many instances these recollections were vivid and specific; as one of my informants remarked, the happenings of the mid 1920s were still fresh in their memories.

As my inquiries progressed it became evident that my critical scrutiny of Mead's conclusions would have to extend to the anthropological paradigm of which *Coming of Age in Samoa* was a part. . . .

My researches were not completed until 1981, when I finally gained access to the archives of the High Court of American Samoa for the 1920s. Thus my refutation of Mead's depiction of Samoa appears some years after her death. In November 1964, however, when Dr. Mead visited the Australian National University, I informed her very fully, during a long private conversation, of the empirical basis of my disagreement with her depiction of Samoa. From that time onward we were in correspondence, and in August 1978, upon its first completion, I offered to send her an early draft of my refutation of the conclusions she had reached in *Coming of Age in Samoa*. I received no reply to this offer before Dr. Mead's death in November of that year.

In September 1981 I returned to Western Samoa with the specific purpose of submitting a draft of [my] book to the critical scrutiny of Samoan scholars. . . . In the course of the refutation of Mead's misleading account of their culture, which many Samoans encouraged me to undertake, I have had to deal realistically with the darker side of Samoan life. During my visit of 1981 I found among contemporary Samoans both a mature appreciation of the need to face these realities and a clear-headed pride in the virtues and strengths of the Samoan way of life. . . .

Mead's Misconstruing of Samoa

. . . [The] notion that cultural determinism was absolute was "so obvious" to Mead that . . . she also avowed it in *Coming of Age in Samoa*, in respect of adolescent behavior.

That this doctrine of the absoluteness of cultural determinism should have seemed "so obvious" to Mead is understandable. Anthropology, when she began its study in 1922, was dominated by Boas' "compelling idea," as Leslie Spier has called it, of "the complete moulding of every human expression—inner thought and external behavior—by social conditioning," and by the time she left for Samoa in 1925 she had become a fervent devotee of the notion that human behavior could be explained in purely cultural terms. Further, although by the time of Mead's recruitment to its ranks cultural anthropology had achieved its independence, it had done so at the cost of becoming an ideology that, in an actively unscientific way, sought totally to exclude biology from the explanation of human behavior. Thus as, [Alfred] Kroeber declared, "the important thing about anthropology is not the science but an attitude of mind"—an attitude of mind, that is, committed to the doctrine of culture as a superorganic entity which incessantly shapes human behavior, "conditioning all responses." It was of this attitude of mind that Mead became a leading proponent, with (as Marvin Harris has observed) her anthropological mission, set for her by Boas, being to defeat the notion of a "panhuman hereditary human nature." She pursued this objective by tirelessly stressing, in publication after publication, "the absence of maturational regularities."

In her own account of this mission, Mead describes it as a battle which she and other Boasians had had to fight with the whole battery at their command, using the most fantastic and startling examples they could muster. It is thus evident that her writings during this period, about Samoa as about other South Seas cultures, had the explicit aim of confuting biological explanations of human behavior and vindicating the doctrines of the Boasian school. By 1939 this battle, according to Mead, had been won. . . .

For Mead's readers in North America and elsewhere in the Western world, there could be no more plausible location for the idyllic society of which she wrote than in the South Seas, a region that since the days of Bougainville has figured in the fantasies of Europeans and Americans as a place of preternatural contentment and sensual delight. So, as Mead reports, her announcement in 1925 that she was going to Samoa caused the same breathless stir as if she had been "setting off for heaven." Indeed, there were many in the 1920s, according to Mead, who longed to go to the South Sea islands "to escape to a kind of divine nothingness in which life would be reduced to the simplest physical terms, to sunshine and the moving shadows of palm trees, to bronze-bodied girls and bronze-bodied boys, food for the asking, no work to do, no obligations to meet."

. . . How did the young Margaret Mead come so to miscronstrue ethos and ethnography of Samoa? The fervency of her belief in cultural determinism and her tendency to view the South Seas as an earthly paradise go some way in accounting for what happened, but manifestly more was involved.

The Ph.D. topic that Boas assigned to Mead was the comparative study of canoe-building, house-building, and tattooing in the Polynesian culture area. During 1924 she gathered information on these activities from the available literature on the Hawaiians, the Marquesans, the Maori, the Tahitians, and the Samoans. These doctoral studies did not have any direct relevance to the quite separate problem of adolescence in Samoa that Boas set her in 1925, and, indeed, the fact that her reading was mainly on Eastern rather than Western Polynesia concealed from her the marked extent to which the traditional culture and values of Samoa differ from those of Tahiti. Again, during the spring of 1925 she had little time for systematic preparation for her Samoan researches. Indeed, the counsel she received from Boas about these researches prior to her departure for Pago Pago lasted, she tells us, for only half an hour. During this brief meeting Boas' principal instruction was that she should concentrate on the problem he had set her and not waste time doing ethnography. Accordingly, when in the second week of November 1925 Mead reached Manu'a, she at once launched into the study of adolescence without first acquiring, either by observation or from inquiry with adult informants, a thorough understanding of the traditional values and customs of the Manu'ans. This, without doubt, was an ill-advised way to proceed, for it meant that Mead was in no position to check the statements of the girls she was studying against a well-informed knowledge of the fa'aSamoa [Samoan way of life].

It is also evident that Mead greatly underestimated the complexity of the culture, society, history, and psychology of the people among whom she was to study adolescence. Samoan society, so Mead would have it, is "very simple," and Samoan culture "uncomplex." . . .

As any one who cares to consult Augustin Krämer's *Die Samoa-Inseln,* Robert Louis Stevenson's *A Footnote to History,* or J. W. Davidson's *Samoa mo Samoa* will quickly discover, Samoan society and culture are by no means simple and uncomplex; they are marked by particularities, intricacies, and subtleties quite as daunting as those which face students of Europe and Asia. Indeed, the fa'aSamoa is so sinuously complex that, as Stevenson's stepdaughter, Isobel Strong, once remarked, "one may live long in Samoa without understanding the whys and wherefores." Mead, however, spent not even a few months on the systematic study of Manu'a before launching upon the study of adolescence immediately upon her arrival in Ta'ū in accordance with Boas' instructions. Thus, she has noted that while on her later field trips she had "the more satisfactory task of learning the culture first and only afterwards working on a special problem" in Samoa this was "not necessary."

. . . Another problem was that of being able to communicate adequately with the people she was to study. Mead had arrived in Pago Pago without any knowledge of the Samoan language. . . . In this situation Mead was plainly at some hazard pursuing her inquiries in Manu'a, for Samoans, when diverted by the stumbling efforts of outsiders to speak their demanding language, are inclined not to take them seriously.

Mead, then, began her inquiries with her girl informants with a far from perfect command of the vernacular, and without systematic prior investigation of Manu'an society and values. Added to this, she elected to live not in a Samoan household but with the handful of expatriate Americans who were the local representatives of the naval government of American Samoa, from which in 1925 many Manu'ans were radically disaffected. . . . Of the immense advantage that an ethnographer gains by living among the people whose values and behavior he is intent on understanding there can be not the slightest doubt. Mead, however, within six weeks of her arrival in Pago Pago, and before she had spent any time actually staying in a traditional household, had come to feel that the food she would have to eat would be too starchy, and the conditions of living she would have to endure too nerve-racking to make residence with a Samoan family bearable. In Ta'ū, she told Boas, she would be able to live "in a white household" and yet be in the midst of one of the villages from which she would be drawing her adolescent subjects. This arrangement to live not in a Samoan household but with the Holt family in their European-style house, which was also the location of the government radio station and medical dispensary, decisively determined the form her researches were to take.

According to Mead her residence in these government quarters furnished her with an absolutely essential neutral base from which she could study all of the individuals in the surrounding village while at the same time remaining "aloof from native feuds and lines of demarcation." Against this exiguous advantage she was, however, depriving herself of the close contacts that speedily develop in Samoa between an ethnographer and the members of the extended family in which he or she lives. Such contacts are essential for the gaining of a thorough understanding of the Samoan language and, most important of all, for the independent verification, by the continuous observation of actual behavior, of the statements being derived from informants. Thus, by living with the Holts, Mead was trapping herself in a situation in which she was forced to rely not on observations of the behavior of Samoans as they lived their lives beyond the precincts of the government station on Ta'ū, but on such hearsay information as she was able to extract from her adolescent subjects. . . .

It is evident then that although, as Mead records, she could "wander freely about the village or go on fishing trips or stop at a house where a woman was weaving" when she was away from the dispensary, her account of adolescence in Samoa was, in the main, derived from the young informants who came to talk with her away from their homes in the villages of Lumā, Si'ufaga, and Faleasao. So, as Mead states, for these three villages, from which all her adolescent informants were drawn, she saw the life that went on "through the eyes" of the group of girls on the details of whose lives she was concentrating. This situation is of crucial significance for the assessment of Mead's researches in Manu'a, for we are clearly faced with the question of the extent to which the lens she fashioned from what she was being told by her adolescent informants and through which she saw Samoan life was a true and accurate lens.

. . . [M]any of the assertions appearing in Mead's depiction of Samoa are fundamentally in error, and some of them preposterously false. How are we to account for the presence of errors of this magnitude? Some Samoans who have read *Coming of Age in Samoa* react, as Shore reports, with anger and the insistence "that Mead lied." This, however, is an interpretation that I have no hesitation in dismissing. The succession of prefaces to *Coming of Age* in Samoa published by Mead in 1949, 1953, 1961, and 1973 indicate clearly, in my judgment, that she did give genuine credence to the view of Samoan life with which she returned to New York in 1926. Moreover, in the 1969 edition of *Social Organization of Manu'a* she freely conceded that there was a serious problem in reconciling the "contradictions" between her own depiction of Samoa and that contained in "other records of historical and contemporary behavior." . . .

Mead's depiction of Samoan culture, as I have shown, is marked by major errors, and her account of the sexual behavior of Samoans by a mind-boggling contradiction, for she asserts that the Samoans have a culture in which female virginity is very highly valued, with a virginity-testing ceremony being "theoretically observed at weddings of all ranks," while at the same time adolescence among females is regarded as a period "appropriate for love-making," with promiscuity before marriage being both permitted and "expected." And, indeed, she actually describes the Samoans as making the "demand" that a female should be "both receptive to the advances of many lovers and yet capable of showing the tokens of virginity at marriage." Something, it becomes plain at this juncture, is emphatically amiss, for surely no human population could be so cognitively disoriented as to conduct their lives in such a schizophrenic way. Nor are the Samoans remotely like this, for . . . they are, in fact, a people who traditionally value virginity highly and so disapprove of premarital promiscuity as to exercise a strict surveillance over the comings and goings of adolescent girls. That these values and this regime were in force in Manu'a in the mid 1920s is, furthermore, clearly established by the testimony of the Manu'ans themselves who, when I discussed this period with those who well remembered it, confirmed that the fa'aSamoa in these matters was operative then as it was both before and after Mead's brief sojourn in Ta'ū. What then can have been the source of Mead's erroneous statement that in Samoa there is great premarital freedom, with promiscuity before marriage among adolescent girls, being both permitted and expected?

The explanation most consistently advanced by the Samoans themselves for the magnitude of the errors in her depiction of their culture and in particular of their sexual morality is, as [Eleanor Ruth] Gerber has reported, "that Mead's informants must have been telling lies in order to tease her." Those Samoans who offer this explanation, which I have heard in Manu'a as well as in other parts of Samoa, are referring to the behavior called *tau fa'ase'e*, to which Samoans are much prone. *Fa'ase'e* (literally "to cause to slip") means "to dupe," as in the example given by Milner, *"e fa'ase'e gofie le teine,* the girl is easily duped"; and the phrase *tau fa'ase'e* refers to the action of deliberately duping someone, a pastime that greatly appeals to the Samoans as a respite from the severities of their authoritarian society.

Because of their strict morality, Samoans show a decided reluctance to discuss sexual matters with outsiders or those in authority, a reticence that is especially marked among female adolescents. Thus, Holmes reports that when he and his wife lived in Manu'a and Tutuila in 1954 "it was never possible to obtain details of sexual experience from unmarried informants, though several of these people were constant companions and part of the household." Further, as Lauifi Ili, Holmes's principal assistant, observes, when it comes to imparting information about sexual activities, Samoan girls are "very close-mouthed and ashamed." Yet it was precisely information of this kind that Mead, a liberated young American newly arrived from New York and resident in the government station at Ta'ū, sought to extract from the adolescent girls she had been sent to study. And when she persisted in this unprecedented probing of a highly embarrassing topic, it is likely that these girls resorted, as Gerber's Samoan informants have averred, to *tau fa'ase'e*, regaling their inquisitor with counterfeit tales of casual love under the palm trees.

This, then, is the explanation that Samoans give for the highly inaccurate portrayal of their sexual morality in Mead's writings. It is an explanation that accounts for how it was that this erroneous portrayal came to be made, as well as for Mead's sincere credence in the account she has given in *Coming of Age in Samoa*, for she was indeed reporting what she had been told by her adolescent informants. The Manu'ans emphasize, however, that the girls who, they claim, plied Mead with these counterfeit tales were only amusing themselves, and had no inkling that their tales would ever find their way into a book.

While we cannot, in the absence of detailed corroborative evidence [but see addendum following], be sure about the truth of this Samoan claim that Mead was mischievously duped by her adolescent informants, we can be certain that she did return to New York in 1926 with tales running directly counter to all other ethnographic accounts of Samoa, from which she constructed her picture of Manu'a as a paradise of free love, and of Samoa as a negative instance, which, so she claimed, validated Boasian doctrine. It was this negative instance that she duly presented to Boas as the ideologically gratifying result of her inquiries in Manu'a. . . .

We are thus confronted in the case of Margaret Mead's Samoan researches with an instructive example of how, as evidence is sought to substantiate a cherished doctrine, the deeply held beliefs of those involved may lead them unwittingly into error. The danger of such an outcome is inherent, it would seem, in the very process of belief formation. . . .

In the case of Mead's Samoan researches, certainly, there is the clearest evidence that it was her deeply convinced belief in the doctrine of extreme cultural determinism, for which she was prepared to fight with the whole battery at her command, that led her to construct an account of Samoa that appeared to substantiate this very doctrine. There is, however, conclusive empirical evidence to demonstrate that Samoa, in numerous respects, is not at all as Mead depicted it to be.

A crucial issue that arises from this historic case for the discipline of anthropology, which has tended to accept the reports of ethnographers as entirely empirical statements, is the extent to which other ethnographic accounts may have been distorted by doctrinal convictions, as well as the methodological question of how such distortion can best be avoided. These are no small problems. I would merely comment that as we look back on Mead's Samoan researches we are able to appreciate anew the wisdom of Karl Popper's admonition that in both science and scholarship it is, above all else, indefatigable rational criticism of our suppositions that is of decisive importance, for such criticism by "bringing out our mistakes . . . makes us understand the difficulties of the problem we are trying to solve," and so saves us from the allure of the "obvious truth" of received doctrine.

Addendum: New Evidence of the Hoaxing of Margaret Mead

In my book *The Fateful Hoaxing of Margaret Mead* (1998) there is an account, based on the sworn testimony of Fa'apua'a, of how Margaret Mead in March of 1926 on the island of Ofu in American Samoa was hoaxed about the sexual mores of the Samoans by her two Samoan traveling companions, Fa'apua'a and Fofoa.

I [have recently discovered] direct evidence, from Mead's own papers, that Margaret Mead was indeed taken in by the "whispered confidences" (as she called them) of Fa'apua'a and Fofoa. This incontrovertible historical evidence finally brings to closure the long-running controversy over Margaret Mead's Samoan fieldwork. . . .

The crucially important direct evidence in question is contained in a little known book entitled *All True! The Record of Actual Adventures That Have Happened To Ten Women of Today* that was published in New York in 1931 by Brewer, Warren and Putnam. The "adventure" by Dr. Margaret Mead is entitled "Life as a Samoan Girl". It begins with a wistful reference to "the group of reverend scientists" who in 1925 sent her to study (Mead, 1925) "the problem of which phenomena of adolescence are culturally and which physiologically determined" among the adolescent girls of Samoa, with "no very clear idea" of how she was "to do this." It ends with an account of her journey to the islands of Ofu and Olosega in March of 1926 with the "two Samoan girls," as she calls them, Fa'apua'a and Fofoa. In fact, Fa'apua'a and Fofoa were both twenty-four years of age and slightly older than Dr. Mead herself. Dr. Mead continues her account of her visit to the islands of Ofu and Olosega with Fa'apua'a and Fofoa by stating: "In all things I had behaved as a Samoan, for only so, only by losing my identity, as far as possible, had I been able to become acquainted with the Samoan girls receive their whispered confidences and learn at the same time the answer to the scientists' questions."

This account, by Mead herself, is fully confirmed by the sworn testimony of Fa'apua'a (cf. Freeman, 1998, Chapter 11). It can be found on p. 141 of the second and paperback edition (1999) of my book *The Fateful Hoaxing of Margaret Mead: A historical analysis of her Samoan research.* It is definitive historical evidence that establishes that Martin Orans is in outright error in asserting (1996:92) that it is "demonstrably false that Mead was taken in by Fa'apua'a and Fofoa." It is also evidence that establishes that *Coming of Age in Samoa,* far from being a "scientific classic" (as Mead herself supposed) is, in certain vitally significant respects (as in its dream-like second chapter), a work of anthropological fiction.

References

Freeman, Derek, 1999, *The Fateful Hoaxing of Margaret Mead,* Boulder: Westview, 2nd edition.

Mead, Margaret, 1925, Plan of Research Submitted to the National Research Council of the U.S.A. (Archives of the National Academy of Sciences).

Mead, Margaret, 1928, *Coming of Age in Samoa.* New York: Morrow.

Mead, Margaret, 1931, "Life as a Samoan Girl," in *All True! The Record of Actual Adventures That Happened to Ten Women of Today.* New York: Brewer, Warren and Putnam.

Orans, Martin, 1996, *Not Even Wrong: Margaret Mead, Derek Freeman and the Samoans,* Novato: Chandler and Sharp.

**Lowell D. Holmes and
Ellen Rhoads Holmes**

Samoan Character and
the Academic World

On January 31, 1983, the *New York Times* carried a front-page article, the headline of which read, "New Samoa Book Challenges Margaret Mead's Conclusions." The book that precipitated this somewhat unexpected turn of events was *Margaret Mead and Samoa: The Making and Unmaking of an Anthropological Myth* by Derek Freeman, an emeritus professor of anthropology at Australian National University in Canberra. This work, which some claim set off the most heated controversy in sociocultural anthropology in one hundred years, is described by its author as a "refutation of Mead's misleading account" of Samoan culture and personality as presented in her 1928 ethnography, *Coming of Age in Samoa.*

The *New York Times* article was of special interest to me because, in 1954, I had conducted a year-long methodological restudy of the Mead data under attack. I had lived in Ta'ū village, where Mead had worked twenty-nine years earlier, and had used many of her informants in a systematic and detailed evaluation of every observation and interpretation she had made about the lifestyle of the people in that Samoan village. A methodological restudy, incidentally, involves a second anthropologist going into the field with the *express purpose* of testing the reliability and validity of the findings of a former investigator. This restudy is made in order to establish what kinds of errors of data collection or interpretation might have been made by certain kinds of people, in certain kinds of field research situations, researching certain kinds of problems. For example, Margaret Mead was a twenty-three-year-old woman investigating a male-dominated society that venerates age. She was a student of Franz Boas and, therefore, went equipped with a particular theoretical frame of reference. She was also on her first field trip—at a time when research methods were crude. My task in this methodological restudy was not only to analyze how my findings might be different from hers (if that would be the case), but I would also attempt to speculate on how differences in the status of the investigators (for example, sex, age, family situation, education) and other personal factors might affect the collection and interpretation of data.

My critique of Margaret Mead's study was presented in my doctoral dissertation, *The Restudy of Manu'an Culture. A Problem in Methodology,* which by 1983 had been collecting dust on a Northwestern University library shelf for some twenty-seven years. I was therefore eager to obtain a copy of Freeman's new evaluation of Mead's work from its publisher, Harvard University Press. In reading the book this is what I found.

In *Margaret Mead and Samoa: The Making and Unmaking of an Anthropological Myth* (1983), Derek Freeman argues that Mead perpetuated a hoax comparable in consequence to that of Piltdown Man when, in 1928, she described Samoa as a paradise where competition, sexual inhibition, and guilt were virtually absent. Refusing to believe that adolescents in all societies inevitably experience emotional crises—storm and stress—because of biological changes associated with puberty (as hypothesized in *Adolescence* in 1904 by psychologist G. Stanley Hall), Mead set out to discover a society where the passage to adulthood was smooth and without trauma. She described such a society in *Coming of Age in Samoa*. In delineating this "negative instance" (which challenged Hall's theory of universal adolescent rebellion and strife), Margaret Mead had in effect established that nurture (culture) is more critical than nature (biology) in accounting for adolescent maturation behavior in the human species. Derek Freeman, on the other hand, rejects the idea that human behavior is largely shaped by culture and believes that Mead and her mentor, Franz Boas (commonly called the "Father of American Anthropology"), were guilty of *totally* ignoring the influence of biological heredity. He believes that Mead's "negative instance" results entirely from faulty data collection and that Mead's Samoan findings have led anthropology, psychology, and education down the primrose path of pseudoscience. Freeman's book, therefore, is an attempt to set the record straight through his own, more accurate, observations of Samoa and Samoans—although his observations of Samoan behavior were in another village, on another island, in another country, and fourteen years later.

Freeman's main theoretical approach in this evaluation of Mead's work derives from the German philosopher of science, Karl Popper, who maintains that science should be deductive, not inductive, and that progress in scientific research should consist essentially of attempts to refute established theories. Thus, Derek Freeman is out to destroy the credibility of what he interprets as the "absolute cultural determinism" to be found in the work of Margaret Mead as well as in much of the work of Boas and his other students. This claim is, of course, spurious, as any student of American anthropological theory knows. For example, in Melville J. Herskovits' biography of Franz Boas, we find the statement that, because of his "rounded view of the problem Boas could perceive so clearly the fallacy of the eugenicist theory, which held the destiny of men to be determined by biological endowment, with little regard for the learned, cultural determinants of behavior." By the same token, he "refused to accept the counter-dogma that man is born with a completely blank slate, on which can be written whatever is willed. He saw both innate endowment and learning—or, as it was called popularly, heredity and environment—as significant factors in the making of the mature individual" (1953:28). Herskovits also points out that "numerous examples can be found, in reports on the various studies he conducted, of how skillfully Boas was able to weave cultural and biological factors into a single fabric" (*Ibid.*).

Marvin Harris concurs: "American anthropology has always been concerned with the relationships between nature (in the guise of habitat and genic programming) and culture (in the guise of traditions encoded in the brain, not in the genes). Neither Boas nor his students ever denied that *Homo sapi-*

ens has a species-specific nature" (1983:26). In his book, *The Rise of Anthropological Theory,* Harris writes, "Boas systematically rejected almost every conceivable form of cultural determinism" (1968:283).

Evaluation of the Mead Data

My restudy experience in Ta'ū village in 1954 led me to conclude that Margaret Mead often overgeneralized; that, in many cases, we interpreted data differently; and that, because of her age and sex, some avenues of investigation apparently were closed to her—particularly those having to do with the more formal aspects of village political organization and ceremonial life. However, her overall characterization of the nature and dynamics of the culture were, in my judgment, quite valid and her contention that it was easier to come of age in Samoa than in America in 1925–1926 was undoubtedly correct. In spite of the greater possibilities for error in a pioneer study, Mead's age (only 23), her sex (in a male-dominated society), and her inexperience, I believe the reliability and validity of the Ta'ū village research is remarkably high.

I look upon an ethnographic account as a kind of map to be used in finding one's way about in a culture—in comprehending and anticipating behavior. Mead's account never left me lost or bewildered in my interactions with Samoan islanders, but I also felt that if one were to come to a decision about the comparative difficulties of coming of age in Samoa and the United States, it would be necessary to know something about what life was like for adolescents in America in 1925–1926. Joseph Folsom's book, *The Family,* published in 1934, but researched about the time Mead was writing *Coming of Age in Samoa,* provided that information. Folsom describes the social environment in which children came of age at that time as follows:

> Children are disciplined and trained with the ideal of absolute obedience to parents. Corporal punishment is used, ideally in cold blood. . . . All sexual behavior on the part of children is prevented by all means at the parents' disposal. . . . For the sake of prevention it has been usual to cultivate in the child, especially the girl, an attitude of horror or disgust toward all aspects of sex. . . . Premarital intercourse is immoral though not abhorrent. . . . Violations are supposedly prevented by the supervision of the girl's parents. . . . Illegitimate children are socially stigmatized. . . . The chief stigma falls upon the unmarried mother, because she has broken an important sex taboo (1934:10–25). . . .

While Freeman contends that Mead was absolutely wrong about nearly everything (partly, he maintains, because the teenage girls she used as informants consistently lied to her), I found discrepancies mainly in such areas as the degree of sexual freedom Samoan young people enjoy, the competitive nature of the society, the aggressiveness of Samoan behavior, and the degree of genuine affection and commitment between lovers and spouses.

I saw Samoan culture as considerably more competitive than Mead, although I never considered it as inflexible or aggressive as Freeman does. I observed a great preoccupation with status, power, and prestige among men of rank and, on more than one occasion, was present at fierce verbal duels between Talking Chiefs trying to enhance their own prestige and, incidentally, that of their village. . . .

I also found that Samoan culture was not as simple as Margaret Mead claimed, nor was Ta'ū village the paradise she would have us believe. She often romanticized, overgeneralized, and, on some occasions, took literary license in her descriptions of Samoan lifeways. For example, her very dramatic chapter, "A Day in Samoa," crowds typical activities (some of which occur only at particular times of the year) into a typical day and thereby presents a village scene that was much more vibrant, bustling, and picturesque than I ever encountered in any twenty-four hour period. Mead's chapter is good prose, but is it good anthropology? . . .

I also did not agree with Mead on the degree of sexual freedom supposedly enjoyed by her informants, but I believe her characterization comes closer to the truth than that of Freeman. Samoans have a very natural and healthy attitude toward sex. Judging by the number of illegitimate children in Ta'ū village when I was there and by the fact that divorce frequently involved claims of adultery, I would conclude that, while Samoans are far from promiscuous, they are not the puritanical prudes Freeman paints them to be. However, I must admit that it was difficult to investigate anything of a sexual nature, primarily because of pressure from the London Missionary Society church. Even today, older Samoans seem more distressed over Mead's claims that they are sexually active than Freeman's claims that they are aggressive with strong passions, even psychopathological tendencies. I would assume, however, that Mead was better able to identify with, and therefore establish rapport with, adolescents and young adults on issues of sexuality than either I (at age 29— married with a wife and child) or Freeman, ten years my senior.

Freeman maintains that Mead imposed her own liberated ideas of sexuality onto the Samoans and that her teenage informants consistently lied to her about these matters solely out of mischief. He has recently made contact with one of Mead's informants, Fa'apua'a Fa'amu, who lived in Fitiuta while Mead was working in Ta'ū village. Freeman believes this informant when she says that she consistently lied to Mead (while also identifying her as a good friend), but Freeman does not seem to consider the possibility that she may be lying to him. The possibility of Mead's informants being successful at such long-term deception is simply not credible considering the fact that Mead was an extremely intelligent, well-trained Ph.D. who constantly cross-checked her data with many informants. Anyone who has studied her field notes in the Library of Congress, as I have, must be impressed with her savvy and sophistication.

I must also disagree with Mead's statements that all love affairs are casual and fleeting, and no one plays for very heavy emotional stakes. Custom dictates that displays of affection between spouses and between lovers not take place in public. However, expressions of love and affection were often observed in the families of my informants. . . .

Although I differed with Margaret Mead on many interpretations, the most important fact that emerged from my methodological restudy of her Samoan research is that, without doubt, Samoan adolescents have a less difficult time negotiating the transition from childhood to adulthood than American adolescents. . . .

Critique of the Freeman Refutation

My objections to Derek Freeman's picture of Samoa are much more substantial than to the picture presented by Margaret Mead. Basically, I question Freeman's objectivity and believe he is guilty of an age-old temptation in science, which was recognized as early as 1787 by Thomas Jefferson—no slouch of a scientist himself. In a letter to his friend Charles Thomson, Jefferson wrote, "The moment a person forms a theory, his imagination sees, in every object, only the traits which favor that theory" (Martin 1952:33).

Not only does Freeman ignore counterevidence, he also ignores time and space and assumes that it is legitimate to assess data obtained by Mead in Manu'a in 1925–1926 in terms of the data he collected in Western Samoa in the 1940s, 1960s, and 1980s.

Time differences   Freeman plays down the fact that Mead did her study of Ta'u village in the Manu'a Island group of American Samoa fourteen years before he arrived as a teacher (not as an anthropologist) in Western Samoa and that he did not return to Samoa with the express purpose of refuting Mead's study until forty-three years after her visit. Minimizing this time gap, he arbitrarily states that "there is no . . . reason to suppose that Samoan society and behavior changed in any fundamental way during the fourteen years between 1926, the year of the completion of Mead's inquiries, and 1940, when I began my own observation of Samoan behavior" (1983:120).

However, Freeman did not visit Ta'u village, the site of Mead's research, until 1968. Having established to his satisfaction that there had been few changes in Samoan culture during this long period of time, Freeman went on to state that he would "draw on evidence of my own research in the 1940s, the years 1965 to 1968, and 1981" (1983:120). I might add that he would draw upon historical sources, some of which go back as far as the early eighteenth century, to prove his points. My own analysis of Samoan cultural change, as published in *Ta'ū, Stability and Change in a Samoan Village* (1958), indicates, however, that while there was relative stability in the culture from 1850 to 1925 and from 1925 to 1954, change definitely did take place, particularly in the twentieth century. There is absolutely no basis for Freeman's dealing with Samoa as though it existed in a totally static condition despite its long history of contact with explorers, whalers, missionaries, colonial officials and bureaucrats, entrepreneurs, anthropologists, and, more recently, educators with Western-style curricula and television networks.

Place differences   It also must be kept in mind that Sa'anapu (where Freeman observed Samoan culture) is not Ta'ū village (where Mead did her study). They are different villages, on different islands, in different countries, and there are great historical and political differences between the island of Upolu in Western Samoa and Ta'ū island in the isolated Manu'a Group of American Samoa. Western Samoa has experienced a long and often oppressive history of colonialism under Germany and New Zealand, while the Manu'a Group and American Samoa in general have been spared this. The U.S. Navy administration (1900–1951) exerted little influence outside the Pago Pago Bay area on the island of Tutuila, and the Department of the Interior, which took over from the Navy, has been an ethnocentric—but still benevolent—force in the political history of the territory. While Sa'anapu is on the opposite side of Upolu from Apia, it has daily bus communication with that port town, with all of its banks, supermarkets, department stores, theaters, bookstores, and nightclubs. Cash cropping has always been more important in Western Samoa than in American Samoa, and today, the economies of the two Samoas are vastly different. . . . On five separate research trips to Manu'a, I have never witnessed a single physical assault or serious argument that threatened to get out of hand. However, urban centers such as Apia in Western Samoa and Pago Pago in American Samoa have a very different character. As early as 1962, there were delinquency problems in the Pago Pago Bay area involving drunkenness, burglary, assaults, and rapes. Young people who migrate to urban areas such as Pago Pago and Apia are no longer under the close supervision and control of their *matai* [chief of the family] and often behave in very nontraditional ways. It is difficult, indeed, to make a blanket statement that all villages in Samoa are the same and that all behavior within the two Samoas is comparable. I have studied several villages during my thirty-seven-year contact with Samoa, and I find each unique in numerous, social, ceremonial, economic, and political respects.

Freeman's subjective use of literature   A serious scientist considers all the literature relating to his or her research problem. One does not select data that supportive and ignore that which is not. Freeman violates that principle repeatedly. . . . When [Ronald Rose's book, *South Seas Magic* (1959)] can be used to corroborate or advance Freeman's position, he is quoted; however, where Rose's statements concerning Samoan sexual behavior run contrary to Freeman's claims, and fall in line with Mead's observations, his work is ignored. For example, while Freeman insists that Samoans are puritanical and sexually inhibited, Rose writes that "sexual adventures begin at an early age. Although virginity is prized, it is insisted on only with the taupo. . . . If a girl hasn't had a succession of lovers by the time she is seventeen or eighteen, she feels she is 'on the shelf' and becomes the laughing stock among her companions" (1959:61).

   With regard to the matter that Freeman believes was Mead's spurious example of a "negative instance"—a culture where coming of age is relatively less stressful—Rose writes (but understandably is not quoted by Freeman) as follows:

> Mental disturbances, stresses and conflicts occur at puberty but, as might be expected. these are not quite as common as in our society where taboos associated with sex abound (*Ibid.*: 164).

One can question the objectivity of a scientist who describes Samoans as "an unusually bellicose people" (1983:157) and attempts to substantiate the claim with citations from the eighteenth century, but fails to quote the favorable impressions of the very first European to come in contact with Samoan islanders from the village of Ta'ū, the very village Mead studied. In 1722, Commodore Jacob Roggeveen anchored his vessel off the village of Ta'ū and allowed a number of the islanders to come aboard. After a two-hour visit, the Commodore wrote in his log:

> They appeared to be a good people, lively in their manner of conversing, gentle in their deportment towards each other, and in their manners nothing was perceived of the savage. . . . It must be acknowledged that this was the nation the most civilized and honest of any that we had seen among the Islands of the South Sea. They were charmed with our arrival amongst them, and received us as divinities. And when they saw us preparing to depart, they testified much regret (Bumey 1816:576).

Rather than quote Roggeveen, Freeman chooses to discuss, as an example of Samoan bellicosity, the La Perouse expedition's visitation at Tutuila in 1787 that ended in tragedy. It is true that Samoans in the village of A'asu attacked a shore party, killing several crew members, but what Freeman fails to mention is that the attack occurred only after crew members punished a Samoan for pilfering by hanging him by his thumbs from the top of the longboat mast. . . .

It also should be noted that the eminent writer, Robert Louis Stevenson, who lived among Samoans the last four years of his life, recorded in his chronicle of Samoan events, *A Footnote to History,* that Samoans were "easy, merry, and pleasure loving; the gayest, though by no means the most capable or the most beautiful of Polynesians" (1892:148) and that their religious sentiment toward conflict was "peace at any price" (*Ibid.*: 147).

Observers contemporary with Mead in Samoa also record descriptions of Samoan chararacter that do not square with Freeman's allegations or his citations from early literature. For example, William Green, the principal of the government school in American Samoa in the 1920s writes:

> Personal combats and fist fights are rather rare today. I believe there has been no murder case in American Samoa since our flag was raised in 1900. Natives will suffer indignities for a long time before resorting to a fight but they remain good fighters. Boxing contests are held occasionally. . . . Respect for elders and magistrates has, I suppose, tended to discourage frequent combats. Life is easy, and one's habitual tendencies and desires are seldom blocked (1924:134).

Professional Reactions

. . . It is questionable whether any anthropology book to date has created such a media circus or produced such a media hero as *Margaret Mead and Samoa, The Making and Unmaking of an Anthropological Myth.* It is also doubtful whether any academic press ever mounted such a campaign of Madison Avenue hype to market a book as did Harvard University Press. The early reviews of the book and feature articles about the controversy were primarily penned by journalists and tended to be highly supportive of Freeman's critique, but once the anthropologists began evaluating the Freeman book, the tide took a definite turn. George Marcus of Rice University called the book a "work of great mischief," the mischief being that Freeman was attempting to reestablish "the importance of biological factors in explanations of human behavior" (1983:2). . . . Marvin Harris observed in his review that Freeman "seems obsessed with the notion that to discredit Mead's Samoan material is to discredit any social scientist who holds that 'nurture' is a more important determinant of the differences and similarities in human social life than nature" (1983:26).

It is only fair to point out that Derek Freeman had, and continues to have, a cadre of anthropological supporters, mostly in Europe and Australia, and the Samoans are mixed in their support of Mead or Freeman. . . .

Like most American anthropologists, and a few scholarly Samoans, we believe the Freeman book has done a disservice to Samoans and to the memory of Margaret Mead. *Margaret Mead and Samoa* is not an objective analysis of Mead's work in Manu'a, but an admitted refutation aimed at discrediting not only Margaret Mead, but Franz Boas and American cultural anthropology in general. Anthropology has often been referred to as a "soft science" throughout much of this rhubarb over Samoa and nature/nurture. It is little wonder, since Freeman's diatribe, published by a supposedly scholarly press, has been accepted by the media, by a select group of anthropologists, and by a number of distinguished ethologists and sociobiologists as legitimate anthropology. Margaret Mead would have loved to have debated the issues with Derek Freeman, but unfortunately, the book was not published while she was alive. It would have been great sport and good for the science of anthropology. As a friend wrote immediately after the publication of Freeman's book, "Whatever else she was, Margaret was a feisty old gal and would have put up a spirited defense which would quickly have turned into a snotty offense." We would have put our money on the plump little lady with the no-nonsense attitude and the compulsion to "get on with it."

References

Burney, James. 1816. *A chronological history of the voyages and discoveries in the South Seas or Pacific Ocean.* London: Luke Hansard and Sons.
Folsom, Joseph K. 1934. *The family: Its sociology and psychiatry.* New York: J. Wiley and Sons.
Freeman, Derek. 1983. *Margaret Mead and Samoa: The making and unmaking of an anthropological myth.* Cambridge, MA: Harvard University Press.
Green, William M. 1924. "Social traits of Samoans." *Journal of Applied Sociology* 9:129 135.
Hall, G. Stanley. 1904. *Adolescence: Its psychology and its relations to physiology, anthropology, sociology, sex, crime, religion and education.* New York: D. Appleton and Company.
Harris, Marvin. 1968. *The rise of anthropological theory.* New York: Thomas Y. Crowell Company.
———. 1983. "The sleep-crawling question." *Psychology Today* May:24–27.
Herskovits, Melville J. 1953. *Franz Boas.* New York: Charles Scribner's Sons.

Holmes, Lowell D. 1958. *Ta'ū: Stability and change in a Samoan village.* Reprint No. 7, Wellington, New Zealand: Polynesian Society.

Marcus, George, 1983. "One man's Mead." *New York Times Book Review* March 27, 1983:2–3, 22–23.

Martin, Edwin T. 1952. *Thomas Jefferson: Scientist.* New York: Henry Schuman.

Rose, Ronald. 1959. *South Seas magic.* London: Hale.

Stevenson, Robert Louis. 1892. *Vailima papers and A footnote to history.* New York: Charles Scribner's Sons.

POSTSCRIPT

Was Margaret Mead's Fieldwork on Samoan Adolescents Fundamentally Flawed?

The response to Freeman's *Margaret Mead and Samoa* was quite extraordinary and included books, journal articles, editorials, and conference papers. Special sessions at the annual meetings of the American Anthropological Association were devoted exclusively to the Mead-Freeman debate. The first reaction was largely defensive. But as the initial shock of Freeman's assertions wore off, scholars began to address some of the specific points of criticism. A representative sample of these would include Lowell D. Holmes's *Quest for the Real Samoa: The Mead/Freeman Controversy and Beyond* (Bergin and Garvey, 1987) and Hiram Caton's edited volume, *The Samoa Reader: Anthropologists Take Stock* (University Press of America, 1990).

A number of scholars have pointed out that Samoan life has changed significantly since Mead's fieldwork. The Christian Church now exerts a much stronger pressure over the very same women that Mead had interviewed. Another point is that Mead's informants themselves have become much more puritanical as old women than they were as girls. These women now have reputations of social propriety to uphold that would not have concerned them in their youth. Can we believe that they had the same views so many years ago?

In the 1980s Freeman returned to Ta'u with an Australian documentary film crew, specifically to interview some of Mead's now elderly informants. When asked what they had told Mead 60 years earlier, the women stated that they fibbed continuously and explained that it is a cherished Samoan custom to trick people in these ways. Freeman and the film crew take such statements as incontrovertible evidence that Mead was hoaxed. But if it is Samoan custom to trick others, how can Freeman and his film crew be certain that they are not victims of a similar hoax?

Another Samoa specialist, Martin Orans, approaches the controversy in his book *Not Even Wrong: Margaret Mead, Derek Freeman, and the Samoans* (Chandler & Sharp, 1996). Orans contends that neither Mead nor Freeman framed their research questions about cultural determinism in ways that can be tested. Arguing that anthropologists must frame their conclusions as testable hypotheses, Orans asserts that Mead and Freeman are so vague that neither makes their case, and both are so ambiguous that they are "not even wrong." But if Orans is correct, how can anthropologists frame the nature-versus-nurture debate in more specific and testable ways in specific field settings?

ISSUE 3

Should Anthropologists Abandon the Concept of Culture?

YES: Lila Abu-Lughod, from "Writing Against Culture," in Richard G. Fox, ed., *Recapturing Anthropology: Working in the Present* (School of American Research Press, 1991)

NO: Christoph Brumann, from "Writing for Culture: Why a Successful Concept Should Not Be Discarded," *Current Anthropology* (Supplement, February 1999)

ISSUE SUMMARY

YES: Cultural anthropologist Lila Abu-Lughod argues that the concept of culture exaggerates the distinctiveness, boundedness, homogeneity, coherence, and timelessness of a society's way of life. In her view, cultural descriptions also place the Western anthropologist in a position superior to the non-Western "other." She suggests that we use descriptions in terms of practices, discourses, connections, and the events of particular people's lives.

NO: Cultural anthropologist Christoph Brumann argues that the problems attributed to the culture concept are not inherent in the concept, but are a result of its being misused. He regards culture as a valuable concept for communication and one that is valid as long as we do not exaggerate the degree to which learned concepts, emotions, and practices are shared in a community.

$\mathbf{T}$he anthropological concept of culture came into existence in the late nineteenth century, along with the development of anthropology as an academic discipline. The culture concept has been modified repeatedly since then in conjunction with changing theoretical trends. In 1952, anthropologists A. L. Kroeber and Clyde Kluckhohn documented and discussed 166 different definitions of culture that had been used in anthropology and other social sciences to that point (*Culture: A Critical Review of Concepts and Definitions,* Harvard University, 1952). Many more definitions have emerged since then.

The first deliberate attempt to define culture in an anthropological sense was the opening line of E. B. Tylor's seminal book *The Origins of Culture*

47

(John Murray, 1871): "Culture, or Civilization, taken in its wide ethnographic sense, is that complex whole which includes knowledge, belief, art, morals, law, custom, and any other capabilities and habits acquired by man as a member of society." Franz Boas, the founder of academic anthropology in America, used Tylor's definition, but clarified that culture was transmitted by learning, not by heredity (race), as most nineteenth-century scholars had believed. Boas's students developed the notion of culture in various directions. Some, like A. L. Kroeber and Ruth Benedict, viewed culture as an emergent phenomenon (not reducible to individual thought and action) whose patterns could be studied without reference to the individual carriers of the culture. Others, like Margaret Mead, became interested in how children learn (internalize) culture. The different theories that rose to prominence in American cultural anthropology have emphasized different aspects of the culture concept and have sometimes redefined culture to fit their concerns. Anthropologists continue to disagree on fundamental questions: Is culture a real thing or merely an abstraction? Is it a set of ideas (beliefs, meanings) or behaviors, and is it found in individuals or only in groups?

Critics of the culture concept, like Lila Abu-Lughod, criticize descriptions of cultures and cultural features for concealing the variations and conflicts in thought and action that lie beneath these generalizations, for exaggerating the differences between the thoughts and behaviors of those inside the group and those outside. Abu-Lughod recommends that we substitute such concepts as "practice" and "discourse" to more accurately reflect social reality. The theory of practice, developed by Pierre Bourdieu, focuses on how observable patterns of behavior are produced. It hypothesizes that people are motivated by sets of dispositions ("habitus"), which influence their behavior in certain directions, but do not rigidly determine the outcome. Discourse refers to a body of statements about a topic that define the topic and influence how people think and act.

Defenders of the culture concept, like Christoph Brumann, believe that the basic concept is sound and that any weaknesses in it can be easily overcome. Brumann argues that anthropologists can describe cultural variations within a society and culture changes without giving up the ability to talk about broad cultural patterns and regularities.

Here are some questions to think about as you read the following selections. Does the existence of individual variations in thought and behavior in all societies mean that all attempts at generalization are worthless? Is all social science research demeaning to the subjects of the studies? Does defining differences between cultures always imply that one is better than the other?

Lila Abu-Lughod

 **YES**

Writing Against Culture

In this [selection] I will argue that "culture" operates in anthropological discourse to enforce separations that inevitably carry a sense of hierarchy. Therefore, anthropologists should now pursue, without exaggerated hopes for the power of their texts to change the world, a variety of strategies for writing *against* culture....

Selves and Others

... Anthropology's avowed goal may be "the study of man [sic]," but it is a dliscipline built on the historically constructed divide between the West and the non-West. It has been and continues to be primarily the study of the non-Western other by the Western self, even if in its new guise it seeks explicitly to give voice to the Other or to present a dialogue between the self and other, either textually or through an explication of the fieldwork encounter.... And the relationship between the West and the non-West, at least since the birth of anthropology, has been constituted by Western domination....

Culture and Difference

... Most American anthropologists believe or act as if "culture," notoriously resistant to definition and ambiguous of referent, is nevertheless the true object of anthropological inquiry. Yet it could also be argued that culture is important to anthropology because the anthropological distinction between self and other rests on it. Culture is the essential tool for making other. As a professional discourse that elaborates on the meaning of culture in order to account for, explain, and understand cultural difference, anthropology also helps construct, produce, and maintain it. Anthropological discourse gives cultural difference (and the separation between groups of people it implies) the air of the self-evident.

In this regard, the concept of culture operates much like its predecessor—race—even though in its twentieth-century form it has some important political advantages. Unlike race, and unlike even the nineteenth-century sense of culture as a synonym for civilization (contrasted to barbarism), the current concept allows for multiple rather than binary differences. This immediately checks—the [easy] move to hierarchizing.... The most important of culture's advantages, however, is that it removes difference from the realm of the natural and the innate. Whether conceived of as a set of behaviors, customs, traditions, rules, plans, recipes, instructions, or programs ... culture is learned and can change.

Despite its anti-essentialist intent, however, the culture concept retains some of the tendencies to freeze difference possessed by concepts like race. This is easier to see if we consider a field in which there has been a shift from one to the other. Orientalism as a scholarly discourse (among other things) is, according to [Edward] Said, "a style of thought based upon an ontological and epistemological distinction made between 'the Orient' and (most of the time) 'the Occident'." What he shows is that in mapping geography, race, and culture onto one another, Orientalism fixes differences between people of "the West" and people of "the East" in ways so rigid that they might as well be considered innate. In the twentieth century, cultural difference, not race, has been the basic subject of Orientalist scholarship devoted now to interpreting the "culture" phenomena (primarily religion and language) to which basic differences in development, economic performance, government, character, and so forth are attributed....

Denied the same capacity for movement, travel, and geographical interaction that Westerners take for granted, the cultures studied by anthropologists have tended to be denied history as well....

[Some scholars] have argued that cultural theories also tend to overemphasize coherence. [James] Clifford notes both that "the discipline of fieldwork-based anthropology, in consulting its authority, constructs and reconstructs coherent cultural others and interpreting selves" and that ethnography is a form of culture collecting (like art collecting) in which "diverse experiences and facts are selected, gathered, detached from their original temporal occasions, and given enduring value in a new arrangement." Organic metaphors of wholeness and the methodology of holism that characterizes anthropology both favor coherence, which in turn contributes to the perception of communities as bounded and discrete.

Certainly discreteness does not have to imply value; the hallmark of twentieth-century anthropology has been its promotion of cultural relativism over evaluation and judgment If anthropology has always to some extent been a form of cultural (self-) critique, that too was an aspect of a refusal to hierarchize difference. Yet neither position would be possible without difference. It would be worth thinking about the implications of the high stakes anthropology has in sustaining and perpetuating a belief in the existence of cultures that are identifiable as discrete, different, and separate from our own. Does difference always smuggle in hierarchy?...

Three Modes of Writing Against Culture

If "culture," shadowed by coherence, timelessness, and discreteness, is the prime anthropological tool for making "other," and difference ... tends to be a relationship of power, then perhaps anthropologists should consider strategies for writing against culture. I will discuss three that I find promising. Although they by no means exhaust the possibilities, the sorts of projects I will describe—theoretical, substantive, and textual—make sense for anthropologists sensitive to issues of positionality and accountability and interested in making anthropological practice something that does not simply shore up global inequalities. I will conclude, however, by considering the limitations of all anthropological reform.

Discourse and Practice

Theoretical discussion, because it is one of the modes in which anthropologists engage each other, provides an important site for contesting "culture." It seems to me that current discussions and deployments of two increasingly popular terms—practice and discourse—do signal a shift away from culture. Although there is always the danger that these terms will come to be used simply as synonyms for culture, they were intended to enable us to analyze social life without presuming the degree of coherence that the culture concept has come to carry.

Practice is associated, in anthropology, with [Pierre] Bourdieu, whose theoretical approach is built around problems of contradiction misunderstanding, and misrecognition, and favors strategies, interests, and improvisations over the more static and homogenizing cultural tropes of rules, models, and texts. Discourse ... has more diverse sources and meanings in anthropology. In its Foucauldian derivation, as it relates to notions of discursive formations, apparatuses, and technologies, it is meant to refuse the distinction between ideas and practices or text and world that the culture concept too readily encourages. In its more sociolinguistic sense, it draws attention to the social uses by individuals of verbal resources. In either case, it allows for the possibility of recognizing within a social group the play of multiple, shifting, and competing statements with practical effects. Both practice and discourse are useful because they work against the assumption of boundedness, not to mention the idealism, of the culture concept.

Connections

Another strategy of writing against culture is to reorient the problems or subject matter anthropologists address. An important focus should be the various connections and interconnections, historical and contemporary, between a community and the anthropologist working there and writing about it, not to mention the world to which he or she belongs and which enables him or her to be in that particular place studying that group. This is more of a political project than an existential one, although the reflexive anthropologists who have taught us to focus on the fieldwork encounter as a site for the construction of the ethnographic "facts" have alerted us to one important dimension of the connection. Other significant sorts of connections have received less attention. [Mary Louise] Pratt notes a regular mystification in ethnographic writing of "the larger agenda of European expansion in which the ethnographer, regardless of his or her own attitudes to it, is caught up, and that determines the ethnographer's own material relationship to the group under study." We need to ask questions about the historical processes by which it came to pass that people like ourselves could be engaged in anthropological studies of people like those, about the current world situation that enables us to engage in this sort of work in this particular place, and about who has preceded us and is even now there with us (tourists, travelers, missionaries, AID consultants, Peace Corps workers). We need to ask what this "will to knowledge" about the Other is connected to in the world.

These questions cannot be asked in general; they should be asked about and answered by tracing through specific situations, configurations, and histories. Even though they do not address directly the place of the ethnographer, and even though they engage in an oversystemization that threatens to erase local interactions, studies like those of [Eric] Wolf on the long history of interaction between particular Western societies and communities in what is now called the Third World represent important means of answering such questions. So do studies like [Sidney] Mintz's that trace the complex processes of transformation and exploitation in which, in Europe and other parts of the world, sugar was involved. The anthropoiogical turn to history, tracing, connections between the present and the past of particular communities, is also an important development.

Not all projects about connections need be historical. Anthropologists are increasingly concerned with national and transnational connections of people, cultural forms, media, techniques, and commodities.... They study the articulation of world capitalism and international politics with the situations of people living in particular communities. All these projects, which involve a shift in gaze to include phenomena of connection, expose the inadequacies of the concept of culture and the elusiveness of the entities designated by the term *cultures*. Although there may be a tendency in the new work merely to widen the object, shifting from culture to nation as locus, ideally there would be attention to the shifting groupings, identities, arid interactions within and across such borders as well. If there was ever a time when anthropologists could consider without too much violence at least some communities as isolated units, certainly the nature of global interactions in the present makes that now impossible!

Ethnographies of the Particular

The third strategy for writing against culture depends on accepting the one insight of [Clifford] Geertz's about anthropology that has been built upon by everyone in this "experimental moment" who takes textuality seriously. Geertz has argued that one of the main things anthropologists do is write, and what they write are fictions (which does not mean they are fictitious). Certainly the practice of ethnographic writing has received an inordinate amount of attention from those involved in *Writing Culture* and an increasing number of others who were not involved. Much of the hostility toward their project arises from the suspicion that in their literary leanings they have too readily collapsed the politics of ethnography into its poetics. And yet they have raised an issue that cannot be ignored. Insofar as anthropologists are in the business of representing others through their ethnographic writing, then surely the degree to which people in the communities they study appear "other" must also be partly function of how anthropologists write about them. Are there ways to write about lives so as to constitute others as less other?

I would argue that one powerful tool for unsettling the culture concept and subverting the process of "othering" it entails is to write "ethnographies of the particular." Generalization, the characteristic mode of operation and style of writing of the social sciences, can no longer be regarded as neutral description It has two unfortunate effects in anthropology that make it worth eschewing. I will explore these before presenting some examples from my own work of what one could hope to accomplish through ethnographies of the particular.

I will not be concerned with several issues frequently raised about generalization. For example, it has often been pointed out that the generalizing mode of social scientific discourse facilitates abstraction and reification. Feminist sociologist Dorothy Smith put the problem vividly in her critique of sociological discourse by noting that

> the complex organization of activities of actual individuals and their actual relations is entered into the discourse through concepts such as class, modernization, formal organization. A realm of theoretically constituted objects is created, freeing the discursive realm from its ground in the lives and work of actual individuals and liberating sociological inquiry to graze on a field of conceptual entities.

Other critics have fixed on different flaws. Interpretive anthropology, for example, in its critique of the search for general laws in positivistic social science, notes a failure to take account of the centrality of meaning to human experience. Yet the result has been to substitute generalization about meanings for generalizations about behavior.

I also want to make clear what the argument for particularity is not: it is not to be mistaken for arguments for privileging micro over macro processes. Ethnomethodologists ... and other students of everyday life seek ways to generalize about microinteractions, while historians might be said to be tracing the particulars of macroprocesses. Nor need a concern with the particulars of individuals' lives imply disregard for forces and dynamics that are not locally based. On the contrary, effects of extralocal and long-term processes are only manifested locally and specifically, produced in the actions of individuals living their particular lives, inscribed in their bodies and their words. What I am arguing for is a form of writing that might better convey that.

There are two reasons for anthropologists to be wary of generalization. The first is that, as part of a professional discourse of "objectivity" and expertise, it is inevitably a language of power. On the one hand, it is the language of those who seem to stand apart from and outside of what they are describing. Again, Smith's critique of sociological discourse is relevant. She has argued that this seemingly detached mode of reflecting on social life is actually located: it represents the perspective of those involved in professional, managerial, and administrative structures and is thus part of "the ruling apparatus of this society." This critique applies as well to anthropology with its inter- rather than intrasocietal perspective and its origins in the exploration and colonization of the non-European world rather than the management of internal social groups like workers, women, blacks, the poor, or prisoners.

On the other hand, even if we withhold judgment on how closely the social sciences can be associated with the apparatuses of management, we have to recognize how all professionalized discourses by nature assert hierarchy. The very gap between the professional and authoritative discourses of generalization and the languages of everyday life (our own and others') establishes a fundamental separation between the anthropologist and the people being written about that facilitates the construction of anthropological objects as simultaneously different and inferior....

The second problem with generalization derives not from its participation in the authoritative discourses of professionalism but from the effects of homogeneity, coherence, and timelessness it tends to produce. When one generalizes from experiences and conversations with a number of specific people in a community, one tends to flatten out differences among them and to homogenize them. The appearance of an absence of internal differentiation makes it easier to conceive of a group of people as a discrete, bounded entity, like the "the Nuer," "the Balinese," and "the Awlad 'Ali Bedouin" who do this or that and believe such-and-such. The effort to produce general ethnographic descriptions of people's beliefs or actions tends to smooth over contradictions, conflicts of interest, and doubts and arguments, not to mention changing motivations and circumstances. The erasure of time and conflict make what is inside the boundary set up by homogenization something essential and fixed. These effects are of special moment to anthropologists because they contribute to the fiction of essentially different and discrete others who can be separated from some sort of equally essential self. Insofar as difference is, as I have argued, hierarchical, and assertions of separation a way of denying responsibility, generalization itself must be treated with suspicion.

For these reasons I propose that we experiment with narrative ethnographies of the particular in a continuing tradition of fieldwork-based writing.... I would expect them to complement rather than replace a range of other types of anthropological projects, from theoretical discussions to the exploration of new topics within anthropology....

Anthropologists commonly generalize about communities by saying that they are characterized by certain institutions, rules, or ways of doing things. For example, we can and often do say things like "The Bongo-Bongo are polygynous." Yet one could refuse to generalize in this way, instead asking how a particular set of individuals—for instance, a man and his three wives in a Bedouin community in Egypt whom I have known for a decade—live the "institution" that we call polygyny. Stressing the particularity of this marriage and building a picture of it through the participants' discussions, recollections, disagreements, and actions would make several theoretical points..

First, refusing to generalize would highlight the constructed quality of that typicality so regularly produced in conventional social scientific accounts. Second, showing the actual circumstances and detailed histories of individuals and their relationships would suggest that such particulars, which are always present (as we know from our own personal experiences), are also always crucial to the constitution of experience. Third, reconstructing people's arguments about, justifications for, and interpretations of what they and others are doing would explain how social life proceeds. It would show that although the terms of their discourses may be set (and, as in any society, include several sometimes contradictory and often historically changing discourses), within these limits, people contest interpretations of what is happening, strategize, feel pain, and live their lives....

By focusing closely on particular individuals and their changing relationships, one would necessarily subvert the most problematic connotations of culture: homogeneity, coherence, and timelessness. Individuals are confronted with choices, struggle with other, make conflicting statements, argue about points of view on the same events, undergo ups and downs in various relationships and changes in their circumstances and desires, face new pressures, and fail to predict what will happen to them or those around them. So, for example, it becomes difficult to think that the term "Bedouin culture" makes sense when one tries to piece together and convey what life is like for one old Bedouin matriarch.

When you ask her to tell the story of her life, she responds that one should only think about God. Yet she tells vivid stories, fixed in memory in particular ways, about her resistances to arranged marriages, her deliveries of children, her worries about sick daughters. She also tells about weddings she has attended, dirty songs sung by certain young men as they sheared the elders' sheep herds, and trips in crowded taxis where she pinched a man's bottom to get him off her lap.

The most regular aspect of her daily life is her wait for prayer times. Is it noon yet? Not yet. Is it afternoon yet? Not yet. Is it sunset yet? Grandmother, you haven't prayed yet? It's already past sunset. She spreads her prayer rug in front of her and prays out loud. At the end, as she folds up her prayer rug, she beseeches God to protect all Muslims. She recites God's names as she goes through her string of prayer beads. The only decoration in her room is a photograph on the wall of herself and her son as pilgrims in Mecca.

Her back so hunched she can hardly stand, she spends her days sitting or lying down on her mattress. She is practically blind and she complains about her many pains. People come and go, her sons, her nephews, her daughter, her nieces, her granddaughters, her great-grandson. They chat, they confer with her about connections between people, marriages, kinship. She gives advice; she scolds them for not doing things properly. And she plays with her great grandson, who is three, by teasing; "Hey, I've run out of snuff. Come here so I can sniff your little tuber."

Being pious and fiercely preserving protocol in the hosting of guests and the exchanging of visits and greetings does not seem to stop her from relishing the outrageous story and the immoral tale. A new favorite when I saw her in 1987 was one she had just picked up from her daughter, herself a married mother of five living near Alamein. It was a tale about an old husband and wife who decide to go visit their daughters, and it was funny for the upsidedown world it evoked.

This tale depicted a world where people did the unthinkable. Instead of the usual candy and biscuits, the couple brought their daughters sacks of dung for gifts. When the first daughter they stayed with went off to draw water from the well, they started dumping out all the large containers of honey and oil in her merchant husband's house. She returned to find them spilling everything and threw them out. So they headed off to visit the second daughter. When she left them minding her baby for a while, the old man killed it just to stop if from crying. She came back, discovered this and threw them out. Next they came across a house with a slaughtered sheep in it. They made belts out of the intestines and caps out of the stomachs and tried them on, admiring each other in their new finery. But when the old woman asked her husband if she didn't look pretty in her new belt he answered, "You'd be really pretty, except for that fly sitting on your nose." With that he smacked the fly, killing his wife. As he wailed in grief he began to fart. Furious at his anus for farting over his dead wife, he heated up a stake and shoved it in, killing himself.

The old woman chuckles as she tells this story, just as she laughs hard over stories about the excessive sexuality of old women. How does this sense of humor, this appreciation of the bawdy, go with devotion to prayer and protocols of honor? How does her nostalgia for the past—when the area was empty and she could see for miles around; when she used to play as a little girl digging up the occasional potsherd or glass bottle in the area now fenced and guarded by the government Antiquities Organization; when her family migrated with the sheep herds and milked and made butter in desert pastures—go with her fierce defense of her favorite grandson, whose father was furious with him because the young man was rumored to have drunk liquor at a local wedding? People do not drink in the community, and drinking is, of course, religiously proscribed. What can "culture" mean, given this old woman's complex responses?

Time is the other important dimension that gets built in if one takes seriously the narrative of people's everyday lives. When the young man's father hits him, the son who has been accused of drinking at the wedding sells his cassette player to a neighbor to raise cash and then disappears. His grandmother cries over him, his aunts discuss it. His father says nothing. It is days before a distant in-law comes to reassure his grandmother that the young man is fine and to indicate that they know his whereabouts (he is working at a construction site about 100 kilometers away). No one knows what the consequences of this event will be. Will he return? What will his father do? Family honor is at stake, reputations for piety, paternal authority. When the young man returns several weeks later, accompanied by a maternal uncle from 50 kilometers west who intervenes to forestall any further punishments, his grandmother weeps in relief. It could easily have turned out differently. Since his disappearance, her days had been taken up with worrying, discussing, waiting, and not knowing what would happen next. That beating and that running away, events that happened in time, become part of the history of that family, the individuals involved, and their relationships. In this sequence of events in a particular family in 1987, we can read what we call the "larger forces" that made it possible, things like growing opportunities for wage labor, the commercialization of Bedouin weddings, and the influx of goods from the cities. Yet because these "forces" are only embodied in the actions of individuals living in time and place, ethnographies of the particular capture them best.

Even ritual, that communal practice for which time seems to have such a different, perhaps cyclical, meaning, that kind of practice which in anthropological discourse so perfectly marks the (exotic, primitive) cultural other as different, turns out to be particular and anything but timeless. If looked at closely in terms of the actual participants and ritual event, it involves unpredictability. Even in ritual the unfolding of what cannot be known beforehand generates great drama and tension. Let me give an example, again from my work. Within the first week of my arrival in the Bedouin community in Egypt where I was to spend years, the young girls in my household outlined for me the exact sequence of events every bride went through in a Bedouin wedding. Over the years, I attended many weddings, all of which followed this outline; yet each of which was distinct. For each bride and groom, not to mention their families, the wedding would mark a moment of major life transformation, not just of status but of associations, daily life, experience, and the future. Each wedding was different in the kinds of families being brought together, the network of relations created and the goods exchanged, spent, and displayed.

More important, the elements of unpredictability were many. Would the bride stay? Would the couple get along? Would there be children? How soon? Even the central rite of the wedding celebration itself—the defloration or public virginity test—was an event of great dramatic tension whose outcome was unknowable in advance.... Events take different courses. That is the nature of "life as lived," everywhere. Generalizations, by producing effects of timelessness and coherence to support the essentialized notion of "cultures" different from ours and peoples separate from us, make us forget this....

NO

Christoph Brumann

Writing for Culture: Why a Successful Concept Should Not Be Discarded

There are times when we still need to be able to speak holistically of Japanese or Trobriand or Moroccan culture in the confidence that we are designating something real and differentially coherent.

JAMES CLIFFORD, The Predicament of Culture

For a long time, defining cultural/social anthropology as the study of the cultural dimension of humans would have raised few objections among the discipline's practitioners. Now the place of culture within that definition is considerably less certain. Within the past decade, or so there has developed what [Marshall] Sahlins calls the "fashionable idea that there is nothing usefully called 'a culture'", and one prominent voice [Lila Abu-Lughod] even advocates "writing against culture", giving a name to a whole "'writing against culture' movement".... Although the scepticism over the culture concept has its origins in deconstructionist and poststructuralist thought, anthropologists sympathizing with it come from an amazing range of theoretical positions that reaches far beyond that specific vantage point.... It turns out that what is being addressed by the critics is certain usages of the culture concept rather than the concept itself and I argue that it is possible—and not very difficult—to disentangle the concept from such misapplications and to find historical precedents for this in anthropology. In a next step I will address what I consider to be the root of the confusion, namely the fact that the sharing of learned traits among humans is never perfect, and how this can be dealt with. Finally, I will present pragmatic reasons for retaining "culture" and also "cultures": the concept has been successful, and other scientific disciplines as well as the general public increasingly employ it in a way we should not be entirely unhappy about. Some of these uses are certainly problematic, but retaining the concept and the common ground it has created will bring us into a better position to challenge them.

The Critique

The major concern of the skeptical discourse on culture is that the concept suggests boundedness, homogeneity, coherence, stability, and structure

From *Current Anthropology,* vol. 40, February 1999, pp. S1–S27. Copyright © 1999 by University of Chicago Press. Reprinted by permission. References and notes omitted.

whereas social reality is characterized by variability, inconsistencies, conflict, change, and individual agency....

Applied in this way, culture—a mere "anthropological abstraction"—is transformed into a thing, an essence, or even a living being or something developing like a living being....

This brings the concept of culture uncomfortably close to ideas such as race that originally it did a great deal to transcend....

As a result, the differences between the anthropologist and the people under study are exaggerated, and the latter are placed in a subordinate position. This increases the distance between the two parties to the ethnographic encounter while enhancing the anthropologist's privileged position as the expert and translator—or even the very creator—of such utter strangeness....

Historical and Optimal Usage

There is no denying that anthropologists in their ethnographic and theoretical work have committed the aforementioned sins in abundance, but I am not convinced that they have done so *because of the culture concept*. To demonstrate this, I will turn to anthropological definitions of culture, since the conception of that term ought to be most clearly expressed there. Modern textbooks define culture as follows:

> A culture is the total socially acquired life-way or life-style of a group of people. It consists of the patterned, repetitive ways of thinking, feeling, and acting that are characteristic of the members of a particular society or segment of a society.

> Culture ... refers ... to learned, accumulated experience. A culture ... refers to those socially transmitted patterns for behavior characteristic of a particular social group.

> Culture is the socially transmitted knowledge and behavior shared by some group of people.

Here and in other textbook definitions, no mention is made of boundaries, universal sharing, immunity to change, or culture's being a thing, an essence, or a living being....

Culture as an Abstraction

Discussing the culture concept, one has to distinguish between "culture" (or "Culture") in the general and "culture/s" in a specific sense. ...The former meaning refers to the general potential of human individuals to share certain not genetically inherited routines of thinking, feeling, and acting with other individuals with whom they are in social contact and/or to the products of that potential. It is not very clear-cut and mentioned only in few definitions; besides, it seems to be derived from the second meaning, on which most of the definitions concentrate. Here a culture is the set of specific learned routines (and/or their material and immaterial products) that are characteristic of a delineated group of people; sometimes these people are tacitly or explicitly included. The existence of any such culture presupposes that of other sets of routines, shared by other groups of people, thus constituting different cultures. The debate in fact focuses almost exclusively on this second meaning, and I will concentrate on it accordingly. It is the act of identifying *discrete* cultures that is held to be empirically unfounded, theoretically misleading, and morally objectionable by the concept's critics.

Of course, cultures are always constructed, but they are so not only because of being "written" within the confines of sociohistorically constituted tropes and discourses but also in a more profound sense. A culture ... is not simply there in the unproblematic way that, for example, a cat or a bicycle is. Rather, the term refers to an abstract aggregate, namely, the prolonged copresence of a set of certain individual items, and thus is employed not too differently from other nouns such as "forest," "crowd," or "city." In identifying a culture, we have to abstract such a set of items from observed instances of thought and behavior, selecting that which occurs repeatedly rather than that which is singular. This is a mental operation that is not in principle different from, say, identifying a style in individual works of art, and the same capabilities of memorizing previously perceived instances and ignoring minor differences for the sake of commonalities are required of anyone who undertakes it. Since in the empirical world no two things are completely identical, the result of any such operation is always contestable, and therefore one can no more prove the existence of Japanese culture than prove that of the Gothic style. Cultures can have no "natural" boundaries but only those that people (anthropologists as well as others) give them, and delimiting a certain set of elements as a culture can therefore be only more or less persuasive, never ultimately "true." Nonetheless, we may consider it expedient to go on using the concept in the same way that we go on speaking of art styles, forests, crowds, or cities; and we may do so in spite of the disagreement that often arises over whether these terms really apply to the specific body of art works, concentration of trees, gathering of people, or settlement that is so designated or where precisely their boundaries are located in a given case.

The core of the problem of identifying cultures can be illustrated with the three diagrams in figure 1. In these, capital letters stand for individuals and number for identifiable ways of thinking, feeling, and acting. In the top diagram, there is perfect sharing among individuals A through F regarding features 1 through 6 and among individuals G through L regarding features 7 through 12. Identifying cultures is not difficult here: Features 1 through 6 represent one culture, features 7 through 12 another. Since there is perfect discreteness between the two groups of features as well as between the two groups of individuals carrying them, this partition represents the only possible way of distinguishing cultures. In contrast, features in the middle diagram are randomly distributed across individuals, and it is impossible to make out cultures in the same unproblematic way or perhaps in any convincing way.

The problems start with a situation such as that of the bottom diagram. This distribution is far from random, yet no discrete blocks can be discerned either. One possible partition would place features 1 through 6 in one culture

	1	2	3	4	5	6	7	8	9	10	11	12
A	x	x	x	x	x	x	.	.	.	.	.	.
B	x	x	x	x	x	x	.	.	.	.	.	.
C	x	x	x	x	x	x	.	.	.	.	.	.
D	x	x	x	x	x	x	.	.	.	.	.	.
E	x	x	x	x	x	x	.	.	.	.	.	.
F	x	x	x	x	x	x	.	.	.	.	.	.
G	.	.	.	.	.	.	x	x	x	x	x	x
H	.	.	.	.	.	.	x	x	x	x	x	x
I	.	.	.	.	.	.	x	x	x	x	x	x
J	.	.	.	.	.	.	x	x	x	x	x	x
K	.	.	.	.	.	.	x	x	x	x	x	x
L	.	.	.	.	.	.	x	x	x	x	x	x

	1	2	3	4	5	6	7	8	9	10	11	12
A	x	x	x	.	x	.	x	.	.	x	.	x
B	.	.	.	x	.	.	x	.	x	.	x	x
C	.	.	x	x	.	x	x	.	x	.	.	.
D	x	.	x	.	.	x	x	.	x	x	.	.
E	.	x	.	.	x	x	.	x	.	x	x	.
F	x	.	x	x	x	.	.	x	.	x	.	.
G	.	x	.	x	.	x	.	x	.	x	x	.
H	x	.	x	.	x	.	x	x	.	x	.	x
I	.	x	.	x	.	x	x	.	x	.	x	.
J	.	x	.	x	x	.	.	x	.	x	x	.
K	x	.	.	x	x	.	.	x	.	x	.	x
L	x	x	.	x	.	.	x	x	x	.	x	.

	1	2	3	4	5	6	7	8	9	10	11	12
A	x	x	x	x	x	x	.	.	.	.	.	.
B	.	x	x	x	x	x	.	.	.	.	.	.
C	x	.	x	.	x	x	.	.	.	.	.	.
D	x	x	x	x	x	x	.	x	.	.	.	x
E	x	x	x	x	.	x	x	.	.	.	.	.
F	x	x	x	x	x	.	x	.	.	.	.	.
G	.	.	.	.	.	.	x	x	.	x	x	x
H	.	.	.	.	.	.	x	x	x	x	x	x
I	.	.	.	.	.	x	.	.	x	x	x	x
J	.	.	.	.	.	.	.	x	x	x	x	x
K	.	.	.	.	x	.	.	.	x	x	.	x
L	.	x	.	.	.	.	.	x.	.	x	x	x

Figure 1   *Three hypothetical distributions of features across individuals*

and features 8 through 12 in a second. Each culture, however, would then contain features that are sometimes associated with features of the other. Moreover, feature 7 does not readily group with either of the two cultures, and individual D may be seen as participating in both.

Incomplete Sharing and the Identification of Cultures

No distribution of learned routines among real people will ever be much clearer than that in the bottom diagram, and consequently there will always be more than one way to cut out cultures from the fuzzy-edged clusters of habits that we observe. I suspect that most of the culture skeptics do not really want to imply that there are no such clusters of habits and that the distribution of cognitive, emotive, and behavioral routines among humans is as in the middle diagram. However, they seem to fear that by identifying cultures when confronted with a distribution like that of the bottom diagram anthropologists will invariably be misunderstood as implying a distribution like that of the top diagram. Ceasing to speak of cultures, however, also entails a cost, namely, being understood as saying that features are distributed randomly, as in the middle diagram. I doubt very much that this kind of misunderstanding is preferable, since it is not borne out by the results of anthropological research. Moreover, it flies in the face of the experience of the billions of amateur anthropologists who inhabit the world, who in their everyday lives continue to identify commonalities in the thought and behavior of different individuals and attribute these to their belonging to the same family, kin group, gender, age-group, neighborhood, class, profession organization, ethnic group, region, nation, etc. Of course, they do so in an on-and-off, often semiconscious way, that—true to its commonsensical nature—cares less about oversimplifications, contradictions, and incompleteness than anthropologists do and often explains difference incorrectly, for example, in terms of genetic or quasi-generic transmission. But many of these amateur anthropologists, would be puzzled indeed if we tried to persuade them that what until recently we would have advised them to call a culture (instead of, for example, "the way we/they do it") does not really exist.

Just as there is no way of deciding whether a glass is half-full or half-empty; there is no ultimate solution to the dilemma of being misunderstood as implying either perfect boundedness and homogeneity (when speaking of cultures) or perfect randomness of distribution (when denying the existence of cultures). Confronted with this dilemma, I propose that we go on using the concept of culture, including the plural form, because of its practical advantages. We should do so in a responsible way, attentive to the specific audience and also to the problem of communicative economy. There are many situations in which "Japanese culture" is a convenient shorthand for designating something like "that which" many or most Japanese irrespective of gender, class, and other differences regularly think, feel, and do by virtue of having been in continuous social contact with other Japanese." And I am confident that at least among contemporary anthropologists the first phrase will very often be understood as equivalent to the second. After all, anthropology did not discover intrasocietal variation only yesterday. While many classic studies of small-scale, out-of-the way societies certainly do not show any awareness of it, peasant studies, explorations of great and little traditions and of center-periphery relations, research on gender, and the ethnographic study of complex societies and cities have been with anthropology for quite some time now and have frequently occupied themselves explicitly with such variation or at least acknowledged its existence. Consequently, the danger of being misunderstood by fellow anthropologists when speaking of a culture is, I think, much smaller than the critics claim.

Moreover, when there is enough time and space, nothing prohibits us from representing the arbitrariness and internal variation of such cultures as faithfully as possible or resorting to formal methods of analysis for delimiting cultures instead of trusting our intuition or—as is commonly done when delimiting ethnic cultures—the judgment of the people we investigate. One could also specify a minimal numerical level of consensus required for a culture and then search for maximal sets of features that fit this requirement (standard statistical procedures such as cluster analysis offer themselves for this task). When describing the two cultures in the bottom diagram, we may distinguish between core features that are shared universally (feature 3 for the first, features 10 and—arguably—12 for the second) or close to universally by the carriers of the culture in question and others that are less widely and unequivocally distributed and may be seen as less central. Nothing prevents us from introducing temporal variation into the picture: searching for the same features in the same individuals at other points in time may produce different distributions which, however, could again be expressed in matrices and superimposed on the previous ones to introduce a third dimension. One may also think of replacing the simple dichotomy of presence/absence with quantitative values, since people will often act differently or with varied intensity in repeated instances of the same situation. All this increases complexity, but the distribution will very likely still be clustered, and we are still not necessarily thrown onto intuition as the only method for finding such clusters. Thus we are also left with the problem of naming them. It may be objected that the total matrix we are dealing with ... has 6 billion rows—one for each living individual in the world, not to mention corporate actors that could also be regarded as culture carriers and dead individuals—and that it has an almost infinite number of columns, there being hardly any limit to identifiable features. On top of that, the matrix changes at a tremendous pace. Nevertheless, from all we know and from what social psychologists have found out about human striving for conformity we can be sure that it will not show a random distribution but will be highly patterned. In an analogy with what I have said about historical and optimal usages, the fact that we are as yet not particularly well equipped to describe and explain this enormous matrix and the clusters therein does not mean that we never will be or that we are better off not even trying, and for this purpose, a word to designate the clusters will be useful....

Everywhere we find sets of certain learned features that are shared more extensively by people who interact with each other than between these people and others with whom they do not interact or among those others. And everywhere we will find that people are aware of this fact, while they are certainly not ignorant of individual variation even among those who have much in common. We should try to describe the unevenness of any such "differential distribution" as well as we can, and it is clear that as yet the precise extent of interindividual conformity and variation within human groups has received insufficient attention, and therefore we do not have a clear theory, for instance, about how much social interaction gives rise to how much culture. We must also face the fact that once culture is found to be incompletely shared it will have that much less explanatory power for specific instances of individual thought and behavior. But sometimes communicative economy may make it expedient to speak of "a culture" and identify the constituent units of such a cluster as "elements," "features," "parts," or "traits" of that culture....

In my view, speaking of culture while making it clear that universal sharing is not implied does not automatically privilege coherence. Just as we may concentrate on explaining why a glass is half-full as well as why it is half-empty, sharing is as good a theme for anthropological research as nonsharing, and I wonder how we can avoid either when attempting to portray and explain people's ways of life realistically. And neither does such an approach preclude temporal variation or presuppose that the always arbitrary, abstract entity that we call a culture becomes a thing, an essence, or a living being. Moreover, defining anthropology as the science of culture does not mean that culture must be the sole focus of analysis: obviously, we do want to know what "events, acts, people, and processes" do with culture and what they let culture do to them. Dropping "culture/s," however, will leave us without a word to name those clusters that, ill-shaped though they may be, are nonetheless out there and do play an important role, and it also makes it difficult to define the discipline in short and positive words, at least if we do not content ourselves with practicing "the fieldwork science."

As pointed out, there is no ultimate logical reason to retain "culture/s" (or to abandon it), but there are pragmatic ones even beyond that of communicative economy. They have to do with the success of the concept, and it is to them that I will now turn.

Pragmatic Reasons for Retaining "Culture/s"

The concept of culture has undoubtedly exerted an influence beyond the borders of the discipline.

> Suddenly people seem to agree with us anthropologists; culture is everywhere. Immigrants have it, business corporations have it, young people have it, women have it, even ordinary middle-aged men have it, all in their own versions.... We see advertising where products are extolled for "bed culture" and "ice cream culture," and something called "the cultural defense plea" is under debate in jurisprudence.

It is concern for the nation's culture that makes the French government establish commissions to search for indigenous equivalents of unwanted loan-words, and it is again in the name of culture that the Chinese and Indonesian leaderships reject the claim to universal application of the Declaration of Human Rights, declaring it a product of Western culture unfit for exportation. "Everyday ways of contemporary talk have been heavily influenced by our anthropological concept of culture."... Moreover, this trend is by no means restricted to postindustrial societies or those aspiring to such a position. On the contrary, Sahlins states that

> the cultural self-consciousness developing among imperialism's erstwhile victims is one of the more remarkable phenomena of world history in the

late twentieth century. "Culture"—the word itself, or some local equivalent—is on everyone's lips.... For centuries they may have hardly noticed it.
But today, as the New Guinean said to the anthropologist, "If we didn't
have *kastom*, we would be just like white men."

Within the academy, the culture concept is also gaining popularity.... Cultural studies has fast established itself in many countries, and its adherents have
moved into a more anthropological direction of conceiving culture, with, for
example, scholars of high literature descending onto the worldly levels of popular novels, comic strips, soap operas, and advertisements....

[T]here is no denying that many ordinary people have grasped at least
part of anthropology's message: culture is there, it is learned, it permeates all
of everyday life, it is important, and it is far more responsible for differences
among human groups than genes. Therefore, I think that retaining the concept will put us in a better strategic position to transmit the other things we
know than we would achieve by denying the existence of culture/s. Choosing
the former strategy, we can try to establish anthropology as the expert on—if
no longer the owner of—culture, whereas opting for the latter places us in the
difficult position of denying something about which we rightly claim to be
more knowledgeable than others....

Therefore, I propose that we retain "culture" the noun in its singular
and plural form and clarify for those non-anthropologists who are willing to
listen what the phenomenon so designated really is—which, as I have tried to
emphasize, requires very clear and definite formulations about all the things
it is not.

Conclusion

There is no immanent justification to be drawn from the empirical world
either for using or for discarding the culture concept. Any set of persons who
have specific routines of thinking, feeling, and acting in common will invariably be different with regard to other such routines, and therefore wherever
we find sharing there is also nonsharing. If we agree, however, to "imagine the
world in which people dwell as a continuous and unbounded landscape, end-
lessly varied in its features and contours, yet without seams or breaks," we will
still need a vocabulary for describing its mountains, plains, rivers, oceans, and
islands. The anthropological concept of culture offers itself for that task, all
the more so since it has persuaded many people outside anthropology of its
usefulness. There is no denying that it has often been applied wrongly and
that it continues to be so, especially in the hands of cultural fundamentalists.
But, weighing the successes and failures, I am not convinced that the concept
really entails the criticized connotations, and I think that it can be dissociated
from them and used "to its best intents." Staying with culture—while emphasizing its problematic reproduction, the limitations imposed on it by the individual and the universal, and its distinctness from ethnicity and identity—will
enable us to retain the common ground it has created within anthropology
and profit from the fact that the general public increasingly understands what

we mean when we employ it. Denying the existence of culture and cultures will be difficult to transmit to the many that see them out there, and they will very likely turn to others who may then disseminate their questionable expertise without serious competitors. Any scientific concept is a simplifying construct and has its costs, but once the advantages have been found to outweigh these costs it should be employed with a clear conscience.

POSTSCRIPT

Should Anthropologists Abandon the Concept of Culture?

Both authors agree that the concept of culture, as commonly used, tends to exaggerate the boundedness, homogeneity, coherence, and stability of the customs, practices, or whole ways of life being described. Lila Abu-Lughod adds that descriptions in terms of culture also exaggerate the degree of difference between the culture of the investigator and the people being studied and imply that the people studied are inferior to the investigator. She concludes that these problems are inherent in the concept of culture and that anthropologists should therefore discard the culture concept altogether. Christoph Brumann, on the other hand, argues that the idea of culture is still very useful for ethnographic description and for communication with scholars and lay people outside the field of anthropology. He believes that it needs only to be repaired, not discarded, by scholars taking care to convey the interconnectedness of cultures, their internal variations and conflicts, and their tendency to change as well as their tendencies to form patterns.

Abu-Lughod's critique of the culture concept is part of a broader self-criticism movement in anthropology—usually termed the "post-modern" movement—which has called into question the epistemological validity of fieldwork and ethnographic writing and has also questioned the morality of Western scholars studying non-Western peoples, seeing it as an extension of colonial domination. Taken to their logical conclusion, these critiques are calling for the end of cultural anthropology as we know it. If we are to eschew all generalization, as Abu-Lughod advises, we would have to stop producing the summary descriptions of other cultures that are the hallmark of our discipline and would have to discard all the comparative categories—such as descent systems, rituals, and exchange systems—that are used for description and cross-cultural comparison. In addition, we would have to discard all the anthropological explanations of sociocultural phenomena (such as the causes of the development of chiefdoms) that are based on the "facts" derived from fieldwork and ethnographic descriptions. (See Carniero's article in Issue 1.) Anthropologists must decide whether the problems and ambiguities in the concept of culture warrant such a radical rebuilding of our discipline.

One of the main challenges for cultural anthropologists today is to adapt the concept of culture to the study of complex societies. Anthropologists first used the concept of culture in the study of relatively independent, small-scale societies (tribes, peasant communities, etc.), so it seemed possible to characterize each society as having a single culture that was relatively uniform throughout the population. As anthropologists have turned their attention to modern, complex societies in a rapidly changing and ever more interconnected world, they have had to face the limitations of that simplistic view. Nowadays anthropologists must think of every definable group or category of people in a complex society as having a culture that often overlaps in its features with the cultures of other groups.

Because individuals are members of many groups and social categories, they each have different combinations of cultures, and they switch them on and off depending on the situation. For example, American college students participate in the cultures of their home area, ethnic group, religious denomination, American youth in general, American college students, their own college in particular, and the various teams and social organizations to which they belong. We realize that we cannot characterize the culture of a complex society, like the United States, in terms of a single set of characteristics that applies to every member of the society. One question raised by this issue is whether that limitation applies to the so-called simple societies studied by earlier anthropologists as well.

The importance, complexity, and problems of the concept of culture are reflected in the fact that anthropologists and other scholars continue to write books and articles about it. A very readable overview of the history of cultural anthropology and the evolution of the culture concept is Adam Kuper's book *Culture: The Anthropologists' Account* (Harvard University Press, 1999). Other recent books on the concept of culture include Lee Cronk's *That Complex Whole: Culture and the Evolution of Human Behavior* (Westview, 1999), Sherry Ortner's edited volume *The Fate of "Culture": Geertz and Beyond* (University of California Press, 1999), and Marvin Harris's *Theories of Culture in Postmodern Times* (Altamira Press, 1999). A valuable starting point for reviewing recent thinking on the culture concept is Sherry Ortner's article "Theory in Anthropology Since the Sixties," *Comparative Studies in Society and History* (1984). Special issues or sections of journals featuring articles on aspects of the culture concept include "Culture: A Second Chance?" *Current Anthropology* (1999); "Comparative Research and Cultural Units," *Ethnology* (2000); "When: A Conversation about Culture," *American Anthropologist* (2001); and "A New Boasian Anthropology: Theory for the 21st Century," *American Anthropologist* (2004). Among many thought-provoking articles are Robert Brightman's "Forget Culture: Replacement, Transcendence, Relexification," *Cultural Anthropology* (1995); Lars Rodseth's "Distributive Models of Culture: A Sapirian Alternative to Essentialism," *American Anthropologist* (1998), W. Penn Handwerker's "The Construct Validity of Cultures: Cultural Diversity, Culture Theory, and a Method for Ethnography," *American Anthropologist* (2002); James Bogg's "The Culture Concept as Theory, in Context," *Current Anthropology* (2004); and F. Allan Hanson's "The New Superorganic," *Current Anthropology* (2004). Reflections by important figures in American anthropology on their views of culture include Marshall Sahlins's "Two or Three Things that I Know about Culture," *Journal of the Royal Anthropological Institute* (1999), and Ward Goodenough's "In Pursuit of Culture," *Annual Review of Anthropology* (2003).

ISSUE 4

Do Native Peoples Today Invent Their Traditions?

YES: Roger M. Keesing, from "Creating the Past: Custom and Identity in the Contemporary Pacific," *The Contemporary Pacific* (Spring/Fall 1989)

NO: Haunani-Kay Trask, from "Natives and Anthropologists: The Colonial Struggle," *The Contemporary Pacific* (Spring 1991)

ISSUE SUMMARY

YES: Cultural anthropologist Roger M. Keesing argues that what native peoples in the Pacific now accept as "traditional culture" is largely an invented and idealized vision of their past. He contends that such fictional images emerge because native peoples are largely unfamiliar with what life was really like in pre-Western times and because such imagery distinguishes native communities from dominant Western culture.

NO: Hawaiian activist and scholar Haunani-Kay Trask asserts that Keesing's critique is fundamentally flawed because he only uses Western documents—and native peoples have oral traditions, genealogies, and other historical sources that are not reflected in Western historical documents. Anthropologists like Keesing, she maintains, are trying to hold on to their privileged position as experts in the face of growing numbers of educated native scholars.

In 1983 Eric Hobsbawm and Terence Ranger published a collection of essays entitled *The Invention of Tradition* (Cambridge University Press). For many anthropologists trained in a structural-functionalist style of research, this volume was striking because it suggested two points that seemed to fly in the face of many cherished anthropological ideas. First, they argued that traditions in all societies change as a response to the political, economic, and social needs of the community. Second, they contended that the "historical" traditions societies celebrated were often invented in the recent past as a way of distinguishing one indigenous group from a dominant one. By 1983 most anthropologists had accepted the axiom that all societies change over time.

Culture and social institutions may work to inhibit changes and keep society functioning as it had in the previous generation, but innovations inevitably occurred. What made Hobsbawm and Ranger's book so important was that it used several Western examples to demonstrate that even in Western countries with rich historical documentation, institutions such as Scottish tartans could become routinized and accepted as a traditional and essential marker of Scottish ethnicity, even though the custom had existed for barely a century. They argued that the idea that tartans had ancient origins was particularly appealing to the Scots because it distinguished them from the dominant English culture that had long oppressed them.

In the following selection, Roger M. Keesing builds on Hobsbawm and Ranger's argument by turning his attention to the "invention of tradition" in Pacific countries. Throughout the Pacific, people now accept as historical traditions and customs practices that could only have emerged following the invasion and conquest of their islands by Western people. Keesing contends that because colonial intrusion has been so comprehensive, Pacific islanders know almost nothing about what their precolonial societies were really like. As a result, islanders have grasped onto certain idealized images of their past as themes and motifs to celebrate the distinctiveness of their cultures from dominant Western society. These idealized and largely fictional images have great political power for oppressed people, and they have often become a rallying point for various social movements. Nevertheless, concludes Keesing, these images of Pacific traditions find little support in historical documents and should largely be understood as modern mythmaking for the political ends of modern Pacific elites.

Hawaiian activist Haunani-Kay Trask attempts to turn Keesing's argument on its head by suggesting that Keesing's assertions about the "inventions" of Hawaiian traditions are yet another example of colonialism, racism, and white presumptions of superiority. She contends that Keesing only accepts Western historical sources, completely ignoring oral tradition, local mythologies, genealogies, and even rituals. Historical documents were biased by Western culture, argues Trask, and often represented an inaccurate understanding of native culture and social institutions. She questions whether or not white anthropologists have a privileged view of native customs, suggesting that most of Keesing's claims are racist attempts to further belittle native understanding and appreciation of the past.

Do native peoples or Western anthropologists have a better understanding of the native past? Have native traditions changed as much as Keesing would have us believe? Have these changes been the direct result of Western colonialism or have native peoples been active agents in such changes? Are Western historical sources biased and inaccurate when describing native practices? Are native oral traditions today accurate and authentic visions of traditional ways of life? Is there an authentic cultural tradition in any society, or, as Keesing suggests, are there different traditions for chiefs and for commoners, for men and for women? And, finally, are these "traditions" powerful as tools to fight oppression?

Roger M. Keesing

 **YES**

Creating the Past: Custom and Identity in the Contemporary Pacific

Across the Pacific, from Hawai'i to New Zealand, in New Caledonia, Aboriginal Australia, Vanuatu, the Solomon Islands, and Papua New Guinea, Pacific peoples are creating pasts, myths of ancestral ways of life that serve as powerful political symbols. In the rhetoric of postcolonial nationalism (and sometimes separatism) and the struggles of indigenous Fourth World peoples, now minorities in their own homelands, visions of the past are being created and evoked.

Scholars of Pacific cultures and history who are sympathetic to these political struggles and quests for identity are in a curious and contradiction-ridden position in relation to these emerging ideologies of the past. The ancestral ways of life being evoked rhetorically may bear little relation to those documented historically, recorded ethnographically, and reconstructed archaeologically—yet their symbolic power and political force are undeniable.

Perhaps it does not matter whether the pasts being recreated and invoked are mythical or "real," in the sense of representing closely what actual people did in actual times and places. Political symbols radically condense and simplify "reality," and are to some extent devoid of content: that is how and why they work. Perhaps it matters only whether such political ideologies are used for just causes, whether they are instruments of liberation or of oppression. In the contemporary Pacific they are being used both to recapture just rights and to deny them. The question is less simple than that.

The process of recapturing the past, of reconstructing, of questioning Western scholarship—historical and anthropological—is important and essential. My intention is neither to defend established versions of the past from a standpoint of vested scholarly interest, nor to debunk emerging political myths by comparing them to actual pasts to which I claim privileged access. Rather, in showing contradictions in this process of political mythmaking and in showing how in many ways the contemporary discourses of cultural identity derive from Western discourses, I seek to promote a more genuinely radical stance in relation to both the more distant and the more recent past—and to Western domination, of minds as well as societies.

The discourse of identity, legitimacy, and historical origins—the political mythmaking of our time—is not as different from the political mythmaking of the pre-European Pacific as it might seem.

The "invention of tradition" has been extensively explored in recent years . . . , in relation to theoretical issues of ideology and representation, questions of political economy (such as the invention and evocation of a symbolically constructed Scottish Highlands culture, replete with woollen kilts from British mills as well as bagpipes . . . , and the dynamics of national-identity construction in postcolonial nation states. These phenomena have not been extensively explored for the Pacific. Nonetheless, they have occurred in other times and places and are going on at present in other settings. Contemporary Malaysia, where a mythic "Malay culture," a conflation of indigenous (but heavily Indianized) court traditions and Islam, is being used to persecute and disenfranchise Chinese and Indian minorities and indigenous ethnic groups, is a case in point.

Modern Mythmaking in the Pacific

Before I turn to some of the important theoretical issues raised by contemporary movements and ideologies of cultural identity, let me sketch briefly the range of phenomena I am concerned with.

Beginning with ideologies of *kastom* in contemporary Melanesia, I will illustrate four variants, or levels, mainly with reference to the Solomon Islands. These phenomena have counterparts in Vanuatu and Papua New Guinea.

First, at a national and regional level, are rhetorical appeals to "The Melanesian Way," and idealizations of custom (most often emanating from a Westernized elite). In Vanuatu in particular, the ideologies and charters of the postcolonial state enshrine customary law and institutions.

Second, are ritualized celebrations of custom in the form of the arts— music, dance, "traditional" dress—as dramatically enacted in art festivals, tourist events, and rituals of state.

Third, the rhetoric of custom is invoked with reference to a particular region or island or province within a postcolonial state. This may take the form of competition for state resources and political power, regional separatism, or even secessionist demands. . . . In the emergence of Papua New Guinea, secessionist claims by North Solomons and East New Britain were cast partly in terms of customary unity. . . .

Fourth, if the field of view is narrowed to particular language groups, particularly on islands like Malaita (or Tanna) where the commitment to "traditional" culture remains strong, we find ideologies of *kastom* used to resolve the contradictions between ancestral ways and Christianity. As Burt has documented, the Kwara'ae of central Malaita have produced origin myths that trace their ancestors back to wandering tribes of Israelites and codify ancestral rules in the style of Biblical commandments. The creation of mythical customs has been encouraged and even demanded by institutions of the postcolonial state that empower and legitimize "paramount chiefs" or other "traditional" leaders: contemporary Melanesia is now filled with "paramount chiefs" in areas that in precolonial times had no systems of chiefly authority or hereditary rank. . . .

In Australia, idealized representations of the pre-European past are used to proclaim Aboriginal identity and the attachment of indigenous peoples to the land, and are being deployed in environmentalist as well as Aboriginal political struggles. In New Zealand, increasingly powerful and successful Maori political movements incorporate idealized and mythicized versions of a precolonial Golden Age, the mystical wisdom of Aotearoa.

Hawai'i and New Caledonia exhibit further variants on the themes of Fourth World political struggle, with idealized representations of precolonial society deployed to assert common identity and to advance and legitimate political demands. In the Hawaiian case, a cultural tradition largely destroyed many decades ago must be reconstituted, reclaimed, revived, reinvented. A denial that so much has been destroyed and lost is achieved by political mythology and the sanctification of what survives, however, altered its forms. In New Caledonia, the issues are not simply the desperate struggle for political power and freedom from colonial oppression, but also the creation of both common bonds and common cultural identity among peoples whose ancestors were deeply divided, culturally and linguistically, into warring tribes speaking mutually unintelligible languages.

Some Theoretical Themes

These discourses of cultural identity in the contemporary Pacific, although they depict the precolonial past and claim to produce countercolonial images, are in many ways derived from Western ideologies.

. . . [C]ontemporary Third World (and Fourth World) representations of their own cultures have been shaped by colonial domination and the perception of Western culture through a less direct reactive process, a dialectic in which elements of indigenous culture are selected and valorized (at the levels of both ideology and practice) as *counters to* or *commentaries on* the intrusive and dominant colonial culture. That is, colonized peoples have distanced themselves from (as well as modeling their conceptual structures on) the culture of domination, selecting and shaping and celebrating the elements of their own traditions that most strikingly differentiate them from Europeans.

. . . Pacific Island elites, and Aboriginal Australians, Maori, and Hawaiians in a position to gain leadership roles and become ideologues, have been heavily exposed, through the educational process, to Western ideologies that idealize primitivity and the wisdom and ecological reverence of those who live close to Nature. Idealizations of the precolonial past in the contemporary Pacific have often been derivatives of Western critiques of modern technology and progress; ironically, those in the Pacific who in their rhetorical moments espouse these idealized views of the past are mainly (in their political actions and life-styles) hell-bent on technology, progress, materialism, and "development."

In the process of objectification, a culture is (at the level of ideology) imagined to consist of "traditional" music, dances, costumes, or artifacts.

Periodically performing or exhibiting these fetishized representations of their cultures, the elites of the new Pacific ritually affirm (to themselves, the tourists, the village voters) that the ancestral cultural heritage lives on.

. . . [A]ssertions of identity based on idealizations of the ancestral past draw heavily on anthropological concepts—particularly ideas about "culture"—as they have entered Western popular thought. It is ironic that cultural nationalist rhetoric often depicts anthropologists as villains who appropriate and exploit, although that anti-anthropological rhetoric is itself squarely shaped by anthropology's concepts and categories. . . .

European scholars are implicated in a more direct way in some of the misrepresentations of ancestral cultures. Some of the classic accounts and generalizations about the cultures of Polynesia and Melanesia by expatriate scholars—to which Islanders have been exposed through books and other media—are misleading. Western scholars' own misrenderings and stereotypes have fed back into contemporary (mis)representations of the Pacific past.

In questioning the political myths of our time, I am not defending the authority of anthropological representations of the Pacific past, or the hegemonic position of scholarly discourse in relation to the aspirations of indigenous peoples to recapture their own pasts. The past . . . is contested ground. I am urging that in contesting it, Pacific Islanders be more relentlessly radical and skeptical—not that they relinquish it to the "experts." (We who claim expertise, too, can well reflect on the politics and epistemology of our privileged authority.)

Finally (and critically), if I seem to imply a gulf between the authenticity of actual precolonial societies and cultures and the inauthenticity of the mythic pasts now being invented in the Pacific, such a characterization in fact perpetuates some of anthropology's own myths. The present political contexts in which talk of custom and ancestral ways goes on are of course very different from precolonial contexts. Nonetheless, such mystification is inherent in political processes, in all times and places. Spurious pasts and false histories were being promulgated in the Pacific long before Europeans arrived, as warrior leaders draped veils of legitimacy over acts of conquest, as leaders sought to validate, reinforce, [and] institutionalize, . . . and as factions battled for dominance. Ironically, then, the "true" and "authentic" cultures of the Pacific past, overlain and distorted by today's political myths, represent, in part at least, cumulations of the political myths of the ancestors.

In Pacific communities on the eve of European invasion, there were multiple "realities"—for commoners and for chiefs, for men and for women, for young and for old, for free persons and for captives or slaves, for victors and for vanquished. Genealogies, cosmologies, rituals were themselves contested spheres. The "authentic" past was never a simple, unambiguous reality. The social worlds of the Pacific prior to European invasion were, like the worlds of the present, multifaceted and complex.

Moreover, however the past may be constructed as a symbol, and however critical it may be for historically dominated peoples to recapture this ground, a people's cultural heritage poses a challenge to radical questioning. We are all to some degree prisoners of "real" pasts as they survive into the present—in the form of patriarchal values and institutions, of patterns of thought, of structures of power. A deeply radical discourse (one that questions basic assumptions) would aspire to liberate us from pasts, both those of our ancestors and those of (colonial or other) domination, as well as to use them as political symbols.

Let me develop these arguments. . . .

The Fetishization of "Culture"

Not only in the Pacific are dramatizations and ritual enactments of cultural traditions being celebrated—in the form of dress, music, dance, handicrafts—while actual cultural traditions are vanishing. The two processes—the celebration of fossilized or fetishized cultures and the destruction of cultures as ways of life and thought—are going on in the Soviet Union, eastern Europe, and China and also in the Andean states, Brazil, Malaysia, and Indonesia. Perhaps it is an essential element in the process of nation building, where populations are ethnically diverse. Most often, a dominant national population imposes its language and cultural tradition on minority groups while appearing to value and preserve minority cultures: they are preserved like specimens in jars. . . . What greater alienation than watching those who dominate and rule you perform symbolically central elements of your cultural heritage: selling *your* culture?

What makes the Pacific distinctive here is the way, particularly in the Melanesian countries, the specimens in the jars are the cultures those with political power have themselves left behind. Members of the Westernized elites are likely to be separated by gulfs of life experience and education from village communities where they have never lived: their ancestral cultures are symbols rather than experienced realities. Bringing the specimens out of the jars on special occasions—cultural festivals, rituals of state—is a denial of alienation at a personal level, and a denial that cultural traditions are being eroded and destroyed in the village hinterlands. . . .

By the same logic, the "cultures" so commoditized and packaged can be sold to tourists. I have commented elsewhere on the way this commoditization shapes Pacific cultures to fit Western fantasies:

> Mass tourism and the media have created a new Pacific in which what is left or reconstructed from the ruins of cultural destruction of earlier decades is commoditized and packaged as exoticism for the tourists. The Pacific [is] Fantasy Land for Europe and the United States (and now for Japan) . . . to be symbolically constructed—and consumed by a consumerist society, to serve its pleasures and needs.
>
> The commoditization of their cultures has left tens of thousands of Pacific Islanders as aliens in their own lands, reduced to tawdry commercialized representations of their ancestors, histories and cultures. Beneath the veneer of fantasy, the Islanders are pauperized in village hinterlands or themselves commoditized as menial employees. Serving the comforts as well as the fantasies of rich tourists, they are constrained to smile and "be happy," because that is part of their symbolic image.

We need only think of tourism in Fiji. There, at least, the elements of culture enacted for tourists represent a version, if an edited and Christianized one (no strangling of widows in the hotel dining rooms), of a past that actually existed. The representations of "Hawaiian culture" for tourists, with hula dances, ukuleles, and pineapples, illustrate that where there is a gulf between historical realities and the expectations of tourists, the fantasies will be packaged and sold.

Invented Pasts and Anthropology

The objectification of a way of life, the reification of the customs of ancestors into a symbol to which a political stance is taken—whether of rejection or idealization—is not new in the Pacific, and is not confined to Islanders who have learned the Western concept of "culture." The so-called Vailala Madness of the Gulf Division of Papua in 1919, where villagers destroyed cult objects in a wave of iconoclasm, and proclaimed their rejection of the ways of ancestors who had withheld material riches from them, is but one example. Other classic "cargo cults" echoed the same theme.

The political stances being taken toward the ways of the ancestors in the contemporary Pacific reflect some of the same mechanisms. When massively confronted with an engulfing or technologically dominating force—whether early colonial invaders or more recently the world capitalist system and late-twentieth-century technology and wealth—one is led to take an objectified, externalized view of one's way of life that would hardly be possible if one were simply *living* it. Land, and spiritual connection to it, *could not* have, other than in a context of invasion and displacement and alienation, the ideological significance it acquires in such a context.

The ideologies of our time, unlike cargo cult ideologies, are phrased in terms of "culture" and other anthropological concepts, as they have passed into Western popular thought and intellectual discourse. This is hardly surprising, given the educational experiences of Pacific Island leaders, but it is problematic nonetheless, because the concepts that have been borrowed oversimplify in ways that have bedeviled anthropology for decades. First, "culture" represents a reification. A complex system of ideas and customs, attributed a false concreteness, is turned into a causal agent. Cultures are viewed as doing things, causing things to happen (or not happen).

In the framework of functionalist anthropology, societies and cultures have been attributed a spurious coherence and integration and portrayed in a timeless equilibrium. The timelessness and integration of the ideologically constructed Pacific pasts represent in part a projection of anthropology's own conceptual simplifications into contemporary political myths.

. . . Pacific Island peoples asserting their identity and their continuity with the past are led to seek, characterize, and proclaim an "essence" that has endured despite a century or more of change and Westernization.

In a different and older anthropological tradition—one that lives on in anthropology museums, hence is represented in the contemporary Pacific—a culture is metonymically represented by its material artifacts. This museological tradition, which has old roots in the nineteenth-century folklorism of Europe, has fed as well into the discourse on cultural identity, as I have noted. From it derives the view that in preserving the material forms and performance genres of a people, one preserves their culture.

In borrowing from anthropological discourse, ideologies of cultural identity in the contemporary Pacific have not only acquired conceptual oversimplifications but have incorporated some empirical distortions and misinterpretations for which anthropologists (and other European scholars) are ultimately responsible.

It is not that Aboriginal or Maori activists, or contemporary Samoans or Trobriand Islanders, are uncritical in their acceptance of what anthropologists have written about them. In Aboriginal struggles for land rights, for example, one of the battles has been waged against orthodox views, deriving ultimately from Radcliffe-Brown, of the patrilineality of local territorial groups—views incorporated into federal land rights legislation. The ironies and contradictions of Aboriginal peoples being denied rights they believe are culturally legitimate on grounds that they do not fit an anthropological model have chilling implications for those of us who would claim privileged authority for our "expertise" or *our* constructions of the past.

There is a further twist of irony when scholarly interpretations that may be faulty, or at least misleadingly oversimplified or overgeneralized, have been incorporated by Pacific Islanders into their conceptions of their own pasts. Let me illustrate with the concept of *mana* in Oceanic religion. . . . When I was at the University of South Pacific in 1984 and spoke on *mana*, I discovered that Polynesian students and faculty had been articulating an ideology of a common Polynesian cultural heritage and identity in which *mana* was central. Yet, as I pointed out, in many languages in Western Polynesia *mana* is used as a noun only to describe thunder, lightning, or other meteorological phenomena. Where *mana is* used as a noun to refer to spiritual power, in a number of Polynesian languages, it seems to be a secondary usage, less common than its usage as a stative verb ('be effective', 'be potent', 'be sacred').

Mana in the sense it has acquired in anthropology seems centrally important only in a few languages of eastern Polynesia, notably Maori and Hawaiian. . . .

The imputation of mystical wisdom to Polynesians (who in the process were distinguished from their dark-skinned, savage, cannibal neighbors to the west) has roots in European theories of race. The construction of the Polynesians in European thought, a process going back to the early explorers, has been brilliantly examined by Bernard Smith. Most striking has been the construction of Maori culture in European imagination. . . . The cosmic philosophy of the Maori, the mystical worldview, is as much a European as a Polynesian creation. Even though contemporary Maori ideologues attempt to discredit some aspects of the representation of Maori culture by Western scholars, the counterrepresentation advanced as authentic seems deeply infused by early Western romanticizations of the Maori. . . .

Political Mythology and Cultural "Authenticity": A Wider View

So far, I have implied that there is a wide gulf between the authentic past—the real ways of life that prevailed in the Pacific on the eve of European invasion— and the representations of the past in contemporary ideologies of cultural identity. This gulf requires a closer look.

. . . My point is . . . that the real past was itself highly political. Pacific societies, in pre-European times, were far from stable and static . . . : they were, as the archaeological record makes very clear, marked by political expansions and contractions, regional systems, warfare, trade—and change. Anthropological models have by and large failed to capture the dynamics of cultural production and change. Cultures are often imagined to be like coral reefs, the gradual accumulation of countless "polyps." . . . To the contrary, . . . cultural production is a highly political process. The symbolic material of cultures—rules imputed to ancestors, rituals, myths—serves ideological ends, reinforcing the power of some, the subordination of others.

From such a viewpoint, the authentic ancestral cultures of the past begin to appear in a different light. The rituals, the myths, the ideologies of hierarchy and the sanctity of chiefs, served political purposes. Conquering chiefs— or their priestly retinues—invented genealogies connecting them to the gods, and discrediting fallen rivals. Those individuals or classes acquiring sufficient political power to control symbolic production could bend cultural rules and roles to their own ends, reinforcing and legitimating their power. (The old Polynesian process whereby ascendant chiefly factions produce and impose versions of the past that legitimate their ascendancy in cosmic and genealogical terms has clearly continued into the latter twentieth century, notably in Tonga.) "Ancestral cultures" themselves represented legitimations of political power and aspirations; cultures were contested spheres. In this sense, the political myths of the contemporary Pacific that refashion the past to advance the interests of the present are not so different from the political myths of the past, dutifully recorded by the early ethnographers.

There are political contexts where it is important for an idealized vision of the past to be used as counter to the present: to the world capitalist system as it incorporates poor Third World countries on its margins as primary producers and consumers; to mindless materialism, disintegration of bonds of kinship and community, narcissistic individualism, destruction of environments for short-term profit. There is a place for pastoral visions, in the West and in the Pacific.

And there is certainly a place for discourses of resistance cast in terms of cultural identity. For Fourth World indigenous minorities in the Pacific— Maori, Aboriginal Australians, Kanaks, Hawaiians—a reverence for what survives of the cultural past (however altered its forms), and for a lost heritage, is a necessary counterpoint to deep anger over the generations of destruction.

But such ideologies become self-delusory if they are not interspersed with visions of "real" pasts that cast into relief not simply their idealized virtues, but their cracks of contradictions. . . . European scholars of the Pacific have been complicit in legitimating and producing male-oriented and elitist representations of societies that were themselves male- and (in many cases) elitedominated. A critical skepticism with regard to pasts and power, and a critical deconstruction of conceptualizations of "a culture" that hide and neutralize subaltern voices and perspectives, should, I think, dialectically confront idealizations of the past. I am encouraged by the emergence, in the last several years, of critical writings in this vein by Pacific Islanders, including Epeli Hau'ofa and a number of feminist critics.

This is not the time to leave the past to the "experts," whether of the present generation or their predecessors. . . .

A more radical Pacific discourse would also be more deeply self-reflexive about the hegemonic force of Western education, of Christianity (an integral part of the colonial-imperialist project), of Western pastoral myths as appropriations of Otherness. . . .

A similar self-reflexivity is a continuing challenge for scholars working in the Pacific. Both the political implications and epistemology of our projects and representations are deeply problematic. The frame of certainty that surrounds scholarly expertise—like mythical history—is less solid than it seems: it dissolves in the right mixture of astute skepticism and self-reflexivity. But specialists on the Pacific do not best serve the interests of a less hegemonic scholarship or best support the political struggles of decolonizing and internally colonized Pacific peoples by suspending their critical judgment or maintaining silence—whether out of liberal guilt or political commitment—regarding mythic pasts evoked in cultural nationalist rhetoric. Our constructions of real pasts are not sacrosanct, but they are important elements in a continuing dialogue and dialectic.

NO    Haunani-Kay Trask

Natives and Anthropologists:
The Colonial Struggle

As a Hawaiian, a long-time outspoken defender of my people's claim to nationhood, a scholar, and a Native who knows her history and people, I found Roger Keesing's article . . . a gem of academic colonialism. Knowing oldfashioned racism too crude to defend but bitterly clinging to his sense of white superiority, Keesing plows the complaining path of the unappreciated missionary who, when confronted by ungrateful, decolonizing Natives, thinly veils his hurt and anger by the high road of lamentation: Alas, poor, bedeviled Natives "invent" their culture in reaction to colonialism, and all in the service of grimy politics!

Keesing's peevishness has a predictably familiar target: Native nationalists—from Australia and New Zealand through the Solomons and New Caledonia to Hawai'i. The problem? These disillusioned souls idealize their pasts for the purpose of political mythmaking in the present. Worse, they are so unoriginal (and, by implication, unfamiliar with what Keesing calls their "real" pasts) as to concoct their myths out of Western categories and values despite their virulent opposition to same. Thus the romanticization of pre-European Native pasts (the "Golden Age" allegedly claimed by the Maori); the assertion of a common Native identity (eg, Fijian "culture"); the "ideology" of land as spiritually significant (supposedly argued by Hawaiians, Solomon Islanders, Kanaks, and Aborigines). The gospel, according to Keesing, is that these claims are "invented." To be specific, there never was a "Golden Age," a common identity, or a spiritual attachment to the land.

Proof? Keesing supplies none, either on the charge that Native nationalists have made such claims or that their claims are false. He merely asserts fabrication then proceeds to belabor, through the mumbo jumbo of academic "discourse," the crying need for Natives (and academics) to face "our" pasts with "skepticism," while pursuing a "critical deconstruction of conceptualizations" to achieve "dialectical confrontation." The final intention should be to "liberate us" from our pasts.

Well, my answer to Keesing has been said by modern-day Natives to would-be White Fathers many times: What do you mean "us," white man?

Among Hawaiians, people like Keesing are described as *maha'oi haole*, that is, rude, intrusive white people who go where they do not belong. In Keesing's case, his factual errors, cultural and political ignorance, and dismissive attitude qualify him perfectly as *maha'oi*. Unlike Keesing; I cannot speak for other Natives. But regarding Hawaiian nationalists, Keesing neither knows whereof he speaks, nor given his *maha'oi* attitude, does he care.

Example.   Keesing only cites works by *haole* academics on the current situation in Hawai'i. Obviously, he hasn't bothered to read our Native nationalists and scholars, including those, like myself, who have been very critical of these same *haole* academics. Indeed, most of his comments on Hawaiian nationalists come from one problematic and contested article (contested by Natives, that is) by anthropologist Jocelyn Linnekin, hardly a sound evidentiary base for sweeping claims that we invent our past.

Beyond his poverty of sources, there is Keesing's willful ignorance of solid evidence from Native forms of history—genealogy—which reveal that in pre-*haole* Hawai'i our people looked on land as a mother, enjoyed a familial relationship with her and other living things, and practiced an economically wise, spiritually based ethic of caring for the land, called *mālama 'āina.*

Contrary to Linnekin's claims, and Keesing's uncritical acceptance of them, the value of *mlama 'ina* has been "documented historically," and "recorded ethnographically," (as Keesing might learn if he read Native sources), two of the criteria Keesing cites as central to any judgment of the accuracy of "ancestral ways of life being evoked rhetorically" by Native nationalists today.[1] If Natives must be held to Keesing's criteria, why should he be allowed to escape them?

The answer is that Keesing, with many Western academics, shares a common assumption: Natives don't know very much, even about their own lifeways, thus there is no need to read them. (The only "real" sources are *haole* sources, hegemony recognizing and reinforcing hegemony).

Keesing's racism is exposed here. Not only has he refused to read what we Native nationalists write and say, he has refused to look at our sources of knowledge. But then, Keesing believes, Natives are so colonized, why bother?

Example.   Keesing has also failed to distinguish between what Hawaiian nationalists say about our ways of life and what the mammoth tourist industry advertises "Hawaiian culture" to be, including "hula dances, ukuleles, and pineapples." Because he is totally ignorant of modern Hawaiian resistance, he is also totally ignorant of the Native criticism of the tourist industry, including the myth of happy Natives waiting to share their "culture" with tourists. In fact, after years of Native resistance to tourism, the churches in Hawai'i (with the push of Native nationalists and international ecumenical groups) sponsored a conference on the impact of tourism on Hawaiian people and culture in 1989. At that conference, Hawaiians from each of our major islands spoke eloquently of tourism's damage to Hawaiian sites, dance, language, economics, land, and way of life. The declaration issued from that conference listed ways to halt this damage, including a ban on all resorts in Hawaiian communities. Keesing should be reading this kind of primary evidence if he wants to learn what Hawaiian nationalists think about tourism and our culture.

Example. Keesing claims that Native nationalists hark back to an "authentic," "simple, unambiguous reality," when, in fact, "there were multiple 'realities'—for commoners and chiefs, for men and for women . . ." in cultures where "genealogies, cosmologies, rituals were themselves contested spheres."

As usual, the critical reader finds not a single reference here to a single Native nationalist statement. More *haole* sources follow, especially Keesing on Keesing. But where are the Natives?

In the dark, naturally.

The truth is that Keesing has made a false charge. Those of us in the current Hawaiian nationalist movement know that genealogies are claimed and contested all the time. Some of the chiefly lineages have legal claims on lands taken by the United States government at the American annexation of Hawai'i in 1898, which means that genealogies have an impact beyond the Hawaiian community. Cosmologies are also contested, with nationalists citing and arguing over accuracy and preferability.[2]

Finally, at the Center for Hawaiian Studies—which generates nationalist positions, sponsors nationalist conferences, and teaches the historical background and political substance of nationalist arguments—students are required to take a course on genealogies.

Given Roger Keesing's shameless claims about us Hawaiian nationalists, I invite him to take this course, or any other offered at our center. We Natives might teach him something.

Example. Keesing asserts that "cultural nationalist rhetoric often depicts anthropologists as villains who appropriate and exploit." In a note, he adds that anthropologists are "imagined to be appropriating and profiting from other people's cultures. . . ."

In Hawai'i, contract work is a major source of funding for archaeologists and anthropologists. These people are hired by investors and state or private institutions to survey areas and deem them ready for use. In highly controversial cases regarding removal of Hawaiian bones and destruction of Hawaiian temple and house sites, many archaeologists and anthropologists have argued *for* development and *against* preservation while receiving substantial sums of money. At its worst, these controversies have exposed the racist paternalism of anthropologists who pit (in their own words) *emotional* Hawaiians who try to stop disinterment and development against *scientific* anthropologists who try to increase the store of (Western) knowledge.

Of course, these *haole* anthropologists would be outraged were we Hawaiians to dig up *their* relatives for osteological analysis, search for evidence of tuberculosis and other diseases, and, not coincidentally, get paid handsomely for our troubles. To my knowledge, no anthropologist has ever dug up missionary bones, despite their plentiful presence. Nor has any haole "expert" ever argued that missionary skeletons should be subjected to osteological analysis, despite historical evidence that missionaries did bring certain diseases to Hawai'i. White colonialism in Hawai'i ensures that it is the colonizers who determine disinterment. Since we are the colonized, we have no power to disinter the bones of the colonizer. Thus, Native remains are dug up and studied. Missionary and explorer remains are sacrosanct.

Apart from contract work, anthropologists make academic careers and employment off Native cultures. Keesing may not think this is "profiting," but anthropologists who secure tenure by studying, publishing, and lecturing about Native peoples are clearly "profiting" through a guaranteed lifetime income. Of course, Keesing is disingenuous, at best. He knows as well as Native nationalists that anthropologists without Natives are like entomologists without insects.

For Hawaiians, anthropologists in general (and Keesing in particular) are part of the colonizing horde because they seek to take away from us the power to define who and what we are, and how we should behave politically and culturally.[3] This theft testifies to the stranglehold of colonialism and explains why self-identity by Natives elicits such strenuous and sometimes vicious denials by members of the dominant culture.

These denials are made in order to undermine the legitimacy of Native nationalists by attacking their motives in asserting their values and institutions. But motivation is laid bare through the struggle for cultural expression. Nationalists offer explanations at every turn: in writing, in public forums, in acts of resistance. To Natives, the burst of creative outpouring that accompanies cultural nationalism is self-explanatory: a choice has been made for things Native over things non-Native. Politically, the choice is one of decolonization.

The direct links between mental and political decolonization are clearly observable to representatives of the dominant culture, like Keesing, who find their status as "experts" on Natives suddenly repudiated by Natives themselves. This is why thinking and acting like a native is a highly politicized reality, one filled with intimate oppositions and psychological tensions. But it is not Natives who create politicization. *That* was begun at the moment of colonization.

In the Hawaiian case, the "invention" criticism has been thrown into the public arena precisely at a time when Hawaiian cultural and political assertion has been both vigorous and strong willed. Since 1970, Hawaiians have been organizing for land rights, including claims to restitution for the American overthrow of our government in 1893 and for forced annexation in 1898. Two decades of struggle have resulted in the contemporary push for Hawaiian sovereignty, with arguments ranging from complete secession to legally incorporated land-based units managed by Hawaiians, to a "nation-within-a-nation" government akin to Native American Indian nations. The US government has issued two reports on the status of Hawaiian trust lands, which encompass nearly half the State of Hawai'i. And finally, a quasi-governmental agency—the Office of Hawaiian Affairs—was created in 1978, partly in response to Hawaiian demands.

This kind of political activity has been accompanied by a flourishing of Hawaiian dance, a move for Hawaiian language immersion schools, and a larger public sensitivity to the destructive Western relationship to the land compared to the indigenous Hawaiian way of caring for the land.

Non-Native response to this Hawaiian resistance has varied from humor, through mild denial that any wrong has been committed against the Hawaiian people and government, to organized counteraction, especially from threatened agencies and actors who hold power over Hawaiian resources. Indeed, representatives of the dominant culture—from historians and anthropologists to bureaucrats and politicians—are quick to feel and perceive danger because, in the colonial context, all Native cultural resistance is political: it challenges hegemony, including that of people like Keesing who claim to encourage a more "radical stance" toward our past by liberating us from it.

But Keesing obviously knows nothing about Hawaiians. He has failed to distinguish land claims from cultural resurgence, although both have nationalist origins. And he has little or no background regarding the theft of Hawaiian domain and dominion by the American government in the nineteenth century. Given this kind of ignorance of both our recent and distant past, Keesing would do better to take a "radical" look at the racism and arrogance of *his* culture which originated anthropology and its "search for the primitive."

As for nationalist Hawaiians, we know our future lies in the ways of our ancestors, not in the colonial world of *haole* experts. Our efforts at "liberation" are directed against the colonizers, whether they be political agencies, like the American government, or academics, like Keesing himself. We do not need, nor do we want to be "liberated" from our past because it is the source of our understanding of the cosmos and of our *mana*.

In our language, the past (*ka wā mamua*) is the time in front or before; the future (*ka wā mahope*) is the time that comes after. In the words of one of our best living Native historians, Lilikalā Kame'eleihiwa (whom Keesing did not read), "The Hawaiian stands firmly in the present, with his back to the future, and his eyes fixed upon the past, seeking historical answers for present-day dilemmas. Such an orientation is to the Hawaiian an eminently practical one, for the future is always unknown whereas the past is rich in glory and knowledge."

Notes

1. In her article, Linnekin writes, "For Hawai'i, 'traditional' properly refers to the precontact era, before Cook's arrival in 1778." But later on the same page, she admits that "tradition is fluid . . ." Despite this confusion she criticizes Hawaiians for a "reconstruction of traditional Hawaiian society" in the present.

    But what constitutes "tradition" to a people is ever-changing. Culture is not static, nor is it frozen in objectified moments in time. Without doubt, Hawaiians were transformed drastically and irreparably after contact, but remnants of earlier lifeways, including values and symbols, have persisted. One of these values is the Hawaiian responsibility to care for the land, to make it flourish, called *mālama 'āina* or *aloha 'āina*. To Linnekin, this value has been invented by modern Hawaiians to protest degradation of the land by developers, the military, and others. What Linnekin has missed here—partly because she has an incomplete grasp of "traditional" values but also because she doesn't understand and thus misapprehends Hawaiian cultural nationalism—is simply this: the Hawaiian relationship to land has persisted into the present. What has changed is ownership and use of the land (from collective use by Hawaiians for subsistence to private use by whites and other non-Natives for profit). Asserting the Hawaiian relationship in this changed context results in politicization. Thus, Hawaiians assert a "traditional" relationship to the land *not* for political ends, as Linnekin (and Keesing) argue, but because they continue to believe in the cultural value of caring for the land. That land use is now contested makes such a belief political. This distinction is crucial because the Hawaiian cultural motivation reveals the persistence of traditional values, the very thing Linnekin (and Keesing) allege modern Hawaiians to have "invented."

2. In Hawai'i the Kawananakoa line contests the loss of governance, since they were heirs to the throne at the time of the American military-backed overthrow of Hawaiian Queen Lili'uokalani. The Salazar family lays claim to part of the Crown lands for similar reasons. Regarding land issues, the Ka'awa family occupied Makapu'u Point in 1988 in protest over its current use. Their argument revolved around their claim to ownership because of their genealogical connection to the Kamehameha line. Among nationalist organizations, 'Ohana o Hawai'i, led by Peggy Ha'o Ross, argues claims to leadership based on genealogy. These examples illustrate the continuity of genealogy as profoundly significant to Hawaiians in establishing mana and, thus, the power to command recognition and leadership. Keesing obviously knows nothing about any of these families or their claims.

3. The United States government defines Native Hawaiians as those with 50 percent or more Hawaiian blood quantum. Those with less than 50 percent Hawaiian blood are not considered to be "Native" and are thus not entitled to lands and monies set aside for 50 percent bloods. Hawaiians are the only human beings in the State of Hawai'i who are categorized by blood quantum, rather like Blacks in South Africa.

    While bureaucrats are happily dividing up who is and is not Native, the substance of *what* constitutes things Hawaiian is constantly asserted by anthropologists against Native nationalists. Of course, the claim to knowledge by anthropologists is their academic training applied to the field. Native nationalists' claim to knowledge is their life experience as Natives.

    The problem is more serious than epistemology, however. In a colonial world, the work of anthropologists and other Western-trained "experts" is used to disparage and exploit Natives. What Linnekin or Keesing or any other anthropologist writes about Hawaiians has more potential power than what Hawaiians write about themselves. Proof of this rests in the use of Linnekin's argument by the US Navy that Hawaiian nationalists have invented the sacred meaning of Kaho'olawe Island (which the US Navy has controlled and bombed since the Second World War) because nationalists need a "political and cultural symbol of protest" in the modern period. Here, the connection between anthropology and the colonial enterprise is explicit. When Natives accuse Western scholars of exploiting them, they have in mind the exact kind of situation I am describing. In fact, the Navy's study was done by an anthropologist who, of course, cited fellow anthropologists, including Linnekin, to argue that the Hawaiian assertion of love and sacredness regarding Kaho'olawe was "fakery." Far from overstating their case, Native nationalists acutely comprehend the structure of their oppression, including that perpetuated by anthropologists.

POSTSCRIPT

Do Native Peoples Today Invent Their Traditions?

Building on Hobsbawm and Ranger's notion of the "invention of tradi-ton," Keesing makes the case that in most—if not all—Pacific societies, the history and cultural traditions that are regarded as authentic are substantially different from the events and practices that actually occurred. In his mind, there can also be little doubt that controlling what is accepted as tradition has become politically important. How does Trask's concern over professional bias impact Keesing's other arguments? What criteria would Trask suggest as a substitute as a way of judging which practices are authentic traditions and which are modern innovations?

Many other anthropologists have addressed the question of the invention of tradition. In Hawaii, the best-known work is by Jocelyn Lin-nekin, especially her 1983 essay "Defining Tradition: Variations on the Hawaiian Identity," *American Ethnologist* (vol. 10) and her book *Children of the Land* (Rutgers University Press, 1985). See also Trask's review of the latter in the *Hawaiian Journal of History* (vol. 20, 1986).

Questions about the invention of traditions have become important in North America as well. In 1997 Brian D. Haley and Larry R. Wilcoxon published an essay in *Current Anthropology* (vol. 38) entitled "Anthropology and the Making of Chumash Tradition." They argued that anthropologists and environmentalists had encouraged Chumash Indians to exaggerate claims that a site proposed for industrial development was traditionally sacred. The following year, archaeologist John McVey Erlandson published a reply to Haley and Wilcoxon in *Current Anthropology* (vol. 39). Like Keesing, Erlandson drew on historical (white American) sources to defend his position that the site was held to be sacred.

Another anthropologist, Alan Hanson, wrote a similar but more focused argument about the invention of tradition among the Maori of New Zealand in "The Making of the Maori: Culture Invention and Its Logic," *American Anthropologist* (vol. 91, no. 4, 1989). This essay prompted a vigorous and at times hostile debate within New Zealand, and at one point some Maori threatened to censure the American Anthropological Association because of this article, which some considered racist and anti-Maori. Stephen Webster discusses this topic in light of the so-called Maori renaissance, a revival of Maori cultural values within the modern bicultural state of New Zealand in his book, *Patrons of Maori Culture: Power, Theory and Ideology in the Maori Renaissance* (University of Otago Press, 1998).

On the Internet . . .

The !Kung of the Kalahari Desert

The !Kung of the Kalahari Desert Web site contains general information about this group of San people who are now called the Ju/'hoansi by most scholars.

> http://www.ucc.uconn.edu/~epsadm03/Kung.html

On Whether Sexually Egalitarian Societies Exist

This Web site by debunker.com takes a somewhat partisan view about this question, but nevertheless offers insights about the debate between Maria Lepowsky and Steven Goldberg.

> http://www.debunker.com/texts/vanatinai.html

Islam for Today

Islam for Today provides basic Information about Islam for non-Muslims. Explore the links to basic Islamic beliefs, Muslim history and civilizations, and articles on Islam.

> http://www.islamfortoday.com/

Collisions of Religions and Violence: Redux

Collisions of Religions and Violence: Redux is a Web site that contains a special issue of the journal *Cross Currents* and deals specifically with the question of whether or not conflict and violence emerge from immutable religious and ethnic differences.

> http://www.crosscurrents.org/violencespecial.htm

Culture-Bound Syndromes

The Culture-Bound Syndromes Web site has links to information on culture-bound psychopathology and a glossary of culture-bound syndromes.

> http://web.utk.edu/~wmorgan/psy573/culture.htm

PART 2

Some Specific Issues
in Cultural Anthropology

*A*lthough some cultural anthropologists are generalists, looking at cultures as wholes, most specialize in one or more subfields, focusing on specific aspects of culture, such as religion or economics. The issues selected here show the range of questions that cultural anthropologists ask, dealing with different kinds of analysis, and asking questions about different aspects of social and cultural life, including linguistic anthropology, economic anthropology, the anthropology of religion, kinship, gender roles, political anthropology, sociobiology, ethnicity, medical anthropology, and museology. These issues illustrate how anthropologists today approach questions from the traditional subfields of cultural anthropology.

- Is Ebonics (Black English) a Distinct Language from Standard English?

- Are San Hunter-Gatherers Basically Pastoralists Who Have Lost Their Herds?

- Does the Natural-Supernatural Distinction Exist in All Cultures?

- Is It Natural for Adopted Children to Want to Find Out About Their Birth Parents?

- Do Sexually Egalitarian Societies Exist?

- Has the Islamic Revolution in Iran Subjugated Women?

- Are Yanomami Violence and Warfare Natural Human Efforts to Maximize Reproductive Fitness?

- Is Ethnic Conflict Inevitable?

- Is Islam a Single Universal Tradition?

- Do Some Illnesses Exist Only Among Members of a Particular Culture?

- Do Museums Misrepresent Ethnic Communities Around the World?

ISSUE 5

Is Ebonics (Black English) a Distinct Language from Standard English?

YES: Ernie Smith, from "What Is Black English? What Is Ebonics?" in Theresa Perry and Lisa Delpit, eds., *The Real Ebonics Debate: Power, Language, and the Education of African-American Children* (Beacon Press, 1998)

NO: John H. McWhorter, from "Wasting Energy on an Illusion," *The Black Scholar* (vol. 27, no. 1, 2001)

ISSUE SUMMARY

YES: Linguist Ernie Smith argues that the speech of many African-Americans is a separate language from English because its grammar is derived from the Niger-Congo languages of Africa. Although most of the vocabulary is borrowed from English, the pronunciations and sentence structures are changed to conform to Niger-Congo forms. Therefore, he says, schools should treat Ebonics-speaking students like other non-English-speaking minority students.

NO: Linguist John McWhorter counters that Black English is just one of many English dialects spoken in America that are mutually intelligible. He argues that the peculiar features of Black English are derived from the dialects of early settlers from Britain, not from African languages. Because African-American children are already familiar with standard English, he concludes, they do not need special language training.

Most Americans now know that some African-Americans, predominantly inner-city poor, speak differently and use different body language than middle-class white Americans. As African-Americans have gained greater exposure through television, films, sports, and music—especially rap and hip-hop—the general population has become familiar with the distinctive vocabulary, rhythm, and style of speaking that has been termed Ebonics or Black English. This manner of speaking has been criticized as substandard English by some educators. Comedian Bill Cosby created a stir by advising young African-Americans to "speak English!" How should we think about this distinctive manner of speaking? Is it ordinary English but full of mistakes and slang? Is it a dialect of English like "Brooklynese"? Or is it an entirely separate language with its own grammar and vocabulary, a vocabulary largely borrowed from standard English but transformed by special rules of pronunciation?

Whether Ebonics is a dialect or a language would normally be of little interest to anyone but linguists. But it has gained social importance because in December 1996, the school board of Oakland, California, passed a resolution stating that Ebonics is not merely a dialect of English, but a separate language, and the primary language of the majority of students in the district. Therefore, they argued, of students should be given special instruction in standard English, like students from other ethnic groups whose home languages were not English. They hoped that this would help improve the low test scores African-American children in the district received on standardized English tests. The resolution caused a media sensation, prompting criticism and even ridicule. Politicians who feared that the Oakland school district would try to claim federal funds for the teaching of English as a foreign language to Ebonics speakers. In January 1997, the board issued several amendments meant to clarify some ambiguous points in the resolution, but reaffirmed their belief that Ebonics is a separate language from English. Thus, the question of whether Ebonics is an English dialect or a separate language has major practical consequences for students across the country. Is this a question for school boards or other legislative bodies to answer, or should it be left to experts on language?

Linguists generally do not draw a sharp distinction between languages and dialects. The general idea is that most languages encompass multiple dialects. These are usually associated with particular regions or with social groups. Which dialect is considered the "standard" version of the language depends on social factors, such as which dialect is spoken by a politically dominant ethnic group, rather than on linguistic characteristics. For example, Cockney English is just as adequate for communication as BBC English, but the latter is considered the standard in Britain because it is spoken by the upper class.

In his selection, Ernie Smith makes the case that Ebonics is a separate language from English because, he argues, its grammar is based on the Niger-Congo languages of West Africa. He acknowledges that most of the vocabulary of Ebonics is borrowed from English, but points out that the pronunciation of the words has been altered to fit Niger-Congo forms. John McWhorter, on the other hand, argues that Black English is just one of many dialects of English spoken in America. He points out that Black English and standard English are mutually intelligible, and he argues that the grammatical peculiarities of Black English can be traced to regional dialects in Britain more convincingly than to African languages.

As you read the following selections, ask yourself whether there is any objective basis for deciding whether two modes of speech are separate languages or just dialects of the same language. What should the criteria be? What kind of evidence would apply? Do you think Black English is more different from standard American English than, say, the speech of white, middle-class teenagers or the speech of poor white people in the rural south?

Ernie Smith  **YES**

What Is Black English? What Is Ebonics?

The features of the language of African Americans—U.S. slave descendants of West and Niger-Congo African origin—have been recognized, described, and discussed for decades. While in recent years the appellations *Vernacular Black English, Black Vernacular English, Black English Vernacular,* and *African American Vernacular English* have gained some popularity, the phrase most prevalently used is *Black English.*

In the 1970s and 1980s, several books appeared on the language of slave descendants of African origin with *Black English* as their title....

Conspicuously, in none of these works is "Black English" defined. By using the word *English*, these works inherently posit that the language of African Americans is "English." And they also tacitly postulate that, being a variant of English, there is a genetic kinship between the language of African Americans with the Germanic language family to which English belongs. Yet, from a historical linguistic perspective, in terms of the "base" from which the grammatical features of "Black English" derive, nothing could be further from the truth. As a number of scholars have argued since the 1930s, African-American speech is an African Language System—the linguistic continuation of Africa in Black America.

What Is "Black English"?

In an attempt to find empirical data supporting the view that the language of African Americans is a dialect of English, I searched the literature on "Black English." Although I found ample debate on whether "Black English" emerged as a result of a pidgin/creole hybridization process or as a result of African slaves being taught Old English "baby talk," I found no empirical evidence that English is even the "base" from which "Black English" derives. This brings us to the issue of what criteria are used for defining and classifying any language, including English, in terms of its "genetic" or familial kinship.

In the *American Heritage Dictionary*, the word English is defined, in part, as "the West Germanic language of the English (people) divided historically into Old English, Middle English, and Modern English and now spoken in the British Isles, the United States and numerous other countries." While the definition tells us that English is a West Germanic language, the question remains: By what criteria was it discerned and decided that English is related to or akin to German and belongs to the West Germanic family of the Indo-

European languages? Was it based on grammar rules, vocabulary, historical origins, or what?

According to Leonard R.Palmer in his text *Descriptive and Comparative Linguistics: A Critical Introduction*, to establish a kinship or "relationship" between languages, one must go beyond vocabulary and look at grammar:

> For ... words are often borrowed by one language from another as a result of cultural contact....What constitutes the most certain evidence of relationship is resemblance of grammatical structure, for languages retain their native structure even after their vocabularies have been swamped by foreign borrowing, such as has been the case for English....

This prompts the question: What precisely is meant by the words *grammar* or *grammatical structure*?...

In linguistics—and for purposes here—the word *grammar* means the phonetic, phonological, morphological, syntactic and semantic systems of a language. Therefore, if English is defined and classified as a Germanic language based on a criterion of continuity in the rules of grammar, then it stands to reason that "Black English" is defined and classified as a dialect of English because there is continuity in the grammar of "Black English" and the English of non-Blacks.

There is, however, an incongruence in the empirical evidence. Those who believe that Black America's language is a dialect of "English" have not documented the existence of a single Black dialect in the African diaspora that has been formed on an English grammar base.

For the sake of argument, let us accept the view of some that "Black English" is a hybrid dialect invented by English-speaking European people during the colonial era as a "contact vernacular" or trade "lingua franca." If one accepts this view, the dialect would have to be based on the grammar of the "English" language. English-speaking people would not have known the grammar of the Niger-Congo African languages and thus could not have invented a hybrid dialect on an African grammar base.

The problem with this view is that there is not a single example of a hybrid dialect that uses African words superimposed on an English grammar. If this view were valid, surely there would be at least one such dialect documented in the diaspora of Niger-Congo African slaves taken by the English.

The fact is, when one analyzes the grammars of the so-called "Black English" dialect and the English spoken by the Europeans and Euro-Americans, the grammars are not the same. While there has been extensive borrowing or adoption of English and other European words, the grammar of the language of the descendants of Niger-Congo African slaves follows the grammar rules of the Niger-Congo African languages. In other words, based on a criterion of continuity in the rules of grammar, there is no empirical evidence that "Black English" ever existed.

An alternative thesis could be that it is not continuity in the rules of "grammar" but the etymology and continuity of the "lexicon" that is the criterion for defining and classifying languages as being related. Logically, if the etymology of the lexicon is the criterion for establishing familial kinship, and the bulk of the vocabulary of "Black English" has been borrowed or adopted from the English language stock, then "Black English" is a dialect of English.

But if one uses such a criterion one must ask: Why is there a double standard? It is universally accepted that English has borrowed the bulk of its lexicon from the Romance or Latin language family. Yet English is not classified as being a Latin or Romance language but as a Germanic language.

Actually, the use of *vocabulary* to classify the language of African Americans is just as incongruent. That is, since Latin and French are the origin of the bulk of the English lexicon, how is it that African-American speech is even classified as an English dialect at all? If the dominant lexicon of the English language is Latin and French, then ipso facto the etymology of the dominant lexicon of so-called "Black English" is Latin and French. By this criterion, it logically follows, that the dialect being called "Black English" would more properly be called "Black Latin" or "Black French."

There is however, another possible definition or meaning of the phrase "Black English"—one that does not hinge on the criteria for classifying a language but rather one that has to do with how the word *Black* is perceived and defined. Those who posit this view contend that "any definition of Black English is closely bound to the problem of defining 'Blackness.'" They posit that there is a wide range of characteristics and experiences among Black people, from those in the street culture to those in the middle class.

Concomitantly, there are many Blacks who are exposed to the English of the upper class and of educated native English speakers, while other Blacks have only been exposed to the dialects of English of the poorer whites. And there are Black people who, though they have not lived in close proximity to Euro-Americans, have had the benefit of an excellent English language instruction.

The argument is made that "Black English" is not merely the Black idiom of the particular English dialect to which a Black has been exposed. "Black English" refers to the English spoken by a Black person who has "mastered" and is ideally competent in his or her use of the grammar and vocabulary of Standard American English.

It must be stressed, however, that this "Black English" is not the "Black English" that is often described as having characteristics distinctively different from the Standard American English idiom. In fact, in terms of its grammatical structure, the "Black English" spoken and written by Blacks who are fluent or ideally competent in Standard American English is identical to that of the Euro-American's Standard American English.

Thus, a critical examination of the literature reveals there are at least three distinct connotations that the appellation "Black English" can have. The first is that "Black English" is a dialect of African Americans that is "based" on mutant ("baby talk") Old English and Middle English archaic forms. The second connotation is that "Black English" is a hybrid dialect of African Americans that has as its genesis the transactional or pidgin/creole language of the West and Niger-Congo African slaves. The third connotation is that "Black

English" is the English spoken by mulattoes, house Negroes, and Black bilinguals who have "mastered" the grammar and vocabulary of Standard English.

Let us now turn to the perspective of the Africologist or Africanist scholars that the native language or mother tongue of the descendants of West and Niger-Congo African slaves is not a dialect of English.

The Meaning and Misuse of the Appellation Ebonics

The term *Ebonics* was coined in January 1973 by Dr. Robert L. Williams, a Professor of Psychology at Washington University in St. Louis, Missouri. Dr. Williams coined the term *Ebonics* during a small group discussion with several African American psychologists, linguists, and speech communications professionals attending a conference convened by Dr. Williams entitled "Cognitive and Language Development of the Black Child."

Etymologically, "Ebonics" is a compound of two words: "Ebony," which means "Black," and "phonics," which means "sounds." Thus Ebonics means, literally, "Black Sounds." As an all encompassing, nonpejorative label, the term *Ebonics* refers to the language of West African, Caribbean, and U.S. slave descendants of Niger-Congo African origin.

In the sense that Ebonics includes both the verbal and paralinguistic communications of African-American people, this means that Ebonics represents an underlying psychological thought process. Hence, the nonverbal sounds, cues, gestures, and so on that are systematically used in the process of communication by African-American people are encompassed by the term as well. This is the original and only intended meaning of the term *Ebonics*.

The consensus among the African-American scholars at the conference was that, owing to their history as slave descendants of West and Niger-Congo African origin, and to the extent that African Americans have been born into, reared in, and continue to live in linguistic environments that are different from the Euro-American English-speaking population, African-American children are not from home environments in which the English language is dominant. The consensus was that, as evidenced by phonetic, phonological, morphological, and syntactical patterns, African-American speech does not follow the grammar rules of English. Rather, it is a West and Niger-Congo African deep structure that has been retained. It is this African deep structure that causes African-American children to score poorly on standardized scales of English proficiency.

In essence, the "genesis" or "origin" of the African-American child's language is the West and Niger-Congo languages of Africa. While being segregated, denied, deprived, and socioeconomically disadvantaged certainly has limited the African American's exposure to and acquisition of Standard English, segregation and poverty is not the "origin" or root cause of the African-American child's limited English proficiency.

When the term *Ebonics* was coined it was not as a mere synonym for the more commonly used appellation *Black English*. Rather, the term *Ebonics* was a repudiation of the lie that Niger-Congo Africans had no fully developed languages originally and that the genesis of human speech for English-speaking

African slaves is an Old English "baby talk" or European-invented pidgin/creole vernacular.

An African Grammar with English Words

Since the 1930s, a number of scholars have posited that African-American speech is an African Language System.... These scholars have consistently maintained that in the hybridization process, it was the grammar of the Niger-Congo African languages that was dominant and that the extensive word borrowing from the English stock does not make Ebonics a dialect of English. In fact, they argue, because it is an African Language System, it is improper to apply terminology that has been devised to describe the grammar of English to describe African-American linguistic structures.

For example, the scholars who view African-American speech as a dialect of English describe the absent final consonant clusters as being "lost," "reduced, " "weakened," "simplified," "deleted," or "omitted" consonant phoneme.

But viewed as an African Language System that has adopted European words, African-American speech is described by Africologists as having retained the canonical form, or shape, of the syllable structure of the Niger-Congo African languages. Thus, in Ebonics homogeneous consonant clusters tend not to occur. This is not because the final phoneme has been "lost," "reduced," "weakened," "simplified," "deleted" or "omitted," but because *they never existed in the first place*. Hence it is by relexification (that is, "the replacement of a vocabulary item in a language with a word from another, without a change in the grammar," that in Ebonics English words such as *west, best, test, last* and *fast* become *wes, bes, tes, las* and *fas*; the words *land, band, sand* and *hand* become *lan, ban, san* and *han*; the words *left, lift, drift* and *swift* become *lef, lif, drif* and *swif*—and so forth.

Similarly, the canonical form, or shape, of syllable structure of Ebonics is that of the Niger-Congo languages of Africa, that is, a strongly consonant vowel, consonant vowel (CV, CV) vocalic pattern. Again, by relexification, in Ebonics entire sentences will have a CV, CV vocalic pattern. In Ebonics a sentence such as, "Did you eat yet?" will exhibit the CV vocalic pattern /ǰ i ǰ E t / or / ǰ u w i ǰ E t /. The reply "No" or "Naw did you?" will exhibit the CV vocalic pattern /n ó ǰu /. The sentence "Did you eat your jello?" will by relexification exhibit the CV pattern / ǰ u w i čo ǰ E l o /.

Because they view African-American speech as an English dialect, Eurocentric scholars contend that in sentences such as "You the teacher" and "That teacher she mean" a copula verbal or the verb *to be* has been "deleted," "dropped," or "omitted." In contrast, because Africologists view the language of African descendants as an African Language System, they contend that there has been no "deleted," "dropped," or "omitted" copula or verb *to be* in the sentences "You the teacher" and "That teacher she mean." As an African Language System that has an equational or equative clause phrase structure, the verb *to be never existed in the first place*.

Absolutely convinced that it is a vernacular dialect of English, Eurocentric scholars have also posited the existence of "double subjects" in so-called Black

English. Viewing Ebonics as an English dialect, Eurocentric scholars mistakenly divide sentences such as "That teacher she mean" and "My sister she smart" into noun phrase (NP) and verb phrase (VP) constituents— as English would be properly divided. In contrast, equally convinced that Black American Language is in fact an African linguistic system, the Africologists do not divide sentences such as "That teacher she mean" and "My sister she smart" into NP and VP constituents. As an African system, the division of an equative clause sentence structure is into "topic" and "comment" constituents. Hence, the pronoun *she* that follows the common nouns *teacher* and *sister* in each sentence is not a constituent of the "topic" segment of the sentence. It is a recapitulative pronoun that belongs to the "comment" segment.

In sum, Ebonics is not a dialect of English. The term *Ebonics* and other Afrocentric appellations such as *Pan African Language* and *African Language Systems* all refer to the linguistic continuity of Africa in Black America. Eurocentric scholars use the term *Ebonics* as a synonym for "Black English." In doing so, they reveal an ignorance of the origin and meaning of the term *Ebonics* that is so profound that their confusion is pathetic....

Eurocentric scholars lack any logical explanation for why, in the entire African diaspora, there is not a single hybrid English and Niger-Congo African dialect that has an English grammar as its base with African words superimposed. They also lack any logical reasons for using vocabulary as their basis for classifying Black American speech, while using grammar as their basis for classifying English. In the process, they are exposed for the academic charlatans they are.

The imperative, however, is to recognize that all pupils are equal and hence, all pupils should to be treated equally. Limited-English-Proficient (LEP) Asian-American, Hispanic-American, Native-American, and other pupils who come from backgrounds where a language other than English is dominant are provided bilingual education and English as a second language (ESL) programs to address their LEP needs. African-American LEP pupils should not, because of their race, be subtly dehumanized, stigmatized, discriminated against or denied. LEP African-American pupils are equally entitled to be provided bilingual education and ESL programs to address their LEP needs.

NO

John H. McWhorter

Wasting Energy on an Illusion

It is a fact that Black English is not different enough from standard English to pose any significant obstacle to speaking, reading, or writing it. Black English is simply a dialect of English, just as standard English is. Any language is actually a bundle of dialects—varieties which all share a core of vocabulary and structure which make them variations on a single theme, even though they differ from one another in particulars. Southern English, Appalachian English, Brooklyn English, and standard English itself are all dialects of English.

Of course, the boundary between dialect and language is not a stark one. Sometimes a variety can diverge so far from the common core of a language X that it becomes impossible to say whether it is a dialect of X or a new language Y. One useful indication of this is when the variety is no longer mutually intelligible with other dialects of X, although this can also happen when varieties remain closely related. There are also cases where geopolitics obscures linguistic reality: Swedish, Norwegian and Danish are really dialects of a single language "Scandinavian," but are considered separate languages because they are spoken in separate countries. Meanwhile, the "dialects" of Chinese, like Mandarin and Cantonese, are actually separate, mutually unintelligible languages, but since they share a writing system and a culture are treated as "dialects."

However, none of this means that there is any "debate" among linguists as to the status of Black English, which is a case in which there is no ambiguity. It is mutually intelligible with standard English both on the page and spoken, and its speakers do not occupy a separate nation. Supporters of the Oakland resolution have often attempted to wave this away by claiming that whether Black English is a dialect or a separate language is merely an arcane issue which we should leave linguists to idly bicker over while the Board "gets on with teaching standard English." However, again, there is no "debate": no credentialed linguist would disagree that Black English is a dialect of English. More importantly, the issue is directly pertinent to the Oakland resolution, not arcane: if Black English were a separate language, the Oakland resolution would be valid. If Black English is simply a dialect, this casts the resolution in a different light.

From *The Black Scholar*, vol. 27, no. 1, 2001, pp. excerpts from 9–14. Copyright © 2001 by THE BLACK SCHOLAR. Reprinted by permission.

However, it must be clear that in arguing against the Oakland resolution on the grounds that Black English is simply a dialect of English, I am not saying that it is a sloppy deviation from the standard. All dialects of all languages are rich, coherent systems. The standard English dialect, like all standard dialects, was chosen out of many solely because of bygone political accidents, not because it is somehow more logical than Black English or any other dialect. Like standard English, Black English is a subtle and complex affair.

To take one of many examples, contrary to popular belief, Black English speakers do not simply insert the verb *be* where standard speakers use conjugated forms like *am, is,* and *are.* In Black English, *be* has the very specific meaning of *habituality.* A Black English speaker would only say *My sister be walkin' by my window* to mean that she walks by on a regular basis. They would never say this to indicate that their sister was walking by at that moment, and anyone who did would sound "funny"—the proper Black English in such an instance would be *My sister walkin' by my window*, with no verb *be* at all. Thus the use of *be* is quite subtle in Black English, and would easily confuse anyone attempting to "learn" the dialect non-natively.

We also must not make the mistake of equating Black English with mere "street slang." Black English speakers indeed often use a colorful slang (lately, *phat* for "good", *fine* for "beautiful," *mackin'* for "cruising for a date," etc.) just as standard English speakers use slang (think of the Valley Girl-speak made popular by the movie *Clueless*, or the parents in the early 1960s' musical *Bye Bye Birdie* despairing of understanding a word their teenage children said). All dialects of all languages have always had slang. Slang, however, changes constantly, and is mere decoration upon an eternal underlying structure. African Americans have been using *be* in the same way for centuries, for example. Black English differs from standard English not only in terms of superficial, evanescent slang, but in fundamental structure.

All of this said, however, Black English simply does not differ *enough* from standard English to impede its child speakers from acquiring the standard. One needs no advanced training to decide on the language/dialect issue here. The very fact that African Americans are often unaware of the very existence of a "Black English" beyond slang words is a clear demonstration that Oakland's resolution is misrepresenting what is in fact an inch-wide gap between two closely related dialects....

The folly of pretending otherwise is revealed by a thought experiment. Imagine that rural, low-income white children were falling similarly behind in Mississippi. The first things we would address would be sociological conditions and quality of schools. African Americans are often aware of the similarity between black speech and that of poor Southern whites. Indeed, such speech is essentially as different from standard English as Black English is. Nevertheless, what would we think of the person who suggested that the reason these children were falling behind was because of the difference between the local dialect and standard English? At best, this would make it into the footnotes of the final resolution addressing the problem.

Thus even without training in linguistics or education, one can perceive the mistake in attributing the poor showing of black students to minor dialect differences. Yet many educators and academics see the Black English situation as somehow an exception....

⋅◈⋅

Another factor which misleads many into conceiving of Black English as a case apart is the highly vaunted "African influences" upon it. While never explicitly stated, the implication is that these influences have left traits so exotic that the jump between Black English and the standard is somehow more difficult to negotiate than that between other dialects and the standard. It is time, however, that the whistle be blown on this claim, which is a vast exaggeration of the facts, based on superannuated and marginal literature. African influence on Black English is light and indirect. Most non-standard features in Black English are directly traceable not to Mende, Yoruba or Kikongo but to regional dialects spoken by the British settlers whose English was what African slaves in America were exposed to. The habitual *be* described above, the use of *done* as in *He done seen her already*, double negation such as *There ain't nothin' stoppin' you*, the simplification of consonant clusters as in *wif* for *with*, the use of *-s* with verbs other than in the third person singular, as in *I walks with Sally*—all of these things can be heard today in Great Britain, and one can sometimes even be surprised by the oddly "African American" sound of some up-country white Britishers.

There are indeed "African Englishes." However, they are spoken not in Detroit, Oakland or Philadelphia, but in the Caribbean and Africa. Examining these reveals the shocking misrepresentation in the claim that Black English is any sense an "African Language System," as the Oakland resolution puts it. A creole language, Srnan, spoken in Surinam, was developed by African slaves, and superimposes English words upon a structure which is fundamentally that of West African languages such as Twi, Ewe, Yoruba and Igbo. Here is a sentence in Sranan: *A hondiman-dati ben bai wan oso gi en mati.* Every word in this sentence is from English: it means *That hunter bought a house for his friend*—literally "the hunter-that been buy one house give him mate." However, West African words tend to consist of sequences of consonant-plus-vowel, and the Surinamese slaves re-fashioned English words to fit this pattern, so that *that* became *dati, mate* became *mati.* The African languages many of the slaves in Surinam spoke place demonstratives like *that* after the noun instead of before it, and thus so does Sranan. Similarly, such languages string verbs together where English uses prepositions, and thus "buy one house give him friend" instead of "buy a house for his friend."

All claims that Black English is somehow an African language with English words must be measured against languages like Sranan. *House* in

Sranan is *oso*. In Black English it is, well, *house*. In Sranan, *bought* is *ben bai*. In Black English—*bought*. And so on.

Of course, some have attempted to get around this by claiming that the "Africanness" of Black English is somehow "hidden," such that only trained scholars could identify it: "It looks like English, but it's not," as I have heard it put. Again, however, this could only be said by someone unfamiliar with, or willfully ignoring, creoles like Jamaican patois. Jamaican patois is not as deeply influenced by African languages as Sranan, but one could indeed say that it "looks like English but isn't." *You ran away from him* in Jamaican patois is *Yu ron go lef im*. All four words are English, but without the translation one would have to blink a few times to figure out the meaning, if one even could (this is another result of the tendency to string verbs in some West African languages). In Black English *You ran away from him* is *You ran away from 'im*. An African language?

⋯⊙⋯

... At best, African influence on Black English is largely restricted to intonation, some vocabulary items (most of them obsolete in urban culture) and patterns of social usage such as the famous call-and-response pattern. Terms such as "Nigritian Ebonics," and the subsuming of Black English into a "Pan-African Communication System," stem not from professional research by trained linguists on Black English, nonstandard British dialects, and several African languages, but from superficial, sociopolitically biased generalizations.

Thus, Black English is not "a case apart" among English dialects. Indeed, students have been castigated for speaking it, but programs have long been in place to address this.... Meanwhile, Black English is not in any sense of the term an "African language": it is simply a dialect of English.

At this point, however, some would argue that bridging Black English and standard English can only help, and that in such a desperate situation we must try anything that works. Indeed, a few scholars have found that black children's reading scores rise somewhat when the "bridging" approach is adopted. Presumably, however, this would be true with children speaking *any* non-standard dialect. The point is that other children do just fine without such help—bridging the gap between the home dialect and the standard is part of the challenge of education, and generally one so minor as to escape notice. Many teachers have told me that dialect was a nonissue when it came to black children's poor performance in schools like Oakland's.

This becomes clear with another thought experiment. Here is a passage in Brooklynese English: *Ain't it great, you an' me sittin' heah tuhgeddah?* Imagine Ed Norton, the sewer worker in *The Honeymooners,* saying it: The face is white, but the dialect is, in fact, as different from standard English as Black English is. Yet none of us are under the impression that the utterer of this sentence is at a disadvantage because school is taught in standard English; we simply imagine that they will unconsciously make the jump. Again, "African influence" does not transform Black English into a case apart: Ed Norton's *together* is *tuhgeddah*; a Black English speaking child's would be *tuhgethah*—

which person is more "disadvantaged" in terms of access to standard English? Linguistically, neither is disadvantaged at all.

꧁꧂

It is natural that linguists might suppose that Black English bars children from the standard, minor dialectal differences having come to loom large in their minds as the result of the long-term study of such things which forms part of everyday linguistic inquiry. However, a wider view shows that this is a mere artifact of the frame of reference which linguistics inevitably creates, as such dialect differences have no effect upon school performance in contexts where sociopolitics and economics are healthy. Around the world, children often bring home dialects to school which are more different from the standard than we could possibly imagine in America. For example, Swiss children speak Swiss German and go to school in High German. The dialects are so divergent that even most Germans cannot understand Swiss German: *Not* is *nicht* in High German, *nüd* in Swiss; *been* is *gewesen* in High German, gsy in Swiss; language is *Sprache* in High German, *Muul* in Swiss. Yet Swiss children learn High German via immersion, and this is not considered oppressive, a slight, or an insult. There are countless similar contexts around the world. An example slightly closer to home is Scottish English: in the current film *Trainspotting*, the near-incomprehensibility of one Scottish-speaking man has attracted much comment. We must recall, however, that this man was schooled in standard English, and surely did not consider it an inconvenience. We are all aware of the alarming rapidity with which children pick up new languages. Imagine, then, how effortlessly they pick up mere dialects of their own language!

"But Swiss children live in a wealthy, well-ordered society," some will object. And this is exactly the point: the conditions under which many African American children in Oakland live are the problem, not Black English....

꧁꧂

... [M]ost of these children already control standard English to a considerable degree. Television is a constant presence in most Americans' lives, and African Americans are no exception. More to the point, few African Americans speak nothing but standard English all day long. Black English and the standard are generally spoken together, often mixed within the same sentence: "I went to get my check today, but the place was closed—(shaking his head) every time I go down there they be closed, man." In other words, black children pick up standard English from parents and siblings right along with Black English. The children and teenagers interviewed by the networks and affiliates in covering the events in Oakland were vivid testimony to this, effortlessly switching between the two dialects and giving the lie to the Board's designation of such children as "Limited English Proficient." African American children resist speaking standard English in the classroom as an expression of the above-mentioned alienation from the mainstream culture. Language is indexed to identity, and thus naturally, children who associate standard English with selling out will refrain from speaking it. However, it is a misinterpretation to suppose that their home dialect has somehow barred them from acquiring a dialect they are bathed in daily from birth. Surely these children can watch "Full House" and "Seinfeld" without subtitles.

❦

... [G]iving African American children help they do not need would be to imply that they are among the stupidest children on earth. If Brooklynese children do not need translation exercises and readers in their home dialect, neither do African American children. If Swiss children are jumping from *Muul* to *Sprache* without a thought, surely African American kids can handle *She my sister* vs. *She's my sister*. African American children, knowing as we all do that their home language is a kind of English, would come to wonder why non-black children, many using non-standard features just as they do, were not given such "translation" lessons. Slavery and discrimination have done enough to create an inferiority complex in the African American race; we need not perpetuate it ourselves. Even worse, the "translation" approach would suppress a basic element of education, challenge—and in this case, a tiny one. Suckled on such overzealous accommodation to their ethnicity, these students would only feel cast adrift later. What felt like natural challenges to non-black students would seem more forbidding to many black students, having been introduced to school via a brand of unnecessary hand-holding which, for better or for worse, they will rarely encounter in the world as we know it.

❦

Finally, if the reader detects a larger philosophical problem lurking behind my statements, they are correct. The language of the Oakland resolution... betray[s] a Black Nationalist sentiment—of the paranoid, anti-intellectual sort— in many leading advocates. Most, I suppose, would dodge the explicit label. However, a depiction of Black English as a hitherto unknown African language spoken on the inner city streets of America is indubitably of a kind with the likes of Martin Bernal's pseudo-scientific *Black Athena*, conspiracy theories claiming that AIDS was set upon blacks by white scientists, and calls by some academics to pardon Al Sharpton's fabrication of the Tawana Brawley story as reflecting a "narrative" reasoning style indigenous to the "African" mind. Such separatist poison is already being taught seriously to African American college students in the guise of "education," turning legions of bright young black minds away from a constructive engagement with the world. More than a few African American academics, while not supporting such perspectives, wink and let them pass in the name of racial solidarity. In my opinion, however, this is settling for mediocrity. For this brand of pernicious nonsense to be extended to seven-year-olds should be chilling to all thinking people....

... [T]he least appropriate thing to waste time, money and energy on, is "teaching" African American children how to translate from their "Nigritian Ebonics" tongue into a separate language known as English. Black children indeed bring a home dialect to the classroom, but so do most children across the country and around the world. We can be certain that if the real causes of educational failure among African American children were addressed, then to future historians, the attention presently paid to "Ebonics" would seem a peculiar little wrinkle in the American timeline.

POSTSCRIPT

Is Ebonics (Black English) a Distinct Language from Standard English?

Ernie Smith and John McWhorter agree that Ebonics and standard American English are different, but they disagree on whether they are different enough to be considered separate languages. Smith contends that Ebonics is a language because its grammar is derived from the languages of West Africa, not from English. He implies that African slaves brought to America retained their basic grammars, but substituted English vocabulary. McWhorter, however, argues that the grammar of Ebonics is actually the same as that of some of the regional dialects of English in rural Britain, the source of many of the people who came to own slaves in the American south. The implication is that African slaves simply learned the dialects of their masters.

This issue raises the questions of how languages come into existence and change over time. One well-documented process is language evolution and divergence. The general idea is that languages slowly change even during stable times, and when a population speaking a certain language splits apart, for whatever reason, its languages gradually become different because the changes taking place are independent. Most of the languages of Europe are thought to have evolved and diverged from a series of common ancestors (Proto-Indo-European, Latin, Proto-Germanic, etc.), which is why linguists can group them into language families (e.g., Germanic), subfamilies (e.g., German and English), and so on. But languages can also influence each other or even merge under some circumstances. For example, English absorbed a large number of French words after the Norman Conquest in AD 1066, which is why English now has a Germanic structure but a partially Romance vocabulary. Because these processes are gradual and continuous, sharp divisions between related languages do not usually exist.

Under some circumstances, people deliberately create new languages, and these may eventually become the mother tongue of a group of people. This is the case with "pidgin" languages, such as Melanesian Pidgin English. Pidgins usually begin as trade languages between groups without a language in common. They have a simplified grammar and a vocabulary drawing on two or more existing languages. Occasionally a pidgin language becomes the primary language of a group, in which case it is referred to as a "creole." It develops a more complex grammar and vocabulary to enable it to serve as a general-purpose language, though its vocabulary may still betray its origin in other languages. McWhorter gives a vivid example of the creole language of the dominant population of Surinam in South America, who mostly descend from freed or escaped African slaves.

Linguists are uncertain whether Black English came from early English dialects in America and then diverged slightly from standard English because of the social isolation of the Africans and their descendants, as McWhorter implies, or from a creole derived from an African grammar combined with English vocabulary, which is the view Smith favors. Information on the speech of early African-American slaves is scarce and hard to interpret. However, one African-American language, Gullah, is quite certainly a creole that combines features of English and several African languages. It is spoken by small numbers of African-Americans living on the Sea Islands and adjacent coastal areas of South Carolina, Georgia, and northern Florida.

A huge literature on Black English/Ebonics and education has sprung up over the last few decades, due in part to the controversy arising from the Oakland school board resolution. A very useful bibliography of nearly 700 references has been compiled by John R. Rickford, Julie Sweetland, and Angela E. Rickford in their article "African American English and Other Vernaculars in Education," *Journal of English Linguistics* (September 2004, pp. 230–320). They code the references under a number of headings, some more relevant to educational issues and others to linguistics issues. An important general work on Black English and education is Geneva Smitherman's *Talking That Talk: Language, Culture and Education in African America* (Routledge, 2000). The edited volume from which Ernie Smith's selection was taken, Theresa Perry and Lisa Delpit's *The Real Ebonics Debate: Power, Language, and the Education of African-American Children* (Beacon Press, 1998) contains a number of valuable articles and documents relating to the Oakland school board resolution. Jacquelyne John Jackson's article "On Oakland's Ebonics: Some Say Gibberish, Some Say Slang, Some Say Dis Den Dat, Me Say Dem Dumb, It Be Mother Tongue," *The Black Scholar* (vol. 27, no. 1, 1997) provides an excellent summary of the events in Oakland and the legal issues involved.

There is also a substantial literature on the history of Black English, based on many decades of research. Two recent edited volumes bringing together a number of important articles are Shana Poplack's *The English History of African American English* (Blackwell Publishers, 2000) and Walt Wolfram and Erik R. Thomas's *The Development of African American English* (Blackwell, 2002).

ISSUE 6

Are San Hunter-Gatherers Basically Pastoralists Who Have Lost Their Herds?

YES: James R. Denbow and Edwin N. Wilmsen, from "Advent and Course of Pastoralism in the Kalahari," *Science* (December 19, 1986)

NO: Richard B. Lee, from *The Dobe Ju/'hoansi,* 3rd ed. (Wadsworth, 2003)

ISSUE SUMMARY

YES: Archaeologists James R. Denbow and Edwin N. Wilmsen argue that the San of the Kalahari Desert in southern Africa have been involved in pastoralism, agriculture, and regional trade networks since at least A.D. 800. They imply that the San, who were hunting and gathering in the twentieth century, were descendants of pastoralists who lost their herds due to subjugation by outsiders, drought, and livestock disease.

NO: Cultural anthropologist Richard B. Lee counters that evidence from oral history, archaeology, and ethnohistory shows that the Ju/'hoansi group of San living in the isolated Nyae Nyae-Dobe area of the Kalahari Desert were autonomous hunter-gatherers until the twentieth century. Although they carried on some trade with outsiders before then, it had minimal impact on their culture.

$\mathbf{C}$an hunter-gatherers (also called "foragers") be economically self-suffcient and politically autonomous even when in contact with more powerful food-producing peoples? This is the basic question behind the "Great Kalahari Debate," which is illustrated by the following selections.

Even in the late nineteenth century, hunting-and-gathering peoples living outside the disruptive influence of complex societies and colonialism were scarce. By then most Native American hunter-gatherers were on reservations or incorporated into the fur trade, and others, like the Veddas of Sri Lanka, had been absorbed and transformed by the dominant societies that surrounded them. The most striking exception was the Australian Aborigines, who were still nomadic hunter-gatherers using stone tools at the time of European contact. Aborigines became the model of the earliest stage of cultural evolution as discussed by Emile Durkheim in *The Elementary Forms of the Religious Life* (George Allen and Unwin Ltd., 1915) and Sigmund Freud in *Totem and Taboo* (Moffat, Yard, 1918). By the 1950s, however, most Aborigines, too, had been settled on ranches, missions, or government settlements, and their cultures had been radically disrupted. Anthropologists' waning hopes of studying other "pristine" foragers were suddenly raised when an American family, the Marshalls, found and studied a group of Ju/'hoansi (!Kung) San living by independent foraging in the Kalahari Desert of Southwest Africa (now Namibia). Lorna Marshall's scholarly articles (later collected in her book *The !Kung of Nyae Nyae* [Harvard University Press, 1976]), her daughter Elizabeth Marshall Thomas's popular book *The Harmless People* (Knopf, 1959) and her son John's films (e.g., *The Hunters*) attracted great attention to the San.

In 1963 then-graduate student Richard B. Lee went to northwestern Bechuanaland (now Botswana) in search of an independent foraging San group. He found such a group in the Ju/'hoansi at Dobe waterhole. Although he recognized that they interacted with Bantu-speaking herding people in the region, his research focused on their adaptation to the natural environment. His findings led to a radically new image of the San and, eventually, of foragers in general. Once thought to live in a precarious struggle for survival, he found that the Ju/'hoansi actually needed to work less than 22 hours a week to get an adequate amount of food. The key to their success was their dependence on plant foods, mostly gathered by women, rather than meat, and the emphasis placed on food sharing.

By the early 1970s, however, some anthropologists had begun to question the popular image of San as isolated people with a continuous history of independent foraging since preagricultural times. In their selection, James R. Denbow and Edwin N. Wilmsen make the case that the Kalahari San have long participated in the regional economy and political system. They argue that the Ju/'hoansi and other inhabitants of the Kalahari Desert were agropastoralists (farmer-herders) and commodity traders until the late nineteenth century, when dominating outsiders, drying climate, and livestock diseases caused some of them to lose their herds and revert (temporarily) to full-time foraging.

Richard B. Lee responds that some San groups—such as the Ju/'hoansi of the Nyae Nyae-Dobe area—were quite isolated from outsiders until the late nineteenth century, when Europeans and Bantu-speaking Africans began to make occasional journeys into their homeland. Thus, his research suggests that foraging societies can live in contact with food-producers without being economically or politically subjugated by them.

This debate raises a number of important questions. Can small-scale, politically weak societies have economic and political ties with powerful outsiders without being dominated and fundamentally changed? Can one generalize from one case like the Dobe Ju/'hoansi to other foraging peoples? If foragers were herders or farmers in the past, can they still tell us something about the hunting-and-gathering way of life before the advent of agriculture?

James R. Denbow and
Edwin N. Wilmsen

 **YES**

Advent and Course of Pastoralism
in the Kalahari

It has long been thought that farming and herding were comparatively recent introductions into the Kalahari and that it has been a preserve of foraging "Bushmen" for thousands of years. Agropastoral Bantu-speakers were thought to have entered this region only within the last two centuries. However, fully developed pastoralism and metallurgy are now shown to have been established in the Kalahari from A.D. 500, with extensive grain agriculture and intracontinental trade added by A.D. 800. Archeological, linguistic, and historical evidence delineates the continuation of mixed economies in the region into the present. Consequences of this revised view for anthropological theory and for policy planning concerning contemporary Kalahari peoples are indicated.

When the principal ethnographic studies of southern African peoples, then called "Bushmen" (1), were undertaken in the 1950's and 1960's, very little was known of their prehistory or of the history of their association with herding and farming peoples; a similar lack of historic depth characterized earlier southern Bantu studies (2). At the time, it was universally assumed that Bantu-speaking farming-herding peoples had intruded into the Kalahari no more than two or three centuries ago. The region was presumed to have been peopled previously only by San-speaking foragers who had, until then, remained isolated from external influences.

Before the mid-1970's, only two systematic archeological investigations had been carried out in Botswana, an area approximately the size of Texas (575,000 square kilometers); only one attempt had been made to integrate the history of relations among hunting and herding Kalahari peoples. In addition, the climatic history of the Kalahari and its potential influence on local economies was entirely unknown. Likewise, linguistic studies, with their implications for revealing the history of social interaction and diversification in the region, were in their infancy. The assumption that pastoralism and social heterogeneity in the Kalahari were very recently introduced appeared to be correct.

Current work in archeology, geology, linguistics, and anthropology renders that assumption untenable. Since 1975, excavations have been carried out at 34 archeological sites in Botswana as well as at other sites in Zimbabwe and Namibia. Seventy-nine radiocarbon dates now delineate the chronology of domesticated food production in Botswana during the past 2000 years. These investigations indicate that cattle (*Bos taurus*) and ovicaprids were introduced

From James R. Denbow and Edwin N. Wilmsen, "Advent and Course of Pastoralism in the Kalahari," *Science*, vol. 234 (December 19, 1986). Copyright © 1986 by The American Association for the Advancement of Science. Reprinted by permission. Some notes omitted.

along with ceramics into the northern Kalahari in the final centuries B.C. and first centuries A.D. Slightly later, grain cultivation and metallurgy were part of the economic repertoire of Early Iron Age (EIA) pastoralists in the region. By the ninth century, these peoples were engaged in trade networks that brought exotic goods such as glass beads and marine shells from the Indian Ocean into the Kalahari.

Geologic evidence suggests that significantly higher rainfall may have created an environment that encouraged the initial establishment of pastoral economies in the region. Linguistic evidence points to the diversification of Khoisan and southern Bantu languages coincident with this agropastoral expansion. Archival sources from the 18th and 19th centuries as well as oral histories document varying conjunctions of pastoralism and foraging in the economies of both Khoisan and Bantu-speakers that existed in precolonial time and characterize the region to this day. These sources also confirm the continued involvement of these peoples in ancient intracontinental trade networks that were not dominated by European colonial merchants until the second half of the 19th century. As a result of these studies, relations among hunters and herders in the Kalahari are shown to be both of longer duration and more integrated than has been thought.

The Context of Initial Pastoralism

Excavations of Late Stone Age (LSA) sites in the Kalahari reveal forager subsistence patterns differing from those recorded ethnographically among San in the region. Brooks and Helgren report that, in at least some LSA sites in the Makgadikgadi Pans area, fish and other aquatic resources complemented land animals in the subsistence of foragers between 4000 and 2000 years ago. At Lotshitshi, on the southeastern edge of the Okavango Delta, a LSA stratum dating within this period was found to contain fish, bullfrogs, and turtles along with large land mammals. Reconnaissance in the Makgadikgadi complex located over 50 additional LSA sites; two of these include small quantities of Bambata ceramics in their assemblages; eight others contain somewhat later EIA Gokomere or Kumadzulo pottery types. At Bambata Cave, in Zimbabwe, ceramics with remains of domesticated sheep are dated tentatively as early as the second century B.C. Maunatlala, in eastern Botswana, has ceramics and pole-and-clay hut remains at the end of the fourth century A.D.

The middle LSA level of Lotshitshi dates in the third century A.D. Faunal remains from this component indicate a broadly based economy including cattle (*B. taurus*) along with zebra, wildebeest, duiker, warthog, smaller game, and fish. Ceramics from this site are too fragmented for accurate identification, but their thin, charcoal-tempered fabric and finely incised decoration are compatible with Bambata types. Farther westward, in Namibia, ceramics (not Bambata ware) were present before A.D. 400 at Mirabib (with domestic sheep) and Falls Rock. Of the sites mentioned thus far, only Maunatlala has yielded evidence of metal use.

Radiocarbon dates placing sheep, and possibly cattle, but not metal, as far south as the Cape of Good Hope in the first century A.D. have been available for some years, consequently, a gap in data existed between these very early pastoralist manifestations in the far south and older centers north of the Okavango and Zambezi Rivers. The early pastoralist sites in the Kalahari and its margins begin to fill that gap. Consistent association of ceramics and domestic animals with LSA assemblages and their early dates indicate that pastoralist elements were introduced from the north into indigenous foraging economies here before the currently documented beginning of the Iron Age in southern Africa.

Recently acquired geomorphological evidence for fluctuating climates in the region has implications for these changes in LSA economies. At the Cwihaba caverns in western Ngamiland, periodically more humid climatic conditions are indicated by episodes of rapid sinter formation. In order to account for these episodes, Cooke suggests that rainfall in western Ngamiland reached 300 percent of the present annual mean between 2500 and 2000 years ago and again around 750 years ago. In general, these dates parallel those obtained for the sequence of beach levels found around the Makgadikgadi, Ngami, and Mababe basins where a number of higher lake levels with intervening regressions are indicated between 3000 and 1500 years ago.

Although it cannot be assumed that these high lake levels were caused solely by increased rainfall, Shaw argues for generally wetter conditions over the delta at dates congruent with those of Cwihaba. He estimates that rainfall over the Okavango increased between 160 and 225 percent. Under such a regime, many currently ephemeral pans and springs would also have contained more constant supplies of available water. Brain and Brain found evidence, in the form of microfaunal proportions, for episodes of climatic amelioration between about 4000 and 500 years ago at Mirabib in Namibia. Thus, several independent studies indicate higher rainfall during the millennium embracing the initial spread of agropastoral economies through the region 2500 to 1500 years ago.

In recent years, studies of Khoe (Central Khoisan) languages have proliferated in the Kalahari; all lead to an estimate that Khoe diversification in this region began about 2000 years ago. Vossen finds words for cattle and milking with apparent Proto-Khoe roots in the Khoe languages of north central Botswana. Köhler finds such words, along with a Khoe crop vocabulary, among the Kxoe (Khoe-speakers of northern Namibia). Both conclude that pastoralism must have been familiar to these peoples for a long time.

Ehret also argues that the basic separation of Khoi and Central Khoisan languages took place in the Botswana-Angola border region shortly after 500 B.C. He proposed further, from lexical evidence, that the basic pastoralist vocabulary of southern Bantu is derived through a Khoisan intermediary in this area, implying that these Bantu-speakers, but not others farther north, acquired cattle and sheep from Khoisan-speaking peoples. Pfouts suggests diversification of the Bantu languages of Namibia and southern Angola beginning about 1500 to 2000 years ago, whereas Ehret and Kinsman specifically place diversification of Proto-southeast Bantu in the EIA of this time frame. These authors suggest that economic factors contributed to this process of linguistic differentiation; their conclusions are compatible with the archeological evidence regarding initiation of pastoralism and socioeconomic heterogeneity in southern Africa. Elphick reconstructs historical data to reach a similar conclusion.

The Early Iron Age

The western sandveld. The presence of Iron Age agropastoral communities in the Kalahari by the middle of the first millennium is now attested for Ngamiland as well as for eastern Botswana. At Tsodilo Hills, in the sandveld, 70 kilometers west of the Okavango, extensive excavations have uncovered settlements that span the period from the 6th to the 11th centuries A.D. Ceramics from the earliest (A.D. 550–730) of these sites, Divuyu, indicate that it belongs to an EIA variant, the distribution of which appears to extend northward into Angola. There are no close parallels in known EIA assemblages to the south, either in Zimbabwe or South Africa. Common decoration motifs consist of multiple parallel bands of combstamping separated by spaces that are either blank or filled-in with incised motifs. Divuyu ceramics are charcoal tempered but have substantial inclusions of calcrete.

A wide variety of iron and copper implements and ornaments were recovered from Divuyu but only a single stone tool. The presence of slag and bloomery waste indicates that metal working took place on the site. An amorphous scatter of friable burned clay fragments with stick impressions marks the probable location of a pole-and-clay hut. Fragments of perforated ceramic strainers indicate that salt was extracted from local sources. Unidentified marine shells provide firm evidence for coastal links, possibly through Angolan sites. Local trade with peoples of the Okavango system is indicated by the presence of fish bones and river mollusk shells (*Unio* sp. or *Aspartharin* sp.). Domesticated ovicaprids made up a large portion of the diet at Divuyu; domesticated *Bos* was rare. Large quantities of carbonized mongongo nut shells (*Ricinodendron rautanenii*) attest to the importance of foraging in the economy.

In the second Iron Age site at Tsodilo, Nqoma, a lower stratum contains Divuyu ceramics contemporary with the final dates at Divuyu itself. The major components at Nqoma stratigraphically overlie this material and are dated in the ninth and tenth centuries. Ceramics from these later components are uniformly charcoal tempered with few inclusions of other materials; decoration is most often applied as bands of interlocking triangles or in pendent triangles filled with hatching, combstamping, or linear punctuating. False-relief chevron designs occur frequently. Only a few dated sites are presently available for comparison. We see affinities with Sioma, in southwestern Zambia, and Dundo, in northeastern Angola, dated to the sixth through eighth centuries in the range of Divuyu and the beginning of Nqoma occupations at Tsodilo, but systematic ceramic comparisons of these sites have yet to be undertaken. Nqoma ceramics are similar to those from the ninth century site at Kapako on the Okavango River in Namibia; charcoal-tempered ceramics have been dated to the same period far out in the sandveld at NxaiNxai and are found in adjacent parts of Botswana and Namibia.

Evidence for metal working is attested at Nqoma by the presence of tuyeres as well as slag and bloom. Iron and copper ornaments are common and include finely made chains and necklaces with alternating links of copper and iron as well as bracelets with designs sometimes preserved by rust and oxidation. Moderate numbers of stone tools of LSA types are present. Dense areas of burned clay with pole and stick impressions mark the locations of substantial house structures.

Cattle (*Bos taurus*) were paramount in the pastoral economy of Nqoma; preliminary analysis suggests they outnumber ovicaprids by a factor of 2. Bifid thoracic vertebrae indicate that at least some of these cattle were of a hump-backed variety. Carbonized seeds of sorghum (*Sorghum bicolor* caffra), pearl millet (*Pennisetum americannum* thyphoides), and perhaps melons (*Cucurbita* sp.) provide direct evidence for cultivation. Remains of wild game along with carbonized mongongo nuts and *Grewia* seeds indicate that foraging continued to form an important part of the diet of this Iron Age population. Fish bones and river mollusk shells document continuing trade connections with the Okavango to the north and east.

Many glass beads and marine shells, primarily cowrie, along with worked ivory, one piece in the shape of a conus shell, provide evidence that Nqoma was an important local center in an intracontinental trade network extending to the Indian Ocean in the ninth century.

The river systems.   Although the origins of the EIA communities at Tsodilo point consistently northward to Angola, contemporary agropastoralist sites on the eastern margins of the Okavango Delta as well as on the Chobe River belong firmly within the Kumadzulo-Dambwa complex documented by Vogel for the Victoria Falls area. This complex forms a regional facies of the widespread Gokomere tradition of western Zimbabwe and northeastern Botswana. Kumadzulo-Dambwa complex ceramics and small clay figurines of humpbacked cattle were found at the eighth century site of Serondela, on the Chobe River, and cattle bones along with LSA lithics and similar ceramics were recovered at Hippo Tooth on the Botletle River dating to the early ninth century. At the island site of Qugana, in the eastern delta, the same ceramic complex with burned, reed-impressed clay hut remains dates to the eighth century; as yet, no domestic fauna have been recovered from this site.

Matlhapaneng, on the southeastern Okavango, is an extensive site dated between the late seventh and tenth centuries, contemporary with the Nqoma sequence at Tsodilo. Ceramics are charcoal tempered with Kumadzulo-Dambwa decoration motifs. Pole-and-clay structures, iron, copper, and ivory ornaments, slag, and bloomery waste mark this as a fully formed EIA community. LSA stone tools are also present. Although this site is not as rich as Nqoma, long-distance trade connections are attested by the presence of cowrie shells and glass beads. Carbonized remains of sorghum (*S. bicolor* caffra), millet (*P. americanum* typhoides), and cow peas (*Vigna unguiculata*) provide evidence for agriculture; cattle and ovicaprids dominate faunal remains. Foraging was important here as it was at Tsodilo; carbonized marula (*Sclerocarya caffra*) and *Grewin* seeds are present and wild animal remains are common.

The eastern hardveld. Similar developments took place simultaneously in the eastern hardveld where thick kraal dung deposits vitrified by burning have been found at more than 200 sites, indicating that large herds were kept in the region. The same EIA suite of materials already described is present, although ceramics are of Gokomere-Zhizo types with affinities eastward to Zimbabwe and northern Transvaal. East coast trade, documented by glass beads and marine shells, is dated in the late first millennium at a number of these sites as well as at contemporary sites in Zimbabwe and the Transvaal.

Major chiefdoms developed along this eastern margin of the Kalahari at the end of the first millennium, marking a transition to later centralized state development. A tripartite hierarchy of settlement size and complexity is discernible at this time. Large towns of approximately 100,000 square meters, Toutswe, K2, and Mapungubwe, dominated extensive hinterlands containing smaller villages and many small hamlets. Rulers of these chiefdoms succeeded in controlling the Indian Ocean trade into the Kalahari; it is possible that a system supplying valued goods in tribute to these chiefdoms from the western sandveld was instituted at this time, displacing previous exchange relations in which foreign imports as well as local exports had circulated widely.

Supporting evidence for changes in social relations of economic production is found in a comparison of age distributions of cattle and ovicaprid remains at the middle-order sites, Nqoma, Matlhapaneng and Taukome, with those at the capital towns, Mapungubwe and K2. At the first set of sites, a bimodal culling pattern is found similar to that of present-day cattle posts in Botswana, where slaughter is highest in nonreproductive age classes. Such a strategy conserves breeding stock and emphasizes rates of herd growth rather than meat production. Producers and consumers of herd products at these sites probably belonged to the same local social units.

In contrast, at Mapungubwe and K2, both primary centers, the majority of cattle slaughtered were in prime age classes; offtake appears not to have followed the conservative strategy found at the secondary sites. In other studies, this form of distribution has been associated with differential social stratification among occupants of a site. This appears to be the most plausible explanation for the contrasting culling patterns observed in our study. Elites at primary centers appear to have been selective consumers of prime rather than very old animals, many of which would have been produced elsewhere.

The Kalahari in the Second Millennium

These eastern Kalahari chiefdoms collapsed around the beginning of the 13th century. Great Zimbabwe emerged at this time, supplanting the political role played earlier at Toutswe, K2, and Mapungubwe. The extent of this new hegemony is indicated by stone-walled Zimbabwe-Khami outposts found far out in the Kalahari on the margins of the Makgadikgadi Pans. Control of trade became the prerogative of this kingdom. The final component at Toutswe (A.D. 1500) is devoid of exotic goods and no long-distance trade items have been recovered from two rock shelters, Qomqoisi and Depression, excavated at Tsodilo and dated to the 16th and 17th centuries, nor in an upper stratum at Lotshitshi, which, though undated, probably falls in this period.

Glass beads reappear at Xaro in Ngamiland at the beginning of the 17th century. These and cowrie shells are abundant at the 18th century site, Kgwebe, as well as in a probably contemporary (though not yet dated) upper stratum at Nqoma. Portuguese, through their Atlantic trade into the Kongo and Angola, were the probable source of these beads, which reached the interior along trade routes that had functioned since the Early Iron Age. Many of the first Europeans to enter the region from the Cape record that this trade in Portuguese goods was active south of the Orange River and to the east at least as far as the Zambezi by the 18th century. Native peoples including San-speakers, not Portuguese themselves, are specified in these records as the interior agents of this trade.

Archival records as well as oral histories testify to the importance of pastoralism throughout the Kalahari long before Europeans arrived. Every European who first observed the region from the 18th century on reports the presence of peoples of different languages, appearance, and group designation—Bantu and Khoissan—everywhere they went. Virtually every one of these Europeans remarks on the importance of pastoralism in all parts of the region and on the involvement of San-speakers in herding; several specifically mention San owners of livestock. Indeed, the herds of subsequently subjugated peoples were one inducement for Tswana expansion into Ngamiland in 1795. So rich in cattle was the northwestern Kalahari that 12,000 head were exported annually from it alone to the Cape during the 1860's through the 1880's, while unknown but apparently large numbers of interior cattle had been supplied to the Atlantic trade since the late 18th century.

In addition to cattle, 100,000 pounds of ivory along with many bales of ostrich feathers and hides are recorded to have been exported annually from the region as a whole during those decades in exchange for guns, tobacco, sugar, coffee, tea, cloth, beads, and other European goods. These were newly developed markets, but the trade networks they followed were continuations of Iron Age systems. Both Khoisan- and Bantu-speakers are reliably recorded by many observers to have been thoroughly involved in production for precolonial regional exchange networks. When first seen by Europeans in the 19th century, the copper mines and salt pans of northern Namibia were exclusively under San control; 50 to 60 tons of ore were estimated to be taken annually from those mines and traded to Bantu smiths. Trade routes were linked to wider subcontinental networks. Salt, manufactured into loaves, was traded far into the interior and is reported to have been at least as important an exchange commodity as copper.

In extension of this economic activity, San are credited with producing the bulk of ivory and ostrich feathers exported through Bantu and Nama middlemen during the 19th century. Relations of production and exchange were thus not strictly bounded by ethnic or linguistic divisions but cut across them. More than anything else, it is this negotiable lattice of relations among peoples and production that characterizes the last two millennia in the Kalahari.

Discussion

We have summarized a large body of data pertaining to prehistoric and historic economies of Kalahari peoples, and those surrounding them, which has been accumulated by a number of investigators. . . . We have concentrated on the early introduction and subsequent local transformations of agropastoralism in the region because these have been the least known aspects of those economies. Pastoralism has been treated in the ethnographies cited at the beginning of this article as if its history in and adjacent to the Kalahari has been recent and separate from that of indigenous foraging. A guiding assumption of these anthropological studies was that 20th-century foraging there is a way of life that has remained unchanged for millennia. Practitioners of these segregated economies have been rather strictly supposed to have had distinct ethnic and racial origins, in contact only for the last two centuries or less. This position can no longer be supported.

Many problems remain to be investigated. Much of the central Kalahari is unexplored archeologically, and the extent to which Iron Age pastoralism penetrated this area is unknown. A hiatus exists in our knowledge of the entire region between the 12th and 16th centuries. While large centralized states with many satellite communities flourished in the east, few if any sites are presently known for this period in the entire western half of southern Africa, with some possible exceptions at the Cape. Drier conditions may have led to shifts in settlement size and location, making detection of sites in the Kalahari difficult under present conditions. A reasonable hypothesis posits a concentration of population along the river systems and permanent springs leaving less densely peopled the drier hinterland, where foraging may have waxed and waned in accordance with changing environmental and regional economic conditions, particularly after European influence penetrated the region. It is unlikely that herders withdrew entirely from the sandveld; more likely, they at least continued to exploit seasonal surface water and grazing. At present, there is no evidence either to support or refute these propositions.

All of the peoples of the Kalahari during the past two millennia have been linked by extensive social and economic networks; thus, during this period of time, the Kalahari was never the isolated refuge of foragers it has been thought to be. It was the vastly intensified extraction of commoditized animal products in the colonial period, abetted by a drying climatic trend and stock diseases, especially rinderpest, which killed 75 percent of all cattle and antelope in southern Africa at the end of the 19th century, that combined to pauperzie the region. These forces became factors leading to increased labor migration to the newly opened South African mines. In the process, the dues and privileges of earlier native states became increasingly translated into private family fortunes of a colonially favored aristocracy, while previously flexible relations among Khoisan and Bantu-speakers were transformed into ethnic categories defined by criteria of race, language, and economic class. The resultant divisions gave, to anthropological observers in the 20th century, the false impression of a Kalahari eternally empty, its peoples long segregated and isolated from each other.

An unresolved problem concerns the presence of Bantu-speakers in the western half of the subcontinent, a presence that now appears to have been more pervasive and much earlier than previously assumed. There is no doubt that the introduction of EIA economies from central Africa brought with it a complex interdigitation of people south of the Zambezi-Okavango-Cunene Rivers. In the eastern half of the subcontinent, it is well established that Iron Age Bantu agropastoralists gained a dominant position over indigenous foragers and pastoralists, ultimately subjugating, absorbing, or eliminating them. This did not happen in the west where, in fact, Khoi-speaking (Nama) herders dominated a large part of the area when first encountered by Europeans. It has been thought that a major reason for this difference lay in the short history of association of these peoples in the west. The perceived isolating severity of the Kalahari environment has been seen as a primary factor protecting San foragers from Bantu pastoralist domination. Neither supposition finds support in the research reported here.

This research has profound implications for understanding relations among contemporary southern African peoples. In particular, those relegated to the ethnographic categories "Bushman" and "hunter-gatherers" are seen to have a history radically different from that hitherto assumed. It is clear that, rather than being static, uniform relics of an ancient way of life, San societies and cultures have undergone transformations in the past 2000 years that have varied in place and time in association with local economic and political alterations involving a variety of peoples.

Two important consequences flow from this new understanding. The first forces reevaluation of models of social evolution based on assumptions brought to the anthropological study of these peoples. At the very least, ethnographic analogies formulated on modern San "foragers" and applied to studies of evolving social forms must be modified to take into account the millennia-long association of these peoples with both pastoralism and Bantu-speakers. Following on this, and more immediately important, is the need to bring the results of this research into the arena of policy planning. In this arena, San are routinely dismissed as rootless "nomads," without legitimate claim to full participation in modern national politics because they are conceived to be unprepared by history to cope with complex decisions involving economic and political alternatives. That this is no more true of them than of any other peoples should be clear in even this brief account of their recent past.

Notes

1. Etymologies of the terms "Bushmen" and "San" are debated; a long-standing derogatory connotation is acknowledged for the first of these, but San, as also "Bantu," has acquired segregating racial and ethnic overtones. To avoid such implications, we use Khoisan and Bantu as adjectives to designate speakers of two different language families, retaining San only where necessary to specify peoples so labeled in ethnographies. We use Setswana spelling, in which c and x represent the front clicks and q the back clicks of Khoisan words.

2.   L. Marshall, *The !Kung of NyaeNyae* (Harvard Univ. Press, Cambridge, MA, 1976); R. Lee, *The !Kung San* (Harvard Univ. Press, Cambridge, MA, 1979); J. Tanaka, *The San* (Univ of Tokyo Press, Tokyo, 1980); G. Silberbauer, *Hunter and Habitat in the Central Kalahari Desert* (Cambridge Univ. Press, Cambridge, 1981); I. Schapera, *The Bantu-Speaking Tribes of Southern Africa* (Routledge, London, 1937); W. Hammond-Tooke, Ed., *The Bantu-Speaking Peoples of Southern Africa* (Routledge, London, 1974).

Richard B. Lee

The Kalahari Debate: Ju/'hoan Images of the Colonial Encounter

The Kalahari Debate, also known as Kalahari revisionism, sprung up in the late 1980s and early 1990s, and has been a topic of discussion among anthropologists ever since. What is at stake in the Kalahari Debate is the question of who the San peoples are historically—autonomous foragers or dependent serfs. The position taken [here] is that the Ju/'hoansi of the Dobe area, despite recent changes, show an unbroken history as independent hunters and gatherers that can be traced back far into the past. The "revisionists" argue that the Nyae Nyae and Dobe area Ju/'hoansi have been bound into regional trade networks and dominated by distant power holders for centuries. In this view they were not even hunters in the past but cattle-keepers, or servants of cattle people, raising the possibility that the Ju/'hoansi's unique cultural features of sharing and egalitarianism come not from their hunting and gathering traditions, but rather from being outcasts, at the bottom of a social hierarchy.

Curiously, until recently, neither the revisionists or their opponents had bothered to systematically ask the Ju people themselves for their views of their own history. How do the Ju/'hoansi interpret their past and how does that picture square with the evidence from archaeology and history? . . .

Beginning in 1986–1987 when the revisionist debate began to heat up, I started to ask Botswana Ju elders focused questions about the time they refer to as *n//a k'aishe* or "first time." The goal was to elicit collective memories of their pre-colonial past, a time we could date historically to the pre-1870s. Subsequently I returned for two more periods of interviewing, in 1995 and 1997, with informants from the Nyae Nyae and Cho/ana areas of Namibia. Now there are five major areas of Ju settlement represented in the oral history accounts. In this discussion, I will draw on three bodies of evidence on the Nyae Nyae-Dobe area Ju/'hoansi: their own oral histories, archaeology, and ethnohistory. . . .

Oral Histories

During my fieldwork in the Dobe area starting in the 1960s, the Ju/'hoansi were acutely aware that they were living under the gaze and control of the Tawana chiefdom and, beyond it, the British colonial authority. However in speaking of the area's past, Ju/'hoansi informants spoke of their own autonomy in the nineteenth century as a given: they were foragers who lived entirely on their own without agriculture or domesticated animals.

The existence of many Later Stone Age archeological sites in the Dobe area with thousands of stone artifacts and debris supports this view. But left unexplained is the presence on these same sites of small quantities of pottery and iron, indicating Iron Age presence or contact with Iron Age cultures. The Ju/'hoansi themselves explain the presence of these goods in terms of their long-standing trade relations with riverine peoples. On the other hand, Kalahari revisionists have argued that these archeological traces are proof positive of domination of the Dobe area by Iron Age peoples and the incorporation of the Ju/'hoansi into a regional polity. Wilmsen has further argued that people labeled Bushmen had raised cattle in centuries past:

> [I]n this century . . . an overwhelming majority of peoples so labeled have pursued a substantially pastoral way of life in symbiosis with, employed by, or enserfed to Bantu-speaking cattle owners . . . this is equally true of earlier centuries.

Remarkably, in all the voluminous writings on the Kalahari Debate . . . , neither side had systematically investigated how the Ju/'hoansi themselves articulate their own history.

An Interview With Kumsa N≠whin

Kumsa n≠whin, a 70-year-old Dobe man, was a former tribal policeman and famous healer I interviewed in 1987. I began by asking him if long ago his ancestors had lived with cattle.

"No," he replied. "My father's father saw them for the first time. My father's father's father did not know them. The first non-San to come to the region were Europeans, not Blacks. We worked for them, got money and obtained our first cattle from the Tswana with that money. The Whites first came to !Kubi [south of Dobe], killed elephants and pulled their teeth [i.e., ivory]. In the old days the Ju/'hoansi also killed elephants with spears for the meat. At least 15 men were required for a hunt. They dumped the tusks [they didn't have a use for them].

"The Whites came by ≠dwa-/twe [lit. "giraffe-horse" [i.e., camels]. The Whites had no cattle, they had horses and camels. 'Janny' came from the south. Another one made a well at Qangwa [also called Lewisfontein]. My father said 'Oh, can water come out of there?' They used metal tools but not engines. This well is not used today. They spoke Burusi [Afrikaans]."

I asked, "Before the Whites came did you know 'Ju sa jo' [Black people] here?" His response was unequivocal: "No. We only knew ourselves. Ju/'hoansi exclusively."

"But when the Blacks did come, who was first?"

"The first Black was Mutibele, a Tswana, and his older brother, Mokgomphata. They came from the east following the paths made by the Whites going in the opposite direction. They were shown the waterholes by Ju/'hoansi including my father/Twi. They were shown the killing sites of the elephants, where the bones lay, the sites where Whites killed. And they said 'Oh, the Whites have already got the n!ore [territory] from us.' Then [Mutibele's] father claimed the land and all the Ju/'hoansi on it, but he deceived us."

"How did he deceive you? When the Tswana claims he is master of you all, do you agree?"

"If he was the master, he didn't give us anything, neither clothes nor pots, or even one calf. The Europeans had given the Ju/'hoansi guns. When the Tswana saw this they decided to give guns to other Ju/'hoansi, so that they could hunt eland and giraffe."

Later in the conversation I explored the nature of San-Black interactions in the precolonial period. What had they received from the Blacks?

"When I was young," Kumsa replied, "we had no iron pots. We used the clay pots of the Goba. We couldn't make them ourselves."

"Then how do you account for the fact that there are many potsherds on old Ju/'hoansi sites around here?"

"Our fathers' fathers and their fathers' fathers got them from the Gobas. They would trade for them with skins. The Gobas didn't come up here. They stayed where they were [on the rivers] and we went to them. This went on for a very long time [so that is why there are so many potsherds]."

"We [always] got two things from them: iron and pots. If you go to Danega today you will find the right earth. But the Gobas didn't come here. We always went to them."

⋅⊙⋅

Kumsa's statements are congruent with a model of autonomy. Others had also made the point that a long-standing trade existed with riverine peoples *in which the Ju did the travelling.* It would be hard to argue that the Blacks could dominate the Dobe area without any physical presence, but I suppose it is not impossible. The trading trips made by the Ju to the east and elsewhere would certainly account for the presence of Iron Age materials on the Dobe area sites. In fact Polly Wiessner has argued that the levels of iron and pottery found on Dobe area Later Stone Age (LSA) sites can be accounted for by *hxaro* trade, a traditional form of delayed exchange still practiced by the Ju/'hoansi that historically has been a vehicle for long-distance trade.

One suggestive point was Kumsa's intriguing statement that the precolonial Ju hunted elephant but discarded the tusks; remarkable because it indicates that the Dobe Ju/'hoansi were hunting elephant for subsistence and were not part of a mercantile *or* a tributary network, since in either case elephant ivory would have been a prime valuable item.

Also interesting is Kumsa's rather dismissive view of the Tswana as overlords. For Kumsa the criterion for being a chief [lit. in San, "wealth-person"] is giving away in this context, not exercising power *per se.* The Europeans were chiefs because they gave guns, the Tswana were "deceivers" because in Kumsa's terms they claimed chiefly status but gave nothing.

A !Goshe Commentary on the Early Days of Contact

/Ti!kai-n!a, aged 80 at the time of the interview (1987), and /Ti!kai-tsau ("tooth") age 63, were two of the leading men of !Goshe, 16 kilometers east of Qangwa, and the easternmost and most economically "progressive" of the

Dobe area villages. !Goshe is the jumping-off point for travel to the east, and the village has kept Tswana cattle since the 1910s. With their strong ties to the east where most Blacks reside, !Goshe people, by reason of history and geography, are the most attuned to links to "Iron Age" peoples.

"Certain Europeans in Gaborone," I began, "argue that long ago you Ju/'hoansi, [that is] your fathers' fathers' fathers' fathers had cattle. Do you agree?"

"No! Not a bit!" was the younger /Ti!kai's emphatic answer. "Long ago our fathers' fathers' fathers' fathers, the only meat *they* had was what they could shoot with arrows. We only got cows from the Tswana."

I persisted. "But when you dig holes deep down beneath where you live, you find pieces of pottery. Where did they come from?"

"Oh those pots were our own work!" replied the elder /Ti!kai. "Our ancestors made them. They would put them on the fire and cook with them. But since we got iron pots from you Europeans we lost the knowledge of pottery making."

Shifting the topic, I asked, "What about iron?"

"We got that from the Mbukushu," said /Ti!kai. "But we learned how to work it ourselves. . . . You stick it in the fire, heat it up, and hammer it. . . . We did it ourselves. We saw how the Gobas did it and we learned from them."

"Where did you get the iron itself from?"

Their answer surprised me. "The Europeans," said /Ti!kai. "The Tswana and Gobas didn't have it. They also got it from the Europeans."

I had to disagree. "But," I said, "in the oldest abandoned villages of the Gobas, iron is there. Long before the Europeans came."

At this point the older /Ti!kai intervened. "Yes! /Tontah is right. Long ago the Mbukushu had the pieces of iron that they worked."

The younger /Ti!kai turned to the older and asked, incredulously, "Well, where did they get the iron from?"

Matter-of-factly, the older man replied, "From the earth."

Much discussion followed on this point. The younger man was unconvinced that the Gobas had iron before the Europeans, but old /Ti!kai stuck to his story.

Shifting topic again, I asked, "Long long ago, did your fathers' fathers' fathers' fathers practice //*hara* [farming]?"

There was no disagreement on this point. "No, we didn't. We just ate the food that we collected from the bush."

The older /Ti!kai added, "When I was a boy we had learned about //*hara* from the Tswanas. They showed us how [to do it]."

The !Goshe interviews corroborate the account of Kumsa on the absence of cattle and agriculture before the twentieth-century arrival of the Tswana. They add detail on Ju/'hoan understandings of the history of pottery and iron use. In the first case they spoke of Ju manufacture of pottery, whereas other informants spoke of it as only imported. In the second case there was an intriguing difference of opinion. There was agreement that iron was imported from the Gobas but only in the recent past, but some believed that iron was so recent that the Gobas only obtained iron *after* the arrival of the Europeans, a view that we were to encounter elsewhere.

N!ae and /Kunta at Cho/ana

Another round of oral history interviews took place in 1995 at Cho/ana, a former Ju/'hoan waterhole, 65 kilometers northwest of Dobe, now located in Namibia's Kaudom Game Reserve. The informants were N!ae and her husband /Kunta (/Tontah) one of my namesakes. Cho/ana has long been known to historians as a meeting point for Ju/'hoansi from several regions. It was a convenient water hole for Ju/'hoan parties engaged in *hxaro* trade to meet.

In tracing the earliest history of the place, /Kunta saw the original owners as Ju/'hoansi, not Blacks or any other ethnic group. In the beginning, asserted /Kunta, only Ju/'hoansi lived here; there were no Gobas. Ju people would come from Nyae Nyae and from the north, to do *hxaro* here. It was a waterhole that always held water. People from the South (Nyae Nyae) would bring /*do* (ostrich eggshell beads). People from the North brought /*an* (glass beads). In /Kunta's words, "*Hxaro* brought them together."

A point of emphasis in our interviews was the question of whether the Gobas made trips to the interior to trade or to make their presence felt. /Kunta was emphatic: "No, [they didn't come to us] we went to them. We saw pots on their fires and wanted them, so they gave us some."

"And what did you give them in return?"

"We gave Gobas /*do* in exchange for pots."

The interior Ju/'hoansis' proximity to Iron Age peoples on their periphery and the use of iron as a marker of Iron Age overlordship has been a particular point of emphasis for the revisionists. I was anxious to hear /Kunta and N!ae's views of the pre-colonial use of iron and its source.

"Did your ancestors have *!ga* (iron)?"

"Are you joking? We didn't know *!ga*. If we needed arrows we used ≠*dwa* (giraffe) or *n!n* (eland) bones."

"Who gave Ju/'hoansi the iron?"

"We visited north and east and saw this wonderful stuff for arrows and knives; we asked Gobas for it and got some. It was very valuable; when others saw it their hearts were sad because they didn't have it; they wanted it so badly they would even fight other Ju for it. Parties went north to seek it; Gobas gave it to them in exchange for steenbok and duiker skins and other things."

"Where did Goba get iron from?"

Without hesitation /Kunta replied, "From the European."

"Are you saying that before Europeans came Gobas had no iron?"

"Yes, they had no iron."

❧⟨◉⟩❧

It is interesting that informants see iron coming ultimately from Europeans; they saw the appearance of iron and Europeans in their areas as so close in time that iron was associated with Europeans. While it is true that the amount of iron on Nyae Nyae-Dobe LSA sites is miniscule, it is striking that the long history of Iron Age occupation on their periphery, for example at the Tsodilo Hills with radiocarbon dates as early as 500 A.D., doesn't have much resonance with the Ju/'hoansi informants. When they did obtain iron from the Gobas, it was clearly an item of trade and not a marker of overlordship. In any event the very (post-European) regency of the trade in iron challenges the revisionist view of a deep antiquity of Ju/'hoan subservience.

Discussion

In all interviews there was repeated insistence that no Gobas or any other Blacks occupied their area or even visited prior to the late nineteenth century; several spoke of the Gobas' preference for staying on the river and avoiding the dry interior. All these accounts illuminate the pragmatic and matter-of-fact approach of Dobe and Nyae Nyae area people to questions of history. These, after all, are questions of the most general nature and the accounts agree closely, not only about the autonomy of the area from outside domination but also about the absence of cattle and agriculture in pre-colonial times (though not of pottery and iron). There are interesting divergences of opinion on whether pottery was imported or locally made, and on whether the Gobas had iron before the Europeans. Taken together these accounts along with others . . . constitute a fair representation of mid and late twentieth-century Ju/'hoan views of their forebearers' nineteenth-century history of autonomy.

One other indication of the Ju sense of their history is the largely positive self-image of their past. They see themselves as actors, not victims, and this contrasts with the negative self-imagery expressed by other San people, (such as Hai//om or Nharo views) of their present and past.

Archaeological Tie-ins

The oral history interviews in both 1995 and 1997 accompanied archaeological excavation, designed to link archaeology with the knowledge that was part of the living tradition of the Ju/'hoansi. Professor Andrew Smith of the University of Cape Town started excavating a rich Later Stone Age archaeological site at Cho/ana, which provided a continual stimulus for oral history as new and interesting materials came to light in the excavations. The Ju informants' comments provided a valuable adjunct to the archaeological work (and vice versa). They identified plant remains, made tentative suggestions regarding fragmentary bone materials, and provided a social context in which the material could be interpreted. For example, the elders described a kind of white glass bead as one of the earliest of the European trade goods obtained through intermediaries to the north. A few days after the interview, precisely such a bead was found in a sealed level in association with an LSA industry.

But the most stunning confirmation of the direct late nineteenth-century encounter between people with advanced stone-working skills and colonialists was a piece of bottle glass (mouth and neck) showing signs of delicate micro-retouching that the South African Later Stone Age is famous for. This gave a further indication of the persistence of LSA stone-working techniques into the colonial contact period.

The oral history's insistence on the absence of cattle and Blacks in the interior was confirmed by the complete lack in the archaeological record of the presence of domesticated animals or of non-Ju/'hoan people in the area prior to the latter part of the nineteenth century. . . .

Colonial Constructions of the Ju/'hoansi

Turning to the third body of evidence, what light do ethnohistoric documents shed on these Ju accounts of their own past? Do they support or contradict Ju accounts of relative autonomy? In general, the few historical accounts we do have support the Ju/'hoansi view of autonomy. . . .

One of the earliest detailed accounts of the Nyae Nyae-Dobe Ju/'hoansi comes relatively late when Hauptman Müller, a German colonial officer, traveled through the Nyae Nyae area in 1911. Müller offers some unusually detailed observations on the situation of the Nyae Nyae-Dobe area Ju/'hoansi some 30 years after colonial trade had been established. In Müller's account (1912) the area remained remote and inaccessible. His visit was the first to the interior from the west in five years.

Most telling is Müller's ethnographic description of the bushman inhabitants of this stretch of land he calls "virginal" [jungfräulich]. He depicts their state as "noch uberuhrt von aller Zivilisation, in alter Ursprunglichkeit" [still untouched by all civilization in their old pristine state]. He reports with amusement how European objects such as matches and mirrors were unknown to them, as well as the camels of his troopers, which startled them and caused the women to grab their children and scatter into the bush. However, he did find them using such things as wooden bowls, glass and iron beads, cooper rings, and "Ovambo knives," all obtained through trade with Black neighbors.

Of particular interest is Müller's descriptions of the Bushman themselves. In his account they were well nourished and relatively tall, thanks to an ample diet of meat (hunted with bone-tipped arrows) and a variety of wild plants. There is no mention in Müller's account of any resident cattle or Bantu-speaking overlords, though BaTswana were visiting the area during his stay. For Müller the association of the Nyae Nyae Bushmen with the BaTswana was not ancient; it was of recent date and was based on trade and assistance rendered at the latters' hunting expeditions. The Bushmen were rewarded with gifts for their services and the relationship with the hunter/herders is described as equitable and friendly:

> The Bushmen seem, however, to be good friends with the BaTswanas. When I asked a Bushman if it didn't bother him that the BaTswanas were killing off so much game every year he said "Yes, but we are getting presents!" . . .

Müller's is one of the earliest accounts to be based on actual reports of what he observed, as distinguished from second-hand accounts at a distance.

And the preceding short quotation is among the very first to cite the actual words of a Ju/'hoan person.

꙳❀꙳

To sum up this section, both German and Ju/'hoan testimony are consistent and mutually supportive. The detail presented by Müller and the others (such as Hans Schinz and James Chapman) attests to five propositions that accord closely with statements made by the Ju/'hoansi themselves:

1. The relative isolation of the Nyae Nyae-Dobe area from the West and the low volume of European traffic, 1880–1911
2. The absence of cattle in pre-colonial Ju subsistence
3. The absence of Bantu overlords or tributary relations
4. The relatively favorable terms of trade between Blacks and San
5. The relatively good foraging subsistence base and nutritional status of the San

These lines of evidence argue the case that the views of the Ju/'hoansi about their historical autonomy are not sharply at odds with the ethnohistoric sources.

Hunter-Gatherer Discourse and Agrarian Discourse

Both the Ju oral histories and the German and other historical texts are cultural constructions, and yet, how are we to account for the correspondences between these two bodies of evidence? Why do they corroborate one another? To argue that both are careful fabrications still leaves open the question of why they agree so closely. One would have to invoke conspiracy or coincidence, in either case a tough sell. Surely it would be more reasonable to assume that they agree because they are describing the same reality. If Kumsa's, the two /Ti!kai's, N!ae and /Kunta's and others' collective accounts of the Ju/'hoansi autonomous past gibe so closely with those of European eyewitnesses such as Müller, then on what grounds rests the view of the historic Ju/'hoansi as enserfed pastoralists? And why has this view gained such currency in anthropological circles?

A more fruitful approach to understanding the recent debates is to attempt to place them in the context of the intellectual currents of the late twentieth century. How does the current conjuncture shape our perceptions of the situation of indigenous "others"?

Obviously, by the 1990s, the processes affecting the Dobe Ju/'hoansi had brought them to becoming clients, laborers, and rural proletarians, subject to and dependent on regional and world economies. Their current predicament is well understood by recourse to theories arising from political economy, dependency theory, or colonial discourse. Current theorizing is much weaker, however, in understanding the antecedent conditions. Part of the inability of contemporary theory to encompass hunters and gatherers as historical subjects is the lack of attention to the *differences* between discourses about hunters and gatherers and the discourses concerning agrarian societies and the emerging world system.

In agrarian discourse the presence of structures of domination are taken as given; it is the *forms* of domination and the modes of exploitation and surplus extraction that are problematic. In the literature on the agrarian societies of the Third World, stratification, class and class struggle, patriarchy, accumulation, and immiseration constitute the basic descriptive and analytical vocabulary.

In hunter-gatherer discourse it is not the forms and modes of domination that are at issue; rather the prior question to be asked is whether domination is *present*. I have been struck by the eagerness of otherwise competent analysts to gloss over, sidestep, or ignore this question.

There is no great mystery about what separates hunter-gatherer from agrarian societies. The former usually live lightly on the land at low densities; they can move and still survive, an escape route not available to sedentary farmers. The latter, with high densities and fixed assets, can no longer reproduce themselves outside the system, and are rendered far more vulnerable to domination.

In the recent debate some analysts seem to have taken the world systems/ political economy position so literally that every culture is seen as nothing more than the sum total of its external relations. But surely there is more to a culture than its links of trade, tribute, domination, and subordination. There is the internal dynamic of the means by which a social group reproduces itself ecologically, socially, and in terms of its collective consciousness. . . .

An historically informed ethnography can offer an alternative to the totalizing discourses of world systems theory. The unself-conscious sense of their own nineteenth- and early twentieth-century autonomy expressed by Ju/ 'hoan hunter-gatherers and its corroboration by contemporaneous colonial observers is one example of how these powerful assumptions can be challenged. They bear testimony that in the not very distant past other ways of being were possible.

That said, autonomy should not be taken as an article of faith, nor is it an all-or-nothing proposition. It is, or should be, an empirical question, and each society may exhibit a complex array of more or less autonomy at stages in its history. Even in agrarian societies spaces are opened up, however small, for the expression of autonomous thought and behavior. Thus it need not be the exclusive preserve of non-hierarchical or noncolonized societies. . . .

With reference to the latter though, a final point: What is desperately needed is to theorize the communal mode of production and its accompanying world view. Without it there is a theoretical vacuum filled far too facilely by imputing capitalist relations of production, bourgeois subjectivity, or "culture of poverty" frameworks to hunter-gatherer peoples.

POSTSCRIPT

Are San Hunter-Gatherers Basically Pastoralists Who Have Lost Their Herds?

These selections express two radically different worldviews. Denbow and Wilmsen's view—which has been called the "revisionist" view—emphasizes the interconnectedness of societies and the tendency for powerful polities to exert control over their less powerful neighbors. On the other hand, Lee's view—called the "traditionalist" view—emphasizes the people's adaptation to their natural environment and sees their relations with outsiders as variable, depending on local circumstances. Most anthropologists recognize that all cultures are influenced by local conditions and by the larger social environment, including, to some extent, the entire "world system." The question is, How much weight should one give to these two types of influence?

The disagreement between these scholars and their supporters is not merely a matter of theoretical emphasis. They also disagree about the facts and their proper interpretation. In subsequent publications Wilmsen and Lee, in particular, have argued over such matters as the precise locations of groups and trade routes mentioned in travelers' journals and whether or not the presence of cattle bones, for example, in an archaeological site indicates trade or outside domination. For elaboration of Wilmsen and Denbow's views see "Paradigmatic History of San-Speaking Peoples and Current Attempts at Revision," *Current Anthropology* (vol. 31, no. 5, 1990) and Wilmsen's book *Land Filled With Flies: A Political Economy of the Kalahari* (University of Chicago Press, 1989). For Lee's critique of these sources see his and Mathias Guenther's "Problems in Kalahari Historical Ethnography and the Tolerance of Error," *History in Africa* (vol. 20, 1993) and "Oxen or Onions? The Search for Trade (and Truth) in the Kalahari," *Current Anthropology* (vol. 32, 1991).

The literature on the San is voluminous. Alan Barnard's book *Hunters and Herders of Southern Africa: A Comparative Ethnography of the Khoisan Peoples* (Cambridge University Press, 1992) is an excellent overview of the various San and Khoi (formerly called "Hottentot") peoples. Important expressions of the revisionist view include Carmel Schrire's article "An Inquiry Into the Evolutionary Status and Apparent Identity of San Hunter-Gatherers," *Human Ecology* (vol. 8, no. 1, 1980) and her chapter entitled "Wild Surmises on Savage Thoughts," in her edited volume *Past and Present in Hunter Gatherer Studies* (Academic Press, 1984). A crucial source on the history of the San is Robert Gordon's *The Bushman Myth: The Making of a Namibian Underclass* (Westview Press, 1992). Works supporting the traditionalist view include Susan Kent's "The Current Forager Controversy: Real vs. Ideal Views of Hunter-Gatherers," *Man* [n.s.] (vol. 27, 1992).

ISSUE 7

Does the Natural–Supernatural Distinction Exist in All Cultures?

YES: Roger Ivar Lohmann, from "The Supernatural Is Everywhere: Defining Qualities of Religion in Melanesia and Beyond," *Anthropological Forum* (November 2003)

NO: Frederick (Fritz) P. Lampe, from "Creating a Second-Storey Woman: Introduced Delineation Between Natural and Supernatural in Melanesia," *Anthropological Forum* (November 2003)

ISSUE SUMMARY

YES: Cultural anthropologist Roger Ivar Lohmann argues that a supernaturalistic worldview or cosmology is at the heart of virtually all religions. For him, the supernatural is a concept that exists everywhere, although it is expressed differently in each society. For him, supernaturalism attributes volition to things that do not have it. He argues that the supernatural is also a part of Western people's daily experience in much the same ways that it is the experience of the Papua New Guineans with whom he worked.

NO: Lutheran pastor and anthropological researcher Frederick (Fritz) P. Lampe argues that "supernatural" is a problematic and inappropriate term like the term "primitive." If we accept the term "supernatural," it is all too easy to become ethnocentric and assume that anything supernatural is unreal and therefore false. He considers a case at the University of Technology in Papua New Guinea to show how use of the term "supernatural" allows us to miss out on how Papua New Guineans actually understand the world in logical, rational, and naturalistic terms that Westerners would generally see as illogical, irrational, and supernaturalistic.

Making sense of other people's religions has been an interest of anthropology from the beginning of the discipline. In his book *Primitive Culture* (J. Murray, 1871), Sir Edward B. Tylor offered the first anthropological definition of religion: the belief in spiritual beings. Since the age of enlightenment in the eighteenth century, scientists had adopted the view that all phenomena could be explained in rational, naturalistic terms. Thus, for Tylor, the belief in ghosts, spirits, demons, demigods, and gods was evidence of irrational thought and misunderstanding of the natural world. He reasoned that people in all societies had dreams, but primitive people mistakenly interpreted these dreams as reality and the characters in them as spiritual beings.

Similarly, Bronislaw Malinowski had distinguished between science on the one hand and magic and religion on the other in his book *Magic, Science, and Religion* (Beacon, 1948). In 1966, American anthropologists Anthony F. C. Wallace defined religion as "beliefs and rituals concerned with supernatural beings, forces, and powers."

Despite these definitions, there is no necessary reason why the notion that there is a distinction between the natural and the supernatural should be present in all societies. Whether people in all societies accept this distinction is an empirical question.

This issue is about whether all societies actually do believe in the supernatural as a category of reality distinct and separate from the natural world. Both essays were presented as part of a panel that was addressing an issue raised by anthropologist Morton Klass in his book *Ordered Universes* (Westview, 1995). Klass, who argued that the use of the term "supernatural" is problematic in many of the same ways that the terms "primitive" and "race" are.

Anthropologist Roger Ivar Lohmann argues that the core of the supernatural is attributing volition to things that do not have it. For him, this is the central feature of religious thinking in all societies around the world. He distinguishes the supernatural as a concept that can be observed empirically in all societies, although its particular cultural expression will vary quite widely in the diverse cultures around the world. For him, attributing volition to things that cannot have volition or to things that do not exist is at the heart of the supernatural. Thus, the supernatural is not limited to spirits, gods, or ghosts, but can also include "luck," "karma," or "the mystical."

Lutheran Pastor Frederick (Fritz) P. Lampe was chaplain at the University of Technology in Papua New Guinea for four years in the 1980s. He draws upon these experiences to challenge whether these Papua New Guineans are using supernatural thinking in responding to such issues as traditional notions of the polluting quality of female menstrual blood for men. For Europeans, the idea that menstrual blood is dangerous is self-evidently wrong; therefore, it is classified as a supernatural idea. But Lampe shows that these New Guinean ideas are based on a naturalistic worldview, not a supernaturalistic one.

In reading these essays, consider how each author understands what is meant by "the supernatural." Do the cases mentioned by Lohmann demonstrate that the supernatural concept is present in every society? What about our own society? Does Lampe's case study actually demonstrate that the supernatural is not a salient part of the worldview he discusses? If it did, would this finding dismiss Lohmann's claim about universality? Even if in one or another case "the supernatural" is not a salient concept, would we necessarily want to abandon the concept as we have the term "primitive?"

Roger Ivar Lohmann  **YES**

The Supernatural Is Everywhere: Defining Qualities of Religion in Melanesia and Beyond

Supernaturalism depicts conscious will or volition as the ultimate cause of phenomena. Supernaturalistic cosmologies are at the heart of virtually all religions. All humans seem to sense a supernatural realm, yet we are unable to detect it scientifically. It is an imagined dimension where volition can exist without brains, and control the physical world. I argue that the concept of 'supernatural' is necessary both to describe particular worldviews accurately, and to understand spirit belief and religion as ubiquitous in human experience.

In conceptualising the supernatural, it is very important at the outset to distinguish between the etic perspectives of scientific observers and the emic views of cultural participants. The supernatural can be viewed as a universal assumption among humans, or as the unique spiritual reality of a given culture. The supernatural is in this regard like sex, which, like all realms of common human experience, is modelled differently in different traditions to produce different gender systems. The distinction between sex and gender is necessary to understand the relationship between objective physicality and cultural models of the physically real. For the same reason that we need to distinguish etic and emic perspectives on reproductive capacity, we need to separate etic and emic definitions of 'supernatural'. As a technical term in anthropology, 'supernatural' serves best as an etic concept describing a universal human experience that is elaborated differently in different traditions.

I define the etic category of supernatural as a ubiquitous mental model that depicts one or more sentient, volitional agencies that are independent of a biological substrate and understood to be the ultimate cause of elements of physical reality. Individual cultural models of the supernatural, like the various forms of gender, are distinctive in different societies. Ethnographers should describe these differences carefully. Some anthropologists, however, argue that the spiritual worlds posited by different peoples are so distinctive that generalising about them with terms like 'supernatural' is inaccurate. I make the case to the contrary that, whereas there is indeed much variation in the spiritualities of different peoples, they are all similar enough to one another that we can recognise virtually all of them as variants of a common human tendency to assume that a supernatural world exists. For example, many Melanesian peoples model the supernatural world as a hidden realm existing inside the material world. While Melanesians typically consider the supernatural to be immanent, some other peoples model the supernatural as being separate from its creation.

People everywhere learn that volition can find expression in physical phenomena, because they routinely experience and witness human creativity. For example, when a man desires a house, his volition brings about the construction of a house. One might call the mental model of this sort of agentive causation the 'volition schema.' Supernaturalism is the extension of the volition schema to phenomena that do not in fact result from will and choice, like the origin of the world. Belief in an afterlife, to give another example, results from extending the volition schema to the dead, who are no longer volitional, to explain our ongoing memories of them.

'Supernatural' is a venerable term in anthropology. However, some criticise it as ethnocentric or misleading, because many peoples do not think spiritual powers are separate from the 'natural' world. Moreover, they point out that, in its etic sense, the term implies that only the natural is real, while the supernatural is not, which does not represent the view of those who believe in a spirit world. These critiques do not demonstrate a problem with the category of 'supernatural'; rather, they point to the dangers of conflating various etic and emic *definitions* of the supernatural. When these are distinguished, the supernatural concept both clarifies a scientific position on a major source of religious behaviour and improves our ability to understand religious worldviews. The supernatural, as I define it, is a real phenomenon with physical causes and effects, which people model differently from one culture to the next. I suggest that all people can distinguish supernaturalistic ideas from naturalistic ones, though they may not find the distinction salient. The distinction is expressed using various idioms, including transcendent vs. tangible, real vs. illusory, sacred vs. profane, living vs. lifeless, ethereal vs. material, and, as I suggest is widespread in Melanesia, hidden vs. exposed, and inside vs. outside.

Critiques of 'supernatural'

Critics of the supernatural concept have two basic arguments. First, they say that it implies condescension toward credulous believers in non-existent beings. Second, they argue that by using the term we erroneously assume that all religions share the West Asian assumption, found in Judaism, Christianity, and Islam, that the natural world is separate from a supernatural creator. These are valid critiques of certain ways of using the term 'supernatural', but they do not damn its usefulness when employed with respect, precision, and a distinction between etic and emic.

To see that this is so, consider an eloquent critique by Morton Klass. Klass points out the similarity between a farmer's offering to the deceased first owner of a field and his rent payment to an absentee landlord. Why, he asks, should we classify the former as supernatural and the latter as natural, when both the first owner and the landlord are invisible and ostensibly require compensation? To do so, he says, merely underlines our disbelief in the efficacy of the offering, and ethnocentrically smears our understanding of the farmer's worldview.

I do not think that seeking an etic explanation requires one to disregard or disrespect the emic one. Nor do we distort the emic perspective by asserting that the farmer can distinguish between dealings with spirits and people. Klass, however, does us a service by emphasising that this distinction may not be salient to the believer, and this should be described in the ethnography.

Having made an analogy with sex above, I consider one with language. In the same way as the pan-human cognitive capability for language is expressed locally as specific languages, and individually as speech, supernaturalism is expressed in local variants as religions, and individually as spirituality. The thousands of different languages all represent one kind of cognitive and behavioural capacity made possible by our neurological apparatus for language. Just as one can distinguish linguistic thought from purely image-based thought, one can likewise distinguish supernaturalism from naturalism. This is so even though both occur simultaneously, mix freely, and may be conflated in ethnopsychologies.

The disregard of Klass's farmer for a distinction that an anthropologist would notice is analogous to a native speaker's inattention to the difference between a voiced and an unvoiced consonant in a language in which this distinction does not carry meaning. Anyone can be made aware of the objective (phonetic) difference between the two sounds, and, for linguists, attention to phonetics is vital. Likewise, for practical purposes, the farmer may not think about the difference between an offering to a dead person and a payment to a living one, but he could make that distinction were it relevant to his task. For anthropologists, it is central to ours. Different peoples emphasise or de-emphasise the distinction between supernatural and natural causation, or mark it in different ways, and critics of the fuzzy use of the concept rightly bring this to our attention.

[Anthropologist Benson] Saler observes that anthropologists often use the term 'supernatural' without defining what they mean, possibly to appear respectful of local beliefs that they in fact consider erroneous. I concur with his view that, if by 'supernatural beings' we mean imaginary ones, we should go ahead and say so. One can openly disagree with others without disrespecting their views. During my fieldwork among the Asabano, a Papua New Guinea people who are enthusiastic Christians, I truthfully told them that I do not believe that Christianity or other religions are true, but that I am nevertheless interested in why they have found them convincing. We had a very amicable and productive exchange of views. Of course, we often disagree with the peoples among whom we work—we are culturally different. Mutual respect and friendship across cultural boundaries are possible, as any anthropologist knows. Cultural relativism serves well as a method to understand another's point of view, but, if used to limit our ability to make comparisons, generalisations, and scientific advances, it closes the mind it has only just opened.

Supernaturalism and the imagination

Granted our right to draw etic conclusions from studies of emic experiences, the question remains as to whether the supernatural is really a product of the human mind. There appears to be little controversy that the imagination is heavily engaged in religious life, but are supernatural worlds made up? [James] Lett declares that, though many anthropologists are loath to admit it, we already know all religious beliefs to be false because they are not based on rationality or objectivity. I am in sympathy with his conclusion about the objective truth of religious beliefs; however, to write supernaturalism off as mere irrationality strikes me as unrealistic. Greenfield shows that, depending on people's knowledge, supernaturalism can offer a reasonable account for cures, and may actually help effect them. A community of believers can agree because they share experiences grounded in similarly biased perception, leading them to see what they expect to see.

Like naturalism, supernaturalism is normally based on rationally structured models of experiential evidence. Supernaturalism is distinctive in that it is based on extended, serious productions of what [Michele] Stephen calls the 'autonomous imagination', imagined realities that we do not recognise as our own inventions. The autonomous imagination, working with the volition schema, produces experiences of and belief in supernatural realms, as revealed in anthropological studies of dreaming. Supernaturalism builds wondrous mental models that could not result only from irrationality and subjectivity gone wild; religions have too much in common for that.

Some anthropologists have referred to spirits as non-empirical beings. Relationships with supernatural beings are central to religion, but these beings are not non-empirical; they are imaginary. The distinction is important, for while the imagination's creations need not accurately *portray* the reality that exists outside of the cogitating brain, they are *themselves* empirical phenomena in that human mental and motor behaviour can be studied scientifically.

Spirit beings are mental models of reality to which the imagination has granted volition. Spirits resemble the objectively real, but are clearly different. We cannot show our friends a spirit the way we can show them a rock. We cannot photograph spirits. Of course, showing a rock and saying it is *really* a spirit allows the listener to create a mental image partially based on the rock; but the imagination must also be invoked to give the rock life. Supernaturalistic models make scientific sense when we see them as arising from the imagination. This is why supernatural beings are often harder to see or touch, act at variance with our everyday knowledge of physics, and are so relevant to human fears and desires.

In so far as volition is a characteristic of humans, and spirits are imagined and related to as though they were people, anthropomorphism is a necessary component of supernatural models, but not all anthropomorphism is supernaturalistic. Non-supernaturalistic anthropomorphism recognises human-like qualities in the exterior or current form of an object that can be directly perceived with the senses, such as a bottle resembling a man in form or function. It includes playful, consciously metaphorical, and surface attributions of human-like qualities to the non-human. However, if one understands the anthropomorphised bottle to have sentience or to have been the result of an extra-biological volition, then one is engaging in supernaturalism. Supernatural anthropomorphism is long-lasting and serious (like the earnest belief among the Asabano that tree spirits are responsible for deaths), rather than brief misapprehensions (such as mistaking a sack for a person), or playful, purposeful fantasy anthropomorphism (like advertisements that endow products, such as Mr Clean cleanser, with human qualities).

Animism, however, defined as attributing spirits (foundational sentient agency) to materials, is by definition the stuff of supernaturalism. More depersonalised notions of mysterious power and meaning, known as *mana*, luck, or animatism—or reverence for persons, places, and things because of their history or symbolic significance ... are not necessarily supernatural. There is a fine line between thinking that one is lucky because of personal circumstances, and attributing one's frequent success to a caring or powerful spirit. Likewise, a place can seem mystical because it evokes strong memories or feelings, with or without the additional notion that this indicates some kind of spiritual presence. Most of us probably cross the border between naturalism and supernaturalism several times each day.

The scientific theory that the supernatural is a natural product of the imagination is supported by the fact that spiritual experiences occur more easily in states of consciousness that allow the autonomous imagination greater play, such as trance and dreams. They also seem more plausible when socially supported: if everyone in the village says that witches are responsible for unfortunate events, witches come to seem very real indeed, as Evans-Pritchard discovered. The weight of tradition grants supernatural beings a veneer of objective reality. A community of believers can see the same spirit, not because it exists as an external being, but because all have similar imaginative hardware and tendencies, and shared instructions on what to picture.

The universality of spiritual experience indeed reveals that there is objective truth to the supernatural. That truth, however, is that the 'spirits' are found *inside* all our heads and not outside any of them. In the same way, all of us experience and can verify with one another that the earth appears to be flat, so it was not unreasonable when people made the jump to conclude that the earth is flat. This conclusion is wrong, of course, as an etic glance from above can show. The more distant perspective and the greater, but never perfect or absolute, objectivity it affords make it plainly visible that the universal experience of flatness, like that of supernaturalism, does reveal a more objective truth, and the truth is not what it first appeared....

Recognising the Supernatural in Melanesia

Melanesians are sometimes characterised as lacking a supernatural concept (e.g., see Lampe). They are not alone in this. In this issue, White argues that supernaturalism can appear and disappear in the history of groups; Shorter notes that others do not divide the world into a supernatural/natural dichotomy; and Aragon points out that some peoples have imminent spiritualities and lack a transcendent supernaturalism in which events are understood to be miraculous. All these authors question the universality of the supernatural on an emic level, and therefore question its status as an etic category. It should be clear from my argument so far that I disagree with these positions in so far as they are using a definition of 'supernatural' similar to my own. I agree with Aragon that the notion of a miracle does not jibe with monistic worldviews but, as her paper makes very clear, even monists habitually apply the volition schema to nonliving things. The Tobaku do not perceive the spirits as miraculously breaking natural laws when they make the land fertile, but, in envisioning the land's fertility as coming from its spirit 'owners', they are attributing volition to something that does not, to the best current scientific knowledge, have it. Thus, by my definition of 'supernatural', Sulawesi highlanders are supernaturalists, but by Aragon's they are not. I prefer my own definition because it captures a universal human propensity that manifests itself within a range of variation.

I am clearly a lumper, while some of my colleagues are splitters, when it comes to categorising spiritual behaviours. To support my position that some lumping (as well as a clear definition) is called for in the case of supernaturalism, I wish to demonstrate that, even in a place that has been considered free of supernaturalism by excellent ethnographers, we can identify versions of the etic supernaturalism that I am at pains to argue exists. It is valuable to examine the bases on which claims of supernatural-free cultures are made. [Peter] Lawrence and [Mervin] Meggitt, for example, rightly note an interpenetration of spiritual and physical among Melanesian peoples. Elaborating, [Peter] Lawrence correctly states that 'gods, spirits, and totems were regarded as a real, if not always visible, part of the ordinary physical environment ... described as more powerful than men but always as corporeal, taking human, animal, or insect form at will'. Based on these characteristics of Melanesian religions, he further describes them as lacking a concept of the supernatural. Yet what he is actually documenting is a conception of supernatural beings as not necessarily separate or ethereal, *not* a lack of supernaturalism per se. Then, somewhat contradictorily, he refers to these rather solid Melanesian spirits as 'non-empirical'.

Many Melanesian peoples believe that spirits can take physical form (*bodi devel* in Tok Pisin) rather than merely inhabiting an object. Kaluli, for example, consider birds to be dead people. Melanesians understand at least some spirits to be tangible and visible, so supernatural beings (volitional entities that are independent of brains and cause physical phenomena) *do* appear in their cosmologies. Stephen observes that Melanesian belief in physical spirits contradicts characterisations of Melanesian spirit beings as either non-empirical or unseen. Both believers and outsiders can verify birds' existence; it is the *significance* of physical phenomena that is disputed. To Kaluli, birds are really the dead, in spite of outer appearances. Interpreting birds as an expression of deceased human volition is supernaturalism. Ethnographers, unable to see the volition, but only its supposed physical manifestation, might conclude that the spirits themselves are non-empirical or unseen. However, even human volition originating in biochemical processes is not visible with the naked eye; only our skins and behaviours are.

Stephen reports that the Mekeo believe in a disembodied 'hidden self ', perceived to leave the body in dreams. While avoiding the terms 'supernatural' and 'natural', Stephen identifies the main idiom in which Melanesians express the dichotomy: hidden vs. external realms. This accords closely with a large Melanesianist literature emphasising the religious role of secrecy and disclosure. To say something is hidden is not to say that it is invisible, ethereal, or non-empirical. A hidden thing, though usually obscured, can appear on occasion. The Asabano described certain beings and powers as hidden. Forest sprites, for example, called *wobuno* ('wild ones'), are alternatively called *balebaleno* ('those who hide'). Traditional Asabano religious knowledge was secret by definition. *Walemaw* means simultaneously secret and sacred. Asabano also believe the dead can become birds who may appear or hide. As reported widely in Melanesia, some Asabano felt at first contact that Whites were spirits: they had great technological and productive powers like the ancestors, and had been hidden until then.

Associated with the idea of hidden in Melanesia is the notion that interiors are more powerful and genuine than exteriors. Ngaing, for example, associate Whites with supernatural power because of their idea that interiors are light, while exteriors are dark. Ngaing discovered in dreams that the land of the Whites is really inside their own land. Inside themselves, they discover, they are white. I recorded an Asabano dream narrative in which the dreamer pulled down a zipper to reveal white skin underneath: an indication of what will happen in the afterlife. This interest in obscured interiors as the locus of the supernatural also resonates with widespread gender separation in Melanesia. Thus, men retain and fan their supernatural powers by isolating and hiding themselves, their rituals, and their sacra from women—a concern with 'purity' that makes sense when seen as an effort to maximise contact with hidden, supernatural interiors. The Telefol male's sacred net bag, for example, is covered with feathers to conceal the human bone sacra secreted inside from the profaning and withering female gaze.

While Melanesian worlds of inside and outside, of hidden and exposed, are deeply intertwined, they are nevertheless distinguished one from the other. Melanesians do not conceive of the distinction as non-empirical vs. empirical, or necessarily as ethereal vs. material or transcendental vs. immanent. Rather, they model the supernatural as a living inside truth, cause, and potential that, like the supernatural envisioned by transcendentalist Christians, is a volition that makes things happen, but is not always visible. Melanesians definitely recognise the supernatural as distinct from the natural, as I have defined the terms.

Conclusion

The natural/supernatural distinction is necessary for understanding religions, from both etic and emic points of view. From a scientific etic perspective, the distinction is between a physically perceived universe of ultimately non-volitional origins (the natural realm) and an imagined universe depicted as having ultimately volitional origins (the supernatural realm).

The refined etic category 'supernatural' defines what ideal typical religions refer to, which all peoples, even those with an immanent spirituality, can recognise, but model differently.

All humans can use the volition schema to think about things. Scientists studying consciousness have to do the opposite and apply physical-chemical schemas to human minds in order to understand how physical matter can give rise to volition. You might find some of those same scientists believing in an afterlife. Klass's farmer, too, knows physical cause and effect: that rain must fall on his crops if they are to grow. He may also think that the ultimate reason the rain falls is because the guardian spirit of the field is pleased with his offering. The supernatural is real, but it is also imaginary, and, while prayer may move spiritual mountains, only work can move physical ones.

Supernaturalism attributes volition to things that do not have it; in this sense it is a kind of cognitive 'dirt'. [Mary] Douglas defines dirt as matter 'out of place', and explains the human fascination with purity as an effort to remove what cannot be placed into our categories. Similarly, the supernatural is *volition* out of place, and this in no small measure accounts for the human fascination with the anomalous idea of spirits. People strive to clean up dirt in order to make their environment 'conform to an idea'. In the realm of religion, however, they accomplish this same parity between ideal and physical worlds by projecting the supernatural—imagined volition out of place—onto the physical world.

Frederick P. Lampe

Creating A Second-Storey Woman: Introduced Delineation Between Natural and Supernatural in Melanesia

Words matter. The use of the term 'supernatural' to describe social activities related to the ethereal maintains a dichotomy that may not be appropriate at this stage in the history of anthropology. I join Morton Klass in suggesting that the time has come to set aside the term 'supernatural', as we have other seemingly descriptive terms like 'race' and 'primitive'. Our continued distinction between natural and supernatural is problematic in that it is relatively easy to succumb to the temptation of labelling natural as real and supernatural as unreal.

In the 1980s, I spent 4 years as the Lutheran chaplain in and around the University of Technology in Lae, Papua New Guinea. The University of Technology, Unitech, was, at that point, one of two government-funded, degree-granting universities in Papua New Guinea. This paper considers the classificatory term 'supernatural' as it relates to men, women and housing at Unitech. The case in point involves the security arrangements for female students, the considered power of vaginal secretions, and the Enlightenment-driven, unilineal, evolutionary schema that contextualises economic and social development in Melanesia. Assuming there to be no natural reason to do otherwise, student living arrangements were organised by administrators without regard, or perhaps in spite of, social taboos prohibiting such things.

The question before us is the descriptive classification 'supernatural'. My argument suggests that on a macro-scale the propensity for anthropologists to impose imprecise distinctions, such as between natural and supernatural, for the sake of classificatory (etic) evaluation is akin to the colonial disregard for social practices and traditions. I contend that its continued use perpetuates an unhealthy power differential between researcher and subject. The use of supernatural retains elements of the colonial legacy that may not be particularly helpful or accurate.

The exploration, colonisation, and conversion of Melanesia by Europeans brought a highly segmented worldview into conflict with a largely cohesive collection of ideas about reality. The European propensity to distinguish between profane and sacred spheres effected a dichotomous differentiation between 'natural' and 'supernatural' in Melanesia. Current higher education

From *Anthropological Forum*, vol. 13, no. 2, 2003, pp. 167–173. Copyright © 2003 by Taylor & Francis Journals. Reprinted by permission. www.tandf.co.uk/journals. References omitted.

in Papua New Guinea reflects this distinction. Melanesian university students participate in a highly differentiated academic context representing a distinct and artificial social experience. An undifferentiated coalition of symbolic elements, with no distinction between supernatural and natural, is forced to contend with a highly differentiated system based upon a post-Enlightenment model of education.

I assume two things: the first is that the Enlightenment is the intellectual and cultural context for those who came to Papua New Guinea as colonisers; the second is that there is power associated with the sexual fluids of women within Melanesian society.

These two frame the subsequent structure for issues that surrounded student housing in the 1980s. The University's housing arrangements, like the intellectual climate of the Enlightenment, effected an artificial ordering of being. The culturally constructed explanation of women's power effects an unauthentic sense of what it means to be human in Melanesia. I join Shorter in this collection, suggesting that as interpreters of culture we must be cautious in our ethnographic reporting, so that we do not perpetuate power differentials through the use of distinctions that are no longer helpful or beneficial. The context of European contact and colonisation and the ontological nature of women vis-à-vis men force a false dichotomy between natural and supernatural. Klass (emphasis in original) observes the following regarding 'supernatural':

> that there is on the one hand a natural—real—universe, and on the other hand there are notions about aspects of the universe that are situated outside the natural and real and are therefore labeled supernatural by the person who *knows* what belongs in which category.

It must be noted that this analysis relies upon a very broad use of the term 'supernatural'. In *Miriam-Webster's collegiate dictionary*, Nature is defined, first, as 'the inherent character or basic constitution of a person or thing' and, second, 'as a creative controlling force in the universe', but neither of these really gets at what this debate is fundamentally about. The second definition of 'natural' states: 'a: being in accordance with or determined by nature b: having or constituting a classification based on features existing in nature'. 'Super' connotes something that is above or beyond. Thus, 'supernatural' refers to something above or beyond that which is a classification of features existing in nature. By using the term to distinguish one thing from another, we separate that which is united in the minds of those with whom we work. This separation is natural in the minds and socio-cultural experience of Europeans but not, perhaps, in the experience of others, specifically Melanesians.

As [Morton] Klass and [Maxine] Weisgrau, [Bengt] Sundkler and [Christopher] Steed and others have argued, the complex of symbols used by social groups was in constant flux. [Deborah] Gewertz and [Fred] Errington, [Donald] Tuzin, [Andrew] Lattas and others documented this creative reflexivity in their recent work in Melanesia. Thus, the introduction of a natural/supernatural dichotomy is one of many imported material and social elements that included technology, ideology and social practice. To suggest that colonial incursion and influence represent a new phenomenon would discount precolonial experience in Melanesia. Change is not the point. Rather, it is the ways in which Melanesians think about themselves, and organise and categorise their universe. What is at issue here is the representation by social scientists of the Melanesian experience. Klass and Weisgrau note: 'One of the most serious problems in the comparative study of religion is the ultimate tendency to impose values and categories deriving from the anthropologist's culture upon the one being studied.' This is at the core of my argument against applying a macro-level classificatory term for the sake of etic clarity.

The colonial context

The Enlightenment played a significant role in the relationship that developed between Melanesians and Europeans. Rationality was a dominant ideology underlying colonial attitudes up to and through 1975 Independence in Papua New Guinea as the country negotiated nationhood and economic development. In its pure form, Reason demanded dissociation from spirits, magic, and polluting elements that were inextricably interwoven in the cultural complex of Melanesia.

Significant European contact on the eastern half of New Guinea began in the mid-nineteenth century. The distinctions between sacred and profane, supernatural and natural, religious and pagan, permeated life among the colonisers. The rationalised dissection of what had previously been undifferentiated meant that, in the minds of colonisers, a clear order of natural facts existed. Understanding what happened in European colonies such as the Territories of Papua and New Guinea is as much about those who came expecting, facilitating and forcing change as it is about the people who lived there. John and Jean Comaroff have reflected on this as it relates to South Africa.

The symbolic systems of Melanesia were under significant pressure to adapt to this incursion. The ways in which food was produced, illness explained, healing facilitated, rites of passage practised, death explained, origins identified, and differences understood existed in a mass of cultural peculiarities. Spirits existed, power was recognised, and social organisation was regulated. There was no distinction between the natural and the supernatural. The ontological nature of men and women in society was defined within this complex social structure. Each ethnic group had a distinct social construction of gender, creating fluid yet distinct references about what it meant to be a man or woman. These ontological constructions reflect distinct ideas about human relationships, the world of spirits and power.

Women of power in Melanesia

One cannot speak of a trans-Melanesian understanding of adult gendered relationships. Yet areas in which male cults were active include respect for the power of the menstrual fluid of women, although the specificity of taboos surrounding female body fluid varies. [Polly] Wiessner and [Akii] Tumu suggest that 'the idea that contact with menstruating females and menstrual blood is harmful to men is widespread throughout the highlands'. General prohibitions are linked to space and time. The preparation or handling of food, physical contact and specific sexual relations between men and girls once they have begun menses appear to be highly regulated. [Terence] Hays and [Patricia] Hays describe the Kwaasi initiation rite among the Ndumba as a time of realisation:

> It is only when a girl becomes a kwaasi that she discovers the extent of men's vulnerability and, because of it, the threat she represents to all. In the seclusion house and in subsequent life, a maturing woman learns that no man is immune to the forces she possesses. From the moment her menstrual blood begins to flow, the new responsibilities attendant upon being the custodian of a lethal weapon are placed squarely upon the initiate's shoulders.

When a woman is menstruating, she retires to the menstrual hut to protect the community. [Philip] Newman and [David] Boyd note that the initiation of Awa women includes warnings to:

> watch where they walk and sit and to be particularly careful in the handling and preparation of food. Menstrual blood is especially dangerous, they are told, and when the signs of a menstrual period appear, they must immediately go to the menstrual hut, [and] remain there until the flow stops.

The consequences of women ignoring these precautions include incapacitation and death for the men: the bones weaken, muscles atrophy and the body withers. Precautions include prohibition of food handling by women in menses, separate and distinct living arrangements, separated sleeping quarters or spaces, spatial orientation including physically higher male position (walking across slopes, within buildings, on ladders, elevations, and so on) and care of waste fluid.

[Mary] Douglas's hypothesis of inter-related symbolic systems of particular societies suggests that, in the case of women's sexual fluids, there appears to be a relationship between prohibitions and the structure of the wider society. More recently, [Thomas] Buckley and [Alma] Gottlieb suggest that menstrual prohibitions reflect the power of women over and against the danger they offer to society. Menstrual rules bring with them social arrangements that are desirable as well as problematic. [Marla] Powers proposes that, when individual rites (seclusion, for example) are taken in isolation 'rather than as a part of the dynamic whole', the result is 'misinterpretation'. Ritual seclusion thus must be viewed within the entire complex of the female life cycle—birth to menarche to death—all associated with creative birth power.

University practicalities and cosmological constructions

The University's distinction between natural and supernatural, as embodied in housing arrangements, fostered an artificial systematic ordering of being and social order in Melanesia.

The University of Technology was founded in 1967, eight years before Independence. In the late 1980s, the faculty was largely expatriate, but the administration and support staff were Papua New Guinean. Unitech served the professional needs of a country that was then, and is now, emerging in global networks of economic trade and resource development. The training of engineers and professionals to work with national and transnational corporations with interests in gold, copper, silver, natural gas, timber, oil and fisheries was the central University mission.

In its early years, the student body was exclusively male. As a part of nation building, Papua New Guinea instituted countrywide educational opportunities for both boys and girls. The goal was to train Papua New Guinean professionals in the technical skills necessary to develop the country socially, politically and economically. These highly trained graduates were ultimately to replace imported expatriates. The student body was composed of men and women from much of Oceania. A Higher School Certificate from a National High School, awarded upon successful completion of Grade 12, was a prerequisite for entry.

Students who attended the University of Technology did so at the invitation of the PNG Department of Education. Papua New Guinea has, along with many former British colonies, adopted a national examination system in which a student's ability to continue beyond Grade 6 is determined through testing. In this land of over 700 languages, English is the language of education.

Female students at Unitech presented a security dilemma for the institution. With a student body that was predominantly male, there was an interest in protecting female students from attack or sexual assault. To this effect, female students were housed on the second floor of two cinderblock dormitories in 1986. Window bars and cyclone-fenced gates secured with heavy chains and padlocks secured these women each night. First-year male students were housed beneath their female counterparts.

The folklore of the campus indicated that this housing arrangement was intentional—upper-division students refused to be housed beneath women; first-year students did not have a choice. Informal interviews I conducted with first-year male students brought to light discomfort at living beneath women. In some cases, these students would sleep on the floor of upper-class male compatriots' dormitories for the duration of the year rather than stay in their own rooms. Upper-division students would regale others with stories about the lengths to which they and current students would go to avoid their housing assignments. Glee was evident in noting the consternation of newly arrived male students who discovered their dormitory arrangements. Upon the successful completion of their first year, male students then moved out to lodge-style dormitories on the outer perimeter of the campus.

The solution to women's security in the late 1980s included ignoring customary cautions regarding the power of highly charged female sexual fluids, and subjecting first-year male students to potential danger. Science, nature, and reason became the primary criteria for distinguishing between things considered to be true.

The dilemma of position

[Edward] Tylor speaks of the ritual practices and beliefs of the 'primitive' as parts of systems that are 'devised by human reason', in other words, of 'natural religions' as those that exist 'without supernatural aid or revelation'. He includes Christianity in this analysis. Belief systems are formed as part of a rational system of thought to make sense of the human place in the cosmos. This position appears to be at the heart of our dialogue here. To follow Tylor suggests that outsiders are able to explain what really occurs in religious systems (etic) vis-à-vis the explanations of participants (emic). In doing so, however, we risk denigrating that which is very real for the actors. At issue is power. In spite of an enlightened postmodern anthropological sensitivity to cultural contexts, distinctive phenomena, reflective positioning, and comparative inclinations, we have not moved far beyond Tylor. [Russell] McCutcheon notes that 'the Enlightenment provides the foundation of a strong outsider position in the study of religion', and goes on to suggest that the study of religion, rooted in the Enlightenment, 'consists in submitting the irrational aspects of human behavior to rational analysis'. Irrationality and rationality, however, exist only within the 'enlightened' etic perspective.

This differential analysis of an integrated system suggests that the human desire for synthesis is mistaken:

> [The Enlightenment's approach] has gone by such names as the scientific or the naturalistic study of religion. By 'naturalistic' one does not mean that this approach is more natural but simply that it presumes from the outset that religion is not *sui generis*, not a special case. Instead, it presumes that when religious people claim to have had supernatural experiences that defy rational explanation they are mistaken in some way.

In the attempt to synthesise the dichotomous relationship between natural and supernatural, European scholars seized upon ritual activity and accompanying mythological construction to define, organise and arrange their cosmos. The study of this language and activity is a recent project. As [Jonathan Z.] Smith (emphasis in original) notes: 'Simply put, the *academic study of religion is a child of the Enlightenment*'.

The issue of power is clearly present in this conversation as it relates to the category of supernatural. By continuing to use 'supernatural' as a classificatory term we perpetuate a false and imposed distinction. While the scientific minds thought they had solved the problem of providing security for arriving female students (their arrival being a significant step in itself), we anthropologists must avoid the temptation to shortcut cultural complexities by creating classifications that are imprecise and alien to the people with whom we work. The natural and supernatural are part of a cultural composite. In the case of housing and higher education in Papua New Guinea, the differentiation may only exist in our own minds.

The histories of both Melanesians and Europeans bring together ideas, practices, and constructions about what it means to be human. Such is the case with descriptive classificatory language that is introduced from without. As anthropologists, we may well be stuck with the awkward yet appropriate obligation of recognising and honouring the complex synthesis of human experience. By avoiding the use of a classificatory schema that perpetuates the positivist tendencies of the Enlightenment, we open the door for honest dialogue about the continual evolution of social experience. The indigenisation of the modern experience can, as a result, proceed with reflective analysis on the part of both insiders and outsiders, using common symbolic imagery that honours the whole.

POSTSCRIPT

Does the Natural–Supernatural Distinction Exist in All Cultures?

Beginning in the late 1960s, many anthropologists challenged the use of many Western terms such as "primitive," "savages," and "barbarism" on the grounds that such terms were pejorative, and that they were based on an ethnocentric bias that prevented anthropologists from understanding other cultures. By the mid-1970s, some anthropologists suggested that even basic categories like kinship, politics, law, art, and religion had to be reexamined because they were based on the fundamental categories of Western societies that were not present in non-Western languages. The argument was that just because we find kinship, politics, or religion in America, there is no reason to believe that in radically different societies such as those in Africa, the Amazon, or New Guinea that people understand or view their societies in these terms. Indeed, several of these abstract categories such as "art," "kinship," and "religion" have no indigenous terms in many societies.

Other anthropologists have challenged this view arguing that whether peoples actually have words for kinship, religion, politics, or law, these are nevertheless useful concepts for analysis and interpretation of non-Western societies. According to this view, these concepts are categories that provide a descriptive language for documenting and analyzing how individual societies operate and how different societies vary from one another. This perspective acknowledges that "kinship," "religion," "law," "politics," "art," and "the economy" are modeled on Western social and cultural practices and do not always represent indigenous categories. But in this view, these criticisms do not limit an anthropologist from understanding the relevant indigenous categories and how they may differ from our own.

The anthropologist Morton Klass (1928–2001) raised this question in his book *Ordered Universes: Approaches to the Anthropology of Religion* (Westview, 1995). He likened the term "supernatural" to the term "race," because it implied a phenomenal reality that simply was not present in the empirical, observable data. In the case of "race," there is no question that physical differences clearly exist from one part of the world to another. But human biological variation is much more complex than most Americans assume it to be, and there is actually more variation within the so-called races than between any two races. The handful of features Americans have come to associate with "race" are some of the least important differences among human populations. In a similar way, the existence of the supernatural is imposed by Western culture, and as Klass suggests, this notion has its roots in the age of enlightenment beginning in the 1700s.

146

Frederick (Fritz) Lampe, who is a Lutheran pastor, suggests that when considering the Papua New Guineans he knows, Klass's view is correct. This is particularly striking given the fact that he is himself a religious man. He acknowledges that New Guineans have beliefs that Lohmann would consider "supernatural," but they do not distinguish the natural and the supernatural as distinct categories of experience or belief.

Roger Ivar Lohmann professes not to be religious, and yet he claims to see the supernatural in all of the Papua New Guinean societies he has encountered. Moreover, Lohmann suggests that even nonreligious Americans may adopt supernatural thinking on a daily basis as they impute conscious motives to non-conscious things. For him, this is the heart of the supernatural. He feels that all societies are consciously aware that supernatural things are similar to natural ones, but are nevertheless different in fundamental ways.

The debate between Lohmann and Lampe appeared in a special issue of the journal *Anthropological Forum* (vol. 13, no. 2, 2003), edited by Lohmann, and including eight other essays that take slightly different positions from these two. Although this is one of the first debates discussing whether the supernatural is a universal human category, others have been discussing similar issues for a number of years. Several of the essays in Morton Klass and Maxine K. Weisgrau's edited volume *Across the Boundaries of Belief* (Westview, 1999) addresses these concerns. Earlier discussions of these topics would include Pascal Boyer's book *The Naturalness of Religious Ideas: A Cognitive Theory of Religion* (University of California Press, 1994), Stewart Guthrie's *Faces in the Clouds: A New Theory of Religion* (Oxford University Press, 1993), and John S. Kennedy's *The New Anthropomorphism* (Cambridge University Press, 1992). Nurit Bird-David's article "'Animism' Revisited: Personhood, Environment, and Relational Epistemology," *Current Anthropology* (vol. 40 supplement, February 1999, pp. S67–S91) and comments about this essay offer some other thoughts.

ISSUE 8

Is It Natural for Adopted Children to Want to Find Out About Their Birth Parents?

YES: **Betty Jean Lifton,** from *Journey of the Adopted Self: A Quest for Wholeness* (Basic Books, 1994)

NO: **John Terrell and Judith Modell,** from "Anthropology and Adoption," *American Anthropologist* (March 1994)

ISSUE SUMMARY

YES: Adoptee and adoption rights advocate Betty Jean Lifton argues that there is a natural need for human beings to know where they came from. Adoption is not a natural human state, she asserts, and it is surrounded by a secrecy that leads to severe social and psychological consequences for adoptees, adoptive parents, and birth parents.

NO: Anthropologists John Terrell and Judith Modell, who are each the parent of an adopted child, contend that the "need" to know one's birth parents is an American (or Western European) cultural construct. They conclude that in other parts of the world, where there is less emphasis placed on biology, adoptees have none of the problems said to be associated with being adopted in America.

T he 1976 television miniseries *Roots*, based on the book by Alex Haley, led many Americans to try to search out their own family stories, to find their own "roots." For most the effort merely meant asking grandparents about their ancestors. But for adopted children in America, information about their forebears was sealed by court order, and there was rarely any knowledge about their birth parents available to them from their adopted parents. Information about birth parents was usually kept secret to protect the birth parents from public scandal, since most adopted children were conceived out of wedlock and quietly put up for adoption with the understanding that the child and the public would never be able to link the birth parents with the adoptee. As social mores have changed in the United States, relatively little stigma now surrounds being an unwed mother or a single parent. But court records for most adoptions remain sealed, leading to a growing movement advocating open adoption records.

For several decades, adoptees' attempts to find their birth parents have become a growing social movement, with advocacy organizations, support groups, and self-help groups all attempting to help adoptees find their birth parents and which often help birth parents find the children they put up for adoption in their youth. Many of these groups insist that there is an inherent human right for adoptees to know their biological parents and for parents to know their natural children. These groups contend that there is a natural bond between parents and children that has been severed by adoption.

In the following selection, Betty Jean Lifton considers the psychological factors at play when children are put up for adoption, where knowledge of their birth parents is denied them. Drawing on her personal experiences as an adoptee as well as on interviews with dozens of other adoptees, Lifton considers how psychologically damaging this veil of secrecy is on adoptees, both as children and as adults. For her, people have a natural need to know where they came from. It is unnatural to grow up separated from and without knowledge of one's natural clan, she argues. The lack of such knowledge of one's roots has a negative impact on the child's psyche and leads them to seek out their roots, concludes Lifton.

Anthropologists John Terrell and Judith Modell counter that the "natural" need to know one's parents, as so often discussed by the adoption rights movement, is an American cultural construct. American and Western European culture emphasizes the difference between biological and adoptive families, viewing adoptive relationships as less real than biological ones. In most non-Western societies, people have very different views of adoption, typically viewing adoptive relationships as equal to biological ones. Citing examples from Hawaii and other parts of Oceania, they challenge the primacy of blood relationships over all other kinds of kinship ties. They argue that in America open adoptions would probably be healthier for all concerned parties but that it would be better still if Americans had a better understanding of the diverse ways other peoples have for understanding and dealing with adoption.

Are kin relations based on biology stronger than relationships based on other ties? Is there something in our genes that makes us have a more important relationship with our biological or birth parents than with others? Are adoptees likely to have stronger bonds with their adopted parents than with their birth parents? What do the experiences of Hawaiians and other Pacific Islanders say about how natural it is to want to know one's birth parents? Is the adoption rights movement in America a social phenomenon that could only emerge in America or does it touch on universal values and psychological needs?

Betwixt and Between

"Then I shan't be exactly human?" Peter asked.
"No."
"What shall I be?"
"You will be Betwixt-and-Between," Solomon said, and certainly he was a wise old fellow, for that is exactly how it turned out.

— James Barrie, *Peter Pan in Kensington Gardens*

Many people identify with the familiar condition of being Betwixt and Between, just as they identify with Peter Pan, the boy who did not want to grow up and face the responsibilities of the real world.

Peter, James Barrie tells us, is "ever so old," but really always the same age: one week. Though he was born "so long ago," he never had a birthday, nor is there the slightest chance of his having one. He escaped from his home when he was seven days old by flying out the window to Kensington Gardens.

Barrie doesn't tell us what was going on in Peter's family that after only seven days he knew he had to take off. But adoptees recognize Peter Pan as a brother. They, too, became lost children when they separated as babies from their natural families and disappeared into a place very much like never-never land. Like Peter, they are fantasy people. Denied the right to see their real birth certificates and the names of those who brought them into the world, they can't be sure they ever had a real *birth* day. They can never grow up because they are always referred to as an "adopted child."

I didn't realize that, like Peter, I wasn't "exactly human" until I was seven *years* old. It was the moment my mother told me I was adopted. Like most adoptive parents faced with breaking such bleak news, she tried to make adoption sound special, but I could feel the penetrating chill of its message. I was not really her child. I had come from somewhere else, a place shrouded in mystery, a place that, like myself, was Betwixt and Between.

As I listened, I could feel a part of myself being pulled into the darkness of that mystery—a place already carved out by Peter and the lost children. I would never be the same again.

This was to be our secret, my mother said. Hers and mine. I was not to share it with anyone—not even my father. It would break his heart if he suspected I knew. In this way I learned that secrecy and adoption were inextricably mixed, as in a witch's brew. By becoming a keeper of the secret, I was to collaborate in the family conspiracy of silence.

I didn't know then that our little family secret was connected to the *big* secret in the closed adoption system, just as our little conspiracy was connected to the larger social conspiracy around adoption. My mother and father had been assured that my birth records would be sealed forever, that I would never be able to learn the identity of my original family. Secrecy was the magic ingredient that would give our adoptive family the aura of a blood-related one. Secrecy was the magic broom that would sweep away all feelings of grief and loss on the part of any of the parties involved.

As I played my role of the good daughter—repressing a natural need to know where I came from—I was unaware that the secrecy inherent in the adoption system was shaping and constricting the self through which I organized my perception of reality. By denying my natural curiosity about where I came from, and my grief for my lost birth parents and for the child I might have been, I was shrinking my emotional space to the size permitted by that system. So, too, were my adoptive parents forced by the secrecy to shrink their emotional space as they denied their need to grieve for the natural child they might have had.

We were trapped in a closed family system where secrecy cut off real communication. We were not unlike those families who keep secrets around alcoholism, divorce, incest, and all the other things that family members are prone to hide from their neighbors and from one another.

I had no idea of this as a child. Having repressed my real feelings, I was not consciously aware of my pain. And as a consequence, I was not consciously aware of myself, except as someone unreal pretending to be real. I did things that my human friends did, even looked real in my high school and college graduation pictures, and in the photographs taken at my wedding, before I flew off with my husband to the Far East.

Perhaps I might have never been in touch with my feelings if, shortly after my return from Japan, a relative, recently married into my adoptive family, had not remarked about something she heard—that my natural parents had been killed in a car accident. Her statement was like a Zen slap, knocking me into another state of consciousness. I had been told my parents were dead, but I had not been told this story. When I tried to clear up the mystery of how they died, I was shocked to learn that they had been very much alive at the time of my adoption—and might still be.

Much that had lain repressed in me now began stirring. I started to wonder how my mind had been able to cut off the primal subject of who my parents were. Even if it were true that they were dead, why had I not asked any questions about them? After all, dead people have names; they have relatives they have left behind; they have graves. Why had I behaved as if death had wiped out all traces of their existence? It was my first conscious brush with the psychological mystery that forms the core of this [selection]: How does a child's mind close down when it senses danger, and stay closed until some life event or crisis inadvertently jars it open? And what traumatic effects does this have on the child's growing sense of self?

⋅✦⋅

As a writer, I set out to explore the psychological complexities of being adopted in my book *Twice Born: Memoirs of an Adopted Daughter.* I was amazed, even alarmed, at what surfaced. The compliant adopted child within, as elusive as ever, was in many ways a stranger to the adult I had become. The anger, barely contained under what passed as irony and wit, could no longer be disguised as I dredged up memories of that child's helplessness in the face of mysteries too dark to comprehend. Even as I wrote about my search and reunion, I felt burdened with guilt, as if it were a disloyalty to my deceased adoptive parents. Nor had I fully absorbed the depths of what I had been through. I found a birth mother who had tried to hold on to me but, as an unmarried seventeen-year-old with no emotional or financial support, finally had to let go. Once she was defeated, she put on the scarlet letter—S for secrecy and shame—and did not tell either of her two husbands or her son about me. We met secretly twice before I had to leave for a summer in Japan. The psychic chaos I felt during those two months in Tokyo—as if I had fallen into a black hole—was so great that when I returned to the States I did not call her for fear of falling back into that dark place: a place, as we will see, that is not unfamiliar to many adoptees who have internalized the taboos of the closed adoption system. At the time of my reunion, there were no books to sanction my search for my mother or to prepare me for what I might experience.

My next book, *Lost and Found, the Adoption Experience,* was an attempt to write such a book and, in so doing, to illuminate the existential condition of being adopted. I explored the psychological pitfalls that await adoptees all through the life cycle when they are forced to close off their real feelings and live *as if* their families of origin were not an inherent part of their identity. I laid out the difficult stages of awakening that adoptees experience before they dare to set out in search of the missing pieces in their lives.

As the search phenomenon was still relatively new at that time, the last part of the book gave an overview of the varieties of reunion experience and the psychological growth and accommodation that everyone—adoptee, adoptive parents, and birth parents—has to make. . . .

⋅✦⋅

[Looking at my own life,] I found an adopted woman waiting there, one who was more sensitive than ever to the lack of respect for the rights of adopted children to know who they are, and who was still absorbed with the psychological mysteries inherent in adoption. Once again I was faced with the same questions I had been grappling with earlier: Why do adopted people feel so alienated? Why do they feel unreal, invisible to themselves and others? Why do they feel unborn? Now, however, I had a new question that I felt would shed light on the others: How do adopted people form a sense of self in the closed adoption system?

The psychoanalyst Karen Horney defined the real self as the alive, unique, personal center of ourselves that wants to grow. When the real self is prevented from free, healthy growth because of abandoning its needs to others, one can become alienated from it. She quotes Kierkegaard on the alienation and loss of self as "sickness unto death." Adoptees, who often say they feel they have no self, can be seen as expressing this despair. Having abandoned their need to know their origins for the sake of their adoptive parents, they are left with a hole in the center of their being. They feel they don't exist.

Of course, everyone has some kind of self. The adoptee born psychologically into the closed adoption system and shaped by its myths, secrets, and taboos from first conscious memory, and even before, has a unique self, an adopted self. But this fragile self has a basic inner division brought about by the need for denial that is built into the closed adoption system.

When I began research for this [selection], I was primarily interested in how secrecy affects the formation of the adopted self. I saw it as emotional abuse (of which adoptive parents are unaware) because it distorts the child's psychic reality. In the course of interviewing adoptees, however, I realized that it is not just secrecy that affects their sense of self but rather a series of traumas. This "cumulative adoption trauma" begins when they are separated from the mother at birth; builds when they learn that they were not born to the people they call mother and father; and is further compounded when they are denied knowledge of the mother and father to whom they were born.

I was not unfamiliar with the literature on trauma. My husband, Robert Jay Lifton, has been preoccupied with trauma on a massive scale. As a journalist, I have reported on the war-wounded, orphaned, and traumatized children of Hiroshima, Korea, Vietnam, and the Holocaust. Still, as an adopted person, loyal to my adoptive parents, I didn't allow myself to see that closed adoption is also a form of trauma—an invisible and subtle one—until years later when I began noticing parallels between adopted children and children of alcoholics, children of survivors (even survivors themselves), and children who have been abused.

There has already been some misunderstanding about the linking of adoption to trauma. Far from being regarded as traumatic, adoption is still widely viewed as fortunate for the child who is rescued from homelessness, and for the adoptive parents who are rescued from childlessness. And in most cases it is. Yet the word *trauma* has been slipping into the psychological literature on adoption with increasing frequency in the last decade as clinicians come to realize the high psychic cost that both parent and child pay when they repress their grief and loss.

I have come to believe in the course of my research that it is unnatural for members of the human species to grow up separated from and without knowledge of their natural clan, that such a lack has a negative influence on a child's psychic reality and relationship with the adoptive parents. By enveloping their origins with secrecy, the closed adoption system asks children to disavow reality, to live *as if* they were born to the parents who raise them. They grow up feeling like anonymous people cut off from the genetic and social heritage that gives everyone else roots.

⋅⟨◉⟩⋅

As I write this, we are Betwixt and Between change and stasis in the adoption field. We are between two systems: the traditional closed one that for almost half a century has cut adopted children off from their heritage, and an open one in which birth mothers choose the adoptive parents of their baby and maintain some contact with the family. It is a time when the best interests of the child, for which the adoption system was originally created, have become subordinate to the best interests of the adults, as fierce custody battles are waged over the few available healthy white infants.

Meanwhile, adoption records remain sealed in all but two states due to the influence of a conservative lobby group, the National Council for Adoption, that has managed to polarize the field by labeling those who seek reform as "anti-adoption." Reformers who are working to open the system, as well as the records, however, are not anti-adoption but rather anti–closed adoption and pro–adopted children.

While no amount of openness can take away the child's trauma of being separated from his mother, or save the child from the trauma of learning she was not born into the adoptive family, we can remove the secrecy that compounds those two traumas. We can begin to demystify the adoptive family and to see it with much of the strengths and weaknesses of other families. The conservatives argue for the myth of the happy adoptive family that has no problems because love conquers all. But we will see that something more is expected of the adopted family: an excess of happiness that is meant to make up for the excess of loss that everyone in the triad experiences, and an excess of denial to cover that loss. Exposing the myths of the adoptive family while still holding on to the very real need and love that parents and child have for each other has been the challenge facing me. . . .

The adoptees [I studied] are mostly successful people in that they are productive in their work and their private lives. But, . . . much of their psychic energy has been taken up with adjusting to the mystery of their origins by disavowing their need to have some knowledge of and contact with their blood kin. . . .

The adoptive family has managed to "pass" until now; it remains, for the most part, an unexplored constellation that has escaped psychological detection. Many professionals regard its psychodynamics as being the same as that of other families, overlooking the trauma that the parents as well as the child experience due to the conspiracy of silence built into the closed system.

Because it is a social rather than a natural construct, we can see the strengths and malfunctions of the adoptive family as a laboratory to illuminate some of the most fundamental issues around mothering and mother loss, attachment and bonding, separation and loss, denial and dissociation, and the human need for origins. We can see the deep need that parents and child fill for each other, but we can also see the problems that occur between parents and child when secrets prevent open communication between them.

In *Lost and Found* I spoke of what I called the Adoption Game, a family system that operates by unspoken rules that require everyone in it to live a double life. While seeming to exist in the real world with their adoptive family, the children are at the same time inhabiting an underground world of fantasies and fears which they can share with no one. The adoptive parents also live a double life. Believing themselves to be doing everything for their children, they withhold from them the very knowledge they need to develop into healthy adults. This double role of savior/withholder eventually works against the adoptive parents, estranging them from their children. So, too, the birth mother is forced to live a double life from the moment she surrenders her baby. Advised to go on as if nothing has happened, she keeps secret what is probably the most important and traumatic event of her life.

In [*Journey of the Adopted Self: A Quest for Wholeness*], I speak not of adoption games but of adoption ghosts. In many ways [the] book is a ghost story, for it tells of the ghosts that haunt the dark crevices of the unconscious and trail each member of the adoption triangle (parents and child alike) wherever they go. Unless one is aware of these ghosts, one will never be able to understand or to help the child who is adopted, the parents who adopt, or the parents who give up a child to adoption.

Who are these ghosts?

The adopted child is always accompanied by the ghost of the child he might have been had he stayed with his birth mother and by the ghost of the fantasy child his adoptive parents might have had. He is also accompanied by the ghost of the birth mother, from whom he has never completely disconnected, and the ghost of the birth father, hidden behind her.

The adoptive mother and father are accompanied by the ghost of the perfect biological child they might have had, who walks beside the adopted child who is taking its place.

The birth mother (and father, to a lesser extent) is accompanied by a retinue of ghosts. The ghost of the baby she gave up. The ghost of her lost lover, whom she connects with the baby. The ghost of the mother she might have been. And the ghosts of the baby's adoptive parents.

All of these ghosts are members of the extended adoptive family, which includes the birth family. . . .

[The] book, then, is about the search for the adopted self. It is not about the literal search in the material world, where one sifts through records and archives for real people with real names and addresses; but rather about the internal search in which one sifts through the pieces of the psyche in an attempt to understand who one was so that one can have some sense of who one is and who one can become. It is the quest for all the missing pieces of the self so that one can become whole.

It is the search for the answer to that universal question—Who am I?—behind which, for the adoptee, lurks: Who is the mother who brought me into this mysterious world?

NO

**John Terrell and
Judith Modell**

Anthropology and Adoption

Anthropologists, we believe, are likely to forget that "what every anthropologist knows" is not necessarily what everyone else knows. In the quest for tenure, professional visibility, and academic achievement, anthropologists may also overlook the possibility that what they know could be important to people who are not anthropologists, too, if only they know. Here is one example.

Adoption in America

In North America, most children grow up living with at least one of the parents they were born to; most children grow up assuming they will live with children born to them. Consequently, perhaps, many people in our society think of adoption as a second-best way of becoming a family (Schaffer and Lindstrom 1989:15). The psychological and social ties binding an adoptive family together are looked on as weaker than "natural" ties of blood. And adoption is seen as difficult and risky. The risk is held to be especially great when a child does not "match"—look like or share the background of—its adoptive parents (Bates 1993). This is preeminently true of transracial and international adoptions, in which a child, who has no say in the matter, is severed not only from its "real" family but also from ethnic roots and cultural heritage: in a word, from its true identity.

Recently, advocates of adoption have been emphasizing the difference between adoptive and biological families (e.g., Melina 1986; Register 1991; Schaffer and Lindstrom 1989), often as a way of helping parents through such "alternative parenthood" (Kirk 1984). Adoptive families are different, for one thing, because adoption is not typical in American society. They are more profoundly different because, it is said, all parties in the "adoption triad" (birth parents, adoptees, and adoptive parents) must cope with psychological pain and feelings of loss. Adoptive parents "lose" the chance to have a biological child and the perpetuation of their blood line. An adopted child loses its natural heritage. And birth parents lose their children.

Moreover, it is presumed that adoptive parents must deal with feelings of inadequacy, and birth parents with feelings of incompetence or frustration. Adoptees, in this argument, suffer throughout their lives because "adoption cuts off people from a part of themselves" (Brodzinsky et al. 1992:3). Even children who were adopted in the first days or weeks of life "grieve not only for the parents they never knew, but for the other aspects of themselves that have been lost through adoption: the loss of origins, of a completed sense of self, of genealogical continuity" (Brodzinsky et al. 1992:11–12). Because they have not been raised by those who gave them life, even the most well-adjusted adoptees, we are told, go through predictable ups and downs of psychological adaptation that distinguish them as a recognizable class of persons who may need special counseling and professional help (Brodzinsky et al. 1992; Samuels 1990:87–113).

Adoption in Oceania

Anthropologists know that what is problematic or self-evident in one society may not be so in another. Oceanic societies—Hawaii among them—are well known in anthropological literature for the frequency and apparent casualness of adoption. What most Americans know about our 50th state, however, does not usually include the information that the last reigning monarch was an adopted, or *hanai,* child. Moreover, this was a crucial fact in her story and remains significant in the interpretations Hawaiians make of their culture and history. In her autobiography, Queen Liliuokalani wrote:

> Immediately after my birth I was wrapped in the finest soft tapa cloth, and taken to the house of another chief, by whom I was adopted. Konia, my foster-mother, was a granddaughter of Kamehameha I., and was married to Paki, also a high chief; their only daughter, Bernice Pauahi, afterwards Mrs. Charles R. Bishop, was therefore my foster-sister. In speaking of our relationship, I have adopted the term customarily used in the English language, but there was no such modification recognized in my native land. I knew no other father or mother than my foster-parents, no other sister than Bernice. [Liliuokalani 1990:4]

She goes on to say that Paki treated her exactly as any other father would treat his child, and that when she would meet her biological parents, she would respond with perhaps more interest, but always with the same demeanor that was due all strangers who noticed her.

Liliuokalani adds that her biological mother and father had other children, ten in all. Most of them were adopted into other chiefs' families. She says it is difficult to explain to outsiders why these adoptions seem perfectly natural to Hawaiians. "As intelligible a reason as can be given is that this alliance by adoption cemented the ties of friendship between chiefs. It spread to the common people, and it has doubtless fostered a community of interest and harmony" (Liliuokalani 1990:4).

Given what anthropologists know about adoption throughout Oceania, (for example, Brady 1976; Carrol 1970; Howard 1990; Levy 1973; Mandeville 1981; Webster 1975), what this royal informant says about the place and popularity of adoption in her native land is not peculiar. For her—and not uniquely—adoption was a loving and generous transaction, not a response to need or crisis. Furthermore, such a loving and generous gesture benefited the whole society as well as the particular individuals involved.

The point of view represented by Queen Liliuokalani—and by other people in Pacific Island societies who share her experiences (Modell 1994a)— ought to be a lesson for Americans, with our quite different story of adoption. As Bartholet (1993) argues, birth parents, adoptive parents, and adoptees should know that people elsewhere in the world may look on adoption in a variety of ways that do not resemble our assumptions and biases about this form of kinship. They need to know that what adoption means, and what it signifies for participants, is malleable, contingent, pragmatic: a "social construction," not a natural fact or a universal cultural given.

Anthropology and Adoption

Anthropologists are likely to find this observation self-evident; adoption is made—*fictio*—by those who practice this mode of child having and child rearing. But, with some exceptions (e.g., Modell 1994b), anthropologists have not been drawn to study the politics and practice of adoption in Western societies: apparently what anthropologists find interesting elsewhere may be less interesting, or deeply private, at home. A glance over the abundant published literature on kinship, in fact, suggests that studying adoption generally plays a peripheral role in anthropology: as a way of illuminating a kinship system, as a mechanism of social mobility, or as a way of transmitting property. Little disciplinary attention has been paid to the diverse ways people think about, react to, and represent the meaning of adoption.

This is not to say that nothing exists on the subject. In the early 20th century, Lowie remarked on the frequency of adoption in Pacific Island societies, forgetting his cultural relativism to claim that child exchange in such societies went "well beyond the rational" (Lowie 1933). His surprise prompted others to inquire into the consequences of the unfamiliar behavior of moving large numbers of children from household to household. Three decades later, in the early 1960s, Levy discovered in a small village in Tahiti that more than 25 percent of children were adopted; this was not untypical for Polynesian societies. Levy went on to analyze the impact of this generous "transaction in parenthood" in his path-breaking account of Tahitian culture and personality (Levy 1973).

Anthropologists such as Marshall picked up other threads in the (slowly) growing tapestry on adoption in the Pacific. In an article examining created kin in Trukese society, Marshall concludes that what is common to kinship is a notion of sharing, differently enacted and represented in different contexts (1977:656–657). To analyze kinship cross-culturally and without bias, he argues, one must explore the nature of nurture and of sharing. His article demonstrates the significance of creating kin through constructed sibling and parent-child bonds for revealing the meanings of kinship. To act like kin is to be kin; to care for reciprocally is to have a relationship. Conduct and performance make (and unmake) kin, with a fluidity that differs from "biogenetic" notions of kinship characteristic of American society (Marshall 1977).

Marshall's article confirms the extent to which kinship is not "natural" but "cultural," representing an intense experience of love and of obligation between individuals. Moreover, these experiences may change over the course of a person's life, depending on circumstances and on perceptions of the "usefulness" and rewards of being related.

Two volumes on adoption in Oceania underscored the importance of created kinship in Pacific Island societies: [Vern] Carroll's *Adoption in Oceania* (1970) and [Ivan] Brady's *Transactions in Kinship* (1976). In both volumes the contributing anthropologists explore the structure and the functions of adoption, with varying degrees of attention to Carroll's initial warning about applying the single term *adoption* to diverse arrangements across cultures. The goal of challenging the universality of a definition of *adoption* is, as Ward Goodenough concludes in the epilogue to the 1970 volume, only imperfectly met. Treating adoption largely as a social institution, the articles in these volumes tended not to explore the meanings of the experience for the individuals involved or to establish a framework for interpretive analysis of the cultural and personal significance of "child exchange" wherever, and however, it occurs.

Silk offers an alternative to the conventional treatment of adoption in anthropological literature. In a 1980 article, she notes the frequency of adoption in Pacific Island societies compared with almost all others in the world, and asks why. Her answer draws on sociobiological theory. Silk argues that as a way of modifying extreme family size, adoption is adaptive for the group, though it may be a risk for the individual child. Following her theoretical premise, the risk lies in the tendency of parents to treat their biological—more *closely related*—children differently from the way they treat an adopted child (Silk 1980:803). She further suggests that, consequently (and necessarily), biological parents retain an interest in the child they have given away; thus, bonds are maintained, not severed, by adoption. In offering a sociobiological explanation, Silk does not mean to exclude the social and cultural factors that affect the transaction; her primary aim is to distinguish societies in which adoption occurs frequently from those in which it occurs rarely (Silk 1980:816). She does not question the concept of adoption itself.

Frequency has continued to be a feature that brings adoption to the attention of anthropologists, most of whom come from a society in which adoption affects "only" about 2 or 3 percent of children in any one year (Adamec and Peirce 1991). Anthropologists of Eskimo (Inuit) societies, sounding rather like anthropologists of the Pacific, remark on the astonishing ease with which children are moved from parent to parent, for shorter or longer stays (Guemple 1979). Several of these studies inquire into the impact of this movement on the affective as well as the structural and functional domains of social life.

The frequency of adoption in large-scale, complex societies has also piqued anthropological interest, though without major impact on the discipline. In 1980, for instance, [Arthur] Wolf and [Chieh-shan] Huang published an exhaustive study of adoption in China whose importance has mainly been acknowledged by other Sinologists. *Marriage and Adoption in China 1845-1945* traces trends in the transactions of women and of children as these reflect social and political changes. With a century's worth of historical records, Wolf and Huang had data other anthropologists might envy. Yet their analysis remains conventional, assuming that the meaning of adoption can be transferred from "us" to "them" and describing the social to the exclusion of the psychological ramifications of the phenomenon.

The silence accorded to full-scale studies of adoption continues. To take a final example: Esther Goody's pioneering analysis of "child exchange" in West African societies and among West Africans in London recognizes the range of meanings and functions moving a child may have (Goody 1982). Discussing numerous particular cases in which parenthood is delegated, Goody reminds her readers that words like *adoption* and *fosterage* are culturally and historically relative as well as individually negotiated. Her book speaks a quiet warning against assuming that the meaning of adoption holds from group to group, time to time, or even person to person.

One cannot, of course, leave the subject of adoption and kinship without referring to the work of Jack Goody—especially his under-appreciated article, "Adoption in Cross Cultural Perspective." The point he made in this 1969 piece remains all too appropriate: "For I know of no attempt to do a systematic survey of the distribution of this phenomenon, which is not for example included in the data recorded in the Ethnographic Atlas (1967) nor mentioned in Goody's study of changing family patterns (1963)" (Goody 1969:56). As far as we know, his agenda for the comparative study of adoption has not been followed. Nor have the issues raised in the ethnographic writings cited above been taken as far as they might.

If anthropologists embrace the goal of examining rather than imposing meanings of core concepts on others—or, for that matter, our own society—then adoption would seem to be a crucial area of study. For it is here that the multivocal meanings of personhood and identity, of kinship and social bonds, can be thoroughly explored—and from the point of view of those who "make" these kinds of relationships. Existing writings on adoption suggest there is more to be said about the self-conscious gesture involved in creating kin and its diverse manifestations. Virtually everywhere it occurs, adoption inscribes and perpetuates understandings of birth, blood, and belonging, of essence and accident or choice. In the late 19th century, the British jurist Sir Henry Maine articulated the premise of his own culture's understanding of adoption: fictive kinship, he wrote, replicates "real" kinship; the bond of law "imitates" the bond of birth and the child is "as if begotten" (Maine 1861). The ramifications of this premise in Western society, and the import of transferring it to other societies, have too rarely been seen as problematic.

The treatment of adoption in anthropological literature perpetuates a sense that the concept is nonproblematic. The transaction of a child, evidently, is not considered either a major social event or a key cultural text; rather, child exchange is analyzed as "only" an aspect of kinship, form of social solidarity, or response to demographic conditions. The neglect also speaks to a conservatism about our methods and categories of analysis, despite (or perhaps because of) the popularity of postmodernist writings in the discipline. Further confirming this is the modest reception given to several recently published radical reexaminations of kinship, of kinship and gender, and of theories of identity and ethnicity (e.g., Collier and Yanagisako 1987; Linnekin and Poyer 1990a; Schneider 1984; Weston 1991). These studies do show, however, that at least some anthropologists are drastically rethinking the context and meaning of fundamental aspects of social life.

Kinship and Adoption

Adoption as a category of meaning, like adoption as social practice, is problematic. Western common sense says the distinction between kin and non-kin is self-evident, a distinction that allows for the concept of "*as if* begotten." Adoption is thus a phenomenological category betwixt categories, a category that straddles the fence, a category in our society that dooms those who fall within it to be both kin and non-kin—real and "fictive." As Schneider has demonstrated through his brilliant analysis of the cultural unit on Yap called *tabinau,* there is much to be gained by recognizing how considerably varied and flexible the meanings of words can be (Schneider 1984:21).

Although Western ideas about kinship and adoption assume the primacy of blood ties and biological inheritance and see people as discrete and bounded individuals (Linnekin and Poyer 1990b:2, 7), anthropologists know that these presuppositions are not universal. Pomponio, for example, notes that while children on Mandok Island, Papua New Guinea, are thought to share the substance of their parents and other kin, "substance" means more than it does in Western thought: not just shared biogenetic endowment but the combination of blood, food, and work. "The transubstantial nature of Mandok personhood is evidenced by their belief that firstborns can be 'created' through adoption, and adoption is not limited to married couples." Many children (13 of 81, or 16 percent of her sample), in fact, are adopted specifically for this purpose. She concludes, "The important substance here is not contained in blood or semen, but food and work (i.e., caretaking). By feeding and caring for a child, the substance of the adult is transferred to that child" (Pomponio 1990:54).

Lieber argues that what Pomponio observes about the nature of kinship and adoption on Mandok may be true of Oceanic societies generally. What it means to be a person in many Pacific Island societies is structured, he says, by local theories of ontogeny (Lieber 1990:71) in which what a person becomes is not "in their blood," but is credited instead to the nurturing social and physical environment within which they mature. In other words, as Howard has summarized the argument, kinship in Oceania is considered to be contingent rather than absolute.

> Thus, on the one hand, kinship has to be validated by social action to be recognized; on the other, kinship status can be achieved through social action (i.e., by consistently acting as kinsmen even though genealogical linkages may be questionable or unknown). [Howard 1990:266]

A similar argument made by Sahlins chastens anthropologists for separating adoption—and kinship—from all aspects of culture and social structure. In Hawaii, where belonging comes from action and relationships are contingent, Sahlins claims: "From family to state, the arrangements of society were in constant flux, a set of relationships constructed on the shifting sands of love" (Sahlins 1985:20). The civil state, he might have added, rests upon chosen attachments much like the relationship between parents and child.

Anthropology and the Public

The process of rethinking theories of the person, of kinship, and of social and cultural life that is essential to our discipline also bears on current debates about multiculturalism occurring throughout the American university environment. Anthropologists have expressed amazement that scholars from across the disciplinary spectrum have discovered "the other," "multivocality," and "multiculturalism" without discovering anthropology (Perry 1992). But it is equally fair to argue that anthropologists have not actively guided the debate or introduced an anthropological vocabulary to a public that will feel the effects of such debate.

Anthropologists—or at least anthropologists who read the *Anthropology Newsletter*—do not need to be told that it is important to be "public or perish" (Givens 1992). Nevertheless—all too often, it seems—anthropologists focus on what their colleagues will say about their work and overlook opportunities to be heard and appreciated by others. Even when they cannot grab newspaper headlines with startling news about lost tribes, missing links, or the oldest potsherds in the world, they need to ask themselves: who might be interested to know what I know?

Thanks to anthropologists such as Schneider, it may no longer be intellectually strategic to study adoption simply to refute the conventional wisdom that the bonds of kinship are genealogical—given by "birth" (Schneider 1984:169–177). Studying adoption can also be a way of discovering the meanings and implications of aspects of culture and social order that remain problematic for both anthropologists and the public. Adoption not only belies what Schneider has called "biologistic" ways of marking and defining human character, human nature, and human behavior (Schneider 1984:175), it also reveals interpretations of concepts like identity, family, and ethnicity.

Thus, for instance, a study of adoption can shed light on definitions of and criteria for "citizenship": What does it mean to belong to a group or nation, and is this linked with ideas about what it means to belong to a family? Nor is adoption irrelevant to larger concerns about assimilation, "true" cultural identity, and ethnic purity, raising as it does the problem of being "*as if* begotten" when contract has been the mode of entry. At core, adoption is about who belongs and how—a subject of immense political as well as disciplinary significance. It is also, and increasingly, about power, privilege, and poverty. Concerns are properly raised about babies moving from the poor to the rich, or, a new version of the old "baby-selling" cry, about residents of impoverished nations and regions putting their babies on the international market. But anthropologists have not addressed those concerns. Moreover, these are issues that touch the lives of a general public, well beyond those who may experience, or know about, an adoptive relationship.

Conclusion

In societies such as ours where caring for children who are not one's own by birth is seen as risky, painful, and unnatural, learning through anthropology's eyes that what adoption does to people is not written in stone would undoubtedly be beneficial to birth parents, adoptive parents, and adoptees. It seems equally apparent that studying adoption in different societies can be a window through which anthropologists may learn about other facets of life.

Our own interest in adoption (beyond the powerful consideration that we are both adoptive parents) lies in both these directions. We are interested in adoption as an empirical question. What are the meanings, values, and contexts of caring for children "other than your own" in different societies? What determines the place and popularity (or lack thereof) of adoption in different societies? The agenda Jack Goody set over twenty years ago can benefit from recent literature on reflexivity and multivocalism, so that adoption is considered not only a social transaction but also a cultural text. The comparative task, then, will involve analyzing the forms of attachment and the representations of experience constituted by adoption—or, broadly, "child exchange"—as practiced by diverse cultural groups.

A study of adoption becomes an inquiry into fundamental beliefs about the person and personal connections as these intertwine with political, economic, and historical developments. Taking the perspective of constructed kinship and making the most of the "construction" it entails, so that adoption is not assumed to be univocal or universal in meaning, can advance theories of culture creativity, human agency, and identity formation. Ideally, studying adoption will preserve the centrality of individual experiences in the composition of social worlds and cultural texts.

We also want to strengthen public awareness of the diverse ways that people in different parts of the world—and in different ethnic communities here in North America—build and value human relationships and family ties and obligations. In the process we should demonstrate that anthropology importantly is, as it historically has been, a "way of seeing" for those other than its practitioners.

References

Adamec, Christine, and William Peirce, 1991, The Encyclopedia of Adoption. New York: Facts on File.

Bartholet, Elizabeth, 1993, Family Bonds. Adoption and the Politics of Parenting. Boston: Houghton Mifflin.

Bates, J. Douglas, 1993, Gift Children. A Story of Race, Family, and Adoption in a Divided America. New York: Ticknor and Fields.

Brady, Ivan, ed., 1976, Transactions in Kinship: Adoption and Fosterage in Oceania. Honolulu: University of Hawaii Press.

Brodzinsky, David M., Marshall D. Schechter, and Robin Marantz Henig, 1992, Being Adopted. The Lifelong Search for Self. New York: Doubleday.

Carrol, Vern, ed., 1970, Adoption in Eastern Oceania. Honolulu: University of Hawaii Press.

Collier, Jane Fishburne, and Sylvia Junko Yanagisako, eds., 1987, Gender and Kinship. Essays toward a Unified Analysis. Stanford: Stanford University Press.

Givens, David B., 1992, Public or Perish. Anthropology Newsletter 33(5):1, 58.

Goody, Esther, 1982, Parenthood and Social Reproduction. New York: Cambridge University Press.

Goody, Jack, 1969, Adoption in Cross-Cultural Perspective. Comparative Studies in Society and History 2:55–78.

Guemple, D. L., 1979, Inuit Adoption. Ottawa: National Museums of Canada.

Howard, Alan, 1990, Cultural Paradigms, History, and the Search for Identity in Oceania, In Cultural Identity and Ethnicity in the Pacific. Jocelyn Linnekin and Lin Poyer, eds. Pp. 259–279. Honolulu: University of Hawaii Press.

Kirk, H. David, 1984, Shared Fate. A Theory and Method of Adoptive Relationships. Port Angeles, WA: Ben-Simon Publications.

Levy, Robert, 1973, The Tahitians: Mind and Experience in the Society Islands. Chicago: University of Chicago Press.

Lieber, Michael D., 1990, Lamarckian Definitions of Identity on Kapingamarangi and Pohnpei. In Cultural Identity and Ethnicity in the Pacific. Jocelyn Linnekin and Lin Poyer, eds. Pp. 71–101. Honolulu: University of Hawaii Press.

Liliuokalani, 1990, Hawaii's Story by Hawaii's Queen. Honolulu: Mutual Publishing.

Linnekin, Jocelyn, and Lin Poyer, 1990a, [eds.] Cultural Identity and Ethnicity in the Pacific. Honolulu: University of Hawaii Press.

———, 1990b, Introduction. In Cultural Identity and Ethnicity in the Pacific. Jocelyn Linnekin and Lin Poyer, eds. Pp. 1–16. Honolulu: University of Hawaii Press.

Lowie, Robert, 1933, Adoption. In Encyclopedia of the Social Sciences. E. A. Seligman and A. Johnson, eds. Pp. 459–460. New York: Macmillan and Company.

Maine, Sir Henry, 1861, Ancient Law. London: Macmillan.

Mandeville, Elizabeth, 1981, Kamano Adoption. Ethnology 20:229–244.

Marshall, Mac, 1977, The Nature of Nurture. American Ethnologist 4(4):643–662.

Melina, Lois Ruskai, 1986, Raising Adopted Children. A Manual for Adoptive Parents. New York: Harper and Row.

Modell, Judith, 1994a, Nowadays Everyone Is *Hanai:* Child Exchange and the Construction of Hawaiian Urban Culture. In Urban Cultures in the Pacific. C. Jourdan and J. M. Philibert, eds. Forthcoming.

———, 1994b, Kenship with Strangers: Adoption and Interpretations of Kinship in American Culture. Berkeley: University of California Press.

Perry, Richard J., 1992, Why Do Multiculturalists Ignore Anthropologists? Chronicle of Higher Education 38(26):A52.

Pomponio, Alice, 1990, Seagulls Don't Fly into the Bush: Cultural Identity and the Negotiations of Development on Mandok Island, Papua New Guinea. In Cultural Identity and Ethnicity in the Pacific. Jocelyn Linnekin and Lin Poyer, eds. Pp. 43–70. Honolulu: University of Hawaii Press.

Register, Cheri, 1991, "Are Those Kids Yours?" American Families with Children Adopted from Other Countries. New York: Free Press.

Sahlins, Marshall, 1985, Islands of History. Chicago: University of Chicago Press.

Samuels, Shirley C., 1990, Ideal Adoption: A Comprehensive Guide to Forming an Adoptive Family. New York: Plenum.

Schaffer, Judith, and Christina Lindstrom, 1989, How to Raise an Adopted Child. A Guide to Help Your Child Flourish from Infancy through Adolescence. New York: Penguin Books.

Schneider, David M., 1984, A Critique of the Study of Kinship. Ann Arbor: University of Michigan Press.

Silk, Joan, 1980, Adoption and Kinship in Oceania. American Anthropologist 82(4): 799–820.

Webster, Steven, 1975, Cognatic Descent Groups and the Contemporary Maori: A Preliminary Reassessment. Journal of the Polynesian Society 84:121–152.

Weston, Kath, 1991, Families We Choose: Lesbians, Gays, Kinship. New York: Columbia University Press.

Wolf, Arthur, and Chieh-shan Huang, 1980, Marriage and Adoption in China, 1845–1945. Stanford: Stanford University Press.

POSTSCRIPT

Is It Natural for Adopted Children to Want to Find Out About Their Birth Parents?

Lifton's argument is clearly situated within the adoption rights movement and draws upon her personal experiences as much as on the experiences of those she has interviewed. She and her American informants clearly have a burning need to know who their birth parents are, and she concludes that it is unnatural for anyone to be deprived of this information. She and her informants feel a certain amount of psychic pain and emptiness, as well as lack of wholeness.

Terrell and Modell, on the other hand, argue that however real such feelings may be, they are cultural constructs rather than natural, biological ones. They cite examples from Pacific Island societies to show that such feelings are not human universals but culturally specific responses to a particular normative kinship structure.

This issue raises questions about just how "natural" are kinship systems in different societies. American society has long placed emphasis on biological families, just as Americans have long accepted biologically or physiologically based illnesses as more real than psychological ones. As Terrell and Modell note, some anthropologists have not found it easy to ignore their own culture's views on adoption. Nevertheless, they argue that anthropologist David Schneider was essentially correct in his description of American kinship. In *American Kinship: A Cultural Account* (Prentice-Hall, 1968), he argues that while Americans contend that kinship is about biological relatedness, in practice it is those who "act" like close kin who are accepted as one's closest kinsmen. Thus, it is the social behavior rather than the genetic relationship that is most important in shaping our social worlds.

To what extent do significantly higher rates of adoption in Oceania or other parts of the world challenge American views that biologically based parent-child relationships are inherently more "real" than socially constructed relationship created by adoption? How are we to explain the strongly held views of Lifton and other adoption rights advocates, who clearly feel something lacking in their own lives if they do not and cannot know who their birth parents are?

Some of Lifton's other books include *Twice Born: Memoirs of an Adopted Daughter* (Penguin, 1977) and *Lost and Found: The Adoption Experience* (HarperCollins, 1988). Somewhat earlier versions of the same argument are provided by John Triseliotis's *In Search of Origins: The Experiences of Adopted People* (Routledge & Kegan Paul, 1973) and H. David Kirk's *Adoptive Kinship: A Modern Institution in Need of Reform* (Butterworths, 1981), as well as his *Shared Fate: A Theory and Method of Adoptive Relationships* (Ben-Simon Publications, 1984). See also David M. Brodzinsky, Marshall D. Schechter, and Robin M. Henig's *Being Adopted: The Lifelong Search for Self* (Doubleday, 1992).

Modell has written a more extended view of the cultural construction of American adoption in *Kinship With Strangers: Adoption and Interpretations of Kinship in American Culture* (University of California Press, 1994). For similar perspectives, see Karen March's *The Stranger Who Bore Me: Adoptee-Birth Mother Relationships* (University of Toronto Press, 1995) and Katarina Wegar's *Adoption, Identity and Kinship: The Debate Over Sealed Birth Records* (Yale University Press, 1997). For a survey of current views of the problems of modern adoption, readers should consult a special issue of *Family Relations* (vol. 49, no. 4, October 2000), edited by Karen March and Charlene Miall.

For discussions of adoption in Pacific Island cultures, see *Adoption in Eastern Oceania* (University of Hawaii Press, 1970), edited by Vern Carroll. See also Jocelyn Linnekin and Lin Poyer's collection, *Cultural Identity and Ethnicity in the Pacific* (University of Hawaii Press, 1990), and Mac Marshall's essay "The Nature of Nurture," *American Ethnologist* (vol. 4, 1977).

ISSUE 9

Do Sexually Egalitarian Societies Exist?

YES: Maria Lepowsky, from *Fruit of the Motherland: Gender in an Egalitarian Society* (Columbia University Press, 1993)

NO: Steven Goldberg, from "Is Patriarchy Inevitable?" *National Review* (November 11, 1996)

ISSUE SUMMARY

YES: Cultural anthropologist Maria Lepowsky argues that among the Vanatinai people of Papua New Guinea, the sexes are basically equal, although minor areas of male advantage exist. Men and women both have personal autonomy; they both have similar access to material possessions, influence, and prestige; and the activities and qualities of males and females are valued equally.

NO: Sociologist Steven Goldberg contends that in all societies men occupy most high positions in hierarchical organizations and most high-status roles, and they dominate women in interpersonal relations. He states that this is because men's hormones cause them to compete more strongly than women for high status and dominance.

In most of the world's societies, men hold the majority of leadership positions in public organizations, from government bodies, to corporations, to religious institutions. In families, husbands usually serve as heads of households and as primary breadwinners, while wives take responsibility for children and homes. Is the predominance of men universal and inevitable, a product of human nature, or is it a cultural fact that might vary or be absent under different circumstances? Are sexually egalitarian societies—in which men and women are equally valued and have equal access to possessions, power, and prestige—even possible?

Some nineteenth-century cultural evolutionists, including J. J. Bachofen and J. F. MacLellan, postulated that a matriarchal stage of evolution, in which women ruled, had preceded the patriarchal stage known to history. Today most anthropologists doubt that matriarchal societies ever existed, but it is well established that some societies trace descent matrilineally, through women, and that in these societies women generally play a more prominent public role than in patrilineal ones, where descent is traced from father to children.

169

Whether or not matriarchal societies ever existed, by the twentieth century European and American societies were firmly patriarchal. Most people considered this state of affairs not only natural but God-given. Both Christian and Jewish religions gave scriptural justification for the predominance of men and the subordination of women.

The anthropology of women (later termed "feminist anthropology"), which arose in the early 1970s, challenged the claim that the subordination of women was either natural or inevitable. The rallying cry of feminists was "Biology is not destiny." Women, it was said, could do anything society permits them to do, and patriarchal society, like any other social institution, could be changed.

Some feminist anthropologists considered male dominance to be universal but attributed it to universal cultural, not biological, causes. The groundbreaking volume *Woman, Culture, and Society*, Michelle Rosaldo and Louise Lamphere, eds. (Stanford University Press, 1974) presents some possible cultural reasons for universal male dominance. Rosaldo and Lamphere proposed that all societies distinguish between "domestic" and "public" domains and that women are always associated with the domestic domain, with the home and the raising of children, while men are active in the public domain, where they have opportunities to obtain wealth, power, and ties with other men.

Some anthropologists contend that sexually egalitarian societies once existed (e.g., Eleanor Leacock's "Women's Status in Egalitarian Society: Implications for Social Evolution," *Current Anthropology* [vol. 19, 1978]). They attribute the scarcity of such societies today to historical circumstances, particularly the spread of European patriarchal culture to the rest of the world through colonialism and Christian missionization.

In her selection, Maria Lepowsky argues that in the Vanatinai culture of Sudest Island in Papua New Guinea, the sexes are basically equal. She describes the numerous features of Vanatinai culture, including social practices and beliefs, that make this possible. She contends that matrilineal descent is one contributing factor, but that it alone does not guarantee sexually egalitarian social relations.

Steven Goldberg counters that males have more of the hormones that cause individuals to strive for dominance than women do. Therefore, regardless of cultural variations, men occupy most positions in hierarchical organizations and most high-status roles, and they are dominant in interpersonal relations with women. Goldberg would argue that even in a matrilineal society like the Vanatinai, more men than women would occupy positions of power and prestige.

While reading these selections, ask yourself whether or not the Vanatinai case actually contradicts Goldberg's assertion that all societies are male dominated. Do you know of any other societies in which men and women are apparently equal? Would a single sexually egalitarian society disprove Goldberg's thesis? If you accept Goldberg's contention that males have an innate tendency toward domination, do you think that any cultural arrangements could neutralize this or keep it in check?

Maria Lepowsky

 **YES**

Gender and Power

Vanatinai customs are generally egalitarian in both philosophy and practice. Women and men have equivalent rights to and control of the means of production, the products of their own labor, and the products of others. Both sexes have access to the symbolic capital of prestige, most visibly through participation in ceremonial exchange and mortuary ritual. Ideologies of male superiority or right of authority over women are notably absent, and ideologies of gender equivalence are clearly articulated. Multiple levels of gender ideologies are largely, but not entirely, congruent. Ideologies in turn are largely congruent with practice and individual actions in expressing gender equivalence, complementarity, and overlap.

There are nevertheless significant differences in social influence and prestige among persons. These are mutable, and they fluctuate over the lifetime of the individual. But Vanatinai social relations are egalitarian overall, and sexually egalitarian in particular, in that at each stage in the life cycle all persons, female and male, have equivalent autonomy and control over their own actions, opportunity to achieve both publicly and privately acknowledged influence and power over the actions of others, and access to valued goods, wealth, and prestige. The quality of generosity, highly valued in both sexes, is explicitly modeled after parental nurture. Women are not viewed as polluting or dangerous to themselves or others in their persons, bodily fluids, or sexuality.

Vanatinai sociality is organized around the principle of personal autonomy. There are no chiefs, and nobody has the right to tell another adult what to do. This philosophy also results in some extremely permissive childrearing and a strong degree of tolerance for the idiosyncrasies of other people's behavior. While working together, sharing, and generosity are admirable, they are strictly voluntary. The selfish and antisocial person might be ostracized, and others will not give to him or her. If kinfolk, in-laws, or neighbors disagree, even with a powerful and influential big man or big woman, they have the option, frequently taken, of moving to another hamlet where they have ties and can expect access to land for gardening and foraging. Land is communally held by matrilineages, but each person has multiple rights to request and be given space to make a garden on land held by others, such as the mother's father's matrilineage. Respect and tolerance for the will and idiosyncrasies of individuals is reinforced by fear of their potential knowledge of witchcraft or sorcery.

Anthropological discussions of women, men, and society over the last one hundred years have been framed largely in terms of "the status of women," presumably unvarying and shared by all women in all social situations. Male dominance and female subordination have thus until recently been perceived as easily identified and often as human universals. If women are indeed universally subordinate, this implies a universal primary cause: hence the search for a single underlying reason for male dominance and female subordination, either material or ideological.

More recent writings in feminist anthropology have stressed multiple and contested gender statuses and ideologies and the impacts of historical forces, variable and changing social contexts, and conflicting gender ideologies. Ambiguity and contradiction, both within and between levels of ideology and social practice, give both women and men room to assert their value and exercise power. Unlike in many cultures where men stress women's innate inferiority, gender relations on Vanatinai are not contested, or antagonistic: there are no male versus female ideologies which vary markedly or directly contradict each other. Vanatinai mythological motifs, beliefs about supernatural power, cultural ideals of the sexual division of labor and of the qualities inherent to men and women, and the customary freedoms and restrictions upon each sex at different points in the life course all provide ideological underpinnings of sexual equality.

Since the 1970s writings on the anthropology of women, in evaluating degrees of female power and influence, have frequently focused on the disparity between the "ideal" sex role pattern of a culture, often based on an ideology of male dominance, publicly proclaimed or enacted by men, and often by women as well, and the "real" one, manifested by the actual behavior of individuals. This approach seeks to uncover female social participation, overt or covert, official or unofficial, in key events and decisions and to learn how women negotiate their social positions. The focus on social and individual "action" or "practice" is prominent more generally in cultural anthropological theory of recent years. Feminist analyses of contradictions between gender ideologies of female inferiority and the realities of women's and men's daily lives—the actual balance of power in household and community—have helped to make this focus on the actual behavior of individuals a wider theoretical concern.

In the Vanatinai case gender ideologies in their multiple levels and contexts emphasize the value of women and provide a mythological charter for the degree of personal autonomy and freedom of choice manifested in real women's lives. Gender ideologies are remarkably similar (though not completely, as I discuss [later]) as they are manifested situationally, in philosophical statements by women and men, in the ideal pattern of the sexual division of labor, in taboos and proscriptions. myth, cosmology, magic, ritual, the supernatural balance of power, and in the codifications of custom. Women are not characterized as weak or inferior. Women and men are valorized for the same qualities of strength, wisdom, and generosity. If possessed of these qualities an individual woman or man will act in ways which bring prestige not only to the actor but to the kin and residence groups to which she or he belongs.

Nevertheless, there is no single relationship between the sexes on Vanatinai. Power relations and relative influence vary with the individuals, sets of roles, situations, and historical moments involved. Gender ideologies embodied in myths, beliefs, prescriptions for role-appropriate behavior, and personal statements sometimes contradict each other or are contradicted by the behavior of individuals.

As Ortner points out, a great deal of recent social science theory emphasizes "the centrality of domination" and the analysis of "asymmetrical social relations" in which one group has more power than the other, as the key to understanding a social system. A focus upon asymmetry and domination also tends to presuppose its universality as a totalizing system of belief and practice and thus to distort analyses of gender roles and ideologies in places with egalitarian relations.

Gender Ideologies

... More men than women are widely known for their wealth of ceremonial valuables and their involvement in exchange and mortuary ritual. Still, Vanatinai is an equal opportunity society where this avenue to prestige and renown is open to both sexes. A few women are well known throughout the archipelago for their exceptional wealth, generosity, and participation in ritualized exchanges. All adult women as well as men are expected to participate in exchange to a certain minimum, particularly when a father, spouse, or close affine dies. Besides the opportunity to be the owner or the eater of a feast, women have an essential ritual role as life-givers, the role of principal female mourner who represents her matrilineage in the ritual work of compensating death to ensure the continuity of life.

Women have a complementary power base as life-givers in other spheres that counterbalances the asymmetry of men's tendency to be more heavily involved in exchange, an advantage that results in part from male powers to bring death. The most exclusive is of course the fact that women give birth to children. These children enrich and enlarge the kin group of the mother and her mothers, sisters, and brothers, ensuring the continuity and the life of the matrilineage itself. Her role of nurturer is highly valued, and the idiom of nurturing or feeding is applied as well to fathers, maternal uncles, and those who give ceremonial valuables to others. In ideological pronouncements she is called, by men and women alike, the owner of the garden, even though garden land is communally held by the matrilineage, and individual plots are usually worked with husbands or unmarried brothers. She is, in verbalized ideology of custom, the giver of yams, the ghanika moli, or true food, with which all human beings are nurtured, whether she grew them or her husband or brother. She is likely to raise pigs, which she exchanges or sacrifices at feasts. She is prominent in the life-giving work of healing, a form of countersorcery. And life-giving, Vanatinai people say, is more highly valued than the life-taking associated with male warfare and sorcery....

An overview of the life courses of males and females on Vanatinai and the ideologies of gender associated with them reveals two more potential sources of contradiction to prevailing ideologies of gender equivalence. One seems clear to an outside observer: men may have more than one wife, if they are strong enough to fulfill multiple affinal obligations and if the co-wives consent to enter into or remain in the marriage. Women may not have two husbands. Even though polygyny is rare, and women need not, and do not necessarily, agree to it, it is a customary and continuing form of marriage and an indication of gender asymmetries. A big man may distribute his procreative power and the strength of his affinal labor and personal wealth to two or more spouses and matrilineages, enlarging his influence and his reputation as a gia. Women may not....

Vanatinai menstrual taboos, such as those prohibiting the menstruating woman from visiting or working in a garden and, especially, from participating in the communal planting of yams, are multivalent cultural markers of female power. The symbolic complexity and multiple meanings of such taboos have been emphasized in recent writings on the anthropology of menstruation. Earlier anthropological constructions have emphasized the relation of menstrual taboos to ideologies of female pollution and thus, directly, of female inferiority or gender asymmetry. In the Vanatinai case there is no ideology of contamination through physical contact with the menstruating woman, who continues to forage, prepare food, and have sexual intercourse. Both men and women who have had intercourse in the last few days are barred from the new yam planting, and the genital fluids of both sexes are inimical, at this earliest and most crucial stage, to the growth of yams. (Later on, marital intercourse in the garden will help the yams to flourish.) Vanatinai menstrual taboos, which bar women from what islanders see as the most tedious form of subsistence labor, weeding gardens, are not regarded by women as a burden or curse but as a welcome interlude of relative leisure. Their predominant cultural meaning may be the ritual separation of the sacred power of female, and human, fertility and regeneration of life from that of plants, especially yams, whose parallels to humans are indicated by anthropomorphizing them in ritual spells. Menstrual taboos further mark woman as the giver of life to human beings.

The Sexual Division of Labor

Vanatinai custom is characterized by a marked degree of overlap in the sexual divisionof labor between what men normally do and what women do. This kind of overlap has been suggested as a primary material basis of gender equality, with the mingling of the sexes in the tasks of daily life working against the rise of male dominance.

Still, sorcerers are almost all male. Witches have less social power on Vanatinai and are blamed for only a small fraction of deaths and misfortunes. Only men build houses or canoes or chop down large trees for construction or clearing garden lands. Women are forbidden by custom to hunt, fish, or make war with spears, although they may hunt for possum and monitor lizard by climbing trees or setting traps and catching them and use a variety of other fishing methods. Despite the suppression of warfare men retain greater control of the powers that come with violence or the coercive threat of violent death.

Some Vanatinai women perceive an inequity in the performance of domestic chores. Almost all adult women are "working wives," who come home tired in the evening, often carrying both a young child in their arms and a heavy basket of yams or other produce on their heads for distances of up to three miles. They sometimes complain to their husbands or to each other that, "We come home after working in the garden all day, and we still have to fetch water, look for firewood, do the cooking and cleaning up and look after the children while all men do is sit on the verandah and chew betel nut!" The men usually retort that these are the work of women. Here is an example of contested gender roles.

Men are tender and loving to their children and often carry them around or take them along on their activities, but they do this only when they feel like it, and childcare is the primary responsibility of a mother, who must delegate it to an older sibling or a kinswoman if she cannot take care of the child herself. Women are also supposed to sweep the house and the hamlet ground every morning and to pick up pig excrement with a sago-bark "shovel" and a coconut-rib broom....

Vanatinai is not a perfectly egalitarian society, either in terms of a lack of difference in the status and power of individuals or in the relations between men and women. Women in young and middle adulthood are likely to spend more time on childcare and supervision of gardens and less on building reputations as prominent transactors of ceremonial valuables. The average woman spends more of her time sweeping up the pig excrement that dots the hamlet from the unfenced domestic pigs wandering through it. The average man spends more time hunting wild boar in the rain forest with his spear (although some men do not like to hunt). His hunting is more highly valued and accorded more prestige by both sexes than her daily maintenance of hamlet cleanliness and household order. The sexual division of labor on Vanatinai is slightly asymmetrical, despite the tremendous overlap in the roles of men and women and the freedom that an individual of either sex has to spend more time on particular activities—gardening, foraging, fishing, caring for children, traveling in quest of ceremonial valuables—and to minimize others.

Yet the average Vanatinai woman owns many of the pigs she cleans up after,and she presentsthempublicly during mortuary rituals and exchanges them with other men and women for shell-disc necklaces, long axe blades of polished greenstone, and other valuables. She then gains status, prestige, and influence over the affairs of others, just as men do and as any adult does who chooses to make the effort to raise pigs, grow large yam gardens, and acquire and distribute ceremonial valuables. Women who achieve prominence and distribute wealth, and thus gain an enhanced ability to mobilize the labor of others, are highly respected by both sexes. An overview of the life course and the sexual division of labor on Vanatinai reveals a striking lack of cultural restrictions upon the autonomy of women as well as men and the openness of island society to a wide variety of lifestyles....

Material and Ideological Bases of Equality

Does equality or inequality, including between men and women, result from material or ideological causes? We cannot say whether an idea preceded or followed specific economic and social circumstances. Does the idea give rise to the act, or does the act generate an ideology that justifies it or mystifies it? ...

On Vanatinai, where there is no ideology of male dominance, the material conditions for gender equality are present. Women—and their brothers—control the means of production. Women own land, and they inherit land, pigs, and valuables from their mothers, their mothers' brothers, and sometimes from their fathers equally with men. They have the ultimate decison-making power over the distribution of staple foods that belong jointly to their kinsmen and that their kinsmen or husbands have helped labor to grow. They are integrated into the prestige economy, the ritualized exchanges of ceremonial valuables. Ideological expressions, such as the common saying that the woman is the owner of the garden, or the well-known myth of the first exchange between two female beings, validate material conditions.

I do not believe it would be possible to have a gender egalitarian society, where prevailing expressions of gender ideology were egalitarian or valorized both sexes to the same degree, without material control by women of land, means of subsistence, or wealth equivalent to that of men. This control would encompass anything from foraging rights, skills, tools, and practical and sacred knowledge to access to high-paying, prestigious jobs and the knowledge and connections it takes to get them. Equal control of the means of production, then, is one necessary precondition of gender equality. Vanatinai women's major disadvantage is their lack of access to a key tool instrumental in gaining power and prestige, the spear. Control of the means of production is potentially greater in a matrilineal society.

Matriliny and Gender

... Matrilineal descent provides the preconditions favorable to the development of female political and economic power, but it does not ensure it. In the cases of Vanatinai, the Nagovisi, the Minangkabau, and the Hopi, matriliny, woman-centered postmarital residence (or the absence of a virilocal residence rule), female autonomy, extradomestic positions of authority, and ideologies of gender that highly value women seem closely connected. Nevertheless matriliny by itself does not necessarily indicate, or generate, gender equality. As earlier comparative studies of matrilineal societies have emphasized, in many cases brothers or husbands control the land, valuables, and persons of sisters and wives....

Gender Ideologies and Practice in Daily Life

... The small scale, fluidity, and mobility of social life on Vanatinai, especially in combination with matriliny, are conducive of egalitarian social relations between men and women and old and young. They promote an ethic of respect for the individual, which must be integrated with the ethic of cooperation essential for survival in a subsistence economy. People must work out conflict through face to face negotiation, or existing social ties will be broken by migration, divorce, or death through sorcery or witchcraft.

Women on Vanatinai are physically mobile, traveling with their families to live with their own kin and then the kin of their spouse, making journeys in quest of valuables, and attending mortuary feasts. They are said to have traveled for these reasons even in precolonial times when the threat of attack was a constant danger. The generally greater physical mobility of men in human societies is a significant factor in sexual asymmetries of power, as it is men who generally negotiate and regulate relationships with outside groups.

Vanatinai women's mobility is not restricted by ideology or by taboo, and women build their own far-ranging personal networks of social relationships. Links in these networks may be activated as needed by the woman to the benefit of her kin or hamlet group. Women are confined little by taboos or community pressures. They travel, choose their own marriage partners or lovers, divorce at will, or develop reputations as wealthy and generous individuals active in exchange.

Big Men, Big Women, and Chiefs

Vanatinai giagia, male and female, match Sahlin's classic description of the Melanesian big man, except that the role of gia is gender-blind. There has been renewed interest among anthropologists in recent years in the big man form of political authority. The Vanatinai case of the female and male giagia offers an intriguing perspective.

In the Massim, except for the Trobriand Islands, the most influential individuals are those who are most successful in exchange and who gain a reputation for public generosity by hosting or contributing significantly to mortuary feasts. Any individual on Vanatinai, male or female, may try to become known as a gia by choosing to exert the extra effort to go beyond the minimum contributions to the mortuary feasts expected of every adult. He or she accumulates ceremonial valuables and other goods both in order to give them away in acts of public generosity and to honor obligations to exchange partners from the local area as well as distant islands. There may be more than one gia in a particular hamlet, or even household, or there may be none. A woman may have considerably more prestige and influence than her husband because of her reputation for acquiring and redistributing valuables. While there are more men than women who are extremely active in exchange, there are some women who are far more active than the majority of men.

Giagia of either sex are only leaders in temporary circumstances and if others wish to follow, as when they host a feast, lead an exchange expedition, or organize the planting of a communal yam garden. Decisions are made by consensus, and the giagia of both sexes influence others through their powers of persuasion, their reputations for ability, and their knowledge, both of beneficial magic and ritual and of sorcery or witchcraft....

Images of Gender and Power

... On Vanatinai power and influence over the actions of others are gained by achievement and demonstrated superior knowledge and skill, whether in the realm of gardening, exchange, healing, or sorcery. Those who accumulate a surplus of resources are expected to be generous and share with their neighbors or face the threat of the sorcery or witchcraft of the envious. Both women and men are free to build their careers through exchange. On the other hand both women and men are free not to strive toward renown as gia-gia but to work for their own families or simply to mind their own business. They can also achieve the respect of their peers, if they seek it at all, as loving parents, responsible and hard-working lineage mates and affines, good gardeners, hunters, or fishers, or skilled healers, carvers, or weavers....

✦❋✦

What can people in other parts of the world learn from the principles of sexual equality in Vanatinai custom and philosophy? Small scale facilitates Vanatinai people's emphasis on face-to-face negotiations of interpersonal conflicts without the delegation of political authority to a small group of middle-aged male elites. It also leaves room for an ethic of respect for the will of the individual regardless of age or sex. A culture that is egalitarian and nonhierarchical overall is more likely to have egalitarian relations between men and women.

Males and females on Vanatinai have equivalent autonomy at each life cycle stage. As adults they have similar opportunities to influence the actions of others. There is a large amount of overlap between the roles and activities of women and men, with women occupying public, prestige-generating roles. Women share control of the production and the distribution of valued goods, and they inherit property. Women as well as men participate in the exchange of valuables, they organize feasts, they officiate at important rituals such as those for yam planting or healing, they counsel their kinfolk, they speak out and are listened to in public meetings, they possess valuable magical knowledge, and they work side by side in most subsistence activities. Women's role as nurturing parent is highly valued and is the dominant metaphor for the generous men and women who gain renown and influence over others by accumulating and then giving away valuable goods.

But these same characteristics of respect for individual autonomy, role overlap, and public participation of women in key subsistence and prestige domains of social life are also possible in large-scale industrial and agricultural societies. The Vanatinai example suggests that sexual equality is facilitated by an overall ethic of respect for and equal treatment of all categories of individuals, the decentralization of political power, and inclusion of all categories of persons (for example, women and ethnic minorities) in public positions of authority and influence. It requires greater role overlap through increased integration of the workforce, increased control by women and minorities of valued goods—property, income, and educational credentials—and increased recognition of the social value of parental care. The example of Vanatinai shows that the subjugation of women by men is not a human universal, and it is not inevitable. Sex role patterns and gender ideologies are closely related to overall social systems of power and prestige. Where these systems stress personal autonomy and egalitarian social relations among all adults, minimizing the formal authority of one person over another, gender equality is possible.

NO

Steven Goldberg

Is Patriarchy Inevitable?

In five hundred years the world, in all likelihood, will have become homogenized. The thousands of varied societies and their dramatically differing methods of socialization, cohesion, family, religion, economy, and politics will have given way to a universal culture. Fortunately, cultural anthropologists have preserved much of our present diversity, which may keep our descendants from too hastily allowing their natural human ego- and ethno-centricity to conclude that theirs is the only way to manage a society.

However, the anthropological sword is two-edged. While diversity is certainly apparent from anthropological investigations, it is also clear that there are realities which manifest themselves no matter what the varied forms of the aforementioned institutions. Because these universal realities cut across cultural lines, they are crucial to our understanding of what society *by its nature* is and, perhaps, of what human beings are. It is important, then, that we ask why, when societies differ as much as do those of the Ituri Pygmy, the Jivaro, the American, the Japanese, and a thousand others, some institutions are universal.

It is always the case that the universal institution serves some need rooted in the deepest nature of human beings. In some cases the explanation of universality is obvious (e.g., why every society has methods of food gathering). But there are other universalities which are apparent, though without any obvious explanation. Of the thousands of societies on which we have any evidence stronger than myth (a form of evidence that would have us believe in cyclopes), there is no evidence that there has ever been a society failing to exhibit three institutions:

1. Primary hierarchies always filled primarily by men.   A Queen Victoria or a Golda Meir is always an exception and is always surrounded by a government of men. Indeed, the constraints of royal lineage may produce more female societal leaders than does democracy—there were more female heads of state in the first two-thirds of the sixteenth century than there were in the first two-thirds of the twentieth.

2. The highest status roles are male.   There are societies in which the women do most of the important economic work and rear the children, while the men seem mostly to hang loose. But, in such societies, hanging loose is given higher status than any non-maternal role primarily served by women. No doubt this is partly due to the fact that the males hold the positions of power. However, it is also likely that high-status roles are male not primarily because they are male (ditch-digging is male and low status), but because they are high status. The high status roles are male because they possess—for whatever socially determined reason in whichever specific society—high status. This high status exerts a more powerful influence on males than it does on females. As a result, males are more willing to sacrifice life's other rewards for status dominance than are females.

In their *Not in Our Genes*, Richard Lewontin, Leon Kamin, and Stephen Rose—who, along with Stephen Jay Gould are the best-known defenders of the view that emphasizes the role of environment and de-emphasizes that of heredity—attempt to find fault with my work by pointing out that most family doctors in the Soviet Union are women. However, they acknowledge that in the Soviet Union "family doctoring [had] lower status than in the United States."

Which is precisely the point. No one doubts that women can be doctors. The question is why doctors (or weavers, or load bearers, etc.) are primarily women only when being a doctor is given lower status than are certain roles played mostly by men—and furthermore, why, even when this is the case (as in Russia) the upper hierarchical positions relevant to that specific area are held by men.

3. Dominance in male-female relationships is always associated with males. "Male dominance" refers to the feeling, of both men and women, that the male is dominant and that the woman must "get around" the male to attain power. Social attitudes may be concordant or discordant with the reality of male dominance. In our own society there was a time when the man's "taking the lead" was positively valued by most women (as 30s' movies attest); today such a view is purportedly detested by many. But attitudes toward male-dominance behavior are causally unimportant to the reality they judge—and are not much more likely to eliminate the reality than would a social dislike of men's being taller be able to eliminate men's being taller.

⁕⊙⁕

Over the past twenty years, I have consulted every original ethnographic work invoked to demonstrate an exception to these societal universalities. Twenty years ago many textbooks spoke cavalierly of "matriarchies" and "Amazons" and pretended that Margaret Mead had claimed to find a society in which sex roles were reversed. Today no serious anthropologist is willing to claim that any specific society has ever been an exception.

It is often claimed that "modern technology renders the physiological differentiation irrelevant." However, there is not a scintilla of evidence that modernization alters the basic "motivational" factors sufficiently to cast doubt on the continued existence of the universals I discuss. The economic needs of modern society probably do set a lower limit on the status of women; no modern society could give women the low status they receive in some non-modern societies. But modernization probably also sets an upper limit;

no modern society is likely to give women the status given to the maternal roles in some other matrilineal societies.

Scandinavian nations, which have long had government agencies devoted to equalizing women's position, are often cited by social scientists as demonstrating modernization's ability to override patriarchy. In fact, however, Norway has 454 municipal councils; 443 are chaired by men. On the Supreme Court, city courts, appellate courts, and in Parliament, there are between five and nine times as many men as there are women. In Sweden, according to government documents, men dominate "senior positions in employer and employee organizations as well as in political and other associations" and only 5 of 82 directors of government agencies, 9 of 83 chairpersons of agency boards, and 9 per cent of judges are women.

One may, of course, hope that all this changes, but one cannot invoke any evidence implying that it will.

Of course, there are those who simply try to assert away the evidence. Lewontin *et al.* write, "Cross cultural universals appear to lie more in the eye of the beholder than in the social reality that is being observed." In fact, with reference to the universalities mentioned above, they do not. If these universals were merely "in the eye of the beholder," the authors would merely have to specify a society in which there was a hierarchy in which males did not predominate and the case would be closed.

The answer to the question of why an institution is universal clearly must be parsimonious. It will not do to ascribe causation of a universal institution to capitalism or Christianity or modernization, because many hundreds of societies lacked these, but not the universal institutions. If the causal explanation is to be at all persuasive, it must invoke some factor present in every society from the most primitive to the most modern. (Invoking the male's physical strength advantage does meet the requirement of parsimony, but does not counter the evidence of the central importance of neuro-endocrinological psycho-physiological factors.)

When sociologists are forced to acknowledge the universals, they nearly always invoke "socialization" as explanation. But this explanation faces two serious problems. First, it does not explain anything, but merely forces us to ask another question: *Why* does socialization of men and women always work in the same direction? Second, the explanation implicitly assumes that the social environment of expectations and norms acts as an *independent* variable capable of acting as counterpoise to the physiological constituents that make us male and female.

In individual cases, of course, anything can happen.

Even when a causation is nearly entirely hereditary, there are many exceptions (as tall women demonstrate). Priests choose to be celibate, but this does not cast doubt on the physiological basis of the "sex drive." To be sure, there is also feedback from the environmental to the physiological, so that association of physical strength with males results in more males lifting weights. However, in principle, a society could find itself with women who were physically stronger than men if women lifted weights throughout their lives and men remained sedentary.

But, in real life, this can't happen because the social environment is a *dependent* variable whose limits are set by our physiological construction. In real life we all observe a male's dominance tendency that is rooted in physiological differences between males and females and, because values and attitudes are not of primary causal importance here, we develop expectations concordant with the male–emale behavioral differences.

Most of the discussion of sex differences has emphasized the neuroendocrinological differentiation of males and females and the cognitive and behavioral differentiation this engenders. This is because there is an enormous amount of evidence demonstrating the role of hormones in fetally differentiating the male and female central nervous systems, CNS response to the potentiating properties of certain hormones, and the thoughts and actions of males and females.

There is not room here for detailed discussion of the neuro-endocrinological mechanism underlying dominance behavior. But a useful analogy is iron and magnet. Iron does not have a "drive" or a "need" to find a magnet, but when there is a magnet in the area, iron, as a result of the very way it is built, tends to react in a certain way. Likewise, the physiological natures of males and females predispose them to have different hierarchies of response to various environmental cues. There is no response that only one sex has; the difference between men and women is the relative strengths of different responses. Males react more readily to hierarchical competitiveness than do females; females react more readily to the needs of an infant-in-distress. Norms and socialization do not cause this difference, but reflect it and make concrete a specific society's specific methods for manifesting the response. (Cleaning a rifle and preparing Spaghetti-Os are not instinctive abilities).

The iron–magnet analogy makes clear the role of social environment. Were there to be a society without hierarchy, status, values, or interdependence of the sexes, there would be no environmental cue to elicit the differentiated, physiologically rooted responses we discuss. But it is difficult to imagine such a society and, indeed, there has never been such a society.

Even if we had no neuro-endocrinological evidence at all, the anthropological evidence alone would be sufficient to force us to posit a mechanism of sexual psycho-physiological differentiation and to predict its discovery. We do, however, possess the neuro-endocrinological evidence and the anthropological evidence permits us to specify the institutional effects—the limits of societal variation that the neuro-endocrinological engenders.

For thousands of years, everyone, save perhaps some social scientists and others ideologically opposed to the idea, have known perfectly well that men and women differ in the physiological factors that underlie masculine and feminine thought and behavior. They may not have known the words to describe the linkage of physiology with thought and behavior, but they knew the linkage was there. (I recently read a comment of a woman in Pennsylvania: "They keep telling us that men and women are the way they are because of what they've been taught, but you can go a hundred miles in any direction and not find a single person who really believes that.") And even the most feminist parent, once she has children, can't help but notice that it is nearly impossible to get small boys to play with dolls not named "Killer Joe, the Marauding Exterminator," or at least with trucks—big trucks.

≈⧉≈

None of this is to deny tremendous variation on the level of roles. Even in our own society, in just a century the role of secretary changed from virtually solely male to virtually solely female. With the exception of roles associated with child nurturance, political leadership, warfare, security, and crime, virtually every specific role is male in some societies and female in others. No one doubts that the women who exhibit the dominance behavior usually exhibited by men encounter discrimination. But the question remains: why is dominance behavior usually exhibited by *men*?

The implication of all this depends on context. Clearly the correctness or incorrectness of the theory I present is important to an understanding of human behavior and society. But to the individual man or woman, on the other hand, the universals are largely irrelevant. The woman who wishes to become President has a sufficient number of real-life equivalents to know that there is not a constraint rendering impossible a female head of state. But there is no more reason for such a woman to deny that the motivation to rule is more often associated with male physiology than there is for the six-foot woman to pretend that women are as tall as men.

POSTSCRIPT

Do Sexually Egalitarian Societies Exist?

In these two selections, Lepowsky and Goldberg disagree both on the interpretation of the facts and on the types of forces, cultural or biological, that determine relations between the sexes. Lepowsky argues that Vanatinai culture is basically sexually egalitarian and that this is due to a particular constellation of social and ideological features of their culture. Goldberg contends that men are dominant in every culture—the Vanatinai people would be no exception—and that men's innate drive to dominate would lead them to occupy most of the positions of authority and high status and to dominate women in interpersonal relations.

During the last 30 years, anthropologists have conducted many studies focusing specifically on gender ideas and roles in particular societies, especially in non-Western and tribal societies. Their general finding is that gender relations are much more complicated and variable than scholars thought in the early days of feminist anthropology. For example, studies have shown that not all societies make a simple distinction between domestic and public domains, associate women exclusively with a domestic domain, or evaluate activities outside the home as superior to those inside it. Scholars have also realized that analytical concepts like "male dominance" and the "status of women" are too crude. They have attempted to break them up into components that can be sought and measured in ethnographic field studies.

The question of whether or not males are dominant in a particular society is not as clear-cut as it once seemed. One important distinction now made, and reflected in Lepowsky's excerpt, is that between the actual practice of male-female roles and interactions and the ideologies that contain bases for evaluating the sexes and their activities. Studies show that in some societies women and men have similar amounts of influence over daily life, but the cultural ideology (or at least the men's ideology) portrays women as inferior to men. In some cases men's and women's spheres of activity and control are separate and independent. Some societies have competing ideologies, in which both men and women portray their own gender as superior. And some societies, such as the Hua of Papua New Guinea, have multiple ideologies, which simultaneously present women as inferior, superior, and equal to men (see Anna Meigs's book *Food, Sex, and Pollution: A New Guinea Religion* [Rutgers University Press, 1984]). Despite these complications, it may still be useful to term a culture in which both practice and ideology consistently point to equality or balance between the sexes as "sexually egalitarian," as Lepowsky does in the case of the Vanatinai. Of course Goldberg would say that such societies do not exist.

For more information on the Vanatinai people, see Lepowsky's book *Fruit of the Motherland: Gender in an Egalitarian Society* (Columbia University Press, 1993). A very readable introduction to feminist anthropology is Henrietta Moore's book *Feminism and Anthropology* (University of Minnesota Press, 1988). An interesting collection of articles showing variations in male-female relations is Peggy Sanday and Ruth Goodenough's edited volume *Beyond the Second Sex: New Directions in the Anthropology of Gender* (University of Pennsylvania Press, 1990). For a discussion of gender equality and inequality among hunter-gatherers, see Karen L. Endicott's article "Gender Relations in Hunter-Gatherer Societies," in *The Cambridge Encyclopedia of Hunters and Gatherers,* Richard B. Lee and Richard Daly, eds. (Cambridge University Press, 1999).

For a full explication of Goldberg's theory of innate male dominance, see his book *Why Men Rule: A Theory of Male Dominance* (Open Court, 1993). Other works that argue for a biological basis for male dominance include Lionel Tiger's book *Men in Groups* (Holt, Rinehart & Winston, 1969); Lionel Tiger and Robin Fox's book *The Imperial Animal* (Holt, Rinehart & Winston, 1971); Robert Wright's article "Feminists Meet Mr. Darwin," *The New Republic* (November 28, 1994); and Barbara Smuts's article "The Origins of Patriarchy: An Evolutionary Perspective," in A. Zagarell's edited volume *Origins of Gender Inequality* (New Issues Press, in press).

ISSUE 10

Has the Islamic Revolution in Iran Subjugated Women?

YES: Parvin Paidar, from "Feminism and Islam in Iran," in Deniz Kandiyoti, ed., *Gendering the Middle East: Emerging Perspectives* (Syracuse University Press, 1996)

NO: Erika Friedl, from "Sources of Female Power in Iran," in Mahnaz Afkhami and Erika Friedl, eds., *In the Eye of the Storm: Women in Post-Revolutionary Iran* (Syracuse University Press, 1994)

ISSUE SUMMARY

YES: Iranian historian Parvin Paidar considers how the position of women suffered following the 1979 Iranian Revolution because of the imposition of Islamic law (*shari'a*), as interpreted by conservative male clerics. She contends that the Islamic Revolution marked a setback in the progressive modernist movements, which had improved women's rights during the secular regime of the Shah; new rights and opportunities have emerged since 1979 only in opposition to conservative interpretations of Islamic law.

NO: American anthropologist Erika Friedl asserts that men in Iran have consistently tried to suppress women's rights since the 1979 Iranian Revolution. Despite these efforts to repress them, women in all levels of society have access to many sources of power. In fact, argues Friedl, women have considerably more power available to them than either Western or Iranian stereotypes might suggest, even though they must work within Islamic law to obtain this power.

Perhaps nowhere has Islam's role in shaping the position of women been more obvious than in Afghanistan where the theocratic Taliban regime prevented women from working outside the home, from attending school, and from participating in the political process in any meaningful way. In Iran one of the effects of the 1979 revolution was that women suddenly lost most of the rights they had gradually obtained over the previous century. In both countries religious leaders have defended their actions and policies in terms of Islamic law, or *shari'a*, leading many Western observers to argue that this legal code inherently subjugates women. However, Muslim clerics have long argued that Islamic law does not subjugate women but merely defines men's and women's roles in society in complementary ways as prescribed by God.

At issue is whether or not Islamic customs, such as wearing head scarves, necessarily subordinate and subjugate women, as many feminist observers have argued. Or does Islamic law as interpreted by conservative male clerics merely delineate complementary social roles for men and women, as many Muslim scholars and religious leaders insist? Most importantly, if *shari'a* does not inherently subjugate women, why is it that the reimposition of *shari'a* law in the late twentieth century has so often included the loss of rights for Muslim women rather than enhancing their legal protections? In these countries, the more anti-Western and fundamentalist the religious and political leaders have become, the lower the apparent position of women.

Islam has traditionally depicted women as the weaker sex, in need of protection from the men in their lives. Such a view has shaped the social roles available to Islamic women in both conservative and progressive Muslim countries. Women in most Muslim countries have a much less obvious political voice in the affairs of the state than in Western countries, since politics is defined in Islamic law as the domain of men. But many observers have argued that within the household, women have considerably more power than Western observers have generally acknowledged.

The following selections consider the role and position of women in Iran. Parvin Paidar, herself an Iranian, documents the changing position of women since the nineteenth century. Here, she shows how women were able to draw on Western feminist ideas during the reign of the Shah to gain individual rights and improve the status of women. But when the Ayatollah Khomeini took control following the 1979 revolution, women's rights were sharply and suddenly curtailed. All of these changes were justified by the need to return to the "true" faith, as outlined in *shari'a* law. For Paidar, improvements in women's position in society have only been possible following Khomeini's death, when less conservative and more secular voices have emerged.

Erika Friedl acknowledges that Iranian women do not have the rights enjoyed by most Western women. But she argues that, working within conservative readings of Islamic law, Iranian women have many sources of power available to them. Such power can emerge in part through resistance to male authority. Or Iranian women can achieve control over their own lives and over the lives of their sons and husbands through work, religion, and the government itself. In a male-dominated society such as Iran, women have many "weapons of the weak" at their disposal, believes Friedl, with which they can achieve power within their households.

Parvin Paidar

 **YES**

Feminism and Islam in Iran

Feminism(s) in the Middle East and their articulations with Islam have attracted substantial interest in recent years. This [selection] will focus on the interaction between feminism and Islam in Iran. It will trace, in general terms, the development of feminism in that country and the ways in which it has interacted with Islam at various historical moments since the turn of the century. While in recent decades feminisms in the Arab Middle East by and large make reference to utopian Islam(s) to defend women's rights, in Iran the interaction between feminism and Islam has taken place in the context of a militant Shi'i state which claims to have implemented 'true Islam'. The contrast between these contexts may provide a useful contribution to an understanding of the interaction between feminism and Islam in various Middle Eastern contexts.

The approach adopted in this [selection] emanates from the view that far from being an optional extra, gender is situated at the heart of political discourses in Iran. Indeed, any political discourse aiming at the social reorganization of Iranian society has necessarily entailed a redefinition of gender relations and of women's position in society. Therefore, this [selection] will place the interaction between Islam and feminism in the broader context of political process in twentieth-century Iran.

Early Twentieth-Century Nationalist Feminism

In tracing the historical development of feminism in relation to Islam, a natural starting point would be the constitutional movement of the early twentieth century, since this was the context within which the 'woman question' was first explicitly raised in Iran.

The Constitutional Revolution of 1906–11 took place against the background of Western intrusion and the rise of nationalism. It revolved around the demand for constitutional monarchy to curb the power of the monarch in favour of the power of parliament and the rule of law on the one hand, and to protect Iran's national interests in the face of Western economic and political intervention on the other. It rested upon a diverse urban alliance which included merchants, traders, land owners, secular intellectuals and the Shi'i clergy. The importance of the constitutional movement for women was in the creation of a particular vision of modern Iran. The concept of modernity encapsulated justice, democracy, independence and women's emancipation. The movement created a conceptual link between national independence and progress and women's emancipation. It constructed women as social actors for the first time and facilitated the formation of a network of women's rights activists which gradually developed into a loosely formed women's movement.

Since the very idea of women's emancipation was grounded in the need for national progress, women activists prioritized the general developmental gains implicit in the improvement of women's position. The main demands of the women's movement included education and the abolition of practices such as seclusion and early marriage, which were regarded as serious impediments to women's contribution to national development. The way in which women's emancipation became associated with national progress during the constitutional period, created a generic link between feminism and nationalism which has shaped the course of Iranian feminism ever since. This has had at least two consequences. First, it has made it impossible to talk about the interaction between feminism and Islam without taking into account the links between Islam and nationalism. Second, this has been one of the main reasons why individualistic types of feminism based on women's personal experience and individual choice, a stance commonly associated with feminism in the West, have not developed in Iran.

The type of nationalism that developed in Iran in the first half of the century was on the whole secular. It was constructed as an alternative discourse, as Islam was associated with traditionalism and backwardness. During the constitutional period, secular intellectuals played an important role in constructing concepts such as constitutionalism, nationalism, modernity and women's emancipation.... Babism was ... one of the main indigenous sources of inspiration for women's emancipation at the turn of the century since one of its female protagonists Tahereh Qorrat ol-Eyn took off her veil in public and challenged the *ulama* (Muslim clergy) to debate women's position with her.

From the beginning of this century, then, the concept of women's emancipation became grounded in concepts associated with nationalism and modernity.... However, the debate on women was conducted in a way which avoided outright confrontation with religion. Feminists of this period complained against social conservatism rather than Islam as such. For example, Bibi Khanum Astarabadi argued that 'The obstacle to women's emancipation is not Islam but the male interest to preserve his privileges....'

Although the secular debate on women avoided outright opposition to Islam, nevertheless the expression of ideas inspired by non-Islamic sources was considered to be a serious threat by many Shi'i clerics. The Shi'i establishment focused on opposing the practical steps taken to emancipate women. For example, the opening of each new school for women was accompanied by a campaign by local mollahs to close it down. This is not to say that the clergy were united on the question of women's education—on the contrary....

[W]hile women's protests against subordination were conducted within an acceptable cultural framework which avoided overt criticism of Islam, the main point of reference for these women was secular nationalism. The secular nature of early twentieth-century feminism was strengthened further in the post-Constitutional period as a result of two particular developments; the rise of socialism and establishment of the Bolshevik state across the border in Russia and the emergence of the state as an agent of social reform....

The emergence of the state as an agent of social reform was an even more important development affecting Iranian feminism in the early part of the century. The state established by Reza Shah Pahlavi in 1925 had a nationalist outlook and valorized pre-Islamic Iran. It set out to transform Iran from a dependent, backward society to a modern, independent nation-state and as a result the state became the initiator and implementor of social reform and assumed responsibility for the health, welfare and education of the population, at least in rhetoric.

Statist Feminism and the Rise of Cultural Nationalism in Mid-Twentieth-Century Iran

However, in imposing reform on women's position, Reza Shah's state adopted a forceful and centralist approach and ended an era of women's independent activities by creating a state-sponsored women's organization to lead the way on women's emancipation. The measures proclaimed included compulsory unveiling, free education and, potentially, the creation of new employment opportunities. These measures had been demanded by many constitutionalists and feminists since the turn of the century, and by implementing them the state took the initiative on women's issues away from independent socialists, liberal nationalists and feminists. With a silent Shi'i establishment, co-opted nationalism, a suppressed socialist movement, and a partly co-opted, partly suppressed women's movement, the only voice allowed on behalf of women was that of the state.

The second Pahlavi state, established in 1941 after the abdication of Reza Shah in favour of his son, Mohammad Reza Shah, continued the same pattern of modernization, co-option and political suppression. The initial period of constitutional rule under the Shah resulted in the formation of a short-lived liberal nationalist government by Mohammad Mosaddeq who led a coalition of nationalist forces. The nationalist government, however, did not have a specific gender agenda and its half-hearted attempt to introduce a new electoral bill which included enfranchisement for women failed. A CIA-sponsored coup in 1953 against Mosaddeq restored the Shah's autocratic rule. The post-coup period of 1960s and 1970s witnessed heightened suppression of most autonomous political groupings. But it also resulted in further state initiatives on women's rights. The campaign for political rights conducted by prominent feminists, such as Fatemeh Sayyah, had some success despite substantial opposition by the clergy.

The 1960s and 1970s also saw the growth of cultural nationalism and Islamic modernism. This occasioned a shift in the interaction between feminism, nationalism and Islam. The rise of cultural nationalism as a new political force closely associated with Islam resulted in the Shi'i establishment reclaiming lost moral ground on women and family issues as a result of several new developments.

First, on the religious front, after the death in 1961 of Ayatollah Borujerdi, the highest Shi'i authority of his time, a group of high-ranking clerics shared similar high status and gained their own followers. These Ayatollahs, including Khomeini, published and circulated widely their religious opinions on a broad range of issues, including women and the family. These religious views about women's position found political expression in a campaign by an Iranian version of the Muslim Brotherhood in the 1960s which presented a new fundamentalist defence of the Shi'i *shari'a* on women.

Second, on the political front, reformist clerics such as Ayatollah Motahhari and lay religious radicals such as Ali Shari'ati articulated new models of Muslim womanhood for Iranian women. The ideas of Shari'ati were adopted by the Mojahedin-e Khalq, who represented the Islamic tendency within the Marxist-Leninist guerrilla movement of the 1960s and 1970s which led a crusade against the Pahlavi state.

The success of these new Islamic trends in regaining the initiative on women and the family was due to both ideological and political factors. The Pahlavi state's unwillingness to introduce fundamental changes on women's position within the family enabled the Shi'i establishment to regain the initiative fairly easily. Both Reza Shah and Mohammad Reza Shah focused their reforms on the civic aspects of women's roles as opposed to the familial ones. Despite tremendous opposition by the Shi'i establishment, both Pahlavi regimes pushed forward with women's education, unveiling and de-segregation, while the reforms that they carried out on the family remained relatively limited. Pahlavi reforms did not go beyond a codification of traditional Shi'i law on women and family as part of the Civil Code of 1936, and an attempt to limit arbitrary male power in the family through the introduction of Family Protection Laws in 1967 and 1975. These limitations were due not so much to clerical opposition as to deeper concerns about the wider implications of granting women real power and independence within the family. The Pahlavi regimes opposed women's independence in the family and their independent presence in the public sphere, and this influenced the logic behind state-sponsored women's organizations which made sure that women's lives inside and outside the home remained under the control of male guardians. This strengthened the clergy's ideological hold over matters concerning women and the family, which was translated so effectively into a successful political campaign by the Shi'i movement during the 1970s.

However, the existence of new Shi'i ideas on women would not by itself have affected feminism in Iran if the political developments of the 1970s had not pushed them to the forefront. The rise of Shi'ism as a serious modern political movement in the context of anti-Shah politics became a major factor in the adoption of Shi'i ideas on women. The revolutionary context provided fertile ground for the first serious confrontation of secular feminisms (such as statist and socialist feminism) by political Islam. For the first time, Islamic activism became a serious political option for Iranian women, and many women from the younger generation who were totally alienated from state feminism took it up. The Pahlavi state's claim to be liberating women was politically untenable; the nationalist opposition was not able to present an alternative gender policy to that of the state and the socialist alternative only attracted a small minority of women. As a result, the campaign on women's issues became the preserve of the Islamic opposition.

The Islamic campaign on women included appeals to reject 'Westernization' and the exploitation of women as 'sex objects' which was seen as the consequence of Iran's economic and cultural dependence on the West. Instead, women were urged to embrace the new Shi'i model of womanhood which represented 'authenticity' and 'independence' and emphasized women's dual role as mothers and revolutionaries. This found credence with large groups among both religious and secular women because it promised political freedom, economic equality, social justice, cultural integrity and personal fulfilment. It facilitated women's massive participation in the Revolution of 1979.

The contrast between women's participation in the 1979 Revolution and the earlier Constitutional Revolution could not be sharper, and was rooted in the different interactions between Islam and feminism in each revolutionary period. The 1979 Revolution was the second attempt in this century, apart from the brief Mosaddeq period, to redefine and change existing relations between the state and Western powers with the aim of establishing independence and democracy in Iran. But while the former revolutionary movement aimed to achieve this through emulation of the Western liberal model of society, the latter aimed to achieve it by constructing an 'indigenous' and 'authentic' Islamic model of society in Iran. Moreover, while the flavour of the first revolutionary discourse was that of a liberal nationalism associated with secularism, the second revolved around a cultural nationalism associated with Islam.

In summary, Iranian feminism was essentially secular until the rise of Shi'i modernism in the 1970s. It was only then that the new trend of Islamist feminism (gender activism within an Islamic framework) joined other feminisms in Iran.

Islamist Feminism and State Policy in the Islamic Republic

Let us now consider the development of Islamist feminism under the Islamic Republic. After the establishment of the Islamic Republic, the new constitution gave a prominent place to women, defining them as mothers and citizens. It stressed that the establishment of an Islamic nation was dependent on the Islamization of women and constructed the ideal Islamic woman in opposition to Western values on womanhood. The constitution attempted to create harmony between the Islamic family and nation by advocating a set of patriarchal relations to strengthen male control over women in the family on the one hand, and granting women the right to be active citizens on the other.

The link between nationalism and Islam was crucial in determining the gender policies of the Islamic Republic. After the Islamic Republic settled into a theocracy, nationalism as a mobilizing force was transformed and re-defined.

The state attempted this by constructing nationalism as synonymous with anti-imperialism on the one hand, and replacing nationalism with Islam as the main mass mobilization force on the other. The new alliance between Islam and anti-imperialism, for which historical precedents existed in Iran, constituted the cornerstone of the Islamization policy of the state. The context of revolutionary populism, anti-imperialism, the effects of a war economy and struggle for state power between Islamic factions determined which concepts and ideas on women were defined as 'Islamic' and which ones as 'un-Islamic'. The result was a significant reversal of the history of clerical opposition to women's participation in politics. For example, the same clerics who had in the 1960s objected to women's enfranchisement on religious grounds were in the 1980s prepared to grant women the right to vote in the name of Islam.

With regard to women's social role, the Islamic Republic formulated policies on women's education, employment and political participation to ensure the continuation of women's mass support. Women's political participation was approved because it legitimized the state's Islamization policies and created an image of popular support and stability internally and internationally. These policies, however, were based on the premise that women's presence outside the home had to be accompanied with a process of de-sexualization of male-female interaction to protect the Islamic family and nation from its harmful moral consequences. A number of policies were developed to ensure this.

First, the protection of the family required the strengthening of male privilege through the Islamization of the Iranian household. The Family Protection Law was abolished and the Civil Code of 1936 was reinstated. This meant that the modest safeguards created for women in matters of divorce, marriage, child custody and abortion were all revoked overnight. Second, an extensive policy of gender segregation and compulsory *hejab* (head cover and loose clothes) for women was implemented. Third, measures were introduced in order to police the integrity of the family. These measures became known as the 'anti-corruption crusade', with a broad definition of corruption covering any social mixing between men and women as well as adultery, homosexuality, consumption of drugs and alcohol, gambling and a whole range of leisure activities.

Having thus structured the social role of women, the post-revolutionary Islamic state encouraged the development of an Islamic women's movement to counter the threat posed by secular feminism. The spontaneous movement of secular women to defend their rights against the Islamic state was crushed and secular feminism was driven into exile. Like preceding secular regimes, the Islamic state has ensured that the women's movement remained under tight state control. Different factions of the state and the state-sponsored revolutionary organizations attempted to harness women's tremendous mobilization potential by creating platforms for Islamic women activists.

The hard-line factions of the state took control of women's mass mobilization by organizing mass rallies in support of state Islamization and against the secular and Islamic opposition. Women's mass support was also manipulated in relation to two other areas of importance to the survival of the state—elections and the war against Iraq.

While women from the lower classes provided the mass support that the Islamic regime needed, Islamic women leaders became involved in philanthropic, religious, and feminist activities. Many of the state-funded welfare agencies, health and education centres, charities and foundations were run by women. Women who managed such organizations often came from clerical families and were well-connected within the circle of Islamic leadership.

A third category of Islamist women took up feminist activities under the patronage of the moderate factions of the state. The Women's Society of the Islamic Revolution (WSIR) was founded soon after the Revolution by a group of women to preserve and build upon the revolutionary demand for a culturally authentic gender identity. The popular, formerly pro-Pahlavi, women's magazine, *Zan-e Ruz* (Woman of Today), was taken over by an editorial board of Islamic feminists and transformed into a popular Islamic women's magazine. These women tended to be highly educated, often with doctorates from Western universities, and professionals in various fields. Their activities included not only publishing women's magazines, but also running women's organizations and formulating Islamic policies on women.

During the post-revolutionary transitional period of 1979–81, Islamist feminists drew their support from the religious faction of the Provisional Government and later, in some cases, the office of President Banisadr. The same period witnessed the forceful imposition of a hasty Islamization programme by Ayatollah Khomeini. This went against the views of Islamist feminists who wanted instead a long-term, gradualist Islamization programme based on educating women about the values of Islam.

Islamist feminists set out to create a vision of the 'ideal Islamic society' and the role of women in it. The idealization of the future Islamic society entailed a critique of the past and the present. The Islamist feminist theory of women's oppression and liberation was constructed in opposition to 'traditional Islam'. 'True Islam', according to Islamic feminists, transcended the 'traditional, deviatory and colonized Islam' in relation to women. The failures of traditional Islam were seen as rooted in male-dominated culture and distorted interpretations of Islamic laws.

Ayatollah Khomeini's Islamization measures received coded criticisms from the Islamist feminists. Azam Taleghani and Zahra Rahnavard, two well-known activists, warned the authorities about the negative effects of forcing women to wear *hejab*. They proposed that the Islamic dress code should not be made specific to women but that both men and women should be required to wear simple and decent clothing which covers the body in a non-arousing, modest fashion. On the Islamic Republic's policy of excluding women from the judiciary, Islamic feminists argued that 'women's emotionality is not an acceptable ground for their exclusion from passing judgement,' and said that 'Muslim women should be able to take their legal problems to female judges as much as possible, just as they take their medical problems to female doctors.'

Despite the enormous enthusiasm of these women and initial expectation that they would make a major contribution to the Islamic Republic's gender policies, Islamist feminists were marginalized by the hard-line factions of the post-revolutionary government. Ayotallah Khomeini's tendency to ignore voices of moderation, together with repressive state policies, resulted in the radicalization of the feminist strand of the Islamist women's movement. During the politically extremist years of 1981–87 the voice of Islamic feminism was thus silenced almost completely.

This took place in the context of a diversity of Islamist opinions, political power struggles, political repression, ideological control, economic stagnation, war and international isolation. These developments affected the ability of the state to establish coherent policies or ensure their effective implementation. Although the general framework of state policies on women was defined by opposition to the Pahlavi regime and 'alien Western values', actual policies of Islamization were formulated in a heterogeneous and adhoc manner by a variety of agents with different and sometimes conflicting interests. The way this affected women can be seen in the pattern of their education and employment in this period. Although strongly encouraged in official rhetoric, in reality women's education and employment suffered from contradictory policies, the imposition of gender quotas and support for male dominance, combined with lack of co-ordination between the multiple centres of decision-making and lack of financial resources. Nevertheless, although the opportunities available to women were reduced, Islamization policies and mismanagement did not stop women's participation in education and employment.

The state also failed to deliver 'Islamic justice' in relation to women's position within the family. Women had been promised support for their 'natural' rights and roles. They were to receive economic and legal protection from the Islamic state and its male representatives in the home. In return, women were expected to prove their credentials as obedient wives, self-sacrificing mothers and active citizens. However, this equation failed to work in the actual political and economic circumstances of the Islamic Republic. On the contrary, measures such as the strengthening of male authority in the family not only failed to increase women's protection, but actually resulted in the reduction of women's familial rights and the deterioration of their material condition. The Islamic Republic may have given its female supporters the opportunity for popular political participation and a sense of righteousness and self-worth, but it seriously undermined women's position within the family and restricted their human rights.

All this gave greater credence to the cause of Islamist feminism. To survive during particularly repressive periods, Islamist feminists tried to be as non-controversial as possible, and in doing so they colluded extensively with state attacks on women's rights. The degree of loyalty to the state expected from Islamist feminists proved to be much higher than that expected from the pro-state feminists of the Pahlavi era. Despite this, the extremist years had a maturing effect on Islamic feminists. They realized that unless they established an autonomous existence and spoke out against state policy, women would continue to get a raw deal despite the state's claim to represent 'true Islam'. Thus, a small but vocal Islamist feminist opposition re-established itself in the late 1980s.

Since the late 1980s, Islamist feminists have been able to campaign for women's rights in a much more open and direct manner than before. They have also proved more successful in pressurizing the policy-makers to revise earlier restrictions on women's legal rights and to consider positive proposals for greater rights for women within an Islamic framework. The issues on which they have campaigned have included family, education, employment, political participation and hejab. On education and employment, which seem to be the most sophisticated and successful issues on which Islamic feminists have campaigned, discriminatory practices towards women have been scrutinized and proposals made for their eradication. One important achievement in this area has been the lifting of restrictions that had been placed on women's entry to technical, scientific and medical fields soon after the Revolution.

Campaigns on the family have focused on improving the balance of power between men and women in the family. The emphasis has been put on the concept of 'partnership between husband and wife' as opposed to the concept of 'male guardianship', which is the basis of the Civil Code. Islamist feminists have protested against the failure of state policy to 'facilitate the growth of women's talents and personality', 'preserve their rights in the sacred institution of family', 'protect the rights of unprotected women' and 'remove obstacles in the way of women's participation in economic, social and political activities.' The policies advocated include state remuneration for housewives and unmarried women, monogamy, automatic custody rights for mothers, protection against divorce without the wife's consent, the right of wives to half the family assets, and women's rights to undertake education, employment or travel without the consent of husbands or other male guardians.

However, despite achieving relative independence for their movement and having some success in persuading policy-makers to extend women's rights, Islamist women leaders have on the whole had limited opportunities to take on decision-making roles and have had a hard time gaining authority or influence in the Islamic polity. Only a handful have entered the Islamic parliament or the government. Eleven elections during the first decade of the Islamic Republic have produced in total only six women representatives in parliament, an even more tokenist minority than in the Pahlavi era....

Conclusion

This incursion into contemporary Iranian history demonstrates that gender issues have been at the heart of Iranian politics and that they have undergone complex and sometimes paradoxical transformations. This has been nowhere more apparent than under the Islamic Republic. Indeed, the transformation of Islamist feminism from post-Revolutionary idealism to realism and pragmatism of thelate1980s has been remarkable. This being the case it is no longer inconceivable to envisage strategic alliances between Iranian strands of secular and Islamist feminisms on women's rights issues. The frames of reference of the two traditions of gender activism are, of course, very different. Iranian Islamist feminism is theoretically rooted in cultural relativism and politically rooted in anti-imperialism, while the direction taken by Iranian secular feminism in exile in the last decade has been largely universalist, anti-religious and increasingly individualistic.

However, the severity and material reality of the problems faced by Iranian women have reduced the importance of these ideological differences. To illustrate this point, it will be useful to compare the experiences of feminists campaigning to improve family laws in the Pahlavi era with those under the Islamic Republic. It took about forty years for secular feminists of the Pahlavi era to change the family law from the Civil Code of 1936 to the Family Protection Law of 1975. In 1979, it took Ayatollah Khomeini one speech to demolish the Family Protection Law in a single blast; and since then it has taken Islamist feminists over twelve years to build it again bit by bit; the task has yet to be completed.

The same family laws which had been historically presented by the Pahlavi state as part of a process of secularization and which were opposed by the clergy as contrary to Islam and therefore demolished, are now being reinstated under the Islamic Republic. The difference does not seem to be in the Islamist or secular nature of the law but in the political priorities of the era. This has created a potential for co-operation and alliance amongst ideologically diverse feminisms. Old ideological enemies may turn into new political allies when it comes to resisting the onslaughts of male supremacy. Although these alliances may be fraught and fragile, they speak of Iranian women's will to act upon their gender interests.

Erika Friedl

Sources of Female Power in Iran

Reports of the position of women in Iran and in other Middle Eastern countries contain a seeming paradox: women are said to be subordinate to men, second-class citizens, oppressed, veiled, and confined, unequal to men legally and in access to resources. This gender inequity further is said to be validated, supported, and mystified by local gender ideologies and a superstructure formed by the teachings of the Quran and other religious scriptures, by Islamic law, and by folk notions about male–female differences. Yet, on the level of everyday life and popular culture, Iranian women, especially mature matrons, are widely perceived as 'powerful.' They are described as running the political affairs of their sons and husbands, as controlling the lives of everyone in the household—omniscient, beloved, respected, and feared matrons much like the stereotypical Jewish mother of western folk culture.

No matter how contradictory the concept of the oppressed-yet-powerful woman might seem, the contradiction is contrived. Indeed, I will even argue that subordinated people, women in this case, not only can be both oppressed and powerful simultaneously, but that they can derive power to effect changes in their own and in others' affairs from the very relations of inequality that define their position: from concrete, adversarial circumstances in their lives, from the existential conditions to which they are confined, unfavorable as they might be.

Women arrive at their position of power vis-à-vis the power elite through dynamic processes, each with its own dialectic logic. In this [selection] I will trace a few of these processes. I will focus on some examples of the power that women in Iran are said to have: on how they access it, how they use it, and where it takes them. In so doing, I will try to show the connection between women's oppression and women's power and will attempt to put the discussion of this seeming paradox into the context of an analytic-methodological frame....

Specifically, I have selected four topics that illustrate the power-potential of women. The first topic, resistance, is an abstract concept, manifested through a bundle of tactics used to counter hegemonic domination. These tactics can be used in all life situations, and create specific power dynamics. The other three topics are concrete and specific: women's work and employment, religion, and political conditions. These three pertain to everyday circumstances of life and are examined for their potential power-content through the use of several brief, illustrative examples.

Resistance as Power

Resistance can take women in three different directions.

1. Power differences between dominants and subordinates—any dominants and their subordinates—inevitably lead to resistance against demands, control, and restrictions of superiors. Dominants in turn perceive the resistance as attempts to challenge, even usurp, their power (in a Zero-Sum game) and thus label resisters as 'bad.' In our case, women do resist domination; their resistance is anticipated, and hence women are said to be by nature obstinate, shameful, foolish, sinful, or childish. As such, it is argued, they must be carefully watched and treated with commensurate firmness if need be ('need' being determined by those in authority), with yet another commensurate backlash of more resistance to be expected. Resistance therefore can, and often does, lead to more suppression: to punishment, discreditation, loss of honor, and confinement rather than freedom, choice, or autonomy.

   For example, in Iran (as elsewhere) women's compliance with the dress code is taken as a measure of both state control on the national level, and of men's control over their families on the individual level. One of the duties of male and female Revolutionary Guards is to publicly enforce the dress code (including the men's dress code, which is much less restrictive and much less focused on than the women's). If a woman's hair shows from under her headscarf the transgression not only is proclaimed a private sin but is also taken as a political statement of resistance to the nation's moral code and to women's place in the social hierarchy of the Islamic Republic, and thus may be punished. By resisting the dress code, individual women do make a statement of protest, but unless they can turn their individual resistance into a mass protest, they cannot use their gesture as a source of power to effect a desired change in the dress code or in their personal position. Their lonely protest is easily quelched.

2. Suicide is one of the most dramatic gestures of resistance. Suicide as a strategy of resistance to demands or to mistreatment by figures of authority (usually within the woman's family) is ineffective for the woman who dies, but the suicide death of one woman can give weight to the resistance efforts of another woman who can use the threat of suicide as a source of power to get her will....

3. The third extreme direction resistance can take is women's own acceptance of the dominants' view of female resistance to hegemonic authority. Women in Iran who accept this view—and there seem to be many—believe that women are inherently weak in body, intellect, and emotional resilience. In extreme but by no means isolated cases, they maintain that all women are inherently 'bad,' probably even hell-bound, and that women's only hope for salvation lies

in proper guidance which will save them from themselves, as it were. Accepting the male paradigm, women paradoxically can turn the male view into a source of power for themselves in relation to others in low positions: women can use the paradigm to control, 'guide,' and subordinate other women. For example, female Revolutionary Guards patrolling the streets to watch over the propriety of other women, mothers-in-law critically watching their daughters-in-law, or *hezbollah* (Party-of-God) women in offices and schools controlling the dress and behavior of officemates or students are enforcing conformity and quelching resistance to male authority. By taking up the cause of male/state authorities, including the expectation of resistance to domination and the perceived need to nip it in the bud, these women can achieve a substantial measure of power over other women. But this support undermines the position of women in general, including their own vis-à-vis their husbands or brothers. Not even the collaborators can easily convert this male-derived power over other subordinates into autonomy in their private lives....

In very rare cases, women manage to turn restrictive orders against the authorities themselves. For example, a woman principal of an all girl's school I know was ordered by her male supervisor not to let any man enter the school premises. When the supervisor appeared a few days later to check on administrative matters, the principal refused him entry on grounds of his own order. Tongue-in-cheek (as in this case) or seriously, women can claim the fool's freedom more easily than men. Although resistance based on the acceptance of male rule in government or in the family may lead to small personal victories for individual women, it cannot be expected to alter the skewed power balance between dominants and subordinates in general. Such resistance is a tactic for getting by and getting even, not for redress.

Resistance can take a great many forms, each with different consequences for the generation of power. I will briefly discuss four such forms which I have found to be used frequently: disobedience, subversion, refusal, and crying for help.

1. Open disobedience of male orders leads to conflict, hidden disobedience to distrust. Both conflict and distrust lead to greater oppression and tighter control, thus creating a vicious circle of tyranny and rebellion.

   For example, a young woman in a small town in southern Iran who disobeyed her husband frequently and for good reasons, as she and many others thought, was often beaten by him in the course of the resulting fights. On one such occasion she fled to her brother, who ordered her to stop arguing and to do her husband's bidding. When she now refused to obey her brother, he beat her, and her relatives and neighbors called her 'crazy' for being disobedient in such a foolishly demonstrative way. Another young woman I know had for years refused all orders by her relatives to marry one of her suitors, on pain of severe punishment at each refusal and near ostracism by her family. Although successful in her resistance, she paid a high price in comfort and reputation. Moreover, when her eventual later marriage to a man of her choosing turned out disastrous, villagers characteristically saw a direct connection between her earlier disobedience and her eventual calamity....

Disobedience as a tool of power for women works best if it is supported by dominants against other dominants: a father supporting his daughter against her husband; a son backing his mother against a half-brother. It can also be successful if one woman's disobedience is backed by other women in an act of solidarity that the men find hard to break. But because solidarity requires more organizational structure than women in Iran, especially rural women, usually have, it is relatively rare outside of the family. Within the family, solidarity is easiest to achieve between mothers and daughters and among sisters, whereas between mothers-in-law and daughters-in-law, and among sisters-in-law, relationships are potentially so fraught with tensions that solidarity seems to be hard to attain.

2. Subversion, in the form of minimal compliance with controversial rules or the outright subversion of such rules is at once a form of testing the limits of the rules and the tolerance of the rule-makers and thus is an expression of one's dissatisfaction with them. This form of resistance can very easily be interpreted as disobedience requiring respective reprisals.

In Iran, for example, the rule for women to cover their hair in front of unrelated men is subverted when a woman drapes a big scarf loosely over her head, holding it in place not by a tight knot or a safety-pin under her chin but by slinging one end of the scarf over the opposite shoulder. The headdress which is meant to conceal has become an ornament; the intent is subverted and the woman who wears it makes a political statement by turning an object of control into one of protest....

3. A woman's refusal to obey her husband's (or father's) orders or to perform expected services challenges the man and inconveniences him. A woman who refuses a demand hopes that her husband will try to prevent the inconvenience and remedy the contested situation before precipitating a showdown. However, any kind of refusal by a woman in everyday situations, from refusing to cook or to fetch a glass of water for her son, to denying sex to her husband, is sanctioned negatively in the Islamic moral code. For a woman, refusing obedience or services to her husband (or, in varying degrees, to other men in positions of authority over her), no matter how extreme the demand, is a sin, and a very 'female' sin at that. It is a sin said to be typical of women, and this notion in turn is part of the script by which women are socialized. Women who resort to refusal as a tool of power are told they are courting punishment in the afterlife as well as in this life.

In the most extreme and most effective case of refusal, a woman leaves her husband to live with her father, brother, or grown son. Her husband then must cope with women's chores, including the care of young children, and is greatly inconvenienced. His difficulty can be compounded if his own mother and other female relatives, in tacit solidarity with his wife, refuse to help him. Sooner or later, out of necessity, he will decide to negotiate for his wife's return, presumably agreeing to measures that will redress his wife's complaints and will improve her situation. Wright reports a case from the Doshman Ziari in which two sisters even left their husbands in order to force them to make a political move the women favored....

4. A cry for help, that is, informing others of wrongs one is suffering, aims to involve outsiders in one's affairs in order to embarrass one's own people into addressing the problem. This form of resistance undermines indirectly a woman's standing, the more so the more people get involved: honorable people take care of their problems themselves.

   For example, a woman who has been beaten may choose to go to the public bathhouse where her bruises will tell her story without a word from her. The news will spread to her father who may then decide to have a word with her husband, usually with a little noise as possible....

These examples suggest that resistance as a source of power for women is considered destructive to self and to others in Iran. Resistance supports the stereotyping of women's power as an inherently dangerous force that must be controlled. Women's resistance is taken by men and women (in what Wright calls the 'dominant model' for behavior and attitudes) as proof of women's inherent weaknesses, their unreliability, recalcitrance, childishness, and antagonism. Although all of these have to be feared as dangerous to the social and moral order, the fear is not a wholesome one, but rather leads to distrust and further curtailment of movement and options for women. Yet, despite its limited, at best short-range, benefits and high costs, resistance is the single most frequently used tactic of power, the most popular 'weapon of the weak' that women use when they feel wronged. Social developments in the Islamic Republic have neither led to equal access to resources for women and men nor to equal opportunities for self-determination and personal autonomy. Given the government's social and gender philosophy, gender equality is not even a sociopolitical agenda. Women therefore can be expected to continue to try to use traditional means to create power, such as resistance, in conducting their lives, even to intensify these power tactics when other sources of power are curtailed.

Work as Power

Women's participation in the labor market is generally taken as an indicator of the status of women, especially in developing countries, and employment of women is considered a means, even a necessity, for women's emancipation. True as this view might be in the long-range processes of women's liberation, my observations in Iran suggest that a woman's labor contribution is not in itself a reliable indicator of a woman's autonomy and power (let alone her status), at least not among the lower classes. This is especially true for manual labor, which generally is regarded as demeaning drudgery. But even clerical work has this connotation, at least among people in the lower classes. Hegland reports from a village in southwest Iran that 'employment outside the home was considered an indication of low socio-economic position and a source of shame both for the women involved and for their relatives.' Such women often find it necessary to assert that they don't have to work, that they are well taken care of and chose employment.

The work women do, be it in- or outside of the home, can be tapped by women as a source of power under certain conditions: (1) The work creates dependencies that the woman can exploit; (2) the work creates resources that the woman can control; (3) the work creates skills that enable the woman to access other sources of power and creates in her the self-confidence to shrewdly exploit them. I will briefly discuss [the first of] these conditions [here].

Dependencies

Within the family, it is easy for a woman to make others, for example, her children, husband, and aged parents-in-law, dependent on her services. A woman in a traditional rural household, by refusing to cook or to milk animals, for example, might force her husband to negotiate with her for better treatment. (This, however, happens at the cost of reinforcement of the negative stereotype of women as nags, or, in extreme cases, the threat of divorce.) On the other hand, as a willing, cooperative, and competent housekeeper, a woman can gain considerable manipulative power. She can gain control over most of the household resources (including even control over a co-wife). By wisely using her resources, she will build up her husband and earn the respect of relatives and others in her social circle, which in turn will empower her to have input in others' and her own affairs. In this way she will also accumulate knowledge about others, which she can incorporate into a power base that includes political as well as economic and emotional resources, and provides many angles for arranging her circumstances to the benefit of herself and her protégés. Hegland reports that the village women she observed used 'their verbal and intellectual skills in gathering information, spying, persuading, taunting, berating, threatening, shaming, discussing, interpreting, encouraging' in order to manipulate their power base. One result of such successful manipulation is the 'powerful' wife-mother figure of popular culture and folklore: the woman who knows everything, who controls children and relatives, who makes and breaks people, who keeps her sons on short emotional reins, and whom everybody loves and fears at the same time. A competent woman in this sense is using her talents, connections, and services—all her assets—to build up her husband (or sons) and herself simultaneously. The most successful will continue to give the impression of overt deferral to male authority, because it is important for the maintenance of 'face' (*aberu*) that her husband's dominance should not be challenged overtly. This pretense of submission in turn has to be accepted by the husband at face value along with his wife's manipulations which, after all, he recognizes as advantageous for himself. This is a power game which so-called successful couples seem to be playing all over the patriarchal world, and which, because of its success, makes other ways of assertion by women, including attempts at emancipation in a western sense, seem superfluous, even foolish, to many men and women in these systems.

In economically depressed post-revolutionary Iran, the household, the kin group, large families are more important than before in structuring the lives of people; the social life as well as economic assistance flow in the kind of close-knit social networks in which women operate very well. Thus, chances for wielding the kind of power that comes from cleverly creating and using dependencies have increased in importance for women....

Religion as Power

Religion can empower women insofar as the religious idiom can provide the means, justifications, and rationalizations for independent actions. Religious concepts thus can be and are used as manipulative devices.

For example, during the revolution, many Iranian women participated in demonstrations against the Pahlavi regime. Hegland reports that the women (and the men who allowed them to do so) saw protest as a religious rather than a political activity: women were giving testimony to Islam by supporting Khomeini.

The paucity of occasions for women in the Islamic Republic to congregate legitimately outside their homes seems to be one of the reasons for the rapid increase in women's participation in graveyard visitation parties on Thursday afternoons. During these visits, women socialize while ostensibly fulfilling a pious obligation. Likewise, *rowzeh* gatherings and *sofrehs* (parties given in honor of a saintly personage) are used extensively for what is elsewhere called women's networking.

Likewise, pilgrimages to saints' shrines are popular among women as religiously motivated social activities. Women consider visits to a neighborhood shrine to be like informal visits to a relative, close to home and easily fit between chores. Pilgrimages to distant, important shrines, however, involve considerable expense and logistical problems, which make male approval, support, and escort necessary for women. Indeed, a woman very likely must use her manipulative powers to make her husband or son take her on a pilgrimage. Frequently a woman can keep her vow to pay a visit to a saint only after she is widowed or has found a separate source of funding for the travel.

For example, an old widow in Deh Koh, an herbalist who had been living precariously on her own for many years, wanted to make the pilgrimage to Mashhad, but was very concerned about the possible impropriety in going alone. On the bus to Mashhad she met a mullah with his eight-year-old son and contracted a temporary, non-sexual marriage with the boy. This allowed her to make the journey as a well-chaperoned married woman. Thus, she used the combination of control over her finances and two religiously sanctioned customs to gain the autonomy to venture into an otherwise inaccessible world. Temporary marriage, which can be taken to demean women, in this case became a source of power that enabled a woman to realize her wish.

Women can use expressions of piety as a manipulative strategy. Since about 1983, a code of piety has developed in Iran, a politically-piously correct way of talking, dressing, reading; a politically correct body of knowledge and phrases that one can use to one's personal advantage.

For example, a young woman (or man for that matter) seeking acceptance at a university or promotion at work will avoid the slightest hint of resistance to the dress code. In public, she will wear the plainest outer garments, correct low-heeled shoes, and a dark scarf pulled over her forehead, completely covering her hairline. She will accept a scholarship to a special Quran course in the summer, no matter how boring she might find it. She will not tell others that at home she is looking at American videos smuggled in from Kuwait. She will pray and observe the fast ostentatiously. She will not be seen with men (other than close family members) in public, and will discourage male attention. Her impeccable behavior will be noted by those who report on her morality, and this will increase her chances for advancement. The restrictive code is thus turned into a tool with which she can manipulate her career.

In the Islamic Republic many women, especially those in the middle class and the former elite, have perfected the art of dissimulation and the use of the code of piety to the extent that their private and public personae are almost totally different.

Since the war, the status of 'Mother of a Martyr' has become a potential source of power for women who have lost a son in the war. The government has given these women the moral right to demand respect and consideration from other people. These women are given preferential treatment in the allocation of subsidized appliances, and they are enlisted as watchers over the correctness of their neighbors' behavior. Some of these women, especially those with limited access to other sources of power and respect, use their position as informer to the point where conversation in a room falters when they enter. These women are seen by others as using a government-bestowed power to the detriment of other women.

In a more traditional religious domain, the prestige of a successful pilgrimage to certain shrines (expressed in the titles *haji, karbela'i, mashhadi*) and that of a descendant of the Prophet Mohammad (*sayyed*) carry respect and are thus a potential source of power for women. A *sayyed* woman often is sought out as a mediator in disputes or as a peacemaker.

For example, in Deh Koh, a man whose wife had fled to her father after a fight enlisted the help of a *sayyed* woman to persuade his father-in-law to send back his wife. Although the young woman's family had vowed they would let her go only if her husband agreed to a list of demands, they found it impossible to resist the *sayyed*, whose invocations of piety, morality, and peace were strengthened greatly by her illustrious descent. In effect, this *sayyed* used her own male-derived powers (from her ancestor, the Prophet) to undermine the protest action of another woman who, as a young wife, had very little power over her fate.

Government as Source of Power

Women in Iran have the right to vote. Yet although voting gives women a voice in political matters equal to men, not all women, especially not rural ones, consider it a source of power. A woman's vote is often regarded as her husband's or father's second vote: he will determine how she is to vote.

Similarly, women do not regard law and the courts as sources of power and rarely use them, even if in a particular instance the law would indeed be on their side. Involving the court in one's affairs is taken as a sign of failure of the informal, traditional, honorable ways of dealing with problems and thus is easily seen as shameful, especially for women. Furthermore, few women have the economic and strategic-assertive resources to go to court alone and plead their case, especially against a male relative.

For example, when in a small town a young woman's husband died, his relatives sent her back to her father without her two infant children. Although the law gave her the right to keep her children at least for a specific time, and although she missed her children badly and fell into serious depression, her father decided not to press the issue in court to avoid the embarrassment of a public fight. The woman felt completely unable to deal with the problem herself, especially over the objection of her father. For similar reasons, women who are denied their legal share of the inheritance of their brothers usually 'pardon' it rather than face a court battle with them.

As mentioned before, politically correct demeanor helps a woman with professional aspirations. In this regard, one could say the government provides a script for women who want to attain power positions, be it as a school principal, a medical professional, an elected member of a village or town council, a Revolutionary Guard, an informer in an office, or an employee of an intelligence agency. In the last three instances, 'successful' women use their government-bestowed powers against other women in the interest of the male dominants, thereby supporting women's domination. Thus, the government makes it possible for some women to advance individually without emancipation....

A final example of a government-generated source of potential power for women comes from an unexpected and controversial circumstance: the mandatory sex-segregation in schools. Although motivated by a restrictive code of sexual morality that otherwise works against women, sex segregated schools have the advantages of all-women's groups in general: they provide young women with an environment where they are not harassed, restricted, challenged, or intimidated by male teachers and male classmates. In such environments women can express themselves freely, they have more opportunity to practice leadership and intellectual skills than they would have if men were present, and they can develop confidence even in such subjects as mathematics and the sciences which in some societies are said to be the domain of men.

Summary

When legitimate sources of power for women become increasingly scarce in an androcentric, male-dominated society such as the Islamic Republic of Iran, and women's realm of action and influence becomes more restricted, women can be expected to intensify their use of the 'weapons of the weak,' that is, manipulation of resources and resistance to restrictive rules to exert control over issues important to them. Both strategies potentially lead to a reinforcement of the popular Iranian stereotype of women's negative character traits, from childishness to outright evil, and reinforce the cycle of antagonism and distrust characteristic of such power constellations. Women who use this system 'well,' that is, in such a way that men feel secure in their claim to control and superiority (regardless of how manipulated or subverted they may be) or else feel that their women's strategies and tactics are advantageous for them, can derive power to the extent that the dominant-subordinate constellation may even seem reversed. Such women are viewed not only as 'powerful' but as de facto rulers of the house. Women who control other women in the interest of dominant authority, either within the family or in public, do so to the detriment of women in general and cannot easily derive autonomy over their own lives from this position. In both cases, that of the successful wife-mother and the wielder of male-derived power, however, the existing hierarchy of domination remains not only unchallenged but is stabilized, and the gendered system of super- and subordination is cemented.

POSTSCRIPT

Has the Islamic Revolution in Iran Subjugated Women?

Since the 1970s feminist anthropologists have increasingly focused attention on the role of women in different societies. Earlier anthropologists, they have argued, had largely written women out of ethnographies, relegating women's roles to the domestic sphere while women's economic and political roles remained largely unstudied. As feminist theory developed in the West, feminist anthropologists attempted to account for and explain the subordination of women in different societies. Radical feminists developed a universal model of patriarchy—a pattern of male domination of women, their labor, their sexuality, and their reproductive capacities. Such models were invoked to explain how women continued to be oppressed in many parts of the world. Explanations of how patriarchal regimes have invoked Islamic law as justification for women being given a subordinate position in society often have emerged from this patriarchal model. Paidar's selection draws on this patriarchal model but avoids the strident, polemical stance that has characterized many feminist interpretations of Muslim society.

The most important reaction to the patriarchal model has been the view that whether these Muslim communities are patriarchal or not, women nevertheless lead rich and rewarding lives in spite of their segregation from men and their limited public role. Some ethnographers have argued that Islamic women even wield considerable informal influence and power. Some anthropologists, such as Lila Abu-Lughod in her *Veiled Sentiments: Honor and Poetry in a Bedouin Society* (University of California Press, 1986) have challenged stereotypes of Islamic women that often depict them as trapped in exploitative gender roles that have emerged from an unchanging form of Islam. Abu-Lughad has argued that we need more descriptive studies of Muslim women before we can understand whether or not these women are subjugated. Friedl suggests that even when women have little direct access to power, as in post revolutionary Iran, women can and have been able to set agendas and define some of the parameters in which public debate over gender policy will be conducted. See *In the Eye of the Story: Women in Post-Revolutionary Iran* (Syracuse University Press, 1994), edited by M. Afkhami and Friedl, for other perspectives on women's rights and roles in Iran.

For a discussion of women's roles in pre-Taliban Afghanistan, see Nancy Tapper's *Bartered Brides: Politics, Gender, and Marriage in an Afghan Tribal Society* (Cambridge University Press, 1991). Ziba Mir-Hosseini's Islam and Gender: *The Religious Debate in Contemporary Iran* (Princeton University Press, 1999) discusses the rise of an indigenous Iranian feminism within postrevolutionary Iranian society. For a discussion of Middle Eastern feminism, see *Remaking*

Women: Feminism and Modernity in the Middle East (Princeton University Press, 1998), edited by Abu-Lughod, and *Gendering the Middle East: Emerging Perspectives* (Syracuse University Press, 1996), edited by Deniz Kandiyoti.

ISSUE 11

Are Yanomami Violence and Warfare Natural Human Efforts to Maximize Reproductive Fitness?

YES: Napoleon A. Chagnon, from "Reproductive and Somatic Conflicts of Interest in the Genesis of Violence and Warfare Among Tribesmen," in Jonathan Haas, ed., *The Anthropology of War* (Cambridge University Press, 1995)

NO: R. Brian Ferguson, from "A Savage Encounter: Western Contact and the Yanomami War Complex," in R. Brian Ferguson and Neil L. Whitehead, eds., *War in the Tribal Zone: Expanding States and Indigenous Warfare* (School of American Research Press, 2000)

ISSUE SUMMARY

YES: Anthropologist and sociobiologist Napoleon A. Chagnon argues that the high incidence of violence and warfare he observed among the Yanomami in the 1960s was directly related to man's inherent drive toward reproductive fitness (i.e., the innate biological drive to have as many offspring as possible). For Chagnon, the Yanomami provide an excellent test of this sociobiological principle because the Yanomami were virtually unaffected by Western colonial expansion and exhibited intense competition for wives.

NO: Anthropologist and cultural materialist R. Brian Ferguson counters that the high incidence of warfare and violence observed by Chagnon in the 1960s was a direct result of contact with Westerners at mission and government stations. Fighting arose in an effort to gain access to steel tools that were increasingly important to the community. Ferguson asserts that fighting is a direct result of colonial circumstances rather than biological drives.

Napoleon Chagnon's work among the Yanomami Indians of the upper Orinoco River basin in Venezuela is one of the best known ethnographic studies of a tribal society. When his books and films first became available in the 1970s, they depicted a society that was intensely competitive and violent.

The Yanomami, according to Chagnon, saw themselves as "the fierce people." Chagnon views the Yanomami as a prototypic tribal society that until very recently operated independently of the forces, processes, and events that affect the rest of the world. For him they represent a pristine example of how tribal communities living in rain forest conditions may have functioned at other times and places in the world.

For many years, Chagnon has periodically revisited the Yanomami, assembling a comprehensive set of data on violence, warfare, movement of local groups, genealogies, and marriage patterns. Since the 1970s Chagnon has championed the cause of sociobiology, which is an effort to bring evolutionary biological theory into anthropology. He uses his database to test whether patterns of warfare and violence can be explained in terms of man's innate desire to reproduce as many offspring as possible, which Chagnon refers to as *reproductive fitness.*

R. Brian Ferguson also studies the Yanomami; however, he routinely uses the term *Yanomami* when discussing linguistically-related tribes studied by Chagnon. Drawing his data from the voluminous books, papers, films, and field reports of others, Ferguson has written a detailed political history of Yanomami warfare. Rather than viewing the Yanomami as innately violent, he interprets the intense violence observed in the 1960s as a direct consequence of changing Yanomami relationships with the outside world. He rejects the notion that the Yanomami of this period represent a pristine tribal society that state societies may have emerged from in the past. Although the foreign influences on the Yanomami may be seen as indirect, Ferguson believes that the Yanomami were nevertheless part of the global system of economic and political relations. Ferguson looks to the control of the material bases of life rather than to biological urges and explains the violent nature of Yanomami culture as the result of a desire to obtain Western products.

This pair of selections raises a number of questions about how anthropologists can explain the sociocultural processes that lead humans to violence. Are there biological drives and urges that lead individuals and groups to engage in violent behavior? Does a growing scarcity of key resources lead individuals to protect their access through increased violence? Is it possible to use contemporary societies as ethnographic analogies to suggest how early prehistoric societies operated? Are there any communities that are not linked to the global system of economic and political relations?

In the following selections, Chagnon develops a model to explain the incidence and character of Yanomami fighting. He asserts that human behavior can be explained in terms of the biological drive to reproduce. This innate drive leads men to maximize their access to women who can bear their children, passing as many of their genes on to the next generation as possible. Ferguson counters Chagnon's position by arguing that the Yanomami have been thoroughly influenced by the flow of steel tools into the region from the outside world. The desire for steel machetes drives Yanomami who live in settlements far from where machetes are available to fight with other Yanomami who have access to this scarce resource.

Napoleon A. Chagnon  **YES**

Reproductive and Somatic Conflicts of Interest in the Genesis of Violence and Warfare Among Tribesmen

Darwin's view of the evolution of life forms by natural selection is now a standard dimension in social and cultural anthropology, modified, of course, to apply to "cultures" or "societies." It is the modification, however, which is today a major issue, since the changes necessary to extend his original arguments by themselves distorted and changed his arguments. Specifically, problems with the "group" versus the "individual" controversy are now beginning to appear in anthropological discussions of the evolved functions of human behavior. This has long been resolved in favour of the individual or lower levels of organization in the field of biology.

Another deficiency in our use of evolutionary theory has to do with our almost exclusive focus on "survival," when, in fact, evolutionary theory is about both survival and reproduction. On the one hand, this is probably related to the difficulty of imagining cultures or societies "reproducing" like organisms. On the other, there is a general bias in materialist/evolutionary anthropology to play down or ignore the issue of the individual's role in shaping societies and cultures. Furthermore, when we deal with survival, our concerns appear to be more about the survival of systems (cultures, groups, populations, etc.) than of individuals. This makes it difficult for us to evaluate and discuss the relationship between societal rules and what individuals actually do. We thereby preclude the possibility of understanding the evolved biological correlates of conventions and institutions.

My proposed approach will treat warfare as only one of a class of conflicts which, in band and village societies, must be examined carefully to determine the extent to which they can be traced back to conflicts of interest among individuals.... [T]he focus will be primarily on individuals, who will be viewed as expending two basic kinds of efforts during their lifetimes: somatic effort (in the interests of survival) and reproductive effort (in the interest of fitness)....

Warfare as a Kind of Conflict

... Conflicts between individuals and groups of individuals break out within many band and tribal societies, but the groups contesting are not always (at the time) politically independent. Indeed, a common consequence of such conflicts is the fissioning of the groups along conflict lines, and an escalation/continuation of the conflict. It is at this point that groups become visibly "independent" of each other and more conveniently fit into categories that enable us to define the *extended* conflicts as "warfare." However, we could not do so initially when the contestants were members of a common group. By insisting that our approach to warfare focus only on conflicts between politically independent groups, we run the risk of losing sight of the genesis of the conflict. We are also tempted to restrict our search for causes to just that inventory of things that "groups" (politically independent societies) might contest over, such as a hunting territory or water hole—resources that may be intimately identified with members of specific local groups.

This is a crucial issue. First, conflicts of interest in band and village societies often occur between individuals within the same group and are provoked by a wide variety of reasons. Second, individuals in kinship-organized societies tend to take sides with close kin and/or those whose reproductive interests overlap significantly with their own (e.g., wife's brothers). "Groups" are therefore often formed on the basis of kinship, marriage, or both, and by definition their members have overlapping reproductive interests. They usually have economic and other interests that overlap as well, but it is theoretically important to keep in mind that, from the perspective of evolution, the ultimate interests of individuals are reproductive in overall scope....

Life Effort

A basic assumption in my model is that the lifetime efforts of individuals can be partitioned into two conceptually distinct categories that incorporate all or nearly all of the activities that an individual (an organism in any species) engages in if it is to be biologically successful. These categories are *somatic effort* and *reproductive effort*. The former has principally to do with those activities, risks, costs, etc. that ensure the survival of the organism in a purely somatic sense—seeking shelter from the elements, protection from predators and conspecifics, obtaining nutrients, maintaining hygiene and health, etc. This would include most items we traditionally focus on in studies of technology, economics, settlement patterns, cultural ecology, grooming, ethnopharmacology, curing, etc.

The second category is one that is not normally considered in traditional cultural ecological/materialist approaches to intergroup conflicts, warfare, and cultural adaptation. While the category's overall content is "reproductive," it includes a number of specific variables not normally considered in traditional anthropological studies of reproduction as such (see Figure 1). Herein lies the value and power of theoretical developments in evolutionary biology that can shed new light on conflicts of interest between individuals and, ultimately, intergroup conflicts between politically independent...

Figure 1

Model of Individual Life Effort From a Darwinian Perspective

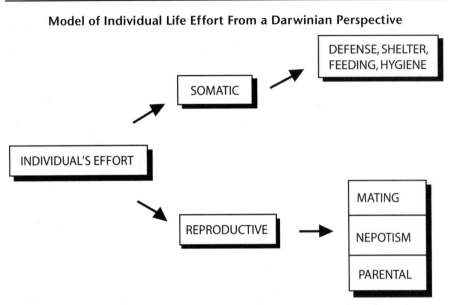

Note: Individuals expend basically two kinds of effort during their lifetimes: Somatic Effort and Reproductive Effort. The former has basically to do with the survival of the organism as such, while the latter has to do with costs, benefits, risks, etc. associated with mating, nepotism (aiding non-descendant kin), and parenting.

A review of the literature pertaining to warfare and conflict in such societies reveals that much of the conflict emanates over such factors as rape, abduction of females, failure to deliver a promised bride, niggardliness in paying bride price or executing bride service, and seduction. Whereas warfare and conflict in industrialized societies and many "ranked" or "stratified" societies can be convincingly shown to be associated with relative scarcity or protection of material resources, the proverbial "means of production," much of the conflict in most band and tribal societies is generated because of contests over the *means of reproduction.*

Let me make one thing perfectly clear at this juncture. I am *not* claiming that all conflicts of interest in band and tribal society derive from conflicts that are reproductive in overall quality, nor am I claiming that conflicts over material resources are not found in such societies. I am simply arguing that conflicts of reproductive interests occur commonly in band and tribal societies and that these often lead, as indicated above, to intergroup conflicts that we traditionally consider to be warfare. I accept (and have always accepted) explanations of specific band and village warfare patterns in which demonstrable and convincing evidence indicates that shortages of material resources are directly implicated in the genesis of the conflicts....

The category "reproductive effort" in my model is advised by and basically derived from the post-1960 theoretical developments in evolutionary biology. Reproduction entails getting copies of one's self into subsequent generations. This can occur in more than the single obvious way we normally think of reproduction: begetting and successfully raising offspring. Since related organisms share identical genes by immediate common descent, organisms can advance their reproductive interests by engaging in activities and behaviours that affect, in a positive way, the reproductive efforts and accomplishments of relatives with whom they share genes. Thus, while the original Darwinian perspective viewed success in terms of fitness measured by numbers of immediate descendants (offspring), the new Darwinian perspective views success in broader, more encompassing terms. What is significant is the number of copies of one's genes that are perpetuated in subsequent generations.

This draws attention to the enormous importance of W. D. Hamilton's now classic papers defining "inclusive fitness." Individual Egos can pass on their genes by direct acts of reproduction (having children) and by aiding genetic relatives, who, by definition, share genes with Ego in proportion to the degree of genetic relatedness between them. If the aid enhances the relatives' reproduction, Ego "benefits" in a reproductive sense by having more copies of his/her genes enter the gene pool of subsequent generations—through the reproductive accomplishments of those relatives.

The study of "reproduction" becomes, then, more than merely the collection of genealogical facts and reproductive histories of individuals. It entails the study of all social interactions that potentially affect the reproductive success of the individual and those with whom he or she is interacting. Such interactions include, for example, taking risks to protect a kinsman in a mortal duel, sharing a piece of food, tendering aid in clearing gardens, and reclassifying a covillager from the kinship category "sister" to "wife."

The study of reproduction also entails the study of both the "rules" and violations of the rules, injunctions, moral prescriptions, etc., which can and often do lead to conflicts and fighting. Thus, failure to give a piece of food might possibly reflect an immediate shortage of food and have, therefore, relevance in a purely somatic context. At the same time, it can reflect a *reproductive* strategy on the part of an individual to enhance his or her political esteem and authority—to insult a reproductive competitor, for example. It thus has relevance in a purely reproductive context as well, often in the absence of resource scarcities. Such affronts are common in meat distributions among the Yanomamö, for example, where there is a chronic struggle among men to establish individual reputations for authority, prestige, esteem, productivity, generosity, and matrimonial success. The "rule" is to give portions of large game away first to the "big men" and then to the lesser. A meat distributor can strategically conduct his distribution to indicate to the assembled that he doesn't consider a particular individual in the group to be as "important" as he himself and others might consider him to be. This can be done by deliberately giving him an unacceptably small portion, an undesirable portion, or presenting a portion after first acknowledging that others are more important than he by distributing to them first. He might even go so far as to give him no portion. This is, of course, remembered and noted by all ... and adds to all those other factors that accumulate eventually into smouldering inter-individual hostilities and conflicts that eventually explode and are expressed in arguments, club fights and, occasionally, homicides.

Reproductive efforts, then, includes a more comprehensive set of variables than traditional anthropological concepts embrace. It can conveniently be partitioned into several broad sub-categories (Figure 1): parental effort, mating effort, and nepotistic effort. Parental effort deals primarily with those factors we are familiar with in our more traditional views of reproduction: all those costs and risks required to rear one's children successfully and, by extension, grandchildren and great-grandchildren, i.e., descendant relatives. Mating effort includes the study of all those variables that affect the success that individuals enjoy in attracting (obtaining) a mate; guarding the mate from the seductive attempts of others; and keeping the kin of that mate satisfied in terms of the expectations that they have regarding bride price, bride service, food sharing, etc. Nepotistic effort includes all those social activities entailing costs and risks that are expended in order to aid non-descendant relatives. These individuals, by virtue of receiving such beneficence, are in a position to translate it into reproductive consequences that ultimately enhance the "inclusive fitness" of the original helper, i.e., by producing additional copies of the helper's genes through their own reproductive accomplishments.

Life Effort Model

... By thinking of an individual's life time as a series of efforts entailing costs and risks on the one hand and benefits on the other, one can more clearly identify the factors that are likely to be significant in terms of the individual's attempts to be successful as both a member of society and as an organism constrained by societal rules. One can see how culture and cultural success is relatable to biology and biological success. The myriad factors that potentially or actually lead to conflicts of somatic and reproductive interests and, ultimately, fighting and warfare can also be appreciated.

By focusing on individual level conflicts of interests, we can more clearly see how the patterns of escalation, found widely in tribal societies, grow in such a way as to enable us to trace the sources of the conflicts back to the individual level and relate them, where possible, to reproductive versus somatic conflicts. This is particularly important for understanding warfare in band and village societies where the initial conflicts are almost always at the level of individuals. The "causes" of specific "wars" in such societies are bound up in complex, often vague, issues that transpired months or even years before the specific raid by "Group A" on "Group B" which we traditionally identify as "war" actually occurs. In contrast, by starting with the "group" as our initial level of analysis (because we usually define warfare as mortal contests between groups), we lose sight of the anterior patterns and are forced to interpret the group level phenomena as having started there.

The focus on individuals not only makes the conflict genesis clearer, it also compels us to consider the history of the conflict and how initial conflicts over one particular cause evolve into newer, more encompassing conflicts that are perpetuated by secondary causes....

Striving for Esteem and Prestige

Kinship and genealogy become significant in understanding conflicts for a variety of reasons. They are as a result central variables in understanding the causes, development and escalation of violence in kinship-organized band and village societies. However, in addition to the variations in one's relative influence in his/her society as determined by the size and structure of one's kinship nexus, individuals are significantly different in their ability to achieve prestige and status through chronic or episodic acts of competition in various arenas of social life. There is marked variation from one society to another in the extent to which there is competition among individuals (viz. Benedict's classic work on patterns of culture [1934]). In some, it is so negligible that ethnographers insist that it is irrelevant or does not occur at all....

This is one area in which we must do more work. Inter-individual conflicts of interest presumably exist in all societies and individuals must therefore resolve them somehow and, we would predict, in fashions that benefit them rather than others. In some societies, it might be very difficult to distinguish the effects that kinship power confers on individuals from those attributes of esteem and prestige that are achieved apart from or in spite of the kinship nexus. Among the Yanomamö, virtually every village I have studied is led by headmen who invariably come from the largest descent groups in the village. Yet in a large number of villages there are men from distant, essentially unrelated villages who, through their individual skills and political abilities, rise to high levels of esteem in spite of their comparatively small number of relatives. In many societies, competition for or striving for high esteem and prestige is obvious and often spectacular.

The benefits for achieving high esteem in most band and village societies normally entail polygynous marriage and/or a more desirable position in the food/labor exchange networks, which can ultimately be related to differential access to mates and differential reproductive success. Among humans, prestige leads to influence and power, and power appears to lead to high reproductive success. Betzig has convincingly demonstrated this in her analysis of a larger number of "despotic" societies, but the extent to which this is true, statistically, in a significant sample of egalitarian societies must yet be established. The correlation has been demonstrated for the Yanomamö in several of my own publications. Large numbers of ethnographic descriptions of tribal societies suggest that polygyny, one spoor of high reproductive success, is usually associated with leadership or other positions of prestige, but none of them document statistical differences in reproductive accomplishments of polygynous versus non-polygynous males. Indeed, variations in male reproductive success have been documented in only a few instances for any species.

Striving for prestige entails taking risks that lead to greater or lesser amounts of success for particular individuals: there will be winners and losers. Those who lose are all the more anxious to establish or reestablish their position. As a result, conflicts and fighting arise, often over issues that appear to have no obvious direct relationship to either somatic or reproductive interests. Whether or not they ultimately do can usually be established by documenting variations in survivorship among the offspring of the successful, as well as differences in numbers of mates and numbers of offspring among the losers and winners, and the comparative reproductive success of the adult off-spring of the esteemed....

A Headmen's Prestige and Reaction to Insult

In about 1980, a particularly devastating war developed between the village of Bisaasi-teri, the group I described in my 1968 monograph *Yanomamö: The Fierce People,* and the village of Daiyari-teri, a smaller, neighboring group described by Lizot in *Tales of the Yanomami.*

The war was provoked by a trivial incident in 1981 that amounted to a gross insult of the Bisaasi-teri headman, but its ultimate origins go back to the mid-1950s. The Daiyari-teri are members of a larger population bloc that includes a village called Mahekodo-teri. The Bisaasi-teri had just recently fissioned from their parent group, the Patanowa-teri, and were attempting to establish themselves as an independent, viable village. To this end, they were cultivating alliances with unrelated villages to their south. Unfortunately, their erstwile allies invited them to a feast and treacherously massacred many of the men and abducted a number of their young women. The survivors fled to and took refuge among the Mahekodo-teri. The Mahekodo-teri, acting from a position of strength, took further advantage of them and appropriated a number of their young women. At the same time, they also tendered them sufficient aid to enable the Bisaasi-teri to recover and regain their independence by making new gardens further away from their enemies. The Daiyari-teri, congeners of the Mahekodo-teri, eventually located their village at a site within a day's walk of the Bisaasi-teri. For the next decade or so, relationships between the two groups varied from friendship and amity to neutrality to overt hostility verging on warfare. In 1965, for example, the Bisaasi-teri spread rumors that the Daiyari-teri were cowards. The Daiyari-teri responded by demanding to have a chest-pounding duel with the more numerous Bisaasi-teri to show them—and the world at large—that they were valiant and would not tolerate insults to their reputations. From that point until about 1980, relationships between the two groups were strained, but the Daiyari-teri were not powerful enough to threaten the Bisaasi-teri militarily. Eventually, visiting between them resumed and they became allies, albeit suspicious allies.

In 1980, the Bisaasi-teri headman decided to take his village on a camping trip up the Orinoco river, near the village of Daiyari-teri. Since they were allies, this headman decided to visit their village and ask them for plantains, a commonly expected courtesy between allies under such circumstances. When he reached the village, there were a large number of Daiyari-teri children and youths playing in the water. They began pelting the headman with mudballs and sticks, harassing him in that fashion all the way into the village—an insult of the first order. What apparently made matters serious was the fact that the Daiyari-teri adults neither scolded the youths nor prevented them from continuing their abuse. The Bisaasi-teri headman left, angry, and without plantains. He moved his people back to the village and cancelled the camping trip.

Some time later, perhaps a few weeks, a large number of Daiyari-teri men visited the Salesian Mission at the mouth of the Mavaca river, immediately across the Orinoco from the Bisaasi-teri village. The Bisaasi-teri spotted them immediately, and challenged them to a fight. They attacked them first with clubs and, ironically, pelted the Daiyari-teri men with lumps of hardened cement that had been discarded from a house-construction project on the mission side of the river. Considerable injury to the Daiyari-teri resulted, and they left for home, bleeding from their numerous wounds, threatening to get revenge. They eventually sent word to the Bisaasi-teri that they wanted to settle their dispute in a chest-pounding duel. The Bisaasi-teri enthusiastically accepted the challenge and went to their village to feast and fight. In the ensuing duel, two young men were killed. The Bisaasi-teri departed immediately, but were intercepted by Daiyari-teri archers who managed to wound one of them with an arrow. Shortly after, the Daiyari-teri raided and wounded a Bisaasi-teri man.

Some weeks later, one of the young men in Bisaasi-teri went on a fishing trip with an employee of the Venezuelan Malarialogia service. He was warned not to go on the trip because it was too close to the Diayari-teri village. He went anyway. While they were fishing from their canoe that night, a party of Daiyari-teri men discovered them and killed the young man with a volley of arrows, three of which struck him in the neck. The Bisaasi-teri recovered his body the next day and, in the ensuing weeks, mounted several unsuccessful raids against the Daiyari-teri, who had fled inland to escape retaliation. The Daiyari-teri eventually returned to their village.

The Bisaasi-teri called on their allies to join them in a raid. One of the allied groups, Iyawei-teri, attacked a day before the main group. The Bisaasi-teri raiding party reached the Daiyari-teri village a short time after the Iyawei-teri raiders had struck and fled, leaving two Daiyari-teri men dead. The Bisaasiteri and their allies, armed with both arrows and shotguns, surrounded the village and set it ablaze, forcing the inhabitants to flee to the bank of the Orinoco river. There they took cover in a large pit they had dug into the ground in the event they were driven from their village by raiders—as they were. They were bombarded with volley after volley of Bisaasi-teri arrows, shot into the air and descending, like mortar rounds, into the open pit. Those who raised up to return the fire were shot with both arrows and shotgun blasts. A number of the adult males were killed; at least two women were deliberately shot as well, and an undetermined number of children and infants were accidentally wounded by the volleys of arrows and random shotgun pellets, some of whom later died. One of the fatalities was a woman who was a sister to the Bisaasi-teri headman and had been appropriated when the Bisaasi-teri took refuge with the Mahekodo-teri in the 1950s.

The survivors fled to an allied village when the raiders left. They solicited aid from the Mahekodo-teri and several other villages to mount revenge raids and eventually managed to ambush a young Bisaasi-teri couple who were on their way to the garden one morning, killing both of them. The Bisaasi-teri were satisfied that they had taught the Daiyari-teri a lesson and have no further interest in raiding them. However, they say they have every intention to exact revenge on the Mahekodo-teri for the two most recent killings and are presently waiting for the most opportune time to do so.

Discussion

In both of the above examples, the notion of prestige and status figure prominently and must be taken into consideration in explaining the conflicts. Moreover, the conflicts are not simply isolated incidents, provoked by a specific single act. They are continuations of smouldering antagonisms that originate in a multitude of previous acts, some involving seduction and male/male competition for women, others involving reactions to insults or testing of resolve and status, and others are purely vindictive and motivated by vengeance. Among the Yanomamö, it is relatively easy to relate all of these variables to reproductive striving, for a village that fails to respond to aggressive acts, even verbal ones, soon finds itself victimized by stronger, more assertive allies who translate their advantage into appropriating reproductively valuable females.

For the leaders, the reproductive rewards for aggressiveness are even more obvious. The above Bisaasi-teri headman, for example, has had 8 wives during his lifetime and has sired 25 children by them (not all survived). At present (1988), he has two wives, one of whom is still young and able to produce his children. Finally, the followers who take risks on behalf of and at the instigation of leaders, benefit in both somatic and reproductive terms as well. By complying with the suggestions and directions of the leaders, they contribute to the reputation of the village, as well as to their own reputations as individuals. By thus establishing the credibility of their claims for being valiant and aggressive, they also manage to prevail in a milieu of chronic aggressive threats and enjoy relatively secure and predictable somatic and reproductive opportunities compared to those who fail to make such demonstrations.

The overall aggregate of groups comprised of competitive status-seeking individuals has its social costs as well. The most obvious one is a domestic condition fraught with relatively constant stress and bickering, particularly in larger groups whose kinship composition might favor factionalism. The chronic fissioning of larger groups along lines of close kinship is a response to this internal social stress and competition whenever external threats are sufficiently low to permit them.

Summary

... Status differentials among individuals are more numerous and dramatic in so-called egalitarian societies than many contemporary theoretical arguments from anthropology assert. These are, in part, inherited in a very real sense. One's fund of kinship power is fixed largely at birth. One cannot, for example, pick his or her parents or descent group, nor alter the reproductive facts of the ascending generations, i.e., how many kin of what kinds or degrees of relatedness he or she will be surrounded by at birth and among whom he or she grows up and must interact socially with on a daily basis. An individual can, as he or she matures, modify the "luck of the kinship draw" in a number of limited ways, but all of them require the cooperation of others. One way is to produce children, but Ego must first find a mate, i.e., have elders who will find a mate for him or her. Another way is to "manipulate" kinship classifications and move people in kinship categories that are socially and reproductively more useful, an act that requires the "endorsement" of co-villagers who will go along with the manipulation by altering their own kin usage to conform to that initiated by the original manipulator. A third way is for particular men to lobby for a village fission that will divide the larger group into smaller ones permitting Ego to surround himself with a mixture of co-resident kin more congenial to his social and reproductive interests. One's ability to influence others, make demands, coerce, garner cooperation, etc. is often a direct function of the individual's kinship nexus and the kinds and numbers of kin-defined allies he or she can draw on to enforce his or her will. Conflicts of interest emerge and develop in a kinship matrix in most band and village societies, necessitating an understanding of genealogical relatedness, reproductive and marital histories, and other features of kinship and descent. In addition, high status and esteem usually confer advantage in matrimonial striving and, therefore, in reproductive success. It thus should be expected that individuals will compete over and have conflicts about relative degrees of esteem, conflicts that may, on the surface, reveal no obvious relationship to either somatic or reproductive resources. Measurements of relative status and relative degrees of reproductive success should be made to determine if there is a positive correlation between them.

R. Brian Ferguson

A Savage Encounter

The lives of the Yanomami of the Orinoco-Mavaca river confluence of southern Venezuela have been presented in the works of Napoleon Chagnon as a kind of morality play. Embroiled in seemingly endless violence fueled by sexual competition, status rivalry, and revenge, the Yanomami are held to exemplify the Hobbesian condition of "'Warre'—the chronic disposition to do battle, to Oppose and dispose of one's sovereign neighbors." Moreover, their lifeways are said to represent "a truly primitive cultural adaptation ... before it was altered or destroyed by our culture." Their warfare is portrayed not as aberrant or unusual, but as the normal state of existence for sovereign tribal peoples, seeming atypical only because other war patterns have been suppressed by colonialism. It is "an expected form of political behavior and no more requires special explanations than do religion or economy." The conditions Chagnon describes are said to resemble those at the dawn of agriculture. The Yanomami are "our contemporary ancestors"; thus, understanding their "quality of life ... can help us understand a large fraction of our own history and behavior." The same insecurities that create Warre among the Yanomami account for warfare among modern nation-states, and the same inference is to be drawn: "the best defense is a good offense."

Chagnon's portrayal is persuasive and has been widely accepted. In the Foreword to his *Yąnomamö: The Fierce People*, one of the most widely read texts in the history of anthropology, the series editors write that the "sovereign tribal" politics of these Yanomami is "a product of long-term sociocultural evolution without intervention from outside alien populations and life ways." Even scholars who have been the most attentive to the violence-provoking possibilities of Western contact accept the Yanomami's relatively "pristine" character. Students of the Yanomami have been more skeptical, many pointing out that the Orinoco-Mavaca area has undergone extensive contact-related changes. None of the critics, however, has shown in any systematic way how those changes relate to observed patterns of violence.

[T]his paper was written ... to explore exactly those relationships, and to challenge the idea that any ethnographic case of indigenous warfare is fully understandable apart from the historical circumstances of contact with an expanding state.... I will not dispute that [Yanomami] are less disrupted and transformed by Western contact than most of the peoples for whom we have ethnographic information. Nevertheless, I will argue that after centuries of sporadic contact with outsiders, Orinoco-Mavaca society was undergoing massive change for some two decades prior to Chagnon's arrival, and that this process of change accelerated during the time period described in Chagnon's monographs (1964–72). His statement that "it is not true, as a few of my colleagues believe, that the Yanomamo were described at a particularly 'turbulent' period of their history" is unsupportable. The "fierce people" immortalized by Chagnon represent a moment in history in which Yanomami culture was pushed into an extreme conflict mode by circumstances related to the intensifying Western presence. Their warfare and other conflicts are manifestations of this larger situation. Where Chagnon tells us that the Yanomami provide "an intimate glimpse beyond history, whither we came," I maintain that they will remain a baffling chimera until they are seen in the light of their own history....

Local History

The ancestors of the Yanomami were raided by slavers, in varying intensity, from probably the mid-seventeenth century to about 1850. The raids drove them deep into the Parima highlands, although some still came down to the rivers to trade. The rubber boom of the latter nineteenth century reached into mountain areas and was accompanied by wars and migrations for the recent ancestors of the Orinoco-Mavaca people. The collapse of rubber production left the region more isolated from Westerners from around 1920 until 1940, a brief interlude which has been misconstrued as a primeval state. For the Orinoco-Mavaca people, this was a time of peace.

Sporadic, sometimes violent, contact began in the area around 1940 and intensified over the decade. The captive woman Helena Valero was in this area, and she describes the intensifying conflicts as new tools and diseases began to filter in. In the late 1940s the Namoweiteri, the population cluster later to host Chagnon's field research, divided into hostile western and eastern (Patanowateri) groups. Then, in 1950, the establishment of the first mission near Mahekodo-teri on the Orinoco was followed almost immediately by the slaughter of a western Namowei-teri trading party by the more isolated Shamatari. Interior groups continued to harry the wealthier villages around the Orinoco until, in 1955, the latter demonstrated their military superiority. During the relatively peaceful half decade to follow, a second mission was established by Iyewei-teri at the mouth of the Ocamo River. The Iyewei-teri are an important contrast to other local groups: although only a few hours by launch downstream from Chagnon's field site, they had a more stable and wealthy Western power base than any upstream village, and enjoyed almost unbroken peace while the upriver villages endured several wars.

In 1958, a government malaria control station was set up at the mouth of the Mavaca River. The Bisaasi-teri, the larger of the western Namowei-teri groups, accepted an invitation to settle by the post. (The other western group, the closely allied Monou-teri, was located a short distance up the Mavaca.)

Almost immediately, the missionaries at Mahekodo-teri moved their main operation to Bisaasi-teri. The Bisaasi-teri and Monou-teri then set out to establish beneficial alliances with Shamatari groups up the Mavaca, and in one instance demonstrated their willingness to use force against potential adversaries. For the next several years, Bisaasi-teri would be the metropolitan center of the far upper Orinoco, especially in late 1964 to early 1966, when Chagnon lived there, and when another mission was attempting to establish itself directly across the Orinoco. But those years also saw the western Namo-wei-teri beleaguered by internal factionalism and external enemies. This was the extraordinary fighting described in *Yąnomamö: The Fierce People....*

Infrastructure

Western contact brings epidemic diseases. In the Orinoco-Mavaca area, epidemics began to occur around 1940, and they continued with devastating frequency. A major outbreak of malaria in 1960 killed an estimated 10 percent of the area population, and another outbreak is indicated for 1963. Chagnon's initial census established the cause of death of 240 individuals: 130 are attributed to malaria and epidemics, and another 25 to "sorcery." A measles epidemic swept through the area in 1968. Among deaths recorded by Chagnon for 1970 to 1974, 82 (69 percent) were due to all infectious diseases (including "magic"). In a different sample gathered at Mavaca for 1969 to 1979, 53 (39.6 percent) were due to malaria.

A single influenza epidemic that hit three remote villages in 1973 shows how terrible the impact can be. One hundred six people died, 27.4 percent of the combined population. One village lost 40 percent. In this epidemic, and presumably in all of them, the young and old died in disproportionate numbers. The contagion apparently was transmitted by men coming back from a trip downstream to obtain machetes....

In sum, in the Orinoco-Mavaca area, a great many families were disrupted by death during the contact period. Only about one-quarter of the children there have both parents alive and coresident by the time they reach the age of 15. For the Yanomami, family, economy, and polity are one, and this many deaths tears at the fabric of society.... The longer-term consequences are described by Chagnon and Melancon:

> Disruption of village life and the resulting coalescence or fusion shatters the social organization and creates chaos, conflict and disorder in the newly-constituted village(s).

... [Another] infrastructural consequence of contact is technological change. Of paramount importance is the introduction of steel cutting tools, which are up to ten times more efficient than stone. As with other Amazonian peoples, Yanomami have gone to great lengths to obtain these tools, relocating villages, sending trading parties on long and hazardous journeys, and raiding vulnerable possessors of steel. All known Yanomami had obtained some metal tools long before any anthropologist visited them, yet these highly valued items remained scarce until very recently. And steel tools are only the beginning. New needs develop rapidly for a range of Western manufactures, in a process that can lead to assimilation into the lowest stratum of the expanding state. In the Orinoco-Mavaca area, those with greatest access to Westerners are seen by other Yanomami as having "turned white."

Machetes, axes, and knives are unlike anything in the indigenous economy. At least at first, their utility and scarcity makes them more precious than items of native manufacture. Furthermore, they are unequally available, their sources restricted to a few points of Western presence, so procurement is the key problem. It is commonly acknowledged that Yanomami villages have moved out of the Parima highlands in order to provide closer access to sources of steel, and that in the Orinoco-Mavaca area, this is why Yanomami moved from the highlands to the insect-infested rivers. And there is more to it than movement.

> Thus there grew up two types of community—those holding manufactured goods acquired directly at source, and those (isolated ones) which were deprived of them. The entire map of economic and matrimonial circuits, along with political alliances, was transformed and flagrant imbalances appeared. Gradually, though scarcely within twenty years ... the economy was disrupted, the society menaced at its roots, and dysfunctional attitudes developed....

Structure

The structural effects of contact on war are here separated into three conventional topics: economics, kinship, and political organization.

Economics

A central problem for all Yanomami economies is how to obtain Western manufactured goods. In different Yanomami areas, these have been obtained by hunting for pelts, traveling to work as farmhands, or producing manioc flour or bananas for sale or trade. In the Orinoco-Mavaca area, the way to obtain Western goods has been to work for the Westerners who come there to live or visit. Missionaries and other resident Westerners regularly give away substantial quantities of manufactures. They make large presentations on special occasions, such as visits to more remote villages, but normally give the manufactures as payment for goods (garden products, meat, firewood), for services (as guides, ground clearers, housebuilders, translators, maids, informants, etc.), and in some instances, for local manufactures with external sale potential. Very few details are available about employment and payments, but one obvious point has important consequences for understanding patterns of conflict: to work for the Westerners in most of these capacities requires that one live close to them.

... [T]he Yanomami generally make great efforts to monopolize access to the Western provider using pleas, threats, and deceptions to keep the distribution of goods within their local group. Beyond the source point, Western manufactures are passed along from village to village through networks of kinship. Often the people in one village use a tool for some time, then pass it along to the next village when they get a new one. The quantities in exchange can only be guessed, but that guess must be high. An incomplete listing of goods distributed from the Catholic mission at Iyewei-teri for 1960 to 1972 includes 3,850 machetes, 620 axes, 2,850 pots, 759,000 fishhooks, and large quantities of other items. Most of these goods were traded to more remote villages. Nevertheless, some villages separated from Western sources by two or three intervening villages are reported as receiving only poor remnants of manufactures....

Most reports indicate that the exchange of Western manufactures is usually without overt contention. A request for an item is made, and that item is given, on the promise of some future compensation. On the other hand, Lizot reports that "the bargaining, however, does not procede without bitter disputes. The partners stay at the brink of rupture." Even the smooth transactions may mask tensions, and the major trading that occurs at feasts is often preceded or followed by violent confrontations. Veiled and not-so-veiled threats are made, as when a man "named the men he had killed on various raids—just before demanding a machete" from Chagnon. "In some communities, to declare, 'I will not give anything' or 'I will not give what you are asking' is to risk a clubbing."...

In exchange for Western manufactures, more isolated Yanomami make and trade local manufactures. Consistent with the earlier quotation from Lizot, this has led to a clear division of labor between Yanomami communities. All the villages around missions have specialized in the trade of Western items; residents of villages without such access have become specialists in producing specific local commodities which they trade to the mission villages.

But does this general pattern apply to the Bisaasi-teri? Admittedly, it would be difficult to infer its existence from reading *The Fierce People*. Cocco, however, like Lizot, describes the pattern as applying to all mission villages in the area, which would include Bisaasi-teri. In a letter written during his initial fieldwork, Chagnon reports the same pattern: "Some villages specialize in making one or another object; others who have special sources of access purvey axes or machetes and pots to the rest." The pattern is also suggested by the captions of two photographs from the same trading session: "Kaobawa trading his steel tools to Shamatari allies" and "Kaobawa ... trading with his Shamatari allies for arrows, baskets, hammocks, and dogs," and it is implied in a passing mention of "steel tools and aluminum pots" being the trade specialization of "several contacted villages." But Chagnon follows this point immediately with a discussion that downplays the utilitarian aspect of trade in local manufactures, arguing that trade specialization is to be understood as a gambit to create political alliances....

[T]he material interest in Bisaai-teri trade is apparent in regard to cotton and hammocks. Woven by men in this area, cotton hammocks are scarce and very valuable. They are traded widely, even into the Parima highlands.

> The Bisaasi-teri obtain much of their spun cotton and curare arrow points from their Shamatari allies. It takes considerable time and labor to accumulate these items. When the Shamatari are visited by the Bisaasi-teri, the

latter make known their desire to have these items, and their hosts promise to produce them. When the items are accumulated, the Shamatari visit the Bisaasi-teri to inform them their cotton and arrow points are ready. A feast is arranged and the items are given over to the Bisaasi-teri after the celebration terminates. The Shamatari then request specific items from their hosts, and the cycle continues.

The Bisaasi-teri export this cotton yarn to another ally, and it is then "brought back in the form of manufactured hammocks, the importer merely contributing labor to the process." In other words, the Bisaasi-teri come to possess a quantity of a very valuable trade item without expending any labor in its production. Curare arrow points, not incidentally, are listed by Cocco as the item Bisaasi-teri uses when trading at Iyewei-teri.

In sum, Yanomami with direct access to sources of Western manufactures make great efforts to monopolize them, sharp tensions surround the exchange of Western items, the quality and quantity of Western manufactures diminishes markedly at each step in the exchange network, and outpost villages acquire large quantities of various local, labor-intensive manufactures. My inference is that those groups who control sources of Western manufactures exploit more isolated peoples who depend on them for metal tools. This inference is reinforced by the more obvious exploitation by middlemen in the realm of marriage relationships, discussed in the next section. Later, we will see how all these factors generate warfare.

Kinship

The main focus of this section is marriage patterns and the much-debated "fighting over women." ...

One of the paramount concerns of a senior man is to find wives for his sons, younger brothers, and other coresident agnates. These men comprise his political supporters. But marriage makers are also vitally concerned with the question of bride service. In terms that are negotiated in advance, a groom is required to live with and labor for his wife's parents for a certain period after marriage, usually one to four years in the Orinoco-Mavaca area, before returning to the husband's village. The main duty of a son-in-law is to hunt, but other obligations are involved, including support of the father-in-law in war. The centrality of marriage arrangements is summed up by Lizot: "The highest cleverness consists in acquiring wives for one's sons by negotiating the briefest possible marital service and in seeking for one's daughters husbands who agree to settle permanently in the community."

Negotiation of marriage arrangements is made far more difficult by the circumstances of Western contact. In the Orinoco-Mavaca area, there is a well-known scarcity of marriageable females. I argue elsewhere that current evidence supports Chagnon's original observation that the intensity of female infanticide is associated with the intensity of warfare, despite his later assertion that sex ratio is skewed at birth. The local scarcity of marriageable women is aggravated by the relative predominance of polygyny. The actual incidence of polygyny is unclear. Some of Chagnon's generalizations, such as "a successful man may have had up to a dozen or more different wives, but rarely more than six wives simultaneously," appear exaggerated....

This relative scarcity of women would make finding a mate for a young man very difficult, and choosing a mate for daughters very political under the best of circumstances. The Yanomami do not live in the best of circumstances. As noted earlier, marriage arrangements are built up over years of negotiations, and they are reduced to chaos by the death waves of epidemics. Many disrupted families must be reconstituted, and arranging new marriages becomes even more difficult when the youngest generation of women dies off.

Simultaneously, the new ordering principle of access to Western goods enters in. Studies of some eastern Yanomami demonstrate a partial substitution of gifts of Western manufactures for actual bride service. The exchange is not a one-time payment. A man who has access to Western goods is expected to obtain them regularly for the wife-giver family. Although most marriages are village-endogamous, intervillage marriages are the firmest basis of alliance. Intermarriage, trade, and political support are all woven together. As noted earlier, the entire map of matrimonial, trade, and alliance networks was redrawn after the introduction of Western manufactures. The basis for this transformation is clear: women flow toward mission and other Western outpost villages. Among the eastern, Brazilian Yanomami, Peters and others describe a dramatic increase in village exogamy, with women going to the mission residents who could make bride payment with Western manufactures. In the northern reaches of their territory, Yanomami seeking Western manufactures from their well-supplied neighbors the Yekuana, gain access by a one-way ceding of women as brides or sexual partners....

The alliance between Chagnon's main field location, Bisaasi-teri and its Shamatari trade-partners to the south is perhaps the best illustration of this general pattern. In the four or five years after it moved to the government malaria station, Bisaasi-teri managed to obtain from the Shamatari "two dozen or so women ... while having given or promised only a half-dozen in return." The chain of trading villages leading out from Bisaasi-teri exhibits a "cline in sex ratios": 0.8, 1.1, 1.2, 1.6. Bisaasi-teri has an unusually high rate of exogamic marriages, 53 percent, compared to 15 percent in Patanowa-teri; and the majority of exogamic marriages in at least one of Bisaasi-teri's two divisions are through alliances, while most of Patanowa-teri's are through abductions of women.

Bisaasi-teri has been equally privileged in terms of bride service.

> The men who have obtained Shamatari wives have, as well, managed to cut short their period of bride service in the Shamatari village. Conversely, Shamatari men who have been promised women of Kaobawa's group are pressed into very lengthy bride service.

The bride service of these Shamatari seems particularly difficult. Chagnon describes one young man who was "expected to do all manner of onerous tasks ... [and] was subject to a considerable amount of ridicule and harsh treatment." His "father-in-law was particularly unpleasant to him. He denied

Wakarabewa sexual access to the girl while at the same time he allowed the young men of the natal village to enjoy these privileges."

Viewing access to Western manufactures as the key to obtaining women from allies is a different perspective than that argued by Chagnon, who has consistently attributed success in obtaining wives to physically aggressive measures. The relevance of the Western manufactures-for-women connection is, however, indicated in a brief comment at the start of his thesis: "the disposition of desirable trade goods may affect the balance in the exchange of women between two villages." Also, in a coauthored article based on team research in another Yanomami area, Chagnon et al. note that control over steel tools gives Makiratare (Yekuana) the ability to "demand and usually obtain sexual access to Yanomama women," both in affairs and as marriage partners.

Political Organization

Having examined the unequal trade and marital relationships that develop on the basis of unequal access to steel tools and other Western items, we can now understand the nature of the antagonisms that lead to war and other political conflicts in the Orinoco-Mavaca area. Steel tools are essential means of production. In the Orinoco-Mavaca area during the period under discussion, they were available from a few source points. Compared to villages dependent on Yanomami middlemen, those with monopolistic access to Westerners received: (1) more Western items, (2) better quality Western items, (3) many local manufactures, (4) more wives, and (5) better bride service terms....

How is force applicable in this context? The most direct application of force is that aimed at obtaining Western manufactures through plunder. That has been done by Yanomami, as by many Amazonian peoples, but it is a high-risk endeavor, and unusual within the Orinoco-Mavaca area. Force is more routinely applied to affect the flow of Western items beyond their source points. This occurs in several ways. Ambush or the threat of ambush is used to discourage travel that would circumvent a middleman village, or raids and surprise attacks at feasts are used to make a village relocate. The latter course can be used by a trade controller against a village that is attempting to move closer to the source of Western goods, and by those without good access to Westerners, in an attempt to make the controlling villages abandon their monopolistic position. Finally, club fights and other violent confrontations are used within established exchange relationships in order to direct the distribution of scarce items, and (more hypothetically) to influence the implicit rates of exchange of Western goods for other valuables.

The Yanomami do not appear at all unusual in this patterning of violence. Very similar considerations shape warfare on the Pacific Northwest Coast.... Conflict over access to Western manufactures fosters intense political conflict not just because of the importance of steel, but because unequal access creates a structured, collective conflict of interest between villages or factions. One man may benefit by capturing a wife, but a whole community benefits by an enhanced flow of machetes, axes, and pots. But turning a community of interest into an action group prepared to do violence is a difficult task, requiring great leadership skills. That brings us to the topic of leaders, and how they too have changed in the circumstances of contact.

Leadership among the Yanomami falls squarely within the general pattern for all recently described Amazonian societies. The headman represents his coresident kin, either a separate settlement or a recognizable cluster of families within a larger village, in interactions with outsiders. He is more likely than other men to be polygynous, and his status relative to other headmen largely depends upon the size of his kin group. In a sense, the group makes the leader, but the leader also makes the group. By his manipulation of marriages and other movements of people, he can gain or lose followers. The headman is the capstone of coresidential group organization, and those groups often dissolve on his death.

Leadership also responds to the changes associated with contact, however. Headmen are the main recipients of Western goods, especially in the more remote villages.... The role of headmen in channeling Western manufactures in outpost villages is less clear, but there are indications that they continue to have special access. To the east, at the Catrimani mission, each mission payment to an individual had to be approved first by the headman. Furthermore, headmen often enjoy the very substantial benefit of explicit backing by resident Westerners....

Another contact-related factor affecting the status of headmen is the intensity of conflict. Increasing danger of war brings an immediate, palpable increase in the authority and jurisdiction of headmen. In a politically charged environment, a leader can be peremptory, even tyrannical, using violence against those who do not obey his orders.

During peaceful times, the need for leadership is limited, but during war and other periods of high tension, the headman has two major responsibilities. One is tending to the necessities of combat, such as organizing raiding parties or checking village perimeters for signs of raiders....

The other responsibility is managing alliances. During peaceful times, political alliances between villages are of limited development and importance. During wartime, they are essential. Allies are needed for survival and success in war, providing both warriors on raids and vital places of refuge. There are often substantial tensions between allies, which the headman must keep under control....

Given the role of the headman as the capstone of the coresidential group, and his centrality in relation to the practice of war and alliance, it is easy to understand a tactic of Yanomami warfare: targeting the headman. Headmen are frequently reported as the intended targets or actual victims of raiders. The effectiveness of this tactic is illustrated by the plight of Monouteri in 1965, when the killing of their headman by raiders left them adrift and dependent on the leadership of self-interested neighbors....

Superstructure

[Chagnon called the Yanomami "the fierce people."] Fierceness is embodied in a commitment to take revenge, in cultivating an image that retaliation will follow any killing. As [one man] reportedly told potential enemies: "We are in this world to avenge ourselves; if you do it to me, I will do it to you." This image has obvious defensive value. In a climate of ongoing wars, the failure to retaliate for a hostile act creates the appearance of weakness, and this can encourage future attacks. But it is necessary to distinguish the tactical value of retaliation from the idea that wars are propelled forward by sentiments of blood revenge. In a recent publication, Chagnon places great emphasis on blood revenge as a factor itself responsible for raiding and other violence. In a commentary on that article, I argue that the vengeance motivation itself is highly malleable, manipulated to suit political needs.

    ... [I]ntensifying hostility between political groups is [also] conceptualized in terms of spirit battles, controlled by their respective shamans. An accusation of witchcraft often precedes combat, so that it may appear that these beliefs are the cause of war. But it has been a consistent finding of witchcraft studies in other parts of the world that accusations of witchcraft *express* existing hostilities rather than cause them. Here too, bad relations lead to suspicions of sorcery and villages "linked by trade and feasting ties ... rarely accuse each other of practicing harmful magic."

    ... [A]ttribution of a death to sorcery is accompanied by a felt need for blood revenge. It may be that witchcraft and revenge are two sides of a coin. Witch beliefs confirm the malevolence of particular outsiders ("them"); vengeance beliefs emphasize the solidarity of the local group ("versus us"). Together, they make up an effective ideological system for the difficult task of mobilizing people for collective violence.

Conclusions

This paper has examined the multiple, interacting effects of Western contact on the war complex of Yanomami of the Orinoco-Mavaca area. Contact both generated war, primarily through conflicting interests in Western manufactures, and led to pervasive reorganization of society and culture, such that all of life became oriented toward violent conflict. Comparing these Yanomami to Yanomami elsewhere, one cannot doubt that they share a fundamental cultural identity. But the "fierce people" represent Yanomami culture in an extreme conflict mode, a mode that is clearly attributable to the exogenous factors of Western contact. These people cannot be taken as "our contemporary ancestors." They do not represent a phase in sociocultural evolution.

    No one can say if the Yanomami ancestors made war before they felt any effects of European contact. But their *known* wars are clearly products of the contact situation, and more specifically, of the infrastructural changes wrought by contact, played out through a changing structure and superstructure.

POSTSCRIPT

Are Yanomami Violence and Warfare Natural Human Efforts to Maximize Reproductive Fitness?

Although no one can dispute the fact that the Yanomami were violent in the 1960s, these selections may lead some to ask whether Yanomami violence was always as pervasive a part of Yanomami culture as Chagnon describes it. Filmmaker Timothy Asch, who helped Chagnon with some of his films, depicts a much more tender side of Yanomami life than is typical in Chagnon's films. What seems to be missing from both of these perspectives, however, is the role of basic cultural values in shaping Yanomami behavior, whether toward violence or toward tenderness. What is also absent in these two accounts is the role of regional patterns of intergroup exchange that may have been disrupted by the introduction of Western machetes.

Ferguson's argument is more fully developed in his book *Yanomami Warfare: A Political History* (School of American Research Press, 1995) in which he draws upon his own research as well as that of many other anthropologists besides Chagnon who have worked with the Yanomami. Other aspects of Ferguson's argument are developed in several papers, including "Game Wars? Ecology and Conflict in Amazonia," *Journal of Anthropological Research* (Summer 1989) and "Do Yanomami Killers Have More Kids?" *American Ethnologist* (August 1989).

Chagnon has published several ethnographic volumes about his research with the Yanomami. These include his original monograph, *Yanomami*, 5th ed. (Harcourt Brace, 1997), originally published with the subtitle "The Fierce People" in 1968, and *Studying the Yanomami* (Holt, Rinehart and Winston, 1974). His most recent monograph deals directly with aspects of cultural change and is entitled *Yanomami: The Last Days of Eden* (Harcourt, Brace, Jovanovich, 1992). He has also published a number of papers supporting his sociobiological interpretations. See "Kin Selection Theory, Kinship, Marriage and Fitness Among the Yanomomö Indians," in G. W. Barlow and J. Silverberg, eds., *Sociobiology: Beyond Natural Selection* (Westview Press, 1980) and "Sociodemographic Attributes of Nepotism in Tribal Populations," *Current Problems in Sociobiology* (Cambridge University Press, 1982).

Two of Bruce Albert's essays, "Yanomami 'Violence': Inclusive Fitness or Ethnographer's Representation," *Current Anthropology* (December 1989) and "On Yanomami Warfare: Rejoinder," *Current Anthropology* (December 1990), deal with the central question of fitness in this issue.

ISSUE 12

Is Ethnic Conflict Inevitable?

YES: Sudhir Kakar, from "Some Unconscious Aspects of Ethnic Violence in India," in Veena Das, ed., *Mirrors of Violence: Communities, Riots and Survivors in South Asia* (Oxford University Press, 1990)

NO: Anthony Oberschall, from "The Manipulation of Ethnicity: From Ethnic Cooperation to Violence and War in Yugoslavia," *Ethnic and Racial Studies* (November 2000)

ISSUE SUMMARY

YES: Indian social researcher Sudhir Kakar analyzes the origins of ethnic conflict from a psychological perspective to argue that ethnic differences are deeply held distinctions that from time to time will inevitably erupt as ethnic conflicts. He maintains that anxiety arises from preconscious fears about cultural differences. In his view, no amount of education or politically correct behavior will eradicate these fears and anxieties about people of differing ethnic backgrounds.

NO: American sociologist Anthony Oberschall considers the ethnic conflicts that have recently emerged in Bosnia and contends that primordial ethnic attachments are insufficient to explain the sudden emergence of violence among Bosnian ethnic groups. He adopts a complex explanation for this violence, identifying circumstances in which fears and anxieties were manipulated by politicians for self-serving ends. It was only in the context of these manipulations that ethnic violence could have erupted, concludes Oberschall.

Since the 1960s anthropologists and other social scientists have debated the causes, origins, and necessary conditions for ethnic differences to erupt into ethnic violence. Such discussions have built on an older debate about the origins of ethnicity. In the earlier debate, two key positions emerged. The first is the *primordialist* view, in which ethnic attachments and sentiments emerge from the fact of being members of the same cultural community. Although cultural in origin, the primordialists see kinship, language, and customary practices as the source of ethnic identity and social bonds between people of the same ethnicity. Ethnicity in this view is something one is born with, or at least born into, because it develops as one learns kinship, language, and culture. A second position, often called the *circumstantialist* perspective, was developed by the Norwegian anthropologist Fredrik Barth in his book *Ethnic Groups and Social Boundaries* (Little, Brown, 1969). For Barth, a person's ethnicity is neither fixed nor a natural condition of his or her birth. One's ethnicity could be (and often was) manipulated under different circumstances. By dressing differently, by learning a different language, and by intermarriage, people in many ethnic groups within a generation or two could become members of another ethnic group and have a different ethnic identity. Later, if it became advantageous to be members of the first ethnic group, these same people could acknowledge their past and become members of the first group.

The following selections shift the ethnicity debate to the problem of whether or not ethnic conflict is inevitable. Sudhir Kakar uses a psychological approach to develop a primordialist argument to explain the frequent and almost continual problems of ethnic violence in India. For Kakar, ethnic sentiments and attachments emerge from deep psychological concerns at the unconscious or even preconscious level. He contends that psychologically there are primordial differences between Indians of different ethnic backgrounds, and such differences lead to conflicts over access to resources, jobs, and the like.

Anthony Oberschall considers possible explanations for the sudden appearance of ethnic conflict in the former Yugoslavia. He acknowledges that the primordialist variables of kinship, religion, and language may play some role in explaining why Serbs, Croats, and Bosnian Muslims behaved as they did once ethnic conflict broke out. Traditional animosities existed for centuries in the Balkans, and they reemerged suddenly after 50 years of peace and cooperation. But such variables cannot explain why these groups started fighting with one another in the first place, says Oberschall, after nearly half a century of living together peacefully, regularly socializing, and even intermarrying with one another; such ties as kinship, language, and religion do not explain why tensions flared up or why neighbors suddenly tried to eliminate people of other ethnic backgrounds from their towns and villages. Drawing on a complex pattern of circumstantial variables, Oberschall develops a circumstantialist model, arguing that politicians were manipulating local sentiments for their own ends. In the context of great uncertainty and crisis, people of all ethnic backgrounds bought into the anxieties suggested by their different leaders.

What leads people to hate people of different ethnic backgrounds? Is it deeply held fears of cultural differences? Or does conflict emerge because individuals fear losing what they have worked hard to obtain? How could people in Yugoslavia live together harmoniously for 50 years and then suddenly participate in the "ethnic cleansing" of their neighborhoods? Could the willingness to commit such acts of violence against neighbors have been suppressed for half a century by a strong central government? What is the source of this kind of group hatred, since differences in skin color and physical features are largely not present in either the Indian or Yugoslavian cases?

Sudhir Kakar

 **YES**

Some Unconscious Aspects of Ethnic Violence in India

The need to integrate social and psychological theory in the analysis of cultural conflicts, i.e. conflicts between ethnic and religious groups, has long been felt while its absence has been equally long deplored. Though everyone agrees on the theoretical questions involved—how do these conflicts originate, develop, and get resolved; how do they result in violent aggression—a general agreement on the answers or even on how to get these answers moves further and further away.

A large part of the problem in the study of these questions lies with the nature of and the crisis within the social sciences. The declining fortunes of logical positivism, hastened in the last twenty years by the widespread circulation and absorption of the views of such thinkers as Gadamer, Habermas, Derrida, Ricouer and Foucault, has led to a plethora of new models in the sciences of man and society. The dominant model of yesteryears—social science as social physics—is now only one among several clamouring for allegiance and adherents. It incorporates only one view among many on the nature of social reality and of social science knowledge. Anthropology, sociology, political science, psychology and even economics are all becoming more pluralistic and scattering into frameworks. In such a situation, the calls for a general theory of ethnic violence or indeed (as Clifford Geertz has remarked) of anything *social,* sound increasingly hollow, and the claims to have one science seem megalomaniacal. Thus, without taking recourse to other disciplines and even ignoring the grand theories of human aggression in psychology itself— those of animal ethology, sociology, Freudian Thanatos and so on—I would like to present some limited 'local knowledge' observations on ethnic violence in India from a psychoanalytic perspective.

In the manner of a clinician, let me begin with the concrete data on which I base my observations on the first question, namely the origins of ethnic conflict. The data for these observations, and those which follow, come from diverse sources: spirit possession in north India, dreams of psychotherapy patients, eavesdropping on group discussions at the Golden Temple complex in July 1984, and finally, personal participation in large religious assemblies.

The Other in Ethnic Conflict

Some years ago, while studying the phenomenon of possession by spirits in rural north India, I was struck by a curious fact. In a very large number of cases, 15 out of 28, the *bhuta* or malignant spirit possessing Hindu men and women turned out to be a Muslim. When, during the healing ritual, the patient went into a trance and the spirit started expressing its wishes, these wishes invariably turned out to be those which would have been horrifying to the patient's conscious self. In one case, the Muslim spirit possessing an elderly Brahmin priest vigorously insisted on eating kababs. The five women surrounding the man who had engaged the *bhuta* in conversation were distinctly disheartened that he had turned out to be a *Sayyad* and one of them lamented: 'These Mussulmans! They have ruined our *dharma* but they are so strong they can withstand our gods.' In another case, the *bhuta* inhabiting a young married woman not only expressed derogatory sentiments towards her 'lord and master' but also openly stated its intentions of bringing the mother-in-law to a violent and preferably bloody end.

Possession by a Muslim *bhuta*, then, seemed to reflect the afflicted person's desperate efforts to convince himself and others that his hunger for forbidden foods and uncontrolled rage towards those who should be loved and respected, as well as all other imagined transgressions and sins of the heart, belonged to the Muslim destroyer of taboos and were furthest away from his 'good' Hindu self. In that Muslim *bhutas* were universally considered to be the strongest, vilest, the most malignant and the most stubborn of the evil spirits, the Muslim seemed to symbolize the alien and the demonic in the unconscious part of the Hindu mind.

The division of humans into mutually exclusive group identities of tribe, nation, caste, religion and class thus seems to serve two important psychological functions. The first is to increase the feeling of well being in the narcissistic realm by locating one's own group at the centre of the universe, superior to others. The shared grandiose self, maintained by legends, myths and rituals, seems to demand a concomitant conviction that other groups are inferior.

India has not been exempt from this universal rule. Whatever idealizing tendencies we might have in viewing our past history, it is difficult to deny that every social group in its tales, ritual and other literature, has sought to portray itself nearer to a purer, divine state while denigrating and banishing others to the periphery. It is also undeniable that sharing a common ego-ideal and giving one's own group a super-individual significance can inspire valued human attributes of loyalty and heroic self-sacrifice. All this is familiar to students of culture and need not detain us further here.

For the psychoanalyst it is the second function of division into ethnic groups, namely the need to have other groups as containers for one's disavowed aspects, which is of greater significance. These disavowed aspects, or the demonic spirits, take birth during that period of our childhood when the child, made conscious of good and bad, right and wrong, begins to divide himself into two parts, one that is the judge and the other that is being judged.

The unacceptable, condemned parts of the self are projected outside, the projective processes being primitive attempts to relieve pain by externalizing it. The expelled parts of the self are then attached to various beings—animals and human—as well as to whole castes, ethnic and religious communities. This early split within our nature, which gives us a future license to view and treat others as if they were no better than the worst in ourselves, is normally completed by the time the child is six to seven years old. The earliest defenses for dealing with the unacceptable aspects of the self—namely their denial, the splitting from awareness and projection onto another group—require the active participation of the members of the child's group-parents and other adults who must support such a denial and projection. They are shared group defenses. The family and extended group of a Hindu upper-caste child, for instance, not only provides him with its myths and rituals which increase his sense of group cohesion and of narcissism in belonging to such an exalted entity, but also help him in elaborating and fleshing out his demonology of other ethnic and religious groups. The *purana* of the Muslim demon, for instance, as elaborated by many Hindu groups, has nothing to do with Sufi saints, the prophet's sayings or the more profound sentiments of Islam. Instead, its stories are of rape and pillage by the legions of Ghazni and Timur as well as other more local accounts of Muslim mayhem.

The Muslim demon is, so to say, the traditional container of Hindu conflicts over aggressive impulses. It is the transgressor of deeply-held taboos, especially over the expression of physical violence. Recent events in Punjab, I am afraid, are creating yet another demon in the Hindu psyche of north India. Over the last few years, tales of [Sikh militant leader] Bhindranwale's dark malevolence and the lore of murderous terrorists has led to a number of reported dreams from patients where Sikhs have appeared as symbols of the patient's own aggressive and sadistic superego. A group of Sikhs with raised swords chasing a patient who has broken into an old woman's shop, a Nihang stabbing a man repeatedly with a spear on the street while another patient as a frightened child looks down upon the scene from an upstairs window—these are two of many such dream images. Leaving aside the role played by these images in the patients' individual dramas, the projection of the feared aggressive parts of the self on the figure of the Sikh is an unhappy portent for the future relationship between the two communities. The fantasy of being overwhelmed by the frightening aggressive strength of the Sikhs can, in periods of upheaval and danger—when widespread regression in ego takes place and the touch with reality is weakened—lead to psychotic delusions about Sikh intentions.

Sikh Militancy

Until this point I have used some psychoanalytic, especially Kleinian, concepts of splitting and projective identification to understand data that bears on the question of ethnic conflict. More specifically, I have outlined the origins of certain pre-conscious attitudes of Hindus towards Muslims and Sikhs.

These attitudes reflect the psychological needs of the child, and the adult, to split off his bad impulses, especially those relating to violence, and to attach them to other communities, a process supported and reinforced by other members of the group. Let me now use another set of analytical concepts of group identity and narcissism, narcissistic hurt and rage, to understand the phenomenon of Sikh militancy. To avoid any misunderstanding let me state at the outset that I am primarily talking about the militant Sikh youth of Punjab, not of all Sikh youths, and certainly not of the Sikh community as a whole. Also, the word narcissism in psychoanalysis is not used in a pejorative sense but, together with sexuality and aggression, as the third major and fundamental motivational factor in human beings which is concerned with the maintenance of self-esteem. The data for these observations comes from being an observer of heated and anguished discussions among randomly formed groups which were being spontaneously held all over the Golden Temple complex in Amritsar, five weeks after Operation Blue Star.* Said elsewhere, the aftermath of Blue Star, which heightened the awareness of their cultural identity among many Sikhs, also brought out in relief one of its less conscious aspects. I have called it the Khalsa warrior element of Sikh identity which, at least since the tenth guru and at least among the Jats, has expressed itself in images of 'lifting up the sword' against the 'oppression of a tyrannical ruler', and whose associated legends only countenance two possible outcomes—complete victory (*fateh*) or martyrdom (*shaheedi*) of those engaged in the battle. The surrounding society has of course reinforced this identity element over the years by its constant talk of Sikh martial process and valour. The Sikh youth's acceptance of these projections of heroic militancy made by the Hindu can lead to his overestimation of this aspect of his identity as he comes to feel that it is his very essence. All other qualities which may compromise heroic militancy, such as yearnings for passivity, softness and patience, will tend to be denied, split off and projected onto other, despised groups. The damage done to the Akal Takht—as much a symbol of corporate militancy as of religious piety—reinforced the two M's—militance and martyrdom—the inner counterparts of the well-known five K's which constitute the outer markers of the Khalsa warrior identity. The exaggerated value placed on martyrdom is hard to understand for Hindus since oppressors in *their* mythology—the Hindu equivalent of Sikh legendary history—tended to be destroyed by divine intervention rather than by the sacrifice of martyrs.

The army action was then a hurt to Sihk religious sentiments in a very different way from the sense in which a Hindu understands the term. It was an affront to group narcissism, to a shared grandiose self. The consequent feelings were of narcissistic hurt and rage. This was brought home to me again and again as I listened to groups of anguished men and women in front of the ruins of the Akal Takht. Most men stood in attitudes of sullen defeat, scorned and derided by the women with such sentences as 'Where is the starch in your moustache now?'

* [Operation 'Blue Star' was the code name for the army action to clear the Golden Temple of Sikh militants in June 1984, in which Bhindranwale died. The operation resulted in extensive damage to the sacred site.—Ed.]

Given the collective need for the preservation of this core of the group identity, the Golden Temple action automatically completed a circle of associations. The army action to clear Akal Takht from desperadoes became an attack on the Sikh nation by a tyrannical 'Delhi durbar'. It was seen as an assault designed to wipe out all its traces, its *nishan*—since this is how it was in the past. The Sikhs killed in the attack were now defenders of the faith and martyrs—since this too is a pattern from the past. The encounter was viewed as a momentous battle, an oppressive empire's defeat of the forces of the Khalsa. The relatively heavy army losses are not a consequence of its restraint but a testimony to the fighting qualities of the Khalsa warrior. Paradoxically, the terrorist losses were exaggerated to simultaneously show the overwhelming strength of the army and the Khalsa readiness to die in martyrdom when victory is not possible.

Bhindranwale, in dramatically exemplifying the two M's of militancy and martyrdom, has touched deep chords. His status with much of the Sikh youth today is very near that of an eleventh guru. Initially, Bhindranwale may have been one of many *sants,* though more militant than most, who dot the countryside in Punjab. What began the process of his elevation was his successful defiance of the government—echoes, again of Sikh history, of defiant gurus contesting state authority. In setting the date and terms of his arrest ('*Santji* gave arrest', and not 'He was arrested', is how the people at the Temple complex put it), and predicting the day of his release, Bhindranwale began to be transformed from a mortal preacher to a 'realized' saint with miraculous powers. (And the reputation of being able to work miracles is, we know, essential for those aspiring to enter the portals of gurudom in all religious traditions.) His 'martyrdom' has now cemented the transformation and made his elevation into the Sikh militant pantheon irreversible. The tortures and murders in the Temple complex or outside are no longer his responsibility, being seen as the doings of deluded associates, acts of which Santji was, of course, unaware.

It is obvious that after the army action there was a threat to the cultural identity of at least a section of the Jat Sikh youth. This led to regressive transformations in the narcissistic realm, where reality is interpreted only as a balm to narcissistic hurt and as a coolant for narcissistic rage. It needs to be asked what precisely constituted this threat. I would tend to see the threat to the Jat Sikh group identity as part of a universal modernizing process to which many groups all over the world have been and continue to be exposed. This group though has preferred to change a social-psychological issue into a political one. The cultural decay and spiritual disintegration talked of in the Anandpur resolution are then viewed as an aspect of majority-minority relations rather than as an existential condition brought on by the workings of a historical fate. A feeling of inner threat is projected outside as oppression, a conflict around tradition and modernity as a conflict around power.

Narcissistic rage, then, is the core of the militancy of Sikh youth and Sikh terrorism. As Kohut says about this rage: 'The need for revenge, for righting a wrong, for undoing a hurt by whatever means, and a deeply anchored, unrelating compulsion in the pursuit of all these aims, gives no rest to those who have suffered a narcissistic injury.' For the analyst, this becomes paramount in the understanding of youthful militancy, the foreground, while political, social and other issues recede into the background.

Let me now make a few observations on the question of ethnic conflict resulting in violent aggression, i.e on mob violence. My data for these remarks is, paradoxically, personal participation in largely peaceful and loving groups engaged in religious and spiritual endeavours. Yet many of the psychological processes are common to the two kinds of groups. Both emotionally charged religious assemblies and mobs on the rampage bring out in relief the vulnerability of human individual ego functions confronted with the power of group processes. In the face of these, the 'integrity', 'autonomy', and 'independence' of the ego seem to be wishful illusions and hypothetical constructs. Mobs, more than religious congregations, provide striking examples of the massive inducement, by group processes, of individuals towards a new identity and behaviour of the sort that would ordinarily be repudiated by a great majority of the individuals so induced. They illustrate, more clearly than in any other comparable social situation, the evanescence of rational thought, the fragility of internalized behavioural controls, values, and moral and ethnical standards.

The most immediate experience in being part of a crowd is the sensual pounding received in the press of other bodies. At first there may be a sense of unease as the body, the container of our individuality and the demarcator of our boundaries in space, is sharply wrenched away from its habitual way of experiencing others. For, as we grow up, the touch of others, once so deliberately courted and responded to with delight, increasingly becomes a problem. Coming from a loved one, touch is deliciously welcomed; with strangers, on the other hand, there is an involuntary shrinking of the body, their touch taking on the menacing air of invasion by the other.

But once the fear of touch disappears in the fierce press of other bodies and the individual lets himself become a part of the crowd's density, the original apprehension is transformed into an expansiveness that stretches to include others. Distances and differences—of class, status, age, caste hierarchy—disappear in an exhilarating feeling that individual boundaries can indeed be transcended and were perhaps illusory in the first place. Of course, touch is only one of the sensual stimuli that hammers at the gate of individual identity. Other excitations, channelled through vision, hearing and smell, are also very much involved. In addition, there are exchanges of body heat, muscle tension and body rhythms which take place in a crowd. In short, the crowd's assault on the sense of individuality, its invitation to transcend one's individual boundaries and its offer of a freedom from personal doubts and anxieties is well nigh irresistible.

The need and search for 'self-transcending' experience, to lose one's self in the group, suspend judgement and reality-testing, is, I believe, the primary motivational factor in both religious assembly and violent mob, even though the stated purpose is spiritual uplift in one and mayhem and murder in the other. Self-transcendence, rooted in the blurring of our body image, not only opens us to the influx of the divine but also heightens our receptivity to the demonic. The surge of love also washes away the defences against the emergence of archaic hates. In psychoanalytic terms, regression in the body image is simultaneous with regression in the superego system. Whether the ego reacts to this regression in a disintegrated fashion with panic that manifests itself (in a mob) in senseless rage and destructive acts—or in a release of love encompassing the group and the world outside—depends on the structure provided to the group. Without the rituals which make tradition palpable and thus extend the group in time by giving assurances of continuity to the beleaguered ego, and without the permanent visibility of leaders whose presence is marked by conspicuous external insignia and who replace the benign and loving functions of the superego, religious crowds can easily turn into marauding mobs. Transcending individuality by merging into a group can generate heroic self-sacrifice but also unimaginable brutality. To get out of one's skin in a devotional assembly is also at the same time to have less regard for saving it in a mob.

Some Implications

The implications of my remark, I know, are not too comforting. The need for communities, our own to take care of our narcissistic needs and of others to serve as recipients for our hostility and destructiveness, are perhaps built into our very ground-plan as human beings. Well meaning educative efforts in classrooms or in national integration seminars are for the most part too late and too little in that they are misdirected. They are too late since most of the evidence indicates that the communal imagination is well entrenched by the time a child enters school. They are misdirected in that they never frankly address the collective—and mostly preconscious—fears and wishes of the various communities. Demons do not much care for 'correct' interpretations of religious texts by scholars, nor are they amenable to humanist pleas of reason to change into good and loving beings. All we can do is accept their existence but reduce their potential for causing actual physical violence and destruction. The routes to this goal, the strategies for struggle with our own inner devils, are many. One strategy strives for the dissolution of small group identities into even large entities. Sikhs and Hindus in Punjab can move towards a group identity around 'Punjabiyyat', in which case the despised demon shifts outside to the *Purubia* or the *Madrasi*. One can go on to progressively larger identities of the nationalist Indian whose *bete-noire* can then be the Pakistani or the Chinese. One can envisage even larger groupings, for instance of the 'Third World', where the sense of narcissistic well being provided by this particular community needs a demonic West as the threatening aggressor.

A second strategy is, in a certain sense, to go the opposite way. By this I mean less the encouragement of various ethnic identities than in ensuring that all manifestations of ethnic group action—assemblies, demonstrations, processions—are given as much religious structure as possible in order to prevent the breakout of archaic hate. Vedic chants and Koranic prayers, *mahants,* *pujaris* and *mullahs* in their full regalia and conspicuous by their presence, are fully encouraged to be in the forefront of religious processions and demonstrations. Traditional religious standards, flags and other symbols are liberally used to bind the religious assemblies.

Yet another strategy (and let me note that none of these are exclusive) is to concentrate all efforts at the containment of the communal demon on the dominant community. We know that the belief of the dominant party in a relationship often becomes a self-fulfilling prophecy, involuntarily changing the very consciousness of the weaker partner. In India the Hindu image of himself and of other communities is apt to be incorporated in the self image of non-Hindu minorities. Even when consciously accepted, the denigrating part of the image is likely to be a source of intensive unconscious rage in other communities. Their rage is stored up over a period of time, till it explodes in all its violent manifestations whenever historical circumstances sanction such eruptions.

Anthony Oberschall

The Manipulation of Ethnicity: From Ethnic Cooperation to Violence and War in Yugoslavia

Four views on ethnicity and ethnic violence are common. In the 'primordial' view, ethnic attachments and identities are a cultural given and a natural affinity, like kinship sentiments. They have an overpowering emotional and non-rational quality. Applied to the former Yugoslavia, the primordialist believes that despite seemingly cooperative relations between nationalities in Yugoslavia, mistrust, enmity, even hatred were just below the surface, as had long been true the Balkans. Triggered by fierce competition for political power during the breakup of Yugoslavia and driven by the uncertainties over state boundaries and minority status, these enmities and hatreds, fuelled by fear and retribution, turned neighbour against neighbour, and district against district, in an expanding spiral of aggression and reprisals. Although the primordial account sounds plausible, and it is true that politicians activated and manipulated latent nationalism and ethnic fears, some evidence contradicts it. Ethnic cleansing was more commonly militias and military against civilians than neighbour against neighbour. In seventeen assaults against villages during the ethnic cleansing of Prijedor district in Bosnia in May/June 1992, we found that the aggressors wore military and paramilitary uniforms and insignia. In fourteen assaults, the survivors did not recognize any of the aggressors, who did not bother to wear masks or disguises. These 'weekend warriors' from central Serbia openly bivouacked at the Prijedor police station. The primordial theory omits the fact that ethnic hatreds can subside as a consequence of statecraft and living together. [President Charles] de Gaulle and [Chancellor Konrad] Adenauer managed to reconcile the French and German people. Why no lasting conciliation in Yugoslavia after forty years of ethnic peace?

In the second, 'instrumentalist' view, ethnic sentiments and loyalties are manipulated by political leaders and intellectuals for political ends, such as state creation. For Yugoslavia, the instrumentalist explanation highlights Serb nationalists' goal of a Greater Serbia, and a similar Croat nationalism. Ethnic cleansing resulted from a historical longing by Serbs in Croatia at first backed moderate nationalists, for a Greater Serbia, with deep cultural roots. [Slobodan] Milosevic and Serb nationalists tried to implement it when the opportunity arose in the late 1980s and early 1990s. Greater Serbia required ethnic cleansing of non-Serbs from

From Anthony Oberschall, "The Manipulation of Ethnicity: From Ethnic Cooperation to Violence and War in Yugoslavia," *Ethnic and Racial Studies,* vol. 23, no. 6 (November 2000). Copyright © 2000 by Routledge Journals, Taylor & Francis Ltd. Reprinted by permission of the author and Taylor & Francis Ltd. http://www.tandf.co.uk/journals. Notes and references omitted.

areas inhabited by a majority of Serbs and the corridors linking Serb population clusters. Although there is evidence that ethnic cleansing was a state policy, orchestrated by the highest authorities in Serbia and the Bosnian Serb leadership, this explanation ignores that many Bosnian Serbs did not want secession, that many Serbs in Croatia at first backed moderate nationalists, and that many Serbs evaded the draft. The instrumentalist view assumes an ethnic consensus that initially does not exist. But if many were reluctant to wage war and to participate in ethnic cleansing, how did ethnic extremists prevail over these moderates?

The third 'constructionist' view of ethnicity and ethnic conflict was originally formulated by [Leo] Kuper. It supplements the insights of the primordial and of the instrumentalist views. Religion or ethnicity are very real social facts, but in ordinary times they are only one of several roles and identities that matter. There is a great deal of variance in a population on ethnic attachments and identities. In the words of [Juan J.] Linz and [Alfred] Stepan 'political identities are less primordial and fixed than contingent and changing. They are amenable to being constructed or eroded by political institutions and political choices'. The constructionist view offers insights but is incomplete. How are nationality and ethnicity constructed and eroded by political mobilization and mass media propaganda?

A fourth model of ethnic violence centres on state breakdown, anarchy, and the security dilemma that such conditions pose to ethnic groups who engage in defensive arming to protect their lives and property against ethnic rivals, which then stimulates arming by other ethnic groups like an arms race between states. The driving motivations are not ethnic hatreds but fear and insecurity. In the Yugoslav crisis Michael Ignatieff puts it thus:

> Once the Yugoslav communist state began to split into its constituent national particles the key question soon became: will the local Croat policeman protect me if I am a Serb? Will I keep my job in the soap factory if my new boss is a Serb or a Muslim? The answer to this question was no, because no state remained to enforce the old ethnic bargain.

There is a security dilemma in ethnic conflict, but why so much ethnic violence without state breakdown? Can insecurity and fear be spread by propaganda even when daily experience contradicts the allegations of ethnic hostility and threat? Can the powerful fear the weak?

Building on the four views and mindful of [Rogers] Brubaker and [David] Laitin's criteria for a satisfactory theory of ethnic violence, I use the idea of latent nationalism at the grass roots, and show how it was activated; I highlight ethnic manipulation by political leaders, and explain why manipulation was successful; I take into account the variance in ethnic identities and analyse why extremists prevailed over moderates; I focus on the security dilemma and ethnic fears and insecurity, and show how fears and insecurity grew from lies and propaganda. To this arsenal of concepts and models for generating the dynamics of ethnicization and collective violence, I add 'cognitive frames'. Combining all, I seek to explain how forty years of cooperative ethnic relations ended with collective violence and war.

Prijedor: A Case-Study

To get a sense of what is to be explained about ethnic conflict and violence at the grass roots, consider the Prijedor district in Northwest Bosnia where major ethnic violence took place in the spring of 1992. In the 1991 Census, Prijedor district was 42.5 percent Serb and 44 percent Muslim. It was surrounded by districts that had either a slight Serb majority or were close to even, as Prijedor was. Prijedor Serbs were not an isolated Serb minority island surrounded by a sea of Muslims and Croats.

There had been no Serb complaints of mistreatment, discrimination, or intimidation in Prijedor by non-Serbs, or vice versa. On the contrary, as a bewildered Muslim refugee from Prijedor stated,

> In Prijedor there were no conflicts between nationalities. We didn't make the distinctions. My colleague at work was an Orthodox Serb, we worked together. When we were children we went to the Orthodox church or the mosque together ... I don't understand. Before there were never any problems between us. We lived together. My sister is married to a Serb, and a brother of my wife is married to a Croat.

According to the [United Nations] Bassiouni Report, Serbs held the leading positions in Prijedor in 1991, as they had done for decades.... In the 1991 elections, the predominantly Muslim SDA [Party of Democratic Union in Bosnia] won thirty seats; the Serb SDS [Serbian Democratic Party] twenty-eight, and thirty-two went to other parties. The Muslims refrained from taking over a number of leading posts to which their electoral victory entitled them because they believed in power-sharing. Even so, the SDS blocked the work of the Prijodor Assembly and organized a parallel governance for Serbs, in alliance with the SDS leaders in nearby Banja Luka. In Bosnia as a whole, the Serbs shared political power and controlled the most important military forces.

As in other towns and cities in Bosnia, the SDS in Prijedor organized a successful Serb plebiscite for Greater Serbia. A parallel Serb governance, called the 'Crisis Committee', secretly created an armed force of Serbs with weapons obtained from Serbia. Serb crisis committees were also formed among Serbs in some of Prijedor district's towns and villages. On the night of 29 April 1992, without any provocation or a shot being fired, 1,775 well-armed Serbs seized the city of Prijedor in a *coup d'état*. By this time the Prijedor local government had completely lost power to various Serb groups. Paramilitaries had seized the radio and television transmitters and cut off all but Serb transmissions. The Serb *coup d'état* in Prijedor is similar to what happened elsewhere in Northern Bosnia.

Non-Serb leaders were arrested and shortly afterwards disappeared, presumed executed. The Muslim police and other officials were fired from their posts. Schools closed; the newspaper ceased publication, and a Serb paper was started. Non-Serbs were harassed, intimidated, fired from their jobs. Amid incessant house searches, weapons, mostly hunting guns, belonging to non-Serbs, were rounded up. After the attempt on 30 May by the Patriotic League of Croats and Muslims—an armed formation of 150 fighters—to retake the old city, many non-Serb inhabitants were arrested and sent to the infamous Omarskca camp. At Omarska, prisoners were tortured, brutalized, starved and killed. The guards were rural Serbs from nearby villages; the interrogators were Prijedor police inspectors.... People were rounded up and some were executed: those shot were Muslim leaders whose names appeared on a list. Atrocities took place elsewhere in the district.

Several observations should be made about the events in Prijedor. Muslims and Serbs had lived in peace before the conflict erupted. The Serbs were neither a numerical minority, nor discriminated against. They not only had a share of power, but they had the biggest share, and they were well armed. Why, then, did Serbs fear their fellow citizens in Prijedor? A cartoon from this period expresses the puzzle well. It shows a bearded Serb paramilitary, armed to the teeth, with guns, hand-granades, ammunition belts, knives, waving a machine gun, looking worried, and yelling at the top of his voice, 'I am being threatened!' There was no anarchy, no state breakdown in Prijedor. The Serbs used the police and military of a functioning government to subdue the non-Serbs. Serbs may have been apprehensive about their future in an independent Bosnia, but even in Bosnia they had a big presence—numerical, military, political, economic. There was no spontaneous violence initiated by Serb civilians against non-Serbs, nor vice-versa. Instead, there was a highly organized, secretly prepared *coup d'état,* like the 1917 Bolshevik seizure of power in Russia.... As in the Russian revolution with the Soviets, the Serb parallel government was not only an instrument for seizing power from non-Serbs but of stripping the moderate Serbs of any influence and authority.

What was the reaction of ordinary Serbs to these events? Though there is no information on Prijedor itself, one can learn from what observers recorded in nearby Banja Luka. Peter Maas reports that a Serb lawyer there estimated that 30 percent of Serbs oppose such things [ethnic cleansing], 60 percent agree or are confused and go along with the 10 percent who 'have the guns and control the television tower'.... An armed, organized 10 percent who control mass communications can have its way when the majority supports it overtly or tacitly or is confused, and when the opposition is unorganized, divided, and scared. One has to explain how it was that 60 percent were supportive of or confused on ethnic cleansing, since their support and quiescence were necessary for the success of the extremist 10 percent.

Was Violent Conflict Inevitable?

In a multinational state such as Yugoslavia, nationality will be a salient dimension of political contention, and there will be leaders and intellectuals with a nationalist ideology and agenda. The Yugoslav constitution and its political institutions were delicately balanced and crafted to deal with nationality. A nationalist challenge would inevitably zero in on stateness, minority rights and power-sharing: if accepted boundaries of political units are renegotiated or remade, who decides which peoples and territories belong to new and old political entities? Will all peoples in the new units be equal citizens for governance, or will majority ethnonational affiliation become the admission ticket for full citizenship?

Once unleashed, nationalism in Yugoslavia set on a collision course the two largest nationalities, the Serbs and the Croats. With a quarter of Serbs living outside Serbia; a centralized Yugoslav state was a guarantor of Serb security. For Croats and their history of opposition to Hapsburg rule, a decentralized state and weak federation meant control of their own destinies, unencumbered by inefficient state agencies and enterprises staffed and controlled by Serbs. Nevertheless, nationality issues could have been sorted out with democratic institutions in a confederation, with collective rights for minorities, and with systems of political representation in elections and collective decision rules in assemblies that would protect minority voice and favour coalitions rather than majority domination. With these reforms, nationalist leaders would have found it difficult to rally the citizenry to their cause.

In a country with great differences in economic development and standards of living between the Republics, there will be disagreements over economic policies, taxation, transfer, subsidies across regions, and abandoning socialism for a market economy. All Republics had experienced dramatic economic gains since World War II. Yugoslavia was not beyond economic repair.

As in other communist states in the late 1980s, the Yugoslav communist leaders wanted to remain in power. Some reprogrammed as reform communists, and hoped to move into European-style social democracy. Others chose ethnonationalism as the issue that would carry them to power and create a new principle of legitimacy for the post-communist regime. Moderate nationalists stood for conciliation among nationalities; extremists were willing to pursue their goals with force and violence. The defeat of the moderates was not inevitable. Why did xenophobic nationalism resonate with the citizenry? How is it that when the media unleashed the war of words and symbols before the war of bullets, so many believed the exaggerations, distortions and fabrications that belied their personal experiences?

Ethnic Relations Before the Crisis

Survey research on ethnic relations in mid-1990 found that in a national sample of 4,232 Yugoslavs, only 17 percent believed that the country would break up into separate states, and 62 percent reported that the 'Yugoslav' affiliation was very or quite important for them. On ethnonational relations, in workplaces, 36 percent characterized them as 'good', 28 percent as 'satisfactory', and only 6 percent said 'bad' and 'very bad'. For ethnonational relations in neighborhoods, 57 percent answered 'good', 28 percent 'satisfactory', and only 12 percent chose 'bad' and 'very bad'. For the majority of Yuogoslavs, on the eve of the Yugoslav wars, nationalist contention in the public arena did not translate into hostile interpersonal ethnic relations....

Ignatieff is puzzled, 'What is difficult to understand about the Balkan tragedy is how ... nationalist lies ever managed to take root in the soil of shared village existence.... In order for war to occur, nationalists had to convince neighbors and friends that in reality they had been massacring each other since time immemorial.'

The Manipulation of Ethnicity

For explaining ethnic manipulation one needs the concept of a cognitive frame. A cognitive frame is a mental structure which situates and connects events, people and groups into a meaningful narrative in which the social world that one inhabits makes sense and can be communicated and shared with others. Yugoslavs experienced ethnic relations through two frames: a normal frame and a crisis frame. People possessed both frames in their minds: in peaceful times the crisis frame was dormant, and in crisis and war the normal frame was suppressed. Both frames were anchored in private and family experiences, in culture and in public life. In the normal frame, which prevailed in [Josip Broz] Tito's Yugoslavia, ethnic relations were cooperative and neighbourly. Colleagues and workers, schoolmates and teammates transacted routinely across nationality. Some did not even know or bother to know another's nationality. Intermarriage was accepted. Holidays were spent in each others' Republics. Except in Kosovo, the normal frame prevailed for most Yugoslavs throughout the 1980s.

The crisis frame was grounded in the experiences and memories of the Balkan wars, the first and second world wars—and other wars before that. In these crises, civilians were not distinguished from combatants. Old people, children, women, priests were not spared. Atrocities, massacres, torture, ethnic cleansing, a scorched-earth policy were the rule. Everyone was held collectively responsible for their nationality and religion, and became a target of revenge and reprisals....

Tito had wanted to eradicate the crisis frame, but it simmered in the memories of older people, the families of victims, intellectuals and religious leaders. Milosevic, Tudjman and other nationalists did not invent the crisis frame; they activated and amplified it....

If the normal frame prevailed in the 1980s as shown by ... survey findings, how did nationalists activate and amplify the crisis frame after decades of dormancy? The emotion that poisons ethnic relations is fear: fear of extinction as a group, fear of assimilation, fear of domination by another group, fear for one's life and property, fear of being a victim once more. After fear comes hate. The threatening others are demonized and dehumanized. The means of awakening and spreading such fears in Yugoslavia were through the newsmedia, politics, education, popular culture, literature, history and the arts.

The crisis frame in Yugoslavia was first resurrected by Serb intellectuals over the plight of the Kosovo Serbs....

Fear of extinction was spread with highly inflated figures on the ethnic killings in World War II....

In my interview with a Serb refugee one can trace how the atrocities discourse switched on the crisis frame: 'We were afraid because nationalists revived the memory of World War II atrocities ... nationalist graffiti on walls awakened fears of past memories; it was a sign that minorities [Serbs in Croatia] would not be respected and safe'.

Fears of domination, oppression and demographic shrinkage were roused by the incessant rape and genocide discourse....

Ordinary people echo the intellectuals' and the media crisis discourse.... Peter Maas asks a Serb refugee couple why they had fled their village. Their answer: Muslims planned to take over, a list of names had been drawn up, Serb women were to be assigned to Muslim harems after the men had been killed. They had heard about it on the radio; the Serb military had uncovered the plan. The journalist probes: 'Did any Muslims in the village ever harm you?' They reply, 'Oh no, our relations with the Muslims in the village were always good, they were decent people'. In the minds of the Serb couple, the crisis frame had eclipsed the normal frame. What under peaceful circumstances were totally implausible events—young women become sexual slaves in harems for breeding janissaries; a fifteenth- and sixteenth-century style Turkish/Islamic invasion of Europe—become credible narratives of ethnic annihilation and domination within the crisis frame.

Fear and the crisis frame provided opportunities for nationalists to mobilize a huge ethnic constituency, get themselves elected to office, and organize aggressive actions against moderates and other ethnics....

Populist nationalism worked. The Vojvodina and Montenegro party leaderships resigned and were replaced by Milosevic loyalists. Abolishing the autonomous provinces of Kosovo and Vojvodina precipitated a constitutional crisis.... The nationality balance in Yugoslav politics was thus disturbed. Serbia gained control of over half the votes in all federal bodies and institutions. Slovenes and Croats reacted with their own nationalism.

There was grass-roots resistance to nationalism and to activation of the crisis frame. A content analysis of news stories in *Oslobodjenje* for 1990 indicates that municipalities, youth and veterans' organizations, and trade unions repeatedly protested against ethnic polarization and hatreds.... Important as this opposition was, it was countered by the spread of populist nationalism. *Oslobodjenje* in 1990 is full of affirmations of national symbols and identities: the renaming of localities; the reburial of bones of atrocity victims from World War II; nationalist graffiti on churches, mosques, monuments and in cemeteries; fights over flags, ethnic insults, nationalist songs, ethnic vandalism. To many, these were signs that normal times were sliding into crisis, and the authorities had lost control.

Mass communications and propaganda research help to explain why ethnic manipulation worked and why the crisis frame eclipsed the normal frame. First, ... fear arousing appeals, originating in a threat, were powerful and effective in changing opinion and belief. Furthermore, the most important reaction to fear is removing the source of threat, precisely what nationalists were promising to do in Yugoslavia. Second, studies of propaganda routinely find that repetition is the single most effective technique of persuasion. It does not matter how big the lie is, so long as it keeps being repeated.

Third, much of what we know is vicarious knowledge and not based on personal experience. We accept the truths of authorities and experts whom we respect and who have socially recognized positions and titles. Who could really tell or check how many Serbs had been massacred by Ustasha? Fourth, outright falsehoods were common and intentional. According to a media analyst, 'In Serbia and Croatia, TV fabricated and shamelessly circulated war crime stories ... the same victims would be identified on Zagreb screens as Croat, on Belgrade screens as Serb'....

Fifth, mass communications studies of the two-step flow of communication show that in ordinary circumstances crude propaganda from 'patriotic journalism' is discounted because people are exposed to a variety of broadcast messages and because they check media messages against the beliefs and opinions in their social milieus in interpersonal relationships and conversations. Ethnic crisis politics breaks down the two-step flow....

Nationalists Win the 1990 Elections

Second only to the mass media wars for the revival of the crisis frame were the 1990 elections. Every town and city experienced the founding of political parties, often at a huge rally in a public building or a sports stadium, during which speaker after speaker gave vent to exaggerated nationalist rhetoric and hostile pronouncements and attacks against other nationalities....

Nationalists persuaded voters not to 'split the ethnic vote' but to vote as a bloc for the nationalists because the other nationalities would bloc-vote and gain power. Bloc-voting became a self-fulfilling prophecy.... The politicians elected were more nationalist than their voters....

Repression of Minorities and Moderates

The demise of the moderates was due to a combination of electoral defeats, loss of credibility about being effective in a crisis, and intimidation and threats from extremists....

The nationalist winners purged their ethnic opponents and moderates of their own nationality from party and state positions. The targets were sent anonymous threat letters, were fired from their jobs, forced into military service, charged with treason, subversion and plotting armed rebellion, and subject to office and house searches for weapons, radio transmitters and 'subversive' literature.... In a Bosnian example reported by [Tadeusz] Mazowiecki, 'According to a witness [from Bosanska Dubica], the elected authorities who were moderates and who tried to prevent acts of violence were dismissed or replaced by Serbian extremists'.

Other methods were cruder.... Ordinary people could not escape ethnic polarization. In an interview a Serb taxi driver explained: 'No one wanted the coming war, but if I don't fight, someone from my side [Serb] will kill me, and if my Muslim friends don't fight, other Muslims will kill them'.

The overthrow of moderates by extremists or radicals is well known in the great revolutions: Girondins were overthrown by the Jacobins in the French revolution and all groups were overthrown by the Bolsheviks in the Russian revolution. The means of seizing power are similar. The radicals create parallel governance to the state and come to exercise *de facto* authority in many institutions, and militias and mutineers execute a *coup d'état*. Then the remaining moderates are purged. It happens in ethnic violence as well. It did so in the mixed ethnic districts of Croatia and Bosnia, and it happened in Prijedor.

Militias Take Over

Militias and paramilitaries roamed far and wide and perpetrated ethnic cleansing, massacres, atrocities and other war crimes, as in the Prijedor district....

Militiamen were not necessarily fanatics filled with hatred to start with. [Tim] Judah described how a Serb militiaman got recruited by his peers from the local SDS who pressured him for weeks: 'We've all got to take up arms, or we'll disappear from here'. He had Muslim and Croat friends. Would they protect him against extremists of all nationalities? Not likely, if it got violent. So he 'took out a gun'. Peer pressure, fear, not only of Muslims but of extremist Serbs who might finger him as a 'traitor', were the major reasons for joining a militia. Some of these men were unemployed and expected a job in the coming Serb government as militia or police.

Once the young man 'took out a gun' he became encapsulated in a quasimilitary unit subject to peer solidarity and ethnic loyalty. He was trained in weapons and indoctrinated with the beliefs and norms of the crisis frame about other ethnics:

a. *Collective guilt:* 'They' act in unison; children grow into adults; women give birth to future warriors; even old people stab you from behind; 'they' will never change.

b. *Revenge and retaliation:* 'They' massacred 'us' in the past, and are about to do it again, in fact they have already started. A setting of scores is justified; an eye for an eye.

c. *Deterrence/first strike:* Disable them before they strike, which is what they are about to do, despite appearances, because they are secretive and treacherous.

d. *Danger/survival:* These are extraordinary times, one's entire nationality is threatened, and extreme measures are justified.

e. *Legitimacy:* Ordinary people and militias are justified in taking extreme measures because the constituted authorities have not come to the defence of our people.

These are the rationalization and the justifying norms for unrestrained, collective, ethnic violence. Other motives for collective violence were economic gain, peer pressure and lack of accountability. From being an ordinary man in normal times the militiaman changed into being a killer at crisis times.

The Bassiouni report (UN Security Council 1994) counted eighty-three paramilitaries in Bosnia alone operating between June 1991 and late 1993, fifty-three for Serbs, with an estimated 20,000–40,000 members, thirteen for Croats, with 12,000–20,000, and fourteen for Bosniac, with 4,000–6,000 men.

In view of 700,000 Bosnian Serb men aged fifteen to thirty-five, militiamen were 10–20 percent of the Serb men of military age in Bosnia. Ten to 20 percent of adult males in militias, added to the military and police, are more than enough for death and destruction against civilians on a massive scale.

Conclusion

My account is not a narrative of events but an analytic explanation for the breakup of Yugoslavia amid collective violence.... On the eve of the wars, Yugoslavs reported cooperative interpersonal ethnic relations and opposed a breakup of the state. Nationalist leaders succeeded in manipulating ethnicity by spreading fear, insecurity and hatred, which advanced their political agenda of separate national states.

To explain their success I draw on elements from the primordialist, instrumentalist and constructionist views on ethnicity and on the theory of ethnic violence originating in fear and insecurity. To these I add the concept of a cognitive frame which clarifies élite-grass-roots linkage and ethnic manipulation. Nationalism, ethnic identity and attachment alone, however intense, do not explain grass-roots ethnic actions. Yugoslavs possessed two frames on ethnic relations: a cooperative frame for normal, peaceful times, as in the decades of the fifties to the eighties. They also possessed a dormant crisis frame anchored in family history and collective memory of wars, ethnic atrocities and brutality. Threats and lies that were implausible and dismissed in the normal frame could resonate when the crisis frame was switched on: they became persuasive, were believed, and inspired fear.

In the waning days of Communism, nationalists activated the crisis frame on ethnicity by playing on fears of ethnic annihilation and oppression in the mass media, in popular culture, in social movements, and in election campaigns. Élite crisis discourse resonated at the grass roots, made for ethnic polarization, and got nationalists elected. Once in office, nationalists suppressed and purged both moderates in their own ethnic group and other ethnics. They organized militias who perpetrated acts of extreme violence against innocent civilians. They conducted war according to the crisis script. Without the tacit, overt or confused support of the majority, the nationalist leaders could not have escalated ethnic rivalry and conflict into massive collective violence.

POSTSCRIPT

Is Ethnic Conflict Inevitable?

Although Kakar's argument draws heavily on psychology, he clearly adopts a primordialist perspective that ethnic differences are inherently threatening; such differences lead to tension and will ultimately emerge as conflict. Individuals may keep their fears and anxieties in check for a time, but preconscious fears and anxiety will eventually emerge. For Kakar, no amount of education or politically correct training will eliminate these anxieties or permanently overcome them.

Oberschall's argument accepts the reality of primordialist variables such as kinship, language, and religion as more important than did Barth in his original formulation of the circumstantialist perspective. But for Oberschall, such variables must be triggered by circumstantialist factors before they can be aroused. The Balkans case is a particularly apt one, as ethnicity in Bosnia is largely based on religious differences. All three "ethnic" communities have emerged from essentially the same pool of genetic material. The language spoken by all three groups is essentially the same language, often called Serbo-Croatian by linguists, though the Serbs use a Cyrillic alphabet and the Croats use a Roman one. The main "ethnic" differences emerge from their three different religions: Eastern Orthodox, Roman Catholic, and Islam. Religious differences in Bosnia correspond to traditional political alliances, but, as in the conflict in Northern Ireland, they are not fundamentally based on significant biological or linguistic differences. In Bosnia, unlike Northern Ireland, people of all three ethnicities had lived and worked side by side; they socialized together and had even intermarried. The primordialist variables are, in Oberschall's view, insufficient to trigger the ethnic violence and brutality that erupted in Bosnia. Ethnic violence, massacres, and ethnic cleansing could only have emerged if people in the towns and villages were manipulated into fearing their neighbors, concludes Oberschall.

Anthropologists and sociologists have long recognized that racial and ethnic tensions in the United States and other countries are linked to issues about access to jobs, land, resources, and opportunities. But it is not clear whether or not such circumstantialist variables are sufficient to explain why social conflict so often allows ethnic affiliations to become so central.

For further reading on genocide and ethnic cleansing, see Alexander L. Hinton's edited volume *Annihilating Difference: The Anthropology of Genocide* (University of California Press, 2002). For another view on ethnic conflict in India, see Ashutosh Varshney's *Ethnic Conflict and Civic Life: Hindus and Muslims in India* (Yale University Press, 2002). For a recent perspective about ethnicity, see André Burguière and Raymond Grew's edited volume *The Construction of Minorities: Cases for Comparison Across Time and Around the World* (University of

Michigan Press, 2001). For more circumstantialist discussions of ethnic conflict, see Jack Eller's *From Culture to Ethnicity to Conflict* (University of Michigan Press, 1999) and *The Myth of "Ethnic Conflict": Politics, Economics, and "Cultural" Violence,* edited by Beverly Crawford and Ronnie D. Lipschutz (International Area Studies, University of California at Berkeley, 1998).

ISSUE 13

Is Islam a Single Universal Tradition?

YES: Francis Robinson, from *Islam and Muslim History in South Asia* (Oxford University Press, 2000)

NO: Veena Das, from "For a Folk-Theology and Theological Anthropology of Islam," *Contributions to Indian Sociology* (July–December 1984)

ISSUE SUMMARY

YES: Historian Francis Robinson argues that Islam is a single, universal tradition, whose proper practices and beliefs can best be understood from the study of religious texts. Islam as practiced in many local communities in India may have numerous syncretic elements borrowed from Hinduism. But these syncretic elements should best be understood as errors in belief and practice that will eventually be weeded out from the single, authentic religious tradition.

NO: Indian sociologist Veena Das counters that the numerous syncretic traditions of Islam found in India and other countries represent important religious differences. Emphasis on textual analysis misses the point that religion as lived and practiced is fundamentally different in various local traditions. Such differences are not likely to disappear through continuing contact with religious leaders in Mecca or other Islamic centers because interpretation will always introduce religious innovation and variation.

The term "syncretism" refers to religious practices and ideas that are a blend of two or more religious traditions. Throughout history, orthodox clergy in many faiths have struggled to eliminate syncretic practices as errors of faith. It has happened in Christianity from at least the second century and in Islam from at least the end of its first century. This issue concerns whether Islam is at its core a single orthodox tradition from which some communities have strayed or whether Islam is better understood as a family of closely related religious traditions that have adopted elements of local practice wherever Islam has emerged.

Travelers to different Muslim countries have long observed that Islam is practiced differently in various places. They have observed that Islam as actually practiced has many elements borrowed from traditional pre-Islamic religions, such as local animistic religions in Indonesia, Hinduism in India, and Christianity or even elements of Christian ritual in the Balkans. Even with modern means of communication, orthodox Islam has not eradicated local syncretic Islamic practices. Thus, like Christianity with its numerous sects and local traditions of ritual, beliefs, and practices, Islam appears in many forms, leading some to speak of the many Islams of the world.

At issue is how we should understand these local Islams. Are the heterodox traditions simply imperfect versions of authentic Muslim faith? Are these syncretic traditions merely temporary manifestations of Islam that over time will become closer to the Islamic ideal? Alternatively, is there something fundamentally different in these diverse local traditions that makes them different from Islam as practiced in Mecca, Cairo, and other centers? Proponents of this latter view, many of whom are anthropologists, have argued that we should study the beliefs and practices as we find them and not be dismissive of them because they diverge from more standard orthodox forms.

Here, historian Francis Robinson comments on a series of studies about the many forms that Islam takes in India. Although Robinson acknowledges that Indian Islam incorporates many Hindu elements, he contends that these foreign elements will over time be eliminated as local people gain more education and contact with authentic Islam. Such a process, he argues, has happened repeatedly as Islam has spread into new areas. At the main Islamic centers, Islam is essentially a single unified tradition with only minor variations in either belief or practice. It has a fixed body of scripture that prescribes how proper Muslims should behave in their daily lives. Thus, non-standard forms of Islam represent only a temporary phase in the conversion process, not religious traditions that are fundamentally different from orthodox Islam.

Sociologist Veena Das argues that Robinson's approach parallels that of most Orientalists who study Middle Eastern religion from written texts rather than from people's actual behavior and beliefs. By primarily considering religious texts, such scholars only get an understanding of literate socioeconomic and political elites. Such approaches tell us little about the religion of common people, who often have quite syncretic beliefs and practices. She has no objection to studying Islamic texts. But she contends that religious texts do not lead to a single religious tradition. All texts must be interpreted, and each interpretation introduces the possibility of new variations in belief and practice. In this sense, she suggests, local versions of Islam in India are fundamentally different from the Islam practiced by religious leaders in Arabia. Attempts to dismiss these variations as temporary deviations ignores many important trends in contemporary Islam.

Does it matter if a local version of Islam incorporates Hindu gods in its practices? Are these practices likely to die out over time? Is Islam fundamentally different from other scriptural religions (Christianity and Judaism) by being able to minimize deviations in practice and belief? Is it possible to convert people from one religion to another without at least some of the earlier beliefs and practices being retained? Can Islam or any other world religion minimize deviation and keep a set of orthodox beliefs through education?

Islam and Muslim History in South Asia

There has been a tendency, in recent years, for some anthropologists ... to emphasize that Muslim society in South Asia, particularly in India, is much more Indian in its beliefs and practice than has been thought in the past. This tendency has its greatest protagonist in Imtiaz Ahmad, a professor of sociology at the Centre for Political Studies in New Delhi's Jawaharlal Nehru University. Since 1975, Ahmad (assisted by both Indian and non-Indian scholars) has been steadily revealing his vision of Indian Islam in what is to be a four volume series of essays.... In the introduction to the third volume, ... Ahmad sets out the main lines of his argument.

He begins with what, for many Islamic sociologists, has come to be an almost obligatory attack on Islamicists. They know languages and texts, but they do not know how Muslims actually behave. They have, in consequence, projected a normative idea of Islam and have deceived us to the great variety of Muslim practices throughout the world. 'The sociological or social anthropological understanding of religion,' we are told, 'is at once more comprehensive and more concrete....'

Ahmad pursues his point by emphasizing the gulf which exists between Islamic law and Muslim practice in India. He observes that all the Muslims he has dealt with acknowledge the five pillars of Islam—creed, prayer, fasting, alms and pilgrimage—and in doing so, acknowledge their duty to follow the pattern for a perfect Muslim existence laid down in the Quran, the example of the Prophet, and the holy law. But, the Islam they practise 'is heavily underlined by elements which are accretions from the local environment and contradict the fundamentalist view of the beliefs and practices to which Muslims must adhere'.

Ahmad notes that, in the past, Islamicists and anthropologists have explained the contradictions between law and local practice by pointing to the historical development of Islamic society. According to them, such contradictions were inevitable for a faith which, by and large, had only slowly intruded into other societies, come to exist side by side with other systems of belief and practice, and often had to accommodate itself to them in order to survive. In such a situation, there were bound to be some who lived lives closer to the Islamic ideal than others, whose religious behavior was profoundly influenced by local custom. Nevertheless, the tendency would be for local custom to give way before the slow but sure progress of the Islamic ideal in Muslim hearts and lives. So Aziz Ahmad, doyen of Muslim scholars of south Asia, considered the folk and syncretic elements in Indian Islam, the worship-

From ISLAM AND MUSLIM SOCIETY IN SOUTH ASIA, 2000, pp. excerpts from 44–52, 56–57, 62. Copyright © 2000 by Oxford University Press India. Reprinted by permission. References and notes omitted.

ping of saints, the barely disguised presence of Hindu godlings, the hint of pollution and the traces of caste, as mere temporary anomalies which would eventually be eliminated by the actions of Muslim reformers. So also the influential anthropologist Clifford Geertz assumed that the process of Islam-ization meant a similar victory of an orthodox, orthoprax great tradition over a heterodox, heteroprax little tradition. 'The typical mode of Islamization,' he declares, is:

> painfully gradual. First comes the Confession of faith, then the other pillars, then a certain degree of observance of the law, and finally, perhaps, espe-cially as a scholarly tradition develops and takes hold, a certain amount of learning in the law and the Quran and Hadith upon which it rests. The intri-cate norms, doctrines, explications, and annotations that make up Islam, or at least Sunni Islam, can be apprehended only step by step, as one comes to control, to a greater or lesser degree, the scriptural sources upon which it rests.... Islamic conversion is not, as a rule, a sudden, total, over-whelming illumination but a slow turning toward a new light.

Ahmad does not accept that the insights of either Aziz Ahmad or Clifford Greetz apply to India. He notes the revivalist and reformist movements of nineteenth- and twentieth-century Islam in India (movements of a kind which Azis Ahmad saw bringing eventual victory to the high Islamic tradi-tion), but discounts their importance because syncretic and folk beliefs are still widely found in Indian Islamic practice. He cannot find Clifford Geertz's pattern in Islamization in India because he finds the orthodox and orthoprax living harmoniously side by side with the heterodox and heteroprax. Ahmad can discover no dynamic situation in which a high Islamic tradition is steadily eating into local custom-centered traditions. Nor, for that matter, does he discover one in which custom-centered traditions are edging into the terri-tory of a high Islamic tradition. He would rather talk of co-existence. High Islamic and custom-centered traditions peacefully 'co-exist as complementary and integral parts of single common religious system'. They do so, and have done so, because of 'the constraints of Islam's own struggle for survival in an alien environment'. Muslims came to India bearing a distinct religious tradi-tion characterized by a vigorous iconoclastic zeal; 'they would probably liked to have conquered the indigenous religious traditions wholesale.' But, he declares, 'this could not be possible to achieve because the indigenous mores and traditions were already an integral part of the life of the people and their total displacement could be achieved only at the cost of Islam's own rejec-tion'. The suggestion seems to be that the co-existence of high Islamic and custom-centered religious traditions developed in the past, is established in the present, and is the distinctive, unique, pattern of Indian Islam which will probably persist into the future....

Ahmad's perspective ... , is important, because it is crucial that Islam should be understood in its Indian, indeed, in its Hindu context. It is a con-text too long neglected.... Nevertheless, the investigations conducted so far do not seem to have explored the subject to the full. They appear limited in understanding, place and time; these limitations raise doubts about Ahmad's conclusions regarding the nature of Indian Islam. I shall examine the nature of these limitations, and put forward alternative conclusions which emerge from investigations conducted along a broader front.

One limitation concerns the style of investigation that Ahmad and his followers have adopted. Much of their purpose is devoted to showing how Muslims actually behave, and how this behaviour is at variance with preferred Islamic practice, indeed is similar to much Hindu practice. In one sense, this emphasis on behaviour is correct because none of the revealed religions place as much emphasis on right conduct (as opposed to right thinking) as Islam. But, if the investigator goes no further than behaviour, understanding of the extent to which genuine shifts in religious orientation may have taken place must be limited. Men often maintain old customs but, as time passes, attach different meanings to them....

Ahmad and some of his fellow scholars make much of Muslim attendance at saint's shrines. Although the possibility of injecting old forms with new content is acknowledged, it is always referred to as 'saint worship' and regarded, despite attendance at shrines in every other Muslim society, as an *essentially* Hindu institution absorbed within Indian Islam. Not once do they refer to the important distinction between the worship of a saint and the worship of God in a saint's presence which is to be found in the writings of the Indian *ulama* and sufis. Many who attend saints' shrines are, of course, either worshipping the *siant* or begging him to intercede for them with God. But there are others who do none of these: they are praying to God in the presence of the saint.... There is, ... considerable literature devoted to conduct at saints' tombs, particular forms of behaviour indicating the proper difference in attitude towards the saints and towards God. It is not good enough to bundle all attendance at saints' tombs into the category of 'saint worship'.... Very few Muslims see anything wrong in such activity. What is crucial is the intention with which it is pursued and the manner in which it is done. Study with the help of interviews would help reveal the intentions of those attending shrines; study with the help of texts would illuminate the significance of different forms of behaviour at shrines. What often might seem to be saint worship would reveal a range of Islamic understandings, a range of positions on the gradient of Islamization. While the thoughts of some still sought the benefit of old superstitions, those of others were coming to be riveted on God.

A second limitation flows from Ahmad's concentration on Indian Muslims alone, which I suspect may have eased his progress towards hinting that Indian Islam has something of a unique quality, in which orthodox, orthoprax Islam co-exists with heterodox, heteroprax Islam as complementary and integral parts of a single common religious system. Of course, Islam in India is unique in one sense; it is only here that we might find a sufi shrine ordering its festivals according to the Hindu calendar, as at the shrine of Hajji Waris Ali Shah of Deva; it is only here that a Hindu festival might be included with Islamic festivals in the celebrations of the year.... But all Islamic societies contain a mixture of local pre-Islamic practice and high Islamic culture. In Java, Muslims are known to pray to the Goddess of the Southern Ocean as well as to Muslim saints and to God himself. In Ottoman Turkey the Bektashi sufi order, which was powerful in the Balkans and Anatolia and closely associated with the famed

Janissary corps of once Christian slave soldiers, recognized an Islamic Trinity of Allah, Muhammad and Ali, and included a version of the Christian communion service in their rites. Further, in nineteenth-century southern Arabia the Swiss Arabist and traveller, Johann Burckhardt, noted that the Bedouin still observed the pre-Islamic practice of sexual hospitality.

Even in long great Islamic centres many dubious customs and beliefs could be found flourishing within earshot and eyeshot of paragons of Islamic right conduct. Consider the picture Snouck Hurgronje paints of late nineteenth century Mecca, the recorded behaviour of its women, the many visits to saints' tombs.... Consider, too, the picture painted by Edward Lane of mid-nineteenth century Cairo; here within a muezzin's cry of al-Azhar he finds every kind of superstition and belief in magic flourishing with vigour. Snapshots of these Muslim worlds taken by investigators at various times in the past two centuries reveal pictures not dissimilar in form from those recently taken by Ahmad and his associates of Muslim communities in India. Far from being unique, the shape of Indian Islam, the relationship between law and actual practice, seems to have much in common with Islamic societies elsewhere.

Mention of the snapshot technique, or what is sometimes called the synchronic view, introduces a crucial third limitation to Ahmad's work which is the little weight he gives to ... the historical dimension[,] a dimension to which scholars as varied as Aziz Ahmad and Clifford Geertz attribute great importance. In the long run we can only understand the relationship between Islam and a particular society by investigating what is happening to that relationship through time. To do this, it is worth digressing to understand how Islamic history moves.

Islam offers a pattern of perfection for man to follow. It is contained in the Quran, the word of God spoken to man through the Prophet Muhammad. It is also contained in the traditions which relate what the Prophet, who is believed to have been divinely inspired, said and did. It is summed up in the law, in which the divine guidance for man is gathered together in a comprehensive system of rules designed to direct all human activity. Although the law came to be formed in the two hundred years following the Prophet's death, and drew on the customary practice of the time, most Muslims have believed that it was fashioned quite independently of historical or social influences. It is known as the *Sharia*, a word derived from Arabic meaning 'the straight way leading to the water'. We should not be deceived into thinking that there are strongly conflicting patterns of perfection by the fact the there are four *mazhab* or ways of Sunni law. There are only minor differences between them and, from the eighteenth century at least, many Muslim scholars, Hanbalis apart, have had little problem drawing from all four. Moreover, we should not be deceived by the fact that in many societies non-Islamic practices had acquired the force of law in Muslim minds. This is often a matter of imperfect knowledge or temporary expedient, although temporary in this sense may well be several hundred years. Nevertheless, such is the desire to follow the true path, a desire noted by many anthropologists, that, as knowledge of the law has grown more widespread, its provisions have tended to oust false practice. Ideally, then, the law stands above society as a pattern of perfection, a standard which all should strive to reach. The more completely a man follows the law in his life, the greater his chance of salvation at the Day of Judgement. The more completely the law is realized in society, the greater the chance that society will be healthy, powerful and just. There is continual tension in Islamic history between the need to strive to realize the pattern of perfection and the necessities of ordinary human life.

The pattern of perfection has been preserved down the ages, and exemplified and administered to Muslim peoples by learned and holy men. The learned men are, of course, the *ulama*, those with *ilm* (knowledge), men learned in the Quran, the traditions and the law, and skilled in ways to make these precious gifts to man socially useful. The holy men are the sufis, or Muslim mystics, men expert in techniques of spiritual development, who teach Muslims how to make God's revelation live in their hearts. I will treat ulama and sufis as different human beings, although often the two functions they perform are united in one man, being no more than the two sides of a fully rounded Islamic personality. But, whether one or two, both are concerted to guard and to broadcast Islamic knowledge in their time, and to raise fresh guardians and transmitters of the central messages of Islamic culture. When a teacher finished teaching a particular book, and was satisfied with his pupil's progress, he gave him an *ejaza* or licence to teach, and on that licence were recorded all the previous teachers of the book back to its author many hundreds of years before. The pupil could see how he had become the most recent bearer of Islamic knowledge transmitted down the ages. Similarly, when a sufi master, or shaikh, decided that a follower was suited to be a disciple, he gave him a *shijra* or mystical genealogy which stated the stages by which mystic knowledge had passed down from the Prophet to the founding saint of the order and from the founding saint to his shaikh, and thence to him. The gratitude, love, respect, veneration of pupil for teacher, and disciple for master was boundless; they know the central importance in Islamic life of the responsibilities which had been bestowed upon them. Their connections, criss-crossing regions and continents, form throughout most of Islamic history the essential moulding framework of the Islamic community.... The central themes of Islamic history focus on the activities of learned and holy men, or their interactions with each other and with the world in which they move. These themes—their attempts to bring Islamic knowledge to pagan and Islamizing societies; their relationships with the state, which are often difficult because ideally the state exists only to put the law as they interpret it into practice; and their connections with each other, in particular the flow of ideas and of knowledge along the connections of pupils and teachers, and of disciples and masters, through time and throughout the Islamic world. The more widely Islamic knowledge was known and acted upon, the more widely Islamic society would be realized on earth.

The extent to which the pattern of perfection is realized in Muslim societies is always changing. There will be learned and holy men eager to raise Muslims to a higher Islamic standard; there will be Muslims who will know that, whether they like it or not, this is what they ought to be striving to achieve but the fate of such a process does not, of course, depend merely on the leadership of learned and holy men or the deepening religious vision of those claiming to be Muslim. It interacts with the wider context—social, economic and political—and it is factors such as these which need to be considered to understand how Islamic knowledge might come to be spread more widely and applied more vigorously. They also suggest how its forward progress might on occasion be checked, and put into reverse.

Consider, for instance, the impact of the social roles which holy men often used to play. They were the pioneers and frontiersmen of the Islamic world, men who from the thirteenth century played the crucial role in drawing new peoples, pagans, Hindus, Buddhists, Shamanists, into an Islamic cultural milieu....

Consider, too, the significance of increasing contact with cultures which are thought to represent more fully the pattern of perfection, cultures in which Islamic knowledge is more widely spread and manifest. Such contact often seems to draw men towards higher Islamic standards, and often, though not always, the stronger and more frequent the contact, the greater the impact on local Islamic practice. One crucial source of contact between the central and the further Islamic lands has been trade....

A second source of contact can be found in the pilgrimage to Mecca, a subject which has only just begun to be studied seriously. Nevertheless, we know enough already to have some idea of its Islamizing effect....

All these processes, and more, have helped in the diffusion and application of Islamic knowledge. It is, as Geertz reminded us in the passage quoted earlier, a painfully slow process. Small changes in the culture of island Java between 1500 and 1800, for instance, mark its slow shift in orientation from a Hindu-Buddhist towards a Muslim world. Men stopped cremating their dead, women danced with more modesty, batik patterns became more formal, the devil-shaped kris handle became stylized, and an Islamic story was included amongst the cycles of the Wayang theatre....

Islamic history, therefore, offers abundant evidence that there is a dynamic relationship between Muslim societies and the pattern of perfection transmitted and exemplified by learned and holy men. More often than not, over the past fourteen centuries, Muslim societies have moved towards a greater realization of that pattern of perfection; on occasion, when they have been cut off from sources of cultural leadership, or when faced with powerful rival cultures, they have slipped away from it. The crucial point is that some form of traffic is always taking place between visions of the ideal Muslim life and the lives which Muslims lead.

Indian Islam is no exception to this rule. Consider what has taken place in the past two hundred and fifty years. This may not appear to be period of great vigour in Islamic life. There is the decline of Mughal power, the rise of the Marattas, the British and the Indian nationalist—a world where Muslim culture and power went hand in hand, comes to be dominated by a culture in part Western, in part secular, and in part Hindu. But, in fact, this has been a period of extraordinary, probably unprecedented, vitality in Indian Islam....

This period of extraordinary vitality coincides with the time when learned and holy men were stronger and more prominent than ever before in Indian history.... It was at this time, when Islam had lost its hold on power in

India, that paradoxically the ulama were best placed to lead their fellow Muslims and to spread knowledge of the faith. Their efforts to respond to Muslim political weakness, and the dangers which it threatened, are the prime source of the vitality of Indian Islam....

One way in which learned and holy men sought to spread Islamic knowledge more widely was through aggressive movements of revival and reform. These were similar to the movements taking place throughout the Islamic world in the nineteenth century; indeed, they had some connections with them....

The main way in which learned and holy men spread Islamic knowledge more widely was by developing a whole new range of new methods of transmission and broadcasting; in doing so, they were quick to exploit new forms of organization and new technological developments. Up to this time, most had taught informally in their homes. Now schools, maktabs and *madrasas* began to be established, institutions which were greater than individuals....

Yet another new method was to make Islamic knowledge immediately comprehensible and readily available. As was happening elsewhere in the Islamic world at the time, learned and holy men were translating Islamic knowledge into languages everyone could understand. In India, the Quran was translated into Persian in the early eighteenth century, into Urdu in the early nineteenth century, and into Bengali in the late nineteenth century. By the 1870s several competing Urdu translations of the Quran were circulating....

Evidently, something remarkable was taking place in nineteenth-century Muslim India. Learned and holy men were developing many new ways of making contact with the Muslim masses; Indian Muslims were able, as never before, to know the pattern of perfect Muslim life....

The evidence set out here raises doubts about Imtiaz Ahmad's conclusion that the high Islamic and the custom-centered traditions have come to be integrated 'to a point that they should come to co-exist as complementary and integral parts of a common religious system'. Rather, it would appear to support the positions of Aziz Ahmad or more especially of Clifford Geertz. In Islamic history, in general, there has been a movement towards, or occasionally away from, the patterns of perfection. In South Asia, in particular, over the past two hundred years, learned and holy men have shown unusual activity and imagination in spreading knowledge of that pattern more widely. The evidence suggests, moreover, that many Muslims have made steps towards realizing that pattern more fully. It may be that over that past thirty-six years the process has continued more obviously in Pakistan and Bangladesh. It may be that in India the process has slackened, even gone into reverse. What there cannot be, as Ahmad asserts, is a state of equilibrium. He is able to make this assertion, one senses, because the case studies he has brought together embrace too short a period of time, because, perhaps, the sociological understanding of religion, and religious change, is not as 'comprehensive' as he would like to think. The historian's extended view suggests that there is continual, if sometimes slow and barely perceptible, movement between visions of perfect Muslim life and those which ordinary Muslims lead.

For a Folk-Theology and Theological Anthropology of Islam

Can we think of Islam as a single unified tradition, or does the historicity of the religious experience of Islam contribute vitally to our understanding of it? This question has great relevance for defining the relation between text and context in the case of all religions that may be said to have 'scripture' in the generic sense, a term that I leave undefined for the moment. Studies on Islam in diverse cultures and in different periods of history have testified to the importance of the Qur'ā n and adherence to the five pillars Islam in the everyday life of Muslims. Beyond this, however, considerable diversity in belief and practice has been observed so as to pose the question: Does a single, true Islam exist at all? Let us examine this question in the context of Islam in Indian society.

The problem of the diversity of observed Islam has been posed most sharply by Imtiaz Ahmad and his colleagues in the several volumes edited by him. We take up here specifically the issues relating to religion and ritual.

Ahmad has tried to show the limitations of an exclusively textual understanding of Islam. He points out that the orientalists have dismissed the 'folk' religion of the Muslims as of little relevance to the understanding of Islam. When they are interested in it, it is only to point to its divergence from normative Islam. He has perhaps overstressed the uniqueness of the syncretic elements in Indian Islam, for these have not only been reported from every society where Islam has spread but also in its original home. In fact, anthropological literature abounds in explanations of these apparent departures from the Islamic ideals, either in terms of psychological needs, compulsions of the unconscious, or exigencies of the socio-political structure. Ahmad and his associates are tolerant and perhaps even indulgent towards these syncretic elements and use simplistic functional explanations for their appearance and persistence.

Taking a somewhat polemic stance against not only Ahmad but also the entire anthropological understanding of Islam is the historian, Francis Robinson. He argues with some force that Islam offers a pattern of perfection, which is readily discernible in the Qur'ā n and the life of the prophet, and provides comprehensive rules of conduct for every Muslim. Further, Robinson states that knowledge of this perfect pattern is spread through holy men and by 'contact with cultures ... in which Islamic knowledge is more widely spread and manifest'; moreover, 'such contact often seems to draw men towards

From contributions to Indian Sociology, vol. 18, no 2, July–December 1984, pp. 293–300. Copyright © 1984 by Sage Publications. Reprinted by permission. References omitted.

higher Islamic standards'. For scholars like Robinson, the course of Islamic history is clear. As knowledge of this perfect Islamic pattern spreads in countries like India, the process of Islamisation will sweep away the various 'dubious' practices that have crept into local Islamic cultures. This, further, is not only a question of fact but also of value.

At the first instance, it may seem that Robinson and Ahmad are on opposite sides of the debate. After all, Robinson is quite unequivocal in his statement that the high Islamic standard being set by holy men ought to be followed by Muslims. Hence a stem admonition to Ahmad and his like '... there will be Muslims who will know that *whether they like it or not*, this is what they ought to be striving to achieve' (emphasis added). Ahmad, on the other hand, has defended syncretism on the ground that people take a pragmatic approach to religion. However, behind this apparent divergence between the views of our two authors, there is a remarkable similarity in the manner in which they construct their basic system of oppositions. Both believe that normative or orthodox Islam constitutes a single pattern of perfection which seems to be in the nature of an unchanging essence.

The first point to be noted here is that it is a gross misrepresentation of the modern scholarship on textual understanding of Islam to argue that there is a consensus of opinion that the Qur'ān reveals a single pattern of perfection. It certainly has the status of scripture, but the notion of scripture in Islam is very different from that in the Judeo-Christian tradition. In the latter, the primary meaning of scripture is the idea of divinely revealed or *written* word of God that has been subjected further to a process of canonisation. In contrast, the Islamic tradition has been well described by Graham:

> The Qur'ānic view is that there have been many 'scriptures' (*kutub*, in the sense of sacred and authoritative, divine revelations), of which the Qur'ān ('Recitation') itself is the final and most complete. All these scriptures have come to the various peoples of history as God's very word, taken in each case from his heavenly scripture (*al-kitāab* or *umm al-kitāb*, 'Mother of Scripture'). This fundamentally generic notion of scripture has not diminished the Muslim's consciousness of the particular ultimacy of their own scripture, but this does give to verbal revelations and scriptural texts a clear status as characteristic, recurring phenomena in the history of God's dealing with humankind.

As I shall try to show later, the notion that scripture has been revealed by God earlier and in different forms has been elaborated in folk theologies to give very different meaning and content to the notion of Islamic perfection, than either Robinson or Ahmad seem prepared to admit.

For the moment, however, let us return to the Qur'ān. This text is not only the source of law for the devout Muslim but is revered as the evidence of the eternal breaking through time. Through this text, the transcendent enters human history. But precisely because the revelation includes a holy and elevated but nevertheless *human* listener, and a language that is spoken by humans, the revelation of God has to be interpreted. It is surely not accidental that the chief Qur'ānic science has been *tafsir*, the phrase-by-phrase exegetical interpretation.

After the great exponent of this art al-Tabari̇ in the ninth century, the Qur'ān has been the subject of continuous reinterpretation. Commentaries have been written in every century, and continue to be written. In view of the ongoing tradition of exegetical interpretation in the constitution of Islamic knowledge, it would be very difficult to maintain that the differences in interpretation are minor. To write a new commentary on a text is to suggest that existing commentaries are inadequate. Now whether we argue that a single interpretation is correct, and all others false, or whether we accept the plurality of meaning as inherent in any act of interpretation, is, I suspect, related to our philosophical moorings. Robinson has great faith that all differences of interpretation would be reduced to minor differences, although this is more a matter of faith than demonstration with him. Wilfred Cantwell Smith the distinguished scholar of Islam, on the other hand argues:

> The writing of formal analytical or exegetical *tafsir*, however, is but one among several ways in which Muslims have set forth one or another specific interpretation of their scripture, or of specific verses within it. Every theologian, jurist, mystic, heresiarch, nationalist, agitator, philosopher, has tended over the centuries, and across the Muslim world, to incorporate the interpretation of the Qur'ān.... And indeed every individual worshipper, quoting this or that verse from the Book in his daily prayers, as he must, sees and feels in that verse something that is in part a function of the meaning for it purveyed to him by his milieu....

Thus when we shift from the meaning of the Qur'ān as a source of law to that as a source of the entire religious life, we can see more readily that meaning is not to be interpreted once, and correctly, but continually reinterpreted, for meanings assigned to the word of God by human efforts can only be approximations.

In thinking of 'holy men' as constituting a single, undifferentiated category, Robinson has done less than justice to the tension between the interpretations of the Qur'ān in terms of their literal and figurative meanings. After all, the distinction between clear and equivocal verses of the Qur'ān is intrinsic to the Islamic tradition and the whole science of elucidation (*ilm-at-Bayān*) addresses itself to the question of an analysis of figures of speech in sacred texts. The tension between knowledge through literal meaning and faith has arisen often in Islamic history, as between the *ulama* and the *sufi* saints. Disputes have thus arisen as to whether the passage relating to the ascent of Mohammad to heaven is to be literally or metaphorically interpreted. The whole distinction between the *zāhiri* and *bātini* meanings, and whether it is the jurist or the man of faith who is more likely to find the hidden meaning of the speech of God cannot be dismissed. These tensions are vital to our understanding of the Qur'ān as a sacred and not merely a jural text. Indeed, the variety of attitudes to revelation is linked to the varieties of religious leadership within Islam as argued cogently by Fazalbhoy and Troll. Robinson's innocence on this whole range of issues is charmingly portrayed in the physical analogies that he uses to depict the process by which Islamic knowledge spreads. For example: 'However, I prefer to think of them (the holy men) as

NO / Veena Das   267

the network of arteries and veins along which life-giving blood of knowledge has flowed through time, and along which it is pumped through the corners of the Islamic world'. This whole view of knowledge as substance, and the holy men as neutral vehicles, is difficult to sustain or defend in view of the legitimacy accorded to the science of interpretation in the Islamic tradition.

The labelling of knowledge as Islamic, without due regard to the content of this knowledge, obscures many important issues. In different periods of history, as in different kinds of societies, the attitude to folk theologies within the Islamic tradition has varied. For instance, the use of Hindu symbols and the evolution of new forms of devotion in *sufiana* music and poetry in medieval India propagated a different way of approaching God than the enunciation of Islamic ideals in the writings and speeches of the leaders of the *tabliki jamā ts* among many Muslim communities today. It is the task of the social scientist to address the problem in terms of the social conditions which bring about these variations in emphasis in the arrangement of ideas as also in the social roles. One cannot dismiss the engagement of medieval Muslim scholars with Hindu symbols as mere guises by which they attracted Hindus to the Islamic faith. This is surely reading history backwards and seeing the concerns of the present as providing motivational forces to the actors of the past.

The intellectual process of labelling as a substitute for delineating the arrangement of relations mars the contributions of Ahmad and his associates also. It is difficult to see why saint-worship is dismissed as un-Islamic without going into the structure of belief within which the reverence is given to a *pir.* This is rightly criticised by Robinson. The same is the case with the customary practices of protection from evil. Without looking into the question of how people explain these and whether there is a difference in the manner in which Hindus and Muslims view magic, the enquiry is foreclosed by providing a simple label. Incidentally, the existence of the evil practices of magicians and the like is testified by the Qur'ā n itself and classified as *sifli amal.* We should see how this notion is developed and what role the text plays in providing protection against evil. The practice of using certain passages in the Qur'ā n by inscribing them on protective amulets has been reported from many parts of the world. As Cassirer has pointed out, the word in the Qur'ā n may be treated as a physical entity as much as a symbolic one. We need many more studies on the manner in which the sacred text is integrated into a variety of religious beliefs and rituals and one hopes we can move from the atomistic approach of labelling items of belief and rituals in terms of received dichotomies—Islamic *vs.* un-Islamic, elite *vs.* folk Islam, great *vs.* little traditional, orthodox *vs.* heterodox. If boundaries have to be found these must reflect the conclusion of an analysis rather than its premises. In different periods of history, the attitudes of the Muslim communities to orthodoxy have varied as have the boundaries of the *ummah,* or the community of believers. But it is precisely our task to find how these boundaries are constructed, a task in which we may be hindered by the application of our preconceived categories.

It seems to me that both Robinson and Ahmad come to identify orthodox Islam with the practice of the elite. It is not surprising that instances of departures from this normative level are always drawn from the religion of the villager, the illiterate, and the women, as for example in Saiyed's descriptions of Moharram. Does an acceptance of normative Islam necessarily commit us to the view that the practice of the poor and the illiterate is always faulty? Incidentally, the movement to fundamentalism in Islam as witnessed in Islamic countries today contrasts completely with the discovery in modem Christianity that the practices of these very sections of society were suppressed in the history of Christianity not because of the truth of revelation but because of the exigencies of power within the organised ecclesiastical hierarchy. Can we think of a theoretical framework which need not commit us irrevocably to the point of view of the religious elite and which may be capable of recognising the active role of the community of believers in sustaining the ideals of Islam?

Let me suggest that between the contrasting dichotomy of elite and folk Islam, or theology and anthropology, we insert the mediating terms, folk-theology and theological anthropology.

The sociology of Islam must apply itself seriously to the investigation of folk theologies, on the one hand, and the meanings and use of scripture in the everyday life of the Muslim, on the other. We must not assume that the folk theologies cannot match the abstraction and cosmological implications of formal theologies. I mention only two directions in which folk theologies may be seen as complementary to formal theology. The first is that revelation has been a recurring phenomenon in the history of God's relation to man although completed in the form of the Qur'ān. Thus folk theology asserts that principles of reality based upon Islamic principles may be articulated by direct reflections on nature, man, and God. The principles of this reality may be also revealed through the experience of mystics and in poetry, music, stories, and proverbs. According to some, the reality of the world according to Islamic principles and the existence of the prophet were known before the historic birth of Mohammad, although lost in the process of history. Hence direct reflection on these ultimate principles of reality, and the variety of ways in which God's majesty impresses itself on man, can reveal the true principles of Islam according to which the world is ordered. The Qur'ān and the *shari'ah* are revered within this paradigm. Institutional theology of the *ulamas,* however, emphasises the formalism by which meaning has to be strictly bounded by one or the other acceptable traditions of exegesis of the Qur'ān, which alone is capable of revealing the Islamic order. It is not the task of the sociologist or the historian to displace either view, for it is in their mutual dialogue that the answer to the question of what constitutes Islam may be found.

The second direction in which folk theologies proceed is in the elaboration of narrative traditions through which Islamic principles have been preserved and communicated. A whole genre of oral and written literature has grown round such narratives. To take an example, Mohammad's instructions to a Bedouin about how to perfom *salā t*—if he had a Qur'ān he should recite it, otherwise he should praise and magnify God—is used as an illustrative analogy to establish that Islamic principles lay greater emphasis on piety and devotion than formal requirements of a ritual. The problem that this kind of literature would pose to Robinson is that it introduces some uncertainty as to the distinctive features of a good Muslim. We may, however, console ourselves by recalling that even God waits till judgement day to make such a pronouncement.

Lastly, a word on Robinson's sociology of knowledge. He says that Ahmad, Mujeeb, Faruqi and Mushirul Hasan can easily be placed in that tradition of scholarship which emphasises that Indian Muslims have their roots deep in Indian society, that they are natural inhabitants of India. As a criticism, this makes no sense since very good studies of Islam have come from scholars who had their roots deep in different kinds of societies. So, what Robinson is implicitly accusing these scholars of is that their view of Islam deliberately emphasises syncretism, and hesitates to condemn it, so that they can establish that 'there is no reason why they (Indian Muslims) cannot be good and loyal citizens of the Republic of India'.

I feel very hesitant to engage in an argument like this in which an insinuation is made that some of our colleagues are manipulating ideas to serve extra-academic interests. But if theories are to be explained by interests, then I am compelled to ask about the interests that Robinson is supporting when he asserts that where 'some form of holy law has come to be applied by the modern state, *with all its great coercive force and power of social penetration* (emphasis added), we may be sure that large groups of Muslims have probably come closer to the pattern of perfection than ever before'. I wonder if this support given to repressive regimes, to the use of torture, war, and punishment, by scholars who themselves enjoy all the privileges of democratic and liberal systems, should be integrated as an important element into Robinson's sociology of knowledge.

POSTSCRIPT

Is Islam a Single Universal Tradition?

At issue in these selections is whether Islam—or any other world religion—is or could be a single unified religious tradition. For Robinson, the answer to this question for Islam is, yes. Conversion of non-Muslims to Islam inevitably introduces heterodox beliefs and heteroprax practices, but historically these have declined and disappeared in older areas as local religious leaders and lay people learn more about the Quran and other scripture. It may be interesting to note that in many parts of India, people practice many different forms of Islam that incorporate dozens of different Hindu elements. But in the long run, these are merely temporary aberrations as communities proceed through the conversion process. In the end, all of these communities will come to embrace authentic, orthodox Islam. For Robinson, Islam represents a fundamentally different religious phenomenon from Christianity, which has long been fragmented into numerous sects, each with different beliefs and practices.

For Das, it is precisely these local differences from Islamic norms that are most interesting. In her view, these religious traditions will change over time, but she questions whether these variations in local Islam will ever totally disappear. Interpretation is at the heart of determining what is proper practice and belief. Since each interpretation introduces innovation, we should expect local Islams to become more divergent. In this way, Islam is no different from any other world religion, divided as it is into Sunni and Shiite sects, with more or less independent Sufi leaders involved in various ways with both congregations. Local Islamic traditions are merely part of a larger pattern in Islam and other world religions.

Can conversion to any religion ever take place without syncretization? And after a local syncretic tradition has emerged, do these local versions ever or inevitably come back into the orthodox fold?

A related question emerges from this discussion: Can any religious tradition remain a single, unified tradition for very long as it moves into new areas and blends with local traditions? Does the fact that orthodox behavior and belief in all world religions are based on interpretation of scripture and/ or teachings allow for the possibility of a stable set of practices? Alternatively, does the importance of interpretation inevitably lead to the formation of sects and religious splinter groups, as has happened in Christianity?

Other works that have addressed these questions in Islam would include Clifford Geertz's *Islam Observed* (University of Chicago Press, 1968) and his *Religion of Java* (Free Press, 1960), Ernest Gelner's *Muslim Society* (Cambridge University Press, 1981), and Aziz Azmah's *Islams and Modernities* (Verso, 1993). Dale Eickelman's *Moroccan Islam* (University of Texas Press, 1976) deals with a similar tension in North Africa, and Robert Launay's *Beyond the Stream: Islam and Society in a West African Town* (University of California Press, 1992) consid-ers one example of a local Islamic tradition in the Ivory Coast.

For a similar issue concerning the conversion of Latin American Indians to Catholocism, see Sabine MacCormack's essay "'The Heart Has Its Reason': The Predicaments of Missionary Christianity in Peru" (*Hispanic American Historical Review*, vo.65, 1985, pp. 443–466).

ISSUE 14

Do Some Illnesses Exist Only Among Members of a Particular Culture?

YES: Sangun Suwanlert, from *"Phii Pob:* Spirit Possession in Rural Thailand,"* in William Lebra, ed., *Culture-Bound Syndromes, Ethnopsychiatry, and Alternate Therapies,* vol. 4 of *Mental Health Research in Asia and the Pacific* (The University Press of Hawaii, 1976)

NO: Robert A. Hahn, from *Sickness and Healing: An Anthropological Perspective* (Yale University Press, 1995)

ISSUE SUMMARY

YES: Physician Sangun Suwanlert from Thailand asks whether or not one particular illness he observed in northern Thai villages, called *phii pob*, corresponds to Western diagnostic categories or is restricted to Thailand. After documenting how this condition does not fit standard psychiatric diagnoses, he concludes that *phii pob* is indeed a "culture-bound syndrome" that can only occur among people who share rural Thai cultural values and beliefs.

NO: Medical anthropologist Robert A. Hahn counters that the very idea of the so-called culture-bound syndrome is flawed. He contends that culture-bound syndromes are reductionist explanations for certain complex illness conditions—that is, explanations that reduce complex phenomena to a single variable. Hahn suggests that such conditions are like any illness condition; they are not so much peculiar diseases but distinctive local cultural expressions of much more common illness conditions that can be found in any culture.

For most of a century anthropologists have observed that people in many tribal societies suffer from peculiar health complaints that seemed to occur only among members of particular cultures. Most of these illnesses were psychiatric in nature, including various kinds of "wild man" behaviors, such as *amok* in Malaysia, the *witiko* (or *windigo*) psychosis of the Ojibwa, the "Arctic hysterias" of some Eskimo and Siberian groups, startle reactions like *latah* in Indonesia and Malaysia, and various panic reactions found among certain Australian aboriginal groups. In some Australian tribes, observers have reported that people have died of no apparent physiological cause after learning that they were victims of sorcery performed against them by an enemy. These diverse conditions appeared quite different from mental illnesses observed in Western countries, and some seemed to have physiological symptoms that were not seen in industrial countries. Such cases raised the possibility that some illnesses might be rooted in a specific culture or even caused by aspects of thecultures themselves. Thus, the idea of the culture-bound syndrome was born.

For medical anthropologists, these culture-bound syndromes seemed to define a special niche in the medical world where anthropologists could contribute valuable insights that physicians, psychologists, and psychiatrists could not provide. Most anthropologists accepted the premise that anthropology could offer few new insights about such conditions like pneumonia, malaria, gastrointestinal diseases, and cancer. But if psychological conditions in different cultures were profoundly shaped by culture or even caused by aspects of a particular culture, then anthropology seemed to have a special role to play in medicine.

For these medical anthropologists the question that confronted them was, How different are these syndromes from Western psychiatric conditions and neuroses? How can such different symptomatologies be explained? How do the details of local cultural traditions actually influence the symptoms of a particular condition, or alternatively, how does culture actually cause such illnesses?

These are some of the questions that Sangun Suwanlert addresses in the following selection. He focuses attention on a particular syndrome called *phii pob*, which he observed in northern Thailand. Rural Thai explain *phii pob* as a kind of spirit possession, which most typically affects married women. Symptoms of possession include numbness of limbs, falling sown (sometimes with convulsions), rigid limbs, clenched fists, and sometimes shaking. While each of these symptoms has been observed in Western culultural contexts, the specific configuration observed in Thailand does not redily map onto any specific Western diagnosis. Suwanlert concludes that phii pob represents a syndrome that is culture-bound and can only emerge among rural Thai.

Robert A. Hahn challenges the very notion that any specific syndrome is so closely linked to any particular culture that it would justify the label "culture-bound syndrome." All illnesses, he argues, are shaped by the local cultures in which they occur. These illnesses would include psychological and psychiatric conditions as well as those we ordinarily assume to be strictly physiological, such as infections, diabetes, chronic pain, and so on. Thus, for Hahn, *phii pob*, *amok*, Arctic hysteria, and the *witiko* psychosis are merely distinctive local symptomatic expressions of conditions that are found in industrialized nations.

Sangun Suwanlert

 **YES**

Phii Pob: Spirit Possession in Rural Thailand

In Thailand, as in all other countries, there are many people who seem to believe in spirits and ghosts. The Thais refer to the spirits and ghosts in general as *phii*. From my experience in treating psychiatric patients, I have found that the patients and their relatives are very much concerned with spirits and ghosts. *Phii* (evil spirit) possession is often found to be a basic cause in mental disease, both functional and organic, and we can divide them into three types:

- Ghosts of the dead: *phii* of grandparents, father, mother, ancestors, or spirits of important and respected people.
- Spirits of sacred things, not emanating from human beings.
- Spirits of the living, such as *phii pong, phii pob, phii ka,* and *phii krasu.*

My paper will be on the spirits of the living, the third type, or *phii pob,* with special emphasis on the psychiatric study of the *phii pob.* The first two kinds of *phii* mentioned above, those that originate from the dead and sacred things, are found to possess people more often than the third kind. . . .

Phii pob ... Uis a common spirit in the northeast, north, and some provinces of the central plain of Thailand. Some say that *phii pob* is nonsubstantial; that nobody can definitely describe its shape. Some say that it is in the shape of a black dog; others say it is shaped more like a monkey. . . .

Phii pob originates in a living person, conceals itself in the body of that person, who is called the originating host, and comes and goes at any time. There are three ways in which a person can become a source of *phii pob:* it may originate in the person himself; he may inherit it from his ancestors; or he may possess an object said to bring good fortune to its owner, and the *phii pob* dwelling in this object may transfer itself to the owner.

Origination within the host. *Phii pob* seems to originate in people who study magic arts and spells, such as the spell for prosperous trading, the spell enabling one to talk cleverly, and the magical love arts, to make a person desire sexual intercourse with the opposite sex or to make one's sexual organs attractive. After a person completes his study, he becomes a teacher in his special field of magic. Almost every teacher of magic observes certain restrictions against doing certain things.... These restrictions may proscribe eating certain kinds of food, accepting fees for treatment and teaching, or going underneath a clothesline. As time passes and such a person forgets these restrictions, the *phii pob* originates automatically within him, although the host may not be aware of it. Since it is believed that the *phii pob* hiding within a person can leave the body of that person to possess another, the new possessed host can discover and make known who the originating host of the *phii pob* is. Usually a person hosts only one *phii pob* of the same sex as himself, but many informants confirm that it is possible for a person to host many and possess both males and females.

Inherited from the host's ancestors.   Although the host grows old and eventually dies, the *phii pob* does not. It goes on hiding in the children of the host, usually the eldest child of the same sex; that is, the father's *phii pob* will transfer to the eldest son and the mother's to the eldest daughter. If the host has no children, the *phii pob* will hide in a close relative and is called *pob chue.*

Origination in objects.   One can become host of *phii pob* by possessing commodities such as *wan krachai* and *wan phii pob,* a tuberous plant, or *see poeng sanei,* a wax charm, which are said to bring good fortune to the possessor. Some believe that *phii pob* dwell in these things and may transfer themselves to the owner.

A person will be possessed by a *phii pob* when he has had an argument with its host, but this is not necessarily the only time. A person or animal can be possessed in four ways:

6. Possession can occur in time of sickness, causing complications, during menopause or at the age of involution, or during the transition from adolescence to adulthood. It is believed that the spirit will eat away at the viscera (kidney, intestines, liver, et cetera) until the individual finally dies.
7. A *phii pob* can possess a boy or a girl under ten years of age and make the child talk irrelevantly. It is believed that most children thus possessed will eventually die.
8. Large domestic animals such as cows, buffalo, and horses can be possessed and die suddenly.
9. A *phii pob* can enter people who have had no previous symptoms, generally women between the ages of 18 and 40, men, less frequently. The possessed host will usually identify the originating host; this is called *ook pak* ("to speak out") in Northeastern Thai.

The Study

At various times from 1967 to 1971, I conducted a study of *phii pob* possession in north and northeast Thailand. My research had the following aims:

- To study the nature of *phii pob* in the upper regions of Thailand, where people believe that *phii pob* is the cause of some illness.
- To study the relationship between the possession syndrome and the environment, the local culture, and the reaction of the people toward this syndrome.

- To determine whether this is a psychiatric syndrome and, if so, how to classify it.
- To study folk treatment for the possessed host and originating host.

This paper reports on sixty-two cases of possessed hosts; six cases of originating hosts; and ten cases of possessed hosts whose *phii pob* refused to leave them....

Symptoms of Possession

The earliest sign of the onset of possession is a numbness of limbs, followed by falling, with or without convulsions. Most who are possessed become unconscious; some become rigid, clench their fists, and must be forced to lie down or sit. After being in this condition for a while, some can answer questions, although somewhat confusedly. There are five categories of symptoms that appear after a person has been possessed:

1. Making noises like "*phii*," shouting out, screaming, weeping.
2. Tensing, clenched fists, or short spasms.
3. Shaking following spasms, (not in all cases).
4. Timidity or shyness, manifested by an inability to speak to or face others. Sometimes facial expressions are similar to those of the originating host.
5. Identifying or speaking out the host's name (*ook pak*).

The fifth is the most important symptom, for it reveals not only the host's name but also the purpose of the possession, whether it is good or bad and whether it is merely passing through the village. Whether this symptom appears depends largely on the ability of the shaman; if he is skillful, he will have the victim talking relevantly.

Possessed Host: Case Illustrations

For illustration, I would like to describe the two cases of possession occurring at the health station that I was able to observe from the onset. . . .

Case 1. A young, unmarried girl, 16 years of age, a Buddhist, with a primary-school education, from the Amnatcharoen District, and of low economic status was admitted to the Class I health station complaining of abdominal pain in the umbilical region. A physical examination revealed no abnormality, and she was referred to me for observation.

In an interview with the girl's mother, it was learned that, although she was very cooperative, the mother knew very little about her daughter because since the age of two the girl had been under her grandmother's care and had lived in another district. When the mother was in her sixth month of pregnancy, the girl's father left home and never returned. After the birth of the child, the mother struggled to make a living for both of them; when the girl was two, the mother remarried, and the child was sent off to her grandmother's. At the age of 15 the girl went to Bangkok with relatives and worked as a servant for six months, but she was unable to cope with her job so went back to live with her mother and stepfather.

Two days after witnessing her drunken stepfather slap her mother during an argument, the girl was possessed by a *phii pob*. The possession, according to the mother, lasted for about an hour. The originating host seemed to be one of the stepfather's friends who lived in the next village, because during possession the girl's general bearing was masculine when she described the kind of husband her stepfather was and when she threatened him with punishment by his ancestors' spirits.

The patient, with decorative cotton strings tied around her neck and wrists, was an attractive girl with sad eyes and a low, soft manner of speaking. During the interview she repeatedly said, "I don't know what my problem is, but I'm anxious about it." Crying, she complained of severe abdominal pain while continually asking her stepfather to do things for her.

The second night after being admitted, about 11:00 P.M., the patient was again possessed by a *phii pob*. When I went to the ward, the relatives, fearful of her falling off the bed, had her lying on the floor, and her mother was massaging her legs. I spoke to her but there was no recognition on her part. However, when she heard me, she sat up immediately in a cross-legged position. Her face became flushed and her eyes widened but did not focus. She raised her hand and said coherently, "I'm Mr. —— (stepfather's friend). I was angry when I heard that my friend did something wrong in the village. I'm here for a visit only." The mother cried out, "Please, go." "No," replied the girl. To the other relatives' suggestion of calling a shaman, the possessed girl answered, "I don't care." Then a relative asked, "Why don't you? This is a government office." (It is a common belief that *phii pob* are afraid of government offices.) The reply was, "I want my friend to behave. I want to let him know that if he doesn't, the ancestors' spirits will break his neck." After the stepfather promised that he would behave, the other relatives asked many questions; an hour later the spirit departed via the mouth, without the help of a shaman.

The patient was treated for ten days with a mild tranquilizer and superficial psychotherapy. She was discharged when she stopped complaining of abdominal pain, and she returned home to her grandmother.

Case 2. A 32-year-old Buddhist woman, wife of a peasant, with a primary-school education, and of low-income status, was admitted to the health station because of manifest muscle twitching in both arms, insomnia, and loss of appetite. A physical examination did not reveal any abnormality.

According to her husband, they had been married for several years. Before their marriage he had been a bachelor and she a divorcée with no children. About a year before admission, the wife was informed that the husband had had a long talk with a girl. Subsequently she began to nag, asking about his relationship with the girl. The more he denied, the more she nagged. A few days later the woman was possessed twice in one day. Ten days before her hospitalization, the husband went to see the girl in question on a business matter. When the wife learned of it she became hysterical, swore at her husband, cried, and ultimately fell into depression. Two days later the muscles in her arms began to twitch.

I visited the patient an hour every morning during her hospitalization because she was on a mild tranquilizer and superficial psychotherapy under my care. Whenever I started talking to her, her husband had to hold on to her arms to prevent them from twitching. Although the patient was pale, she looked younger than her years. She seemed to understand me well enough to make me think that she was not confused. However, she often said, "I'm quite worried about my future."

On the fourth night after admission, she became possessed by a female *phii pob*. The spirit claimed that it had come for a visit and asked the husband how things were going at home and how he had been behaving lately. Approximately fifteen minutes later the patient became silent and fell into depression, indicating that the spirit had departed. After ten days at the health station, the patient felt much better and the muscle twitching disappeared; she was discharged.

I consider the two cases cited above simple cases, but only when the precipitating cause of possession is taken into consideration. The cause was a kind of wish-fulfillment for people living in a noncomplex society. . . .

Originating Hosts

Case 1. Mrs. S., age 65, was from Amphur Wapee Patum, Mahasarakam Province. She looked slightly younger than her age, was dressed neatly in a long-sleeved blouse and a local type of skirt and wore the Northeastern type of earrings. Throughout the interview she sat properly and was very cooperative.

According to her, about five years ago in 1963, one of her sons who was working at Amphur Barn Pai in Kohnkaen Province befriended a man who had fallen off a car and broken his leg. The man had run out of money and wanted to sell a box containing a small image of Buddha on one side and a closely knitted gold fabric on the other. The man wanted 100 baht (US$5) for it but took the 20 baht offered. The man told him to take good care of it since it was valuable. When her son returned home, he placed the object on the shelf for worship. About a month later Mrs. S. began to have headaches and insomnia, so she consulted a shaman. He advised her that the object was the cause of the ailment and to get rid of it. One neighbor suggested that she throw it away but another asked for it so she gave it to the latter. Her headaches and insomnia soon disappeared.

After she disposed of the object in 1967, three of her neighbors, girls aged 14–15, were entered by *phii pob*. All of them claimed that it was a *phii pob* from Mrs. S. Mrs. S. felt very uneasy and asked the head of the village to find an expert who could expel the *phii pob* from her. She was referred to someone and paid over 1,000 baht (US$50) for his service. Because she feared that she might not be completely cured, she continued to receive a treatment of "holy water" at least once a month.

When asked how she felt after the shaman had beaten her with a stick and the *phii pob* had supposedly left, although the neighbors still accused her of being a *phii pob*, Mrs. S. said that she felt no pain nor anything else but shame and worry. She did not want to see anybody. She was worried about her seven sons who would have to bear the accusation for a long time. This is why she made her way to Wat Dhat Panom for the expulsion of *phii pob* from her. The person she consulted told her that if she would gather together a small Buddhist image, holy thread, and a fallen fragment of a pagoda, she would be protected from *phii pob*. She replied that she had spent all her money and could not purchase the necessary articles. I bought and gave them to her, and it seemed to lift up her spirits.

Case 2. A 36-year-old man, Mr. B., married and living in Amphur Boor Kaw, Kalasinthu Province, came to Wat Dhat Panom to have *phii pob* driven out of his body. He was told that he had two *phii pob,* both in the shape of monkeys, perched on his shoulder. In our interview, Mr. B. reported that about five years before, when he was unmarried, he bought a wax charm to attract women and make them fall in love with him. He did not think much more about it until he discovered that his *phii pob* was going around possessing the neighborhood women.

When asked how he felt when the *phii pob* left his body to enter into another, he said that he trembled with no apparent cause, but did not feel anything leave his body. He was not concerned that his neighbors would do any harm to him. Whenever he thought about it, he said, he felt sad and worried, but he strongly denied having any illness.

I then asked him about his wife's and children's reaction to his being called the host. He said they were all ashamed and worried about it, especially when one of his children overheard the villagers talking about him.

About a month before he came for treatment at Wat Pra Dhat, someone in the village became possessed again. At that time a villager fired a shot into the sky, and Mr. B. began to fear for his life. Until then, he was sad and worried about the situation he was in, but he never thought anyone would do him any harm. (The probable reason for this was that he had a relative in a monastery who was highly respected by the villagers.) After this incident, he was unable to sleep well and often dreamed of monkeys and black dogs. Finally he decided to seek help at Wat Pra Dhat since the two spirit doctors who had treated him did not help him feel better.

I studied the symptoms of depression in the six cases of originating hosts to see whether illness such as depression existed in the distant villages. A questionnaire based on Cleghorn and Curtis' depression study was used. Results suggested that the patients came for treatment out of worry over bodily harm that they might receive and out of depression manifested by the symptoms such as sadness, insomnia, and loss of appetite. These symptoms lead one to conclude that villagers do become depressed and try to avoid other people when they are accused of being a *phii pob*....

Villagers' Attitude toward *Phii Pob*

Belief in spirits has become a part of village tradition. The spirits, both good and bad, are perceived as superhuman beings, so good spirits are worshipped or respected and the bad ones are driven away as quickly as possible. The modernization introduced by education and communication has not changed these beliefs much. The villagers justify their belief in spirits by declaring that it is not harmful to anyone.

Actually there are three groups of people with respect to belief in spirits. (1) Nonbelievers include persons who have had some training in Buddhism, those who have been educated in cities or towns, and those whose families were troubled by spirits and have become good Buddhists. (2) Partial believers usually have a little more formal education than the average villager and often talk about true and false spirit possession and have tried to prove it. (3) Full believers include those who have lived only in the village, those who have experienced spirit possession, and those persuaded by others to believe in spirits. In actual number there are more full believers than nonbelievers and partial believers put together.

One may conclude that *phii pob* are considered suprahuman but bad spirits that should not be dwelling inside a human being. The method of driving out the bad spirit is either by physical punishment, beating the possessed with a cane, or by luring the bad spirits with the good because if the spirit is in a person too long the person can die or become mentally ill (*phii ba'*). Once a person's spirit has been expelled, he is considered cured and can continue to live in the village without prejudice....

Analysis

Possessed host group 1.   Working in the health station and in the villages, I was soon able to recognize a person who had been possessed by a *phii pob*. A possessed woman was usually distinguished in her beauty, dramatic in manner, and charmingly seductive. It was common to see her with cotton strings tied around her neck and wrists. While being interviewed, I noted, the possessed hosts were sensitive and easily stimulated, quick-tempered, self-centered, and susceptible to suggestions. These characteristics may be classified as belonging to a "hysterical personality," which is generally found more in women than in men. Perhaps this could be one of the reasons for the predominance of women among the 50 possessed hosts whom I studied in 1967. Fully 96 per cent of them were women, and only 4 per cent were men; 38 per cent were 21–30 years old; 76 per cent were married. They may have had problems before being possessed. It seems that the mechanism of *phii pob* possession is a socially accepted way of solving social and internal conflicts.

The feeling of numbness prior to possession experienced by 42 per cent of the possessed was, I feel, a result of emotional tension rather than malnutrition, because most of the possessed hosts were physically healthy (see Table 1). After exhibiting other symptoms, such as depression and visual and auditory hallucinations, they went through a state of which they had no recollec-

Table 1

Pre- and Post-Possession Symptoms (ranked by frequency)

Pre-Possession Symptoms (frequency rate = 42-2)*	Post-Possession Symptoms (frequency rate = 41-2)**
1. Felt numbness throughout the body and limbs.	1. Felt quite well.
2. Felt like crying.	2. Felt aches and pains all over the body.
3. Felt dizzy.	3. Felt weary.
4. Had vision of round shapes.	4. Became frightened and worried.
5. Felt sick at heart.	5. Developed insomnia.
6. Had headaches and chills.	6. Felt heart palpitations.
7. Had vision of a monkey.	7. Became groggy and befuddled.
8. Had vision of a man.	
9. Had vision of a dog or a cat.	
10. Heard voices calling.	
11. Felt stiffness in chest.	
12. Had vision of a chicken.	
13. Heard a dog barking.	
14. None.	

*Some symptoms appeared in combination, e.g., numbness and having vision of a monkey, but here they are listed separately.
**Most of the possessed could not remember what they said or did while being possessed, but some felt pains as though beaten with a cane, although very vaguely. Their gestures were similar to those of the originating host.

tion. This syndrome should without question be considered psychiatric, although there was not much content to their hallucination. Mainly they saw round objects, monkeys, cats, men, or dogs, suggesting toxic psychosis. But the symptom that makes it different from toxic psychosis is the state of trance, during which the patients could talk relevantly.

While being possessed, the patients seemed to take on a "double personality" for a short period, not more than an hour (see Table 2). At this time the possessed seemed to be in a state of trance as if hypnotized, which I would classify as "dissociative reaction". *Phii pob* possession may be a type of hysteria, but I feel that it is a kind of "dissociative reaction" that occurs only in specific Thai cultural groups but has not yet been geographically localized or classified, unlike *amok* or *latah*.

An originating host is considered a clever person who practices many kinds of spells and is respected by the villagers. Because he is considered a clever person, the possessed identifies with the host and does not feel that any harm will come about. Identification is said to be an important mental mechanism in hysteria and it occurs in people who have had a previous relationship with each other. Characterization appears to be on the conscious level.

The villagers feel that *phii pob* possession is a genuine occurrence—everyone in my investigation believed in it. They might be smiling and giggling, but when asked about *phii pob*, their facial expression at once becomes solemn. They also believe that the *phii pob* or the hosts have their central location in

Table 2

Characteristics of Possession Episode (Group 1, 1957: N = 50)

Characteristic	Number	Percent
Duration:		
Momentary	13	26
1 hour	16	32
2 hours	7	14
3 hours	5	10
8 hours	2	4
48 hours	1	2
Undetermined	6	12
Departure Point:		
Unknown	16	32
Mouth (vomiting)	9	18
Bladder (urinating)	7	14
Another part of the body	18	36
Number of times Possessed:		
1	22	44
2	6	12
3	10	20
> 3	12	24

Baan Chyak, Tambon Nacik, which perhaps accounts for the fact that more patients come from south of Amnat Charoen than from north of it.

Possessed host group 2.   Group 2 includes ten possessed hosts, whose *phii pob* refused to depart after 48 hours, whom I studied in 1969–1971. After receiving treatment at the hospital for about a week, these persons felt much better. In their case, the diagnosis might be hysterical psychosis and the mechanism of *phii pob* is more complicated and difficult to generalize than for group 1.

Originating hosts.   It was very difficult to get information from originating hosts at the beginning of the study, because I presumed that my clients would resent inquiries from a total stranger. In addition, there were always others around when I conducted the interviews, and I felt that harm might result. However, through the cooperation of the Buddhist monks, I was able to interview six originating hosts (*phii pob*).

Through the interviews it was established that one could become a *phii pob* by three means: through inheritance, incantation study, and possession of "sacred" things. Although the *phii pob* accepted the causes, they could not see how the spirits in their bodies could go and possess others. They admitted to worrying and feeling depressed and ashamed about what had happened, but they had no other feelings or reactions.

Being a *phii pob* seemed to last from one to five years. All of those affected earnestly sought to expel the spirits in them. I felt that the only time the villagers noticed that one of them was a *phii pob* was when the *pob* possessed another and "spoke." On the other hand, such identification could have been a vindictive fabrication. Once identified, though, the only way out for the accused was to announce that he was going to have treatments to expel the *phii pob*.

Judging from the six cases I studied, the mental health of the accused was poor, affecting the immediate family members and other relatives. I often wonder what was the basic cause of the one case where the healing process was completed and the *phii pob* was supposedly buried only to have the woman go and dig it up. Was it the power over others that she enjoyed, or was she really overpowered by the spirits, as claimed? These questions still remain unanswered.

Some people are sympathetic toward *phii pob* but will not live under the same roof with them and will try to exile them. Tolo Village in Roi-Et Province seemed to accept the exiles; no one in that village seemed possessed, although the majority of the villagers were known to be *phii pobs*.

Phii pob possession is both good and bad. It may be a socially acceptable way of solving social and interpersonal conflicts. On the other hand, it is quite simple for a person to falsely accuse another of being *phii pob*, with disastrous consequences. Usually the only way out for the accused is to admit that he is a *phii pob* and to promise to undergo treatment to drive out the spirit, or move to another place. I believe that public reaction profoundly affects a person's mental health.

Conclusion

... Sixty-two cases of possessed hosts were studied in the villages of two provinces in Northeast Thailand; ten were admitted by relatives for treatment at Srithunya Hospital, Nondhaburi, because shamans could not drive the spirits off.

With group 1, 50 cases studied in 1967, *phii pob* possession occurred in the village, and the duration of possession was momentary to 48 hours. After the spirit was driven off, the possessed hosts became their former selves and felt quite well. The personalities of hosts who were repeatedly possessed were hysterical, precipitating various kinds of causes for illness. During the period of possession, the symptoms were similar to hysterical trance or a dissociative phenomenon. The diagnosis might be a hysterical neurosis that occurs only in specific Thai cultural groups. It seemed that the mechanism of *phii pob* possession was a socially accepted way of solving social and internal conflicts.

Group 2, studied in 1969–1971, comprised ten cases of *phii pob* who refused to depart from their possessed hosts within 48 hours. The possessed hosts were brought into the psychiatric hospital as psychotics. After receiving treatment for about a week, they felt much better. The diagnosis might be hysterical psychosis. The mechanism of *phii pob* possession for this group is more complicated than for group 1....

Robert A. Hahn

Culture-Bound Syndromes Unbound

One of the jumpers while sitting in his chair with a knife in his hand was told to throw it, and he threw it quickly, so that it stuck in a beam opposite; at the same time he repeated the order to throw it, with cry or utterance of alarm resembling that of hysteria or epilepsy. He also threw away his pipe when filling it with tobacco when he was slapped upon the shoulder.... They [the jumpers] could not help repeating the word or sound that came from the person that ordered them any more than they could help striking, dropping, throwing, jumping, or starting; all of these phenomena were indeed but parts of the general condition known as jumping.... All of the jumpers agree that it tires them to be jumped and they dread it, but they were constantly annoyed by their companions.

— "Jumpers," Moosehead Lake, Maine, described by Beard

E. A. B. at the time of the event was 20 years old, unmarried, the third of four siblings and an Iban. At the time he ran amok he had been uprooted from his normal surrounding, a longhouse in one of the upper reaches of the Batang Lupar river. He was working in an oil drilling camp, approximately 200 miles from home with no direct communication. One night, while living on a barge near the camp, he grabbed a knife and slashed five of his fellow workers, three Malay and two Chinese.

— A man with *amok* in Malaysia, described [by] Schmidt

A man, about age 45, with wife and children, took a second wife. Afraid of the first wife's jealousy, he tried to keep the new relationship secret, but in time the second marriage became known. One evening, he came home tired and fatigued. He got the shivers, broke out in a cold sweat, and felt that his penis was shrinking. At his cry for help, the neighbors came running. Only men helped him. One man tightly held the patient's penis while another went for a sanro, *a native healer. The* sanro *performed one ritual and after a while the anxiety disappeared, ending the day's attack.*

— An Indonesian man with *koro*, reported [by] Chabot

Observers of seemingly strange behavior have distinguished a variety of behavioral syndromes that, because of their apparent uniqueness and fit to local cultural conditions, are described as culture-bound. The observers of such behavior have most often been from Western settings, the behavior

From Robert A. Hahn, *Sickness and Healing: An Anthropological Perspective* (Yale University Press, 1995). Copyright © 1995 by Yale University. Reprinted by permission of Yale University Press. References omitted.

observed principally in non-Western ones. In this [selection], I examine the logic by which the generic diagnostic label "culture-bound syndrome" is ascribed to some conditions and not to others. I claim that the idea of culture-bound syndromes is a conceptual mistake, confusing rather than clarifying our understanding of the role of culture in sickness and fostering a false dichotomy of events and the disciplines in which they are studied. All conditions of sickness are affected in many ways, and none is exhaustively determined by its cultural setting. Physiology, medicine, psychology, and anthropology are complementary rather than contrary and exclusive; all are relevant and necessary to the comprehensive understanding of human phenomena of sickness and healing....

The very notion of a culture-bound syndrome indicates a form of reductionism—the explanation of a given phenomenon by a single principle or body of knowledge. Other explanatory principles are thus denied relevance. Reductionists may claim that they have fully explained a culture-bound syndrome and that, in consequence, this phenomenon falls exclusively within their domain of inquiry. This mistaken effort is apparent in versions of anthropology as well as in Western medicine, psychiatry, psychoanalysis, and psychology. I argue that such claims fragment human function and its study into falsely opposed divisions.

Although anthropologists may believe that they have established a firm position by appropriating culture-bound syndromes to their own domain of explanation, their claims are at once excessive and too modest, claiming too much for culture-bound syndromes and too little for the diseases staked out by Biomedicine. I argue that full explanation requires an opening of the inner sanctum of Biomedicine to anthropological review and a concomitant recognition of pervasive physiological constraint in the workings of culture. Humans are bound by their cultures—but not rigidly. Nor is culture the only binding principle; body, mind, society, and the broader environment also bind. An exploration of culture-bound syndromes thus reaches the variety of forms of sickness and the range of human disciplinary approaches.

To assess the notion of culture-bound syndrome, I briefly define *syndrome* and *culture* and suggest how syndromes might be *bound* by culture. I distinguish three ways in which culture-bound syndromes have been understood.... I propose that we discard the misleading concept of culture-bound syndrome in favor of a broader study of the role of human mind, physiology, culture, and society in pathology and its relief.

Syndromes, Cultures, and Binds

A *syndrome* (from the Latin "things that run together") is a group of conditions, generally pathological, that may be physical and/or mental, signs and/or symptoms, and that is thought to constitute a discrete entity. One syndrome, AIDS (acquired immunodeficiency syndrome), has gained recent attention; it is defined by a complex set of signs and symptoms that has evolved with changing knowledge as well as political-economic circumstances. Numerous other syndromes are named in Biomedicine, some after their discoverer, others after their symptoms. Syndromes are distinguished from other events that co-occur in that their co-occurrence is thought to be not simply coincidental; a syndrome is a part of a unifying phenomenon—for example, a recognized biological process. The constituents of a syndrome may reflect a group of similar causes. What makes AIDS a syndrome is the acquisition of a specific virus, the human immunodeficiency virus, which causes a range of outcomes constituting AIDS.

The specificity with which a syndrome is defined will substantially affect what can validly be said about it—its distribution by nation and ethnic group, and other characteristics....

A culture, in the anthropological sense, is the set of beliefs, rules of behavior, and customary behaviors maintained, practiced, and transmitted in a given society. Different cultures may be found in a society as a whole or in its segments—for example, in its ethnic groups or social classes.

A syndrome may be regarded as culture-bound if particular cultural conditions are *necessary* for the occurrence of that syndrome; thus the culture-bound syndrome is thought not to occur in the absence of these cultural conditions. Some analysts of culture-bound syndromes may regard specific cultural conditions as *sufficient* for the syndrome's occurrence; in this view, no conditions other than these cultural ones (for example, other cultural conditions or noncultural ones) are necessary to provoke the occurrence of the culture-bound syndrome.

A Hypothetical Ethnography of the Diagnosis Culture-Bound Syndrome

Some of the dilemmas inherent in the notion of culture-bound syndrome are apparent in the ethnographic sources of this diagnosis. The history of specific terms and interpretations of these conditions is most often lost in the memories and notes of colonial settlers. Winzeler provides a rare historical account of the development of notions of latah. Edwards formulates the history of another condition, koro, its multiple names, and purported cases; as in the example of koro described at the outset of this [selection], a person who experiences koro is usually under great stress or anxiety, suffers a retraction of the genitals, and may fear death.

In general, we may guess that the application of the generic label culturebound syndrome and of terms for specific conditions, such as latah, and "wildman behavior," occurs in a sequence approximating the following:

1. Observers, most often trained in Western medicine, psychiatry, or psychoanalysis, or in anthropology or psychology, visit a foreign setting or an ethnic setting at home. Most often, ethnic settings are those that differ in their culture from the observers' own. Most often, though not always, the observers are white Americans or Europeans.

2. The observers notice behavior that seems strange (that is, unusual by their standards of normality) and indicative of deviance and disturbance. According to their interpretive bent, the observers are likely to take the observed behavior as pathological in some way—medically, psychiatrically, psychodynamically, behaviorally, and so on. Yet they may not know how to diagnose this pathology since it does not fit the familiar criteria of Western nosology. The culture-bound syndromes were early described as "exotic," a term that may tell us more about its users than about its intended referent.

3. The people among whom the strange behavior occur may offer a solution to the diagnostic dilemma. They may distinguish and label the observed behavior, although recognition of such labels in an unfamiliar setting is problematic. A response to an observer's question (such as, "What and I observing, and what is it called?"), which perhaps is not well understood, may not truly indicate what nevertheless comes to be accepted as an indigenous label for the observed condition. Vallee, for example, suggests that the term for one such condition, *pibloqtoq* (also referred to as "Arctic hysteria"), is the fabrication of early explorers rather than a usual term of Eskimo usage....

4. The observers return home with their prized possession: a new syndrome that, because it seems to be found only in the cultural setting from which they have returned, is labeled culture-bound. Culture-bound syndromes are residual; they are conditions that do not fit the nosological scheme of a Western observer. Rather than questioning the completeness or validity of the Western nosology, the new syndrome is set apart as an oddity from another culture.

5. The observers now face the ambiguous challenge of showing how this culture-bound syndrome actually fits into their own explanatory paradigm. The dilemma here is that, as the phenomenon is encompassed by the observers' explanatory system, it may lose its uniqueness and become a version of the broader phenomenon. Explanatory gain may be culture-specific loss. Analysts of culture-bound syndromes have attempted to keep their syndrome while reducing it also, by showing how social, cultural, and psychological conditions—general elements of their own scheme—are so distinctively configured in the local scene as to make this particular syndrome unlikely to occur elsewhere. Their reductions combine the universal principles of their own discipline—for example, the learning theories of psychology—with the unique cultural peculiarities of the local setting—for example, the specifics of who teaches, what is taught, and how. The local fit and indigenous label appear to give these conditions an immunity from spreading elsewhere; they may *look* like the "xyz" syndrome found elsewhere, but they are really different.

6. Having established a new condition, often distinguished by an ascribed indigenous term, the "discoverer" of this syndrome (or other observers) may then find further instances of similar conditions in new settings, applying the established term, but now crossing cultural boundaries. Amok is the most notorious condition to be exported....

Understanding Culture-Bound Syndromes

Three alternative understandings of culture-bound phenomena are plausible. One may be described as "exclusionist," the other two as "inclusionist." I refer to one inclusionist position as "nature-culture continuum," to the second as "multiple-aspect."

The exclusionist interpretation of culture-bound syndromes is suggested by the phrase "culture-bound syndrome" itself. The phrase implies or assumes that some conditions are culture-bound and others are not. Conditions that are not culture-bound may be regarded as culture-free, culture-blind; perhaps they are thought of as nature-, physiology-, or materiality-bound. In the exclusionist view, that a condition falls in one-half of this divide implies that it does not fall in the other, and vice versa. Latah and amok are culture-bound syndromes; measles and lung cancer are not. This division is held to correspond to disciplinary divisions as well, so that culture-bound syndromes are the concern of anthropological and/or psychological or psychiatric expertise and culture-free syndromes are the subject of medical or physiological examination.

Kenny provides an excellent example of the exclusionist position in his analysis of latah. In Kenny's work, some conditions are regarded as clearly culture-bound and others as clearly universal (though universal conditions may be differently interpreted in different settings).

> Measles or smallpox, for example, are clearly identifiable disease entities, but receive very different cultural interpretations. Is this also true for "latah," "amok," and other ostensibly culture-bound syndromes? In short, are latah-like startle responses better considered [quoting Simons 1980] as the "exploitation of a neurophysiological potential," *or* are they themselves more plausibly considered as the outcome of social *rather than* biological factors? (emphasis added)

Kenny's "or" and "rather than" are exclusive connections. "Disease entities" are regarded as universal phenomena, the results of biological factors; culture-bound syndromes, in contrast, are not diseaselike and result from social factors. Kenny claims that cultural patterns "fully explain" latah; it would thus seem that biological explanation has no room....

Kenny believes the "true" nature of latah to be dramaturgic, an arena he believes unrelated or exclusive of human biology.... Kenny writes: "If this is the case, then the latah performance is taken out of the province of biomedical reductionism and is seen in what I take to be its true light—as theater." Kenny here replaces biomedical reductionism with theatrical reductionism.

Psychologist John Carr's interpretation of another Southeast Asian condition, amok, represents a version of the exclusionist position distinct from Kenny's. Though Carr writes that some syndromes are culture-bound, he goes on to formulate a plausible interpretation of amok behavior based on a theory of learning from Western psychology. Carr applies universal principles to the Malay setting, asserting that amok is a learned behavior response to a highly ambiguous yet demanding culture situation. Langness claims that similar

Table 3

Explanatory Principle

	Culture	Nature
Condition	Culture-bound syndrome Illness	Culture-free syndrome Disease
Discipline	Psychology Anthropology	Physiology Medicine Psychiatry

cultural conditions—"contradictory demands and discontinuities"—account for "wildman behavior" in New Guinea.

Yet although Carr relates this culture-bound syndrome to universal principles of learning, like Kenny, he explicitly dissociates it from universal processes of disease, as formulated in Biomedicine: "The notion that culture-bound syndromes share underlying common disease forms is rejected. Instead, the ethno-behavioral model postulates that culture-bound syndromes consist of culturally specific behavioral repertoires legitimated by culturally sanctioned norms and concepts, but with both behavior and norms acquired in accordance with basic principles of human learning universal to all cultures."

Using notions of disease and illness developed by Kleinman, Carr associates culture-bound syndromes with illness behavior, which, "as distinct from the disease process, is always culturally determined." He concludes that a culture-bound syndrome is "a distinct repertoire of behaviors that (1) have evolved as the result of a social learning process in which the conceptual and value systems, and the social structural forms that mediate their effects, have served to define the conditions under which such behavior is an appropriate response, and (2) have been legitimated within the indigenous system as *illness* primarily in terms of extreme deviation from the behavioral norm as defined by preeminent culturally-specific conceptual dimensions governing social behavior."

This description of culture-bound syndromes parallels Kleinman's distinction between disease and illness and corresponds to disciplines appropriate to each [as seen in Table 3]. Carr notes, however, that culture-bound syndromes "may be precipitated by any number of etiological factors, among them physical, as well as sociocultural determinants." Thus, the basic cause of amok is thought to be psychological; the particular elements that are psychologically incorporated are culturally specific, and given this established syndrome, a number of precipitants, including physical ones, may elicit this behavior. Carr regards diseases as phenomena that appear universally, in "inviolate" form, and that are the legitimate concern of medicine and psychiatry, whereas illnesses are "always culturally determined" and are thus the legitimate concern of psychology and anthropology....

The inclusionist nature-culture continuum position maintains that all human events, including the supposed culture-bound ones, have cultural *and* biological *and* cognitive *and* psychodynamic aspects, though some events are more profoundly shaped by one of these aspects than by others. Thus, although no conditions are exclusively culture-bound or culture-free, some may be largely culturally shaped and others principally determined by universal physiology. In this conception, the notion of culture-bound syndrome remains a valid one. An example of the nature-culture continuum position is the work of Leighton and Murphy:

> So far as the total process in the development of psychiatric disorder is concerned, it would seem best to assume that heredity, biological, and psychological factors are all three engaged. To claim dominance for one, or for any subarea within one, *as a matter of general theory,* is to express a linear conception of cause and effect which is out of keeping with what we know about all the processes in the world around us. More germane is an approach to the topic that aims to discover and map out the interrelated factors and the nature of their interrelationships.

The recommendation that the relative importance of heredity, biology, and psychology cannot be theoretically determined in advance but must be empirically analyzed suggests that these factors may have more or less weight for different sicknesses.

The continuum understanding would make the extent to which a condition is culture-bound a matter of degree. It might be possible, at least theoretically, to quantify the proportions in which different factors contribute to given outcome conditions. Measles might occupy the natural, physiological end of this spectrum, the culture-bound syndromes the other; it is not clear what sorts of conditions might fall between—perhaps depression and alcoholism....

Anthropological Queries and Logical Doubts ...

Defining Syndromes: Category and Context

The prevailing view of culture-bound syndromes is that these behaviors are distinctive of their cultural circumstances. Taken to its extreme, this view has implications that make scientific comparison impossible. All phenomena and events are unique, each differentiable from all others by some or, more likely, by many characteristics: each screw produced in a factory, every case of depression and tuberculosis, every episode of latah. The variations of each occurrence of a phenomenon are explicable, though perhaps not by current knowledge, in terms of the context of that occurrence. Indeed, such explanation is what we mean by "context"—a phenomenon's context is its circumstance, its environment. It is the explanatory power of a phenomenon rather than its simple physical contiguity that constitutes the context of something to be explained. Because one phenomenon is significant in the explanation of another, however, does not bind the two to the exclusion of other explanatory principles. Occurrences of latah may well be different in large and small communities, as manifested by older and younger performers, by one person and another, even by an individual person at different times or in different circumstances. Do we then talk of community-bound, age-bound, person-bound, person-time-circumstance-bound syndromes?

By contextualizing in this way, we end up with a list of occurrences-for-persons-at-times-in-circumstances, and so on, ad infinitum....

In Search of the Whole: Interpretive and Causal Explanation

The exclusionist claim that some behavioral complexes are culture-bound and that others are not, and that the latter fit into some universal scheme, suggests that the culture-bound phenomena are so distinctive that they are beyond comparison. The explanation of such phenomena, exclusionists assume, connects them with other local phenomena and patterns of meaning, rather than with phenomena and patterns elsewhere. This perspective parallels one of two radically different positions that divide anthropology as well as literary studies, historiography, and psychology: interpretive and causal. Culture-bound syndromes provide a perfect example of the interpretive school, since they are thought to be explicable only by their local context.

According to the interpretive understanding, a position also called hermeneutic and phenomenological and sometimes associated with the philosopher Ludwig Wittgenstein, social and cultural phenomena are fully explained when they are shown to fit with their local phenomena in a system that "makes sense." In this view, questions about the causes of the phenomena of interest are regarded as misconceived or tangential. Thus, Kenny objects to attempts to explain culture-bound syndromes by universal, causal principles: "These medical or pseudo-medical labels evoke the notion that there is some kind of causal process underlying *latah*. The interpreters of *latah* seek to identify factors in the life experience of the victim which make her condition inevitable." It is implied that no kind of causality underlies latah. In a more general vein, Geertz writes, "Believing, with Max Weber, that man is an animal suspended in webs or significance he himself has spun, I take culture to be those webs, and the analysis of it to be therefore not an experimental science in search of law but an interpretive one in search of meaning."

Although it is obvious that anthropology is not an experimental science, Geertz goes further to assert that a search for law, presumably causal, excludes a search for interpretation. Interpretation is deemed appropriate only in the study of the workings of culture. Thus Geertz distinguishes blinks, which may be causally analyzed by science, from winks, which are intentional acts shaped by cultural systems to be analyzed by an interpretation of meaning in society and the circumstances of the winker. Yet, at some level, human biology is the mechanism of winks and may be involved in their motivation as well, and blinks, too, may express a symbolic meaning; these two forms of eye movement are not as distinctive as Geertz claims them to be.

... [I]f comprehensive explanation rests with those who perform an action, we become ensnared in webs of meaning that lead logically to solipsism [a theory holding that the self can know nothing but its own modifications and that the self is the only existent thing]. If local phenomena and labels for them can be understood only in terms of other local phenomena and their labels, then research across localities, as in much of anthropology, becomes impossible. Anthropologists may pursue their own tales, but not those of others.

Anthropology, Sibling Disciplines, and the Spectrum of Sickness

A conceptual and theoretical solution to the troubles of the exclusionist position might be founded in four principles:

1. A cross-cultural theory of sickness should begin, though not necessarily end, with the indigenous and personal understandings of the sufferer. Forms of suffering that do not fit the Biomedical mold will not be excluded as culture-bound. Patients at home will not be rejected as superstitious or as "crocks" because they fail to fall into Biomedical diagnostics. Pathology would be defined by the experience of the patient rather than by principles that seem a priori universal because they work fairly well among some groups at home and because they can be significantly explained by physiology, also apparently universal. Although a person may be (asymptomatically) unaware of the conditions that might later affect his or her well-being, still the state of well-being itself, and thus the sources of threat to it, are defined by the thought world of the patient him- or herself.
2. Interpreting a human act or syndrome—that is, showing its fit to the understandings and to the local circumstances in which it occurs—may be necessary, but it is not sufficient for full understanding. Minimally, an explanation that some phenomenon occurs in one place because of such-and-such conditions must also show that it does not occur elsewhere, where these conditions are not met. Comparison is a necessity and requires the development of comparative categories so that we may say that this is found here but not there, and that that is found there but not here. Even interpretation itself requires comparative categories; without them, the terms of one language and culture (say, the interpreter's) could not apply to those of another; translation would be impossible; and interpretation could thus be made only in local terms and only for local consumption. Exclusionism, by insisting on the exclusive local fit of all cultural phenomena, thereby precludes comparison; indeed it precludes communication across cultural boundaries.

   The difficulties of causal explanation are notorious, though perhaps better recognized than the hazards of interpretation. Nevertheless causal explanation, however systematic and nonlinear, must be pursued. In this way a universal scheme will come to take local meaning into account.
3. The course of human events is inevitably many-leveled, so that neither our disciplines—such as anthropology, physiology, psychology—nor their central concepts—culture, biochemical exchanges, human experience—can exclusively appropriate any event. That is, human

events are not simply cultural or psychological, but inevitably bear these aspects and others.

4. ... [T]here are several ways in which the organization and culture of societies affect their processes of pathogenesis and healing. Societies inform their members about how the world is divided up and put together. With regard to pathogenic and healthful processes I have recommended three forms of understanding: *disease* models, *illness* models, and *disorder* models. Societies also engage in the production of sickness because of the ways in which they organize cultural beliefs and social relations. Carr's psychosocial analysis of amok illustrates the pathogenic powers of the social environment.

Such a sociocultural framework applies not only to conditions that are obviously affected, but to the purportedly hard-core diseases as well. The Biomedical model has obscured rather than enlightened such effects. Yet the history of tuberculosis, as brilliantly portrayed by René and Jean Dubos forty years ago, illustrates sociocultural effects in this condition whose biological characteristics appear to be clearly defined. The variety and power of ideology in tuberculosis-like conditions in European society are visible in a great range of attitudes toward this former (and reemerging) "captain of the men of death," its victims sometimes believed to manifest intensified creative powers as they were "consumed." Ideologies continue to be modified. The Duboses suggest that the term *tuberculosis,* already bearing a denotation not directly indicative of contemporary etiological conceptions, could be modified to fit current knowledge. The bacterium itself was then being shown to be neither necessary nor sufficient to the symptomatic complex that we call tuberculosis. The Duboses insisted on the causative importance of the host's sociocultural and natural environment. They also noted that though psychological factors were likely to be of importance, their extent and workings were unknown. A great variety of remedial efforts have also followed beliefs about this condition and about the broader order of social life. Tubercular patients have been revered and isolated, placed in dry climates and wet ones, required to rest and to exercise exhaustively.

Culture, nature, and the human mind between play central roles in diseases commonly thought of in terms of microorganisms and toxins as well as in apparently strange behavioral complexes. Only an inclusionist framework can encompass the range of pathological (and healthy) forms.

Culture-bound syndromes constitute an important frontier between anthropology, Biomedicine, and the medical systems of other societies. Built in premises different from our own, they challenge our standard divisions of things. In striking fashion they have reminded us that our own forms of sickness and of reacting to events do not cover the spectrum of the humanly possible. A comprehensive theory of human reactions and pathology must take them into account.

I have argued that the exclusionist understanding of culture-bound syndromes, implicit in the term, yet not intended by early proponents, distorts the role of culture and of physiology in human affairs. It claims too much of culture at the margin of our nosological scheme and too little of culture at medicine's core. Medical professionals, anthropologists, and others have conspired in a false division of labor. False divisions obstruct understanding. The abandonment of the erroneous category, culture-bound syndrome, might serve to redirect our attention to the formulation of a theory of human sickness in which culture, psychology, and physiology were regarded as mutually relevant across cultural and nosological boundaries.

POSTSCRIPT

Do Some Illnesses Exist Only Among Members of a Particular Culture?

In discussing *phii pob,* Suwanlert accepts this condition as a medical problem that he believes occurs ony among rural Thai people. As he outlines the syndrome, he links its occurrence to cultural factors specific to rural communities in transition that are not found in industrial societies. He does not find any systematic correspondence between *phii pob* and psychological diagnoses in the West, and thus he concludes that *phii pob* is a culture-bound syndrome. Hahn, in contrast, steps back from the details of specific conditions described as culture-bound syndromes to ask what they all have in common rather than focus simply on one condition like *phii pob.* He asks, In what sense can these syndromes be seen as distinct from Western diagnostic categories? Hahn concludes that authors like Suwanlert have typically reduced what must be complex illness experiences to a single set of cultural factors. He concludes that there are no culture-bound syndromes; all illness conditions are rooted in the biology and psychology of individual patients but shaped by the cultures in which they live. Thus, culture plays no more important role in *phii pob* than in malaria, pneumonia, cancer, or depression.

Suwanlert and Hahn differ on whether or not conditions like *phii pob* are really so different that they cannot be explained as manifestations or local cultural expressions of more common psychological problems. Suwanlert argues that *phii pob* is unlike anything described in the standard reference manual, *Diagnostic and Statistical Manual of Mental Disorders (DSM-IV),* (American Psychiatric Association, 1994). Hahn contends that the symptoms associated with conditions such as *phii pob* are typically so vague and ambiguous that they only seem to not fit *DSM-IV.* In this instance, patients with *phii pob* may have any subset of the symptoms that include numbness, falling sown, convulsions, tensing, clenched fists, short spasms, timidity, and a distinctive kind of vocalizations. Non of these symptoms by itself is sufficient to define the condition as *phii pob,* and no particular set of these symptoms are required for the case to be defined as spirit possession.

A similar issue concerns whether or not we could actually compare culture-bound syndromes if they genuinely were bound to particular cultures. Hahn argues that if they were truly culture-bound, comparisons among different kinds of hysterias, wild man behaviors, startle reactions, and the like would be impossible. Such syndromes would have no common basis for comparison since it is the distinctive cultures, not something in the bodies and psyches of patients, that are causing the conditions. Hahn suggests that comparison among different conditions, such as the comparison Cawte provides in his selection, would be impossible.

Ronald C. Simons and Charles C. Hughes edited *The Culture-Bound Syndromes: Folk Illnesses of Psychiatric and Anthropological Interest* (D. Reidel, 1985), which surveys the various syndromes and attempts to sort them into general patterns. This volume has an exhaustive bibliography of primary sources about most culture-bound syndromes. Although Simons and Hughes accept the premise of the culture-bound syndrome, they conclude that some conditions probably should not be considered culture-bound, while others, such as Arctic hysteria, *amok*, and *latah*, probably should be accepted as legitimate culture-bound syndromes. Despite thefactthatthis volumeaccepts some culture-bound syndromes as distinctive, Hughes challenges the suitability of using this terminology, since most of the conditions can be related to conditions described in the *DSM-IV*.

Suwanlert's selection comes from one of the first collections to document many of the culture-bound syndromes: *Culture-Bound Syndromes, Ethnopsychiatry, and Alternate Therapies*, William P. Lebra, ed. (University Press of Hawaii, 1985). The collection contains detailed discussions of *latah, amok, witiko* psychosis, Arctic hysteria, and other syndromes mentioned here. Another volume of interest to psychological anthropologists and students interested in the relationship between culture and mental health is *Cultural Conceptions of Mental Health and Therapy*, edited by Anthony J. Marsella and Geoffrey M. White (D. Reidel, 1982). For a good discussion of *latah*, see Robert L. Winzeler's *Latah in Southeast Asia: The History and Ethnography of a Culture-Bound Syndrome* (Cambridge University Press, 1995).

ISSUE 15

Do Museums Misrepresent Ethnic Communities Around the World?

YES: James Clifford, from *The Predicament of Culture: Twentieth-Century Ethnography, Literature, and Art* (Harvard University Press, 1988)

NO: Denis Dutton, from "Mythologies of Tribal Art," *African Arts* (Summer 1995)

ISSUE SUMMARY

YES: Postmodernist anthropologist James Clifford argues that the very act of removing objects from their ethnographic contexts distorts the meaning of objects held in museums. He contends that whether these objects are displayed in art museums or anthropological museums, exhibitions misrepresent ethnic communities by omitting important aspects of contemporary life, especially involvement with the colonial or Western world.

NO: Anthropologist Denis Dutton asserts that no exhibition can provide a complete context for ethnographic objects, but that does not mean that museum exhibitions are fundamentally flawed. Dutton suggests that postmodernists misunderstand traditional approaches to interpreting museum collections, and what they offer as a replacement actually minimizes what we can understand of ethnic communities from museum collections.

In the late nineteenth and early twentieth centuries, museums were a major focus of anthropological research. In the United States, for example, until after the First World War more anthropologists were employed in museums than in universities. By 1940 cultural anthropologists had largely moved out of museums as they focused on intensive fieldwork. This change was directly related to a shift in paradigms from cultural evolution to functionalism, which happened in the 1920s and 1930s.

As anthropologists later began to focus on functional questions about how societies and their institutions worked, museum collections became increasingly unimportant. Many anthropologists believed that differences in the bindings of stone axes have little to say about how marriages were contracted or how clans were linked together; objects cannot explain how leadership worked or what role religious ideas might have had in maintaining social order.

The following selections deal with the question of how museums should exhibit and interpret ethnographic collections that were obtained during the "museum period" of anthropology. Both authors are critical of certain exhibitions, particularly art historian William Rubin's "Primitivism" show from 1984, and both feel that a good exhibition should contextualize museum objects historically. But the authors differ profoundly in their approach to the study of museum objects.

James Clifford surveys several different kinds of museum exhibits in New York and asks, Do any of them do justice to the peoples who made and used these objects? For Clifford, objects and the cultures from which they come have histories. He questions how much of these histories are present in the several exhibitions he visited. By definition, each and every non-Western object in a Western museum has been removed from its original ethnographic context, a process often referred to as "decontextualization."

Clifford explains in his selection how museums offer a "representation" of tribal peoples as if these societies were timeless and without history. By focusing on particular features of tribal culture, each exhibition makes statements about the relationship between modern Americans and "primitive" peoples. For him, these are fundamentally misleading representations.

Denis Dutton accepts that exhibitions such as those discussed by Clifford are inevitably incomplete, but the lack of a full context does not completely invalidate the exercise of exhibiting objects from tribal societies. He argues that Clifford and the other postmodernist critics of museum exhibitions go too far in their criticisms and that they, too, have an agenda that is itself misleading. Referring to this postmodernist agenda as a "new mythology" about tribal art, Dutton contends that the new mythologists have exaggerated their interpretations of museum exhibitions.

Dutton argues that museums can never offer complete representations of ethnic communities; but this does not mean that exhibitions cannot be both informative and enlightening even if they are incomplete. He asserts that Clifford's analysis leads us away from any understanding of museum objects; instead Clifford prefers to present his understandings of the culture through museum curators in our own modern culture. For Dutton, the goal should be to discover the meanings and significance of objects from the point of view of their original communities, and such meanings will never emerge from critiques of museum exhibitions like Clifford's.

How serious are the inevitable distortions of a museum exhibit? Does the omission of the current historical and global economic context misinform the public? How much context can a museum exhibition realistically provide? If such misrepresentations do occur, would it be better not to exhibit "primitive" art at all? What solutions to the problem of distortion do Clifford and Dutton propose?

James Clifford  **YES**

Histories of the Tribal
and the Modern

During the winter of 1984-85 one could encounter tribal objects in an
unusual number of locations around New York City. This [selection] surveys a half-dozen, focusing on the most controversial: the major exhibition held at the Museum of Modern Art (MOMA), "'Primitivism' in 20th
Century Art: Affinity of the Tribal and the Modern." The ..."ethnographic
present" is late December 1984.

The "tribal" objects gathered on West Fifty-third Street have been around.
They are travelers—some arriving from folklore and ethnographic museums in
Europe, others from art galleries and private collections. They have traveled
first class to the Museum of Modern Art, elaborately crated and insured for
important sums. Previous accommodations have been less luxurious: some
were stolen, others "purchased" for a song by colonial administrators, travelers, anthropologists, missionaries, sailors in African ports. These non-Western
objects have been by turns curiosities, ethnographic specimens, major art creations. After 1900 they began to turn up in European flea markets, thereafter
moving between avant-garde studios and collectors' apartments. Some came
to rest in the unheated basements or "laboratories" of anthropology museums, surrounded by objects made in the same region of the world. Others
encountered odd fellow travelers, lighted and labeled in strange display cases.
Now on West Fifty-third Street they intermingle with works by European masters—Picasso, Giacometti, Brancusi, and others. A three-dimensional Eskimo
mask with twelve arms and a number of holes hangs beside a canvas on which
Joan Miró has painted colored shapes. The people in New York look at the two
objects and see that they are alike.

Travelers tell different stories in different places, and on West Fifty-third
Street an origin story of modernism is featured. Around 1910 Picasso and his
cohort suddenly, intuitively recognize that "primitive" objects are in fact
powerful "art." They collect, imitate, and are affected by these objects. Their
own work, even when not directly influenced, seems oddly reminiscent of
non-Western forms. The modern and the primitive converse across the centuries and continents. At the Museum of Modern Art an exact history is told featuring individual artists and objects, their encounters in specific studios at
precise moments. Photographs document the crucial influences of non-West-

ern artifacts on the pioneer modernists. This focused story is surrounded and infused with another—a loose allegory of relationship centering on the word *affinity*. The word is a kinship term, suggesting a deeper or more natural relationship than mere resemblance or juxtaposition. It connotes a common quality or essence joining the tribal to the modern. A Family of Art is brought together, global, diverse, richly inventive, and miraculously unified, for every object displayed on West Fifty-third Street looks modern.

The exhibition at MOMA is historical and didactic. It is complemented by a comprehensive, scholarly catalogue, which includes divergent views of its topic and in which the show's organizers, William Rubin and Kirk Varnedoe, argue at length its underlying premises. One of the virtues of an exhibition that blatantly makes a case or tells a story is that it encourages debate and makes possible the suggestion of other stories. Thus in what follows different histories of the tribal and the modern will be proposed in response to the sharply focused history on display at the Museum of Modern Art. But before that history can be seen for what it is, however—a specific story that excludes other stories—the universalizing allegory of affinity must be cleared away.

This allegory, the story of the Modernist Family of Art, is not rigorously argued at MOMA. (That would require some explicit form of either an archetypal or structural analysis.) The allegory is, rather, built into the exhibition's form, featured suggestively in its publicity, left uncontradicted, repetitiously asserted—"Affinity of the Tribal and the Modern." The allegory has a hero, whose virtuoso work, an exhibit caption tells us, contains more affinities with the tribal than that of any other pioneer modernist. These affinities "measure the depth of Picasso's grasp of the informing principles of tribal sculpture, and reflect his profound identity of spirit with the tribal peoples." Modernism is thus presented as a search for "informing principles" that transcend culture, politics, and history. Beneath this generous umbrella the tribal is modern and the modern more richly, more diversely human.

‹⊙›

The power of the affinity idea is such (it becomes almost self-evident in the MOMA juxtapositions) that it is worth reviewing the major objections to it. Anthropologists, long familiar with the issue of cultural diffusion versus independent invention, are not likely to find anything special in the similarities between selected tribal and modern objects. An established principle of anthropological comparative method asserts that the greater the range of cultures, the more likely one is to find similar traits. MOMA's sample is very large, embracing African, Oceanian, North American, and Arctic "tribal" groups. A second principle, that of the "limitation of possibilities," recognizes that invention, while highly diverse, is not infinite. The human body, for example, with its two eyes, four limbs, bilateral arrangement of features, front and back, and so on, will be represented and stylized in a limited number of ways. There is thus a priori no reason to claim evidence for affinity (rather than mere resemblance or coincidence) because an exhibition of tribal works that seem impressively "modern" in style can be gathered. An equally striking collection could be made demonstrating sharp dissimilarities between tribal and modern objects.

The qualities most often said to link these objects are their "conceptualism" and "abstraction" (but a very long and ultimately incoherent list of shared traits, including "magic," "ritualism," "environmentalism," use of "natural" materials, and so on, can be derived from the show and especially from its catalogue). Actually the tribal and modern artifacts are similar only in that they do *not* feature the pictorial illusionism or sculptural naturalism that came to dominate Western European art after the Renaissance. Abstraction and conceptualism are, of course, pervasive in the arts of the non-Western World. To say that they share with modernism a rejection of certain naturalist projects is not to show anything like an affinity. Indeed the "tribalism" selected in the exhibition to resemble modernism is itself a construction designed to accomplish the task of resemblance. Ife and Benin sculptures, highly naturalistic in style, are excluded from the "tribal" and placed in a somewhat arbitrary category of "court" society (which does not, however, include large chieftainships). Moreover, pre-Columbian works, though they have a place in the catalogue, are largely omitted from the exhibition. One can question other selections and exclusions that result in a collection of only "modern"-looking tribal objects. Why, for example, are there relatively few "impure" objects constructed from the debris of colonial culture contacts? And is there not an overall bias toward clean, abstract forms as against rough or crude work?

The "Affinities" room of the exhibition is an intriguing but entirely problematic exercise in formal mix-and-match. The short introductory text begins well: "AFFINITIES presents a group of tribal objects notable for their appeal to modern taste." Indeed this is all that can rigorously be said of the objects in this room. The text continues, however, "Selected pairings of modern and tribal objects demonstrate common denominators of these arts that are independent of direct influence." The phrase *common denominators* implies something more systematic than intriguing resemblance. What can it possibly mean? ... The affinity idea itself is wide-ranging and promiscuous, as are allusions to universal human capacities retrieved in the encounter between modern and tribal or invocations of the expansive human mind—the healthy capacity of modernist consciousness to question its limits and engage otherness.

... The affinities shown at MOMA are all on modernist terms. The great modernist "pioneers" (and their museum) are shown promoting formerly despised tribal "fetishes" or mere ethnographic "specimens" to the status of high art and in the process discovering new dimensions of their ("our") creative potential. The capacity of art to transcend its cultural and historical context is asserted repeatedly....

At West Fifth-third Street modernist primitivism is a going Western concern....

Indeed an unintended effect of the exhibition's comprehensive catalogue is to show once and for all the incoherence of the modern Rorschach of "the primitive." ... [T]he catalogue succeeds in demonstrating not any essential affinity between tribal and modern or even a coherent modernist attitude toward the primitive but rather the restless desire and power of the modern West to collect the world.

⊸◈⊷

... If we ignore the "Affinities" room at MOMA, however, and focus on the "serious" historical part of the exhibition, new critical questions emerge. What is excluded by the specific focus of the history? Isn't this factual narration still infused with the affinity allegory, since it is cast as a story of creative genius recognizing the greatness of tribal works, discovering common artistic "informing principles"? Could the story of this intercultural encounter be told differently? It is worth making the effort to extract another story from the materials in the exhibition—a history not of redemption or of discovery but of reclassification. This other history assumes that "art" is not universal but is a changing Western cultural category. The fact that rather abruptly, in the space of a few decades, a large class of non-Western artifacts came to be redefined as art is a taxonomic shift that requires critical historical discussion, not celebration. That this construction of a generous category of art pitched at a global scale occurred just as the planet's tribal peoples came massively under European political, economic, and evangelical dominion cannot be irrelevant. But there is no room for such complexities at the MOMA show. Obviously the modernist appropriation of tribal productions as art is not simply imperialist. The project involves too many strong critiques of colonialist, evolutionist assumptions. As we shall see, though, the scope and underlying logic of the "discovery" of tribal art reproduces hegemonic Western assumptions rooted in the colonial and neocolonial epoch.

Picasso, Léger, Apollinaire, and many others came to recognize the elemental, "magical" power of African sculptures in a period of growing *négrophilie,* a context that would see the irruption onto the European scene of other evocative black figures: the jazzman, the boxer (Al Brown), the *sauvage* Josephine Baker. To tell the history of modernism's recognition of African "art" in this broader context would raise ambiguous and disturbing questions about aesthetic appropriation of non-Western others, issues of race, gender, and power. This other story is largely invisible at MOMA.... Overall one would be hard pressed to deduce from the exhibition that all the enthusiasm for things *nègre,* for the "magic" of African art, had anything to do with race. Art in this focused history has no essential link with coded perceptions of black bodies—their vitalism, rhythm, magic, erotic power, etc.—as seen by whites. The modernism represented here is concerned only with artistic invention, a positive category separable from a negative primitivism of the irrational, the savage, the base, the flight from civilization.

A different historical focus might bring a photograph of Josephine Baker into the vicinity of the African statues that were exciting the Parisian avant-garde in the 1910s and 1920s; but such a juxtaposition would be unthinkable in the MOMA history, for it evokes different affinities from those contributing to the category of great art. The black body in Paris of the twenties was an ideological artifact. Archaic Africa (which came to Paris by way of the future— that is, America) was sexed, gendered, and invested with "magic" in specific ways. Standard poses adopted by "La Bakaire," like Léger's designs and costumes, evoked a recognizable "Africanity"—the naked form emphasizing pelvis and buttocks, a segmented stylization suggesting a strangely mechanical vitality. The inclusion of so ideologically loaded a form as the body of Josephine Baker among the figures classified as art on West Fifty-third Street would suggest a different account of modernist primitivism, a different analysis of the category *nègre* in *l'art nègre* and an exploration of the "taste" that was something more than just a backdrop for the discovery of tribal art in the opening decades of this century.

Such a focus would treat art as a category defined and redefined in specific historical contexts and relations of power....

Since 1900 non-Western objects have generally been classified as either primitive art *or* ethnographic specimens. Before the modernist revolution associated with Picasso and the simultaneous rise of cultural anthropology associated with Boas and Malinowski, these objects were differently sorted—as antiquities, exotic curiosities, orientalia, the remains of early man, and so on. With the emergence of twentieth-century modernism and anthropology figures formerly called "fetishes" (to take just one class of object) became works either of "sculpture" or of "material culture." The distinction between the aesthetic and the anthropological was soon institutionally reinforced. In art galleries non-Western objects were displayed for their formal and aesthetic qualities; in ethnographic museums they were represented in a "cultural" context. In the latter an African statue was a ritual object belonging to a distinct group; it was displayed in ways that elucidated its use, symbolism, and function. The institutionalized distinction between aesthetic and anthropological discourses took form during the years documented at MOMA, years that saw the complementary discovery of primitive "art" and of an anthropological concept of culture." ...

Cultural background is not essential to correct aesthetic appreciation and analysis: good art, the masterpiece, is universally recognizable. The pioneer modernists themselves knew little or nothing of these objects' ethnographic meaning. What was good enough for Picasso is good enough for MOMA. Indeed an ignorance of cultural context seems almost a precondition for artistic appreciation. In this object system a tribal piece is detached from one milieu in order to circulate freely in another, a world of art—of museums, markets, and connoisseurship.

Since the early years of modernism and cultural anthropology non-Western objects have found a "home" either within the discourses and institutions of art or within those of anthropology.... Both discourses assume a primitive world in need of preservation, redemption, and representation. The concrete, inventive existence of tribal cultures and artists is suppressed in the process of either constituting authentic, "traditional" worlds or appreciating their products in the timeless category of "art."

◆◎◆

Nothing on West Fifty-third Street suggests that good tribal art is being produced in the 1980s. The non-Western artifacts on display are located either in
a vague past (reminiscent of the label "nineteenth-twentieth century" that
accompanies African and Oceanian pieces in the Metropolitan Museum's
Rockefeller Wing) or in a purely conceptual space defined by "primitive"
qualities: magic, ritualism, closeness to nature, mythic or cosmological aims.
In this relegation of the tribal or primitive to either a vanishing past or an
ahistorical, conceptual present, modernist appreciation reproduces common
ethnographic categories.

The same structure can be seen in the Hall of Pacific Peoples, dedicated
to Margaret Mead, at the American Museum of Natural History. This new permanent hall is a superbly refurbished anthropological stopping place for non-
Western objects. In *Rotunda* (December 1984), the museum's publication, an
article announcing the installation contains the following paragraph:

> Margaret Mead once referred to the cultures of Pacific peoples as "a world
> that once was and now is no more." Prior to her death in 1978 she
> approved the basic plans for the new *Hall of Pacific Peoples.* (p. 1)

We are offered treasures saved from a destructive history, relics of a vanishing world. Visitors to the installation (and especially members of *present*
Pacific cultures) may find a "world that is no more" more appropriately
evoked in two charming display cases just outside the hall. It is the world of a
dated anthropology. Here one finds a neatly typed page of notes from Mead's
much-disputed Samoan research, a picture of the fieldworker interacting
"closely" with Melanesians (she is carrying a child on her back), a box of
brightly colored discs and triangles once used for psychological testing, a copy
of Mead's column in *Redbook*. In the Hall of Pacific Peoples artifacts suggesting change and syncretism are set apart in a small display entitled "Culture
Contact." It is noted that Western influence and indigenous response have
been active in the Pacific since the eighteenth century. Yet few signs of this
involvement appear anywhere else in the large hall, despite the fact that many
of the objects were made in the past 150 years in situations of contact, and
despite the fact that the museum's ethnographic explanations reflect quite
recent research on the cultures of the Pacific. The historical contacts and
impurities that are part of ethnographic work—and that may signal the life,
not the death, of societies—are systematically excluded.

The tenses of the hall's explanatory captions are revealing. A recent color
photograph of a Samoan *kava* ceremony is accompanied by the words: "STATUS
and RANK were [sic] important features of Samoan society," a statement that
will seem strange to anyone who knows how important they remain in Samoa
today. Elsewhere in the hall a black-and-white photograph of an Australian
Arunta woman and child, taken around 1900 by the pioneer ethnographers
Spencer and Gillen, is captioned in the *present* tense. Aboriginals apparently
must always inhabit a mythic time. Many other examples of temporal incoher-

ence could be cited—old Sepik objects described in the present, recent Trobri-
and photos labeled in the past, and so forth.

The point is not simply that the image of Samoan *kava* drinking and status
society presented here is a distortion or that in most of the Hall of Pacific Peoples history has been airbrushed out. (No Samoan men at the *kava* ceremony
are wearing wristwatches; Trobriand face painting is shown without noting that
it is worn at cricket matches.) Beyond such questions of accuracy is an issue of
systematic ideological coding. To locate "tribal" peoples in a nonhistorical time
and ourselves in a different, historical time is clearly tendentious and no longer
credible (Fabian 1983). This recognition throws doubt on the perception of a
vanishing tribal world, rescued, made valuable and meaningful, either as ethnographic "culture" or as primitive/modern "art."...

At the Hall of Pacific Peoples or the Rockefeller Wing the actual ongoing-
life and "impure" inventions of tribal peoples are erased in the name of cultural or artistic "authenticity." Similarly at MOMA the production of tribal
"art" is entirely in the past. Turning up in the flea markets and museums of
late nineteenth-century Europe, these objects are destined to be aesthetically
redeemed, given new value in the object system of a generous modernism.

⊰◈⊱

The story retold at MOMA, the struggle to gain recognition for tribal art, for its
capacity "like all great art ... to show images of man that transcend the particular lives and times of their creators," is taken for granted at another stopping
place for tribal travelers in Manhattan, the Center for African Art on East Sixty-
eighth Street. Susan Vogel, the executive director, proclaims in her introduction
to the catalogue of its inaugural exhibition, "African Masterpieces from the
Musee de l'Homme," that the "aesthetic-anthropological debate" has been
resolved. It is now widely accepted that "ethnographic specimens" can be distinguished from "works of art" and that within the latter category a limited
number of "masterpieces" are to be found. Vogel correctly notes that the aesthetic recognition of tribal objects depends on changes in Western taste. For
example it took the work of Francis Bacon, Lucas Samaras, and others to make it
possible to exhibit as art "rough and horrifying [African] works as well as
refined and lyrical ones." Once recognized, though, art is apparently art. Thus
the selection at the Center is made on aesthetic criteria alone. A prominent plac-
ard affirms that the ability of these objects "to transcend the limitations of time
and place, to speak to us across time and culture ... places them among the
highest points of human achievement. It is as works of art that we regard them
here and as a testament to the greatness of their creators."

There could be no clearer statement of one side of the aesthetic anthropological "debate" (or better, *system*). On the other (anthropological) side,
across town, the Hall of Pacific Peoples presents collective rather than individual productions—the work of "cultures." At the American Museum of Natural
History ethnographic exhibits have come increasingly to resemble art shows.
Indeed the Hall of Pacific Peoples represents the latest in aestheticized scient-
ism. Objects are displayed in ways that highlight their formal properties....

While these artistically displayed artifacts are scientifically explained, an older, functionalist attempt to present an integrated picture of specific societies or culture areas is no longer seriously pursued. There is an almost dadaist quality to the labels on eight cases devoted to Australian aboriginal society (I cite the complete series in order): "CEREMONY, SPIRIT FIGURE, MAGICIANS AND SORCERERS, SACRED ART, SPEAR THROWERS, STONE AXES AND KNIVES, WOMEN, BOOMERANGS." Elsewhere the hall's pieces of culture have been recontextualized within a new cybernetic, anthropological discourse. For instance flutes and stringed instruments are captioned: "MUSIC is a system of organized sound in man's [sic] aural environment" or nearby: "COMMUNICATION is an important function of organized sound."

In the anthropological Hall of Pacific Peoples non-Western objects still have primarily scientific value. They are in addition beautiful. Conversely, at the Center for African Art artifacts are essentially defined as "masterpieces," their makers as great artists. The discourse of connoisseurship reigns. Yet once the story of art told at MOMA becomes dogma, it is possible to reintroduce and co-opt the discourse of ethnography. At the Center tribal contexts and functions are described along with individual histories of the objects on display. Now firmly classified as masterpieces, African objects escape the vague, ahistorical location of the "tribal" or the "primitive." The catalogue, a sort of *catalogue raisonné,* discusses each work intensively. The category of the masterpiece individuates: the pieces on display are not typical; some are one of a kind. The famous Fon god of war or the Abomey shark-man lend themselves to precise histories of individual creation and appropriation in visible colonial situations. Captions specify *which* Griaule expedition to West Africa in the 1930s acquired each Dogon statue.... We learn in the catalogue that a superb Bamileke mother and child was carved by an artist named Kwayep, that the statue was bought by the colonial administrator and anthropologist Henri Labouret from King N'Jike. While tribal names predominate at MOMA, the Rockefeller Wing, and the American Museum of Natural History, here personal names make their appearance.

In the "African Masterpieces" catalogue we learn of an ethnographer's excitement on finding a Dogon hermaphrodite figure that would later become famous. The letter recording this excitement, written by Denise Paulme in 1935, serves as evidence of the aesthetic concerns of many early ethnographic collectors. These individuals, we are told, could intuitively distinguish masterpieces from mere art or ethnographic specimens. (Actually many of the individual ethnographers behind the Musée de l'Homme collection, such as Paulme, Michel Leiris, Marcel Griaule, and André Schaeffner, were friends and collaborators of the same "pioneer modernist" artists who, in the story told at MOMA, constructed the category of primitive art. Thus the intuitive aesthetic sense in question is the product of a historically specific milieu.) The "African Masterpieces" catalogue insists that the founders of the Musée de l'Homme were art connoisseurs, that this great anthropological museum never treated all its contents as "ethnographic specimens." The Musee de l'Homme was and is secretly an art museum. The taxonomic split between art and artifact is thus healed, at least for self-evident "masterpieces," entirely in terms of the aesthetic code. Art is art in any museum....

The non-Western objects that excited Picasso, Derain, and Léger broke into the realm of official Western art from outside. They were quickly integrated, recognized as masterpieces, given homes within an anthropological-aesthetic object system. By now this process has been sufficiently celebrated. We need exhibitions that question the boundaries of art and of the art world, an influx of truly indigestible "outside" artifacts. The relations of power whereby one portion of humanity can select, value, and collect the pure products of others need to be criticized and transformed. This is no small task. In the meantime one can at least imagine shows that feature the impure, "inauthentic" productions of past and present tribal life; exhibitions radically heterogeneous in their global mix of styles; exhibitions that locate themselves in specific multicultural junctures; exhibitions in which nature remains "unnatural"; exhibitions whose principles of incorporation are openly questionable. The following would be my contribution to a different show on "affinities of the tribal and the postmodern." I offer just the first paragraph from Barbara Tedlock's superb description of the Zuni Shalako ceremony, a festival that is only part of a complex, living tradition.

Imagine a small western New Mexican village, its snow-lit streets lined with white Mercedes, quarter-ton pickups and Dodge vans. Villagers wrapped in black blankets and flowered shawls are standing next to visitors in blue velveteen blouses with rows of dime buttons and voluminous satin skirts. Their men are in black Stetson silver-banded hats, pressed jeans, Tony Lama boots and multicolored Pendleton blankets. Strangers dressed in dayglo orange, pink and green ski jackets, stocking caps, hiking boots and mittens. All crowded together they are looking into newly constructed houses illuminated by bare light bulbs dangling from raw rafters edged with Woolworth's red fabric and flowered blue print calico. Cinderblock and plasterboard white walls are layered with striped serapes, Chimayó blankets, Navajo rugs, flowered fringed embroidered shawls, black silk from Mexico and purple, red and blue rayon from Czechoslovakia. Rows of Hopi cotton dance kilts and rain sashes; Isleta woven red and green belts; Navajo and Zuni silver concha belts and black mantas covered with silver brooches set with carved lapidary, rainbow mosaic, channel inlay, turquoise needlepoint, pink agate, alabaster, black cannel coal and bakelite from old '78s, coral, abalone shell, mother-of-pearl and horned oyster hang from poles suspended from the ceiling. Mule and white-tailed deer trophy-heads wearing squash-blossom, coral and chunk-turquoise necklaces are hammered up around the room over rearing buckskins above Arabian tapestries of Martin Luther King and the Kennedy brothers, The Last Supper, a herd of sheep with a haloed herder, horses, peacocks.

Mythologies of Tribal Art

Forty years ago Roland Barthes defined a mythology as those "falsely obvious" ideas which an age so takes for granted that it is unaware of its own belief. An example of what he means can be seen in his 1957 critique of Edward Steichen's celebrated photographic assemblage "The Family of Man." Barthes declares that the myth this exhibition promotes first seems to stress exoticism, projecting a Babel of human diversity over the globe. From this picture of diversity, however, a pluralistic humanism "is magically produced: man is born, works, laughs and dies everywhere in the same way...." The implicit mythological background of the show postulates "a human essence."

Barthes is exactly on target about the philosophic intentions of "The Family of Man." In his introduction to the published version of the exhibition, Steichen had written that the show was "conceived as a mirror of the universal elements and emotions in the everydayness of life—as a mirror of the essential oneness of mankind throughout the world." Such juxtapositions as that which places Nina Leen's *Life* magazine image of an American farm family next to a family in Bechuanaland (now Botswana), photographed by another *Life* photographer, Nat Farbman, are therefore meant to convey the idea that despite all differences of exterior form, of cultural surface, the underlying nature of all families and peoples is essentially the same. This position is what Barthes views as the sentimentalized mythology of "classic humanism," and he contrasts it with his own "progressive humanism," which must try "constantly to scour nature, its 'laws' and its 'limits' in order to discover History there, and at last to establish Nature itself as historical." While classic humanism regards the American and African families as embodying, beneath culture and skin color, abiding natural relationships of kin and affection, progressive humanism would insist that these bourgeois conceptions of the natural are themselves historically determined. Barthes claims that such imperialistic juxtapositions ignore the political and economic roots of diversity.

Although "The Family of Man" had a potently relevant message for the generation that had witnessed the genocidal horrors of the Second World War, it was also worth paying attention to Barthes's claim that Steichen's collection, for all its antiracism and humanist charms, conveyed an implicit illusion of equality of power among the cultures it portrayed. It is now two generations later, however, and critics who accept the importance of exposing cultural mythologies and covert ideologies have new work to do. One area of criticism that especially stands in need of fresh examination is the shell-pocked field where battles have raged over the status and understanding of ethnographic arts. Barthes's reaction to MOMA's "The Family of Man" is particularly pertinent in this regard, because much of what he says adumbrates reactions to another exhibition, " 'Primitivism' in 20th Century Art," which took place over a quarter of a century later in that same museum. That show displayed side-by-side images of Africa and Europe, not photographs of people, but works of art. And it too was denounced as complacently positing, without regard to cultural difference, a specious universalism—aesthetic instead of moral.

But a sea change in academic thinking separates Barthes's critique of "The Family of Man" from the more strident critics of the "Primitivism" show. In the middle 1950s, Barthes was nearly alone in his dissent against a much loved and widely praised exhibition. The generation of critics who questioned (or denounced) "Primitivism" represented a manner of thinking that had become a virtual academic fashion. Some of these later critics were arguing from a set of ideas that had themselves come to embody a virtual mythology in precisely the Barthesian sense. Their views presuppose and constitute, in point of fact, a New Mythology of tribal arts—a prevailing set of presuppositions, prejudices, and articles of political and philosophical faith which govern many discussions of these arts and their relations to European criticism, art, and aesthetics. A contemporary Africanist art historian [Sidney Kasfir] for example, writes in a recent *African Arts* article on the authenticity of African masks and carvings: "That from an African perspective, these objects are *not* art in the current Western sense is too well known to discuss here." The phrase "too well known to discuss here" is symptomatic of a mythology. Barthes claimed his intention to unmask "the mystification which transforms petit-bourgeois culture into universal nature." Today we should be just as willing to deal with those mystifications that transform prevailing conventions of academic culture into validated truth.

This vigorous New Mythology of tribal arts takes on its life against the backdrop of what it posits as the Old Mythology. As with other ideologies, the New Mythology would no more describe its precepts as "mythology" than would the Old: both operate according to the familiar adage "Your views are so much mythology; mine speak the truth." Nevertheless, much contemporary theorizing and criticism about tribal arts are founded on a complacent acceptance of a substrate of givens and unsupported hypotheses which constitute the central tenets of the New Mythology. To be sure, not all of the theses are false. On the other hand, not all of the beliefs the New Mythologists stigmatize as Old Mythology are false either. Independent, critical thinkers should want to choose the component ideas of these mythologies that are worth rejecting, preserving, or reviving.

Providing a disinterested assessment of these ideas is not easy in the present ideologically charged and factious atmosphere. This indeed is part of the problem: so many contemporary theorists of tribal arts posit enemies who have it all wrong, in contrast to themselves, who have it right. This lack of any generosity whatsoever toward one's perceived (or invented) opposition increasingly stultifies writing in this area. The New Mythology finds itself expressed by a wide range of writers, including, for example, the more vociferous critics of the "Primitivism" show such as Thomas McEvilley and Hal Foster; James Clifford in his treatment of museums and ethnographic art; Arnold Krupat in *Ethnocriticism;* Sidney Kasfir in her article "African Art and Authenticity," published in this journal; Sally Price in *Primitive Art in Civilized Places;* Marianna Torgovnick in *Gone Primitive;* and Christopher B. Steiner in *African Art in Transit.*

Mythologies, Old and New

There are actually two phases of the Old Mythology to which these writers tend to react. What I will call *premodernist* or *colonialist* Old Mythology includes the elements of nineteenth-century imperialism—racism, contempt for "childish" artifacts, and regard for "primitive" art as representing a lower evolutionary stage of human development, with missionaries burning "fetishes" and the wholesale looting of indigenous art, as in Benin. The later, more enlightened, *modernist* Old Mythology, exemplified by such figures as Picasso, Roger Fry, and the "Primitivism" exhibition itself, is, from a New Mythological perspective, perhaps even more insidious, because while it pretends to valorize these arts, it perpetuates acts of imperialism, appropriation, and ethnocentric insensitivity toward Third World peoples—all in the name of enlightened, magnanimous liberalism. The grounds for my three-fold distinction—between premodernist/colonialist Old Mythology, modernist Old Mythology, and the New Mythology—can be usefully developed in terms of the following key ideas. Again, some of these notions included within these mythologies are entirely valid, some constitute half-truths, and some are plainly false; no one of these sets of ideas has a monopoly on truth.

> *(1) According to the premodernist Old Mythology, at least as the New Mythology likes to imagine it, tribal artifacts weren't works of art at all, but merely "fetishes," "idols," "fertility symbols," "ancestor figures," and the like, which colonialists collected as they might botanical specimens. The later, post-Picasso modernist version of the Old Mythology insists, on the contrary, that they are works of art, embodying universal aesthetic values.*

Curiously, the New Mythology frequently sides with the colonialist Old Mythology by aggressively questioning the status of tribal artifacts as works of art: in the New Mythological view, the Old Mythology at least acknowledged difference. This convergence of opinion, however, is complicated. Philistine colonialists often regarded artifacts as demonstrating little skill and no sense of form: the colonialists were applying nineteenth-century European aesthetic criteria to genres of work they did not begin to comprehend, and so were reluctant to call them "art." The New Mythologists' reluctance to identify tribal artifact genres as "art" is based on the notion that this would be hegemonic or imperialistic. Such reluctance is frequently supported by unthinking repetition of the folk legend that pretechnological peoples have no art because they have no word that refers to what Europeans call "art."

Patrick R. McNaughton recognizes another aspect of this New Mythologists' doctrine and has stressed the importance of challenging it, "because so many scholars still recite what has become a kind of maxim asserted by outsiders about Africans, that they unlike us treat what we call art as a functional part of life" rather than something for aesthetic contemplation.

(2) The Old Mythology essentialized the primitive, subsuming the endless variety of tribal cultures under a few crude stereotypes.

The New Mythology, on the other hand, while eager to recognize the diverse and frequently unique characteristics that distinguish tribal societies, essentializes "the West," creating, in an inversion of Edward Said's familiar formulation, a kind of Occidentalism. Thus, in the example cited earlier, Kasfir qualifies her discussion of authenticity with the remark that the artifacts in question should not be considered art "in the current Western sense." The quaintness of this last phrase should not go unnoticed: among Praxiteles, Donatello, Rembrandt, Judy Chicago, Duchamp, and Koons—not to mention the myriad genres of European folk craft and popular art—there is no "current Western sense" of art, but various, radically different, and rival senses of the concept, each partially implicated in competing social practices and theories of art. In fact, in its crudity, the very phrase "the West" is the New Mythologists' answer to "the Primitive" as that term might have been used a century ago. The latter was a lazy and misleading way of lumping together such cultures as Hopi, Sepik, Benin, and !Kung—even Aztec, in some understandings of "primitive." In the New Mythology, "the West" refers to twelfth-century French villages, horror movies, the Industrial Revolution, the theology of St. Augustine, New Zealand public education, the international banking system, modern toy retailing, medieval concepts of disease, Thanksgiving dinner, electronic mail, Gregorian chants, Linnaean botany, napalm, the Chopin études, and bar codes—as though the values and ideologies found therein can be the subject of useful generalization. The New Mythology replaces one set of stereotypes with another set, equally banal.

(3) In the Old Mythology, precontact tribal societies were seen as largely isolated, unchanging, coherent, and unbroken in their cultural tradition. Colonialism was supposed to have destroyed their structure and belief base. Their Golden Age of aesthetic and cultural achievement, and hence authenticity, predates European contact. Postcolonial culture and artifacts are culturally "inauthentic."

The New Mythology asserts to the contrary that these societies never were isolated, were not necessarily "unified" or "coherent," and underwent profound breaks in their traditions before European contact. The Old Mythology's " people without a history" view was a convenient colonialist construction. The New Mythology responds to claims of "inauthenticity" by variously claiming (a) indigenous belief systems were not destroyed but only occulted during the colonial period, and are now coming again into flower; (b) what is truly authentic is now found in the process of mutual appropriation by indigenous and colonial cultures; and in any event, (c) authentic cultural values must always be defined by the people who hold them: therefore, whatever indigenous people claim as authentic is, *ipso facto,* authentic, whether traditional, postcolonial, or merely imported.

Old and New Mythologists for the most part agree that small-scale indigenous societies have been permanently altered or obliterated by the encounter with the West's political systems, media, missionaries, technology, commerce, wage labor, and so forth. New Mythologists, however, are especially keen to emphasize that this has involved imperialist domination and exploitation. What is awkward for them is the fact that less desirable elements of culture change have been enthusiastically (and voluntarily) embraced by many indigenous peoples: cigarettes, soft drinks, movies, pop music, and Jack Daniels. By stressing that tribal cultures were always borrowing and in a state of flux, the New Mythology places in benign perspective the obliteration (or active abandonment) of traditional indigenous values: all cultures, it seems, are in the process of being altered by history.

(4) The Old Mythology, especially in its colonial form, held it unproblematic that traders or travelers might buy or barter for artifacts. Alternatively, artifacts might be accepted as gifts. None of this disturbs their meanings in the Old Mythology, and if anything the native should be thankful for receiving payment for the work before the termites got to it.

The New Mythology sees buying, selling, and trading as essentially Western concepts. Even to accept these objects as gifts is to become, as Kasfir puts it, implicated in "the web of conflicting interests that surround them." There is hence no "noninterventionist" way of obtaining these artifacts, since somewhere in the scheme power relations will obtrude, leading to the exploitation of the indigenous maker or owner of the object. In other words, the native always gets cheated. The New Mythology seems to impute to precontact tribal societies a premercantile edenic state, as though trade and barter (not to mention theft or conquest) of ritual or other valuable artifacts did not occur among these peoples until Europeans came along.

(5) The only reason to collect primitive artifacts, according to premodernist Old Mythology, was as curiosities, examples perhaps of an early stage of Social Darwinist development: they were to be placed in a cabinet alongside fossils and tropical insects. After Picasso & Co., the Old Mythology proclaimed that primitive art embodied the aesthetic sensibilities found in all art, and therefore was as much worth collecting as Constables or Utamaros, and for precisely the same reasons.

The New Mythology displays an oddly ambivalent attitude toward collecting. On the one hand, collecting is persistently disparaged, for instance as a "hegemonic activity, an act of appropriation . . . a largely colonial enterprise ... the logical outcome of a social-evolutionary view of the Other." McEvilley speaks of "captured" tribal objects, a trope suggesting they exist in Western collections as prisoners or slaves. Given the reprehensible nature of collecting, one would expect New Mythologists to demand that the trade in ethnographic art cease, but I have not encountered any such suggestions (except, of course, for the criminal trade in looted antiquities). Even those writers who take moral satisfaction from criticizing collecting appear themselves to have "captured" the occasional artifact.

> *(6) On puritanical grounds the Old Mythology often forbade taking pleasure in works of tribal art: the sexual element in carvings offended missionary and nineteenth-century colonial sensibilities. In New Zealand, as elsewhere, genitals were hacked off Maori figures, and some overtly sexual carvings were simply burned, lest prurient pleasure be aroused.*

The New Mythology replaces this attitude with a new and asexual form of puritanism. Enjoyment of any sort derived from the experience of ethnographic art is considered a cultural mistake at best, a form of visual imperialism at worst: "the colonialist gaze." Angst-ridden New Mythologists are reluctant to record appreciation or enthusiastic emotional reactions to artifacts. Thus Torgovnick heaps contempt on Roger Fry, among many others, for his "insensitive" and "racist" readings in praise of African art, but she never provides, in her own voice, nonracist, sensitive readings to instruct us on how to do it right. Nicholas Thomas is simply bemused: of the museums crammed with indigenous artifacts—"carved bowls, clubs, spears, baskets, pots," etc.—he honestly admits that "I have never understood why people want to look at such things (although I often look at them myself)." Christopher B. Steiner makes the bizarre claim that the objects are valued by Westerners as a way to "celebrate" the loss of the utility they had in their original cultural contexts. Other New Mythologists, such as James Clifford and James Boon (whose article title "Why Museums Make Me Sad" is clear enough), write about ethnographic arts with such a brooding sense of guilt about the historical treatment of conquered cultures that no sense of joy or love for the art is ever allowed to emerge.

> *(7) Colonialist Old Mythology held that though primitive cultures were to some degree capable of adopting Western technologies and manufactured articles, they could not possibly understand Western culture. In fact, having no adequate comparative perspective, the primitives could not even fully understand their own cultures. Their simple little societies were, however, transparent to the educated, sophisticated Westerner.*

The New Mythology, on the contrary, contends that it is the "educated" West which fails to grasp the vast subtleties offered by these cultures, ranging from ethnobotany and folk medicines to spiritual wisdom. Instead, the West ethnocentrically imposes on them its own categories, such as "individual," "religion," or "work of art," when in actuality these concepts have no place in the cultural landscape of the Other. In the matter of borrowing, the New Mythology holds that indigenous artists are, in its preferred parlance, free to appropriate from European culture, infusing their new work with "transformed meanings," fresh associations given to foreign elements introduced into a new cultural context. The reverse—Europeans borrowing from indigenous arts—is to be discouraged. This inversion of the Old Mythology means that an innovative Sepik dancer who incorporates cigarette wrappers in an elaborate headdress is participating in an exciting fusion of cultures, while a

Swedish office-worker who wears a New Guinea dog-tooth necklace is implicated in hegemonic, colonialist appropriation.

As a frontispiece for *Gone Primitive,* Torgovnick presents a heavily ironic,
not to say sneering, painting (by Ed Rihacek) of a stylish European woman
wearing sunglasses and sitting before a zebra skin, surrounded by a collection
of "primitive art." In his derisory essay on the "Primitivism" exhibition, Clifford reproduces a 1929 photograph of Mrs. Pierre Loeb, seated in her Paris apart-
ment filled with Melanesian and African carvings. Clifford labels this as an
"appropriation" which was "not included in the 'Primitivism' Show" (a curious
observation inasmuch as this very photograph appears in the show's catalogue).
Both of these images suggest a kind of disapproval of European cultural appropriation that it would be unthinkable to direct toward their cultural inversion—
for example, the 1970s posed village photograph Susan Vogel has published
showing a Côte d'Ivoire man seated before a wrinkled, painted backdrop of an
airplane, a cassette radio proudly displayed on his lap.

> *(8) The Old Mythology at its colonialist worst posited an ethnocentric aes-
> thetic absolutism: advanced, naturalistic European art forms were seen, espe-
> cially because of their naturalism, as demonstrating a higher stage in the
> evolution of art. Modernist Old Mythology retained the idea of universal aes-
> thetic standards, but argued that tribal arts fully met these criteria for excel-
> lence, which were formalist rather than naturalistic.*

In rejecting both these positions, some New Mythologists urge the abandonment of any idea of transcultural aesthetic criteria (which would be
implicitly imperialistic) in favor of complete aesthetic relativism. McEvilley
imputes to Kant an epistemology which "tacitly supported the violent
progress of 19th- and 20th-century imperialisms" and which justified a view
of the Western aesthetic sense as superior to that of non-Western cultures. The
New Mythology owes its aesthetic relativism entirely to the climate of poststructural thought rather than to any empirical study of ethnographic and
other world arts.

> *(9) More generally, both colonialist and modernist Old Mythologies imply or
> presuppose an epistemic realism: they both presume to describe the actual, exis-
> tent characteristics of tribal societies and their arts.*

Under the influence of poststructuralism, the New Mythology often presupposes various forms of constructivism, the idea that categories of human
existence are constituted entirely by our own mental activity: we "invent" or
"construct" the "primitive," tribal "art," "religion," and so on. The knots into
which theorists become tied in trying to introduce such poststructural rhetoric into the study of indigenous arts is illustrated by Barbara Kirshenblatt-
Gimblett who writes: "Ethnographic artifacts are objects of ethnography. They
are artifacts created by ethnographers. Objects become ethnographic by virtue
of being defined, segmented, detached, and carried away by ethnographers."
From her first sentence, a dictionary definition, Kirshenblatt-Gimblett
deduces a constructivist howler: the trivial fact that ethnographers define the

ethnographic status of artifacts does not entail that *they create the artifacts.* Nor do they create the artifacts' meanings; it is the people being studied who determine that, and this awkward reality gets obviously in the way of attempts by New Mythologists to relativize cultural knowledge and meaning. Constructivism is a strong force among New Mythologists most influenced by literary theory, and is less persistent among those who come from a background of academic anthropology. Despite their tendency to toy with the jargon of literary theory, anthropologists generally acquire a robust respect for the independent existence and integrity of the peoples they study.

> (10) Finally, premodernist Old Mythology, especially in its Victorian colonialist guises, preached the superiority of Western culture. It proposed to bring moral enlightenment to people it viewed as savages, mainly through Christianity, but also with science and modern medicine. In this, it stands starkly apart from modernist Old Mythology, and even from some eighteenth-century explorers of the South Pacific, who claimed that the moral sense and intellectual capacities of "primitive man" were at least equal to those of Europeans.

The air of smug moral superiority has returned with a vengeance with the arrival of the New Mythology, whose champions patronize, censure, and jeer at any Old Mythology text they find wanting. The New Mythology of tribal arts displays a sense of righteous certitude that would fit the most zealous Victorian missionary.

At Play in the Fields of the Text

In some respects, the New Mythology's frequent borrowing from poststructuralism and the general intellectual climate of postmodernism is healthy and appropriate. For example, the approach to tribal arts must necessarily involve "blurred genres" and fused disciplines, bringing together ethnography, art history, philosophical aesthetics, and general cultural, including literary, criticism. This is fully in the poststructural/postmodern spirit, as is calling into question the peculiarly European distinction between the so-called fine arts and the popular and folk arts and crafts, which normally has no clear application in understanding tribal arts. But there are other aspects of poststructuralism which sit uneasily with the study of tribal arts.

One such notion is the pervasive poststructuralist attack on the authority of the artist or author in aesthetic interpretation. Barthes, whose thinking was again seminal in this regard, proclaimed the death of the god-author, along with the end of the ideologies of objectivity and truth, insisting that the meaning of a literary text is a critical construction instead of a discovered fact. In the theory of literature and the practice of criticism, such constructivist ideas have had their uses, liberating criticism from traditional demands to invoke authorial intention as a validating principle for critical interpretation.

However, the poststructural abandonment of the notion that texts contain meanings placed there by their authors (which it is criticism's job to determine) is only possible in a cultural landscape in which there is enough

prior agreement on meanings to allow criticism to become thus freely creative. The poststructural death of the author could only take hold in literary
theory because there was already in place an extensive tradition of interpretation of, say, *Madame Bovary* or *Moby Dick*. These novels enjoy a canonical status as works of literary art: they observe the conventions of established genres
and were written in European languages by recognized literary artists. The
cultural conditions that form the context of their creation and reception are
solid enough to enable a generation of critics—notably Barthes, Foucault, and
Derrida, but also the New Critics of the Anglo-American world—to declare the
hypothetical death of the author and advocate a liberated, creative criticism of
jouissance.

But do these doctrines and strategies of contemporary theory provide
useful models for the critical ethnography of indigenous arts? Hardly. Poststructuralism's image of the free-spirited critic at play in textual fields goes
counter to one of the most strongly held (indeed, in my opinion, indispens-
able) principles of the New Mythology: respect for the autonomous existence
of tribal artists, including respect for their intentions and cultural values.
Declaring the death of the (European) author may be jolly sport for jaded literary theorists, but an analogous ideological death of the tribal artist is not
nearly so welcome in the New Mythology, nor should it be in any anthropology department. The study of tribal arts—indeed, all non-Western arts—cannot
presuppose a sufficiently stable, shared background understanding against
which one might declare artists' intentions irrelevant or passé. Moreover, the
New Mythology gains its sense of identity by pitting itself against what it
takes to be the Old Mythology's ethnocentric disregard not only for the intentions of tribal artists but for their very names as well. (Price calls this "the
anonymization of Primitive Art," and it was a major complaint lodged against
the "'Primitivism' in 20th Century Art" exhibition. If such ethnocentrism is
not to be actively encouraged, the tribal artist's interpretations *must* enjoy
special status, defining in the first instance the object of study. In order to
respect the cultures and people from which tribal works of art are drawn, the
New Mythology must treat indigenous intentions— ascertained or, where
unavailable, at least postulated—as constituting the beginning of all interpretation, if not its exhaustive or validating end.

This deep conflict between doctrines of the New Mythology and the
poststructuralism it seems so eager to appropriate keeps breaking out despite
efforts to paper it over. McEvilley and Clifford enthusiastically adopt the discourse of constructivism, so long as they are talking about how "we," or "the
West," or the "omniscient" curatorial mind, construct the generalized primitive, but New Mythologists are not nearly so keen to revert to constructivist
parlance when it comes to discussing the actual meanings of works of tribal
art. Thus Kasfir asks, "Who creates meaning for African art?," where "for"
indicates "on behalf of," implying that Western collectors and exhibitors make
a meaning for African art to satisfy the Western eye and mind.

This, however, avoids the more obvious wording of the question "Who
creates the meaning *of* African art?" If there is any answer at all to this ques-

tion, it must begin with the artists and cultures that produce the art. The West can "construct" in the poststructuralist manner to its heart's content, but its understandings will always be about the indigenous constructions of the cultures from which African works derive. It is indigenous intentions, values, descriptions, and constructions which must be awarded theoretical primacy. If an African carving is intended by its maker to embody a spirit, and that is an ascertainable fact about it, then any ethnography that constructs its meaning in contradiction to that fact is false. Of course, ethnography need not culminate with indigenous meanings and intentions, any more than literary criticism comes to an end when an author's intended meaning for a work of fiction has been determined. But ethnography has no choice except to begin with indigenous meanings, which it does not construct, but discovers.

POSTSCRIPT

Do Museums Misrepresent Ethnic Communities Around the World?

Clifford, like many critical theorists, is deeply suspicious of all representations of others. Dutton, in contrast, seems to question both the motives and the logic of this suspicion. He is especially critical of Clifford's lack of historical accuracy when describing the goals and motivations of museums and their curators. Are Clifford's postmodernist conclusions guilty of misrepresenting the museum world in ways that parallel his critique of particular exhibits? Does Dutton's critique of the postmodernists solve the historical problems that are present in both museums and the writings of their critics? Is there a middle ground that would allow for exhibitions with more sensitive context?

Clifford has also dealt with museum exhibits in his book *Routes: Travel and Translation in the Late Twentieth Century* (Harvard University Press, 1997). Related approaches to the problem of representation in museums include Sally Price's *Primitive Art in Civilized Places* (University of Chicago Press, 1989) and Shelly Errington's *The Death of Authentic Primitive Art and Other Tales of Progress* (University of California Press, 1998).

Nicholas Thomas's *Entangled Objects: Exchange, Material Culture and Colonialism in the Pacific* (Harvard University Press, 1991) considers the problem of representation among ethnographic objects in the Pacific. Enid Schildkraut and Curtis A. Keim's *The Scramble for Art in Central Africa* (Cambridge University Press, 1998), Ruth B. Phillips and Christopher B. Steiner's *Unpacking Culture: Art and Commodity in Colonial and Post Colonial Worlds* (University of California Press, 1999), and Michael O'Hanlon and Robert L. Welsch's *Hunting the Gatherers: Ethnographic Collectors, Agents, and Agency in Melanesia* (Berghahn, 2000) provide examples of the rich historical context of museum collections of the sort Dutton seeks.

Both Clifford and Dutton build their arguments on the premise that objects have complex histories, an idea that was originally developed in slightly different ways by anthropological historian George W. Stocking, Jr.'s *Objects and Others: Essays on Museums and Material Culture* (University of Wisconsin Press, 1985) and by anthropologist Arjun Appadurai's *The Social Life of Things: Commodities in Cultural Perspective* (Cambridge University Press, 1986). Both books make two crucial points: objects have histories, and the meanings of objects change when the objects themselves move from one context to another. Also, both argue that objects can take on many different meanings depending on context and viewpoint. Together these books have redefined museological studies and transformed what had been an anthropological backwater into a thriving specialization within the discipline.

Darkness in El Dorado (The Anthropological Niche of Douglas W. Hume)

This Web site brings together nearly all of the documents about the Patrick Tierney/ Napoleon controversy.

http://members.aol.com/archaeodog/darkness_in_el_dorado/ index.htm

Hands Around the World: Yanomamo Indians

The Hands Around the World: Yanomamo Indians Web Site provides useful links to dozens of Web sites dealing with the Yanomamo (currently called the Yanomami) Indians of Venezuela and Brazil.

http://indian-cultures.com/Cultures/yanomamo.html

The Yanomamö

Created by Brian Schwimmer, this Yanomamö (also spelled Yanomami) Web site explores intergroup relations, alliances, and the role of warfare among the Yanomamö. This site also provides links to additional sites on the subject.

http://www.umanitoba.ca/faculties/arts/anthropology/ tutor/case_studies/yanomamo/

Endangered Languages, Endangered Knowledge, Endangered Environments

This Web site offers links to papers from a conference on endangered languages and their relationship to endangered knowledge systems and natural species. The conference was sponsored by the National Museum of Natural History at the Smithsonian Institute and held at Berkeley, California.

http://ucjeps.berkeley.edu/Endangered_Lang_Conf/ Endangered_Lang.html

Endangered Languages

This Web site sponsored by the Summer Institute of Linguistics offers links and pages about various endangered languages in the Third World.

http://www.sil.org/sociolx/ndg-lg-home.html

American Anthropological Association Statements on Ethics

Created by the American Anthropological Association, the largest organization of anthropologists in the world, this Statements on Ethics Web site provides a code of ethics for its members and a handbook on ethical issues faced by anthropologists.

http://www.aaanet.org/stmts/ethstmnt.htm

PART 3

Ethics in Cultural Anthropology

*T*he ethical treatment of other peoples has come to play an increasingly important role in contemporary anthropology. Ethical issues directly affect how cultural anthropologists should treat their human subjects. Nowhere has this concern become more visible in cultural anthropology than in the case of the Yanomami Indians of Venezuela where journalist Patrick Tierney has accused anthropologist Napoleon Chagnon and other researchers of harming the people they studied. This issue created considerable discussion and debate within the discipline, launching task forces to investigate the allegations that have still not concluded their work. In a rather different way, anthropologists and linguists have recently raised questions about the responsibility of researchers to be more proactive in addressing indigenous concerns. Here we consider the plight of endangered languages. Some have argued that scholars should work to change governmental policies that encourage people to abandon their indigenous languages, while others suggest that it is paternalistic for scholars to decide what language indigenous people should speak. Similarly, we may ask what the ethical responsibilities of Western anthropologists should be when they find certain cultural practices abhorrent or unjust. Should anthropologists work to change these practices? All of these issues raise questions about how involved anthropologists should become with the people with whom they work. Should anthropologists take a passive, objective, and even scientific position, or should they use what they know to support or change these native communities?

- Did Napoleon Chagnon and Other Researchers Adversely Affect the Yanomami Indians of Venezuela?

- Should Anthropologists and Linguists Be Concerned About Losing Endangered Languages?

- Should Anthropologists Work to Eliminate the Practice of Female Circumcision?

ISSUE 16

Did Napoleon Chagnon and Other Researchers Adversely Affect the Yanomami Indians of Venezuela?

YES: Terence Turner, from *The Yanomami and the Ethics of Anthropological Practice* (Cornell University Latin American Studies Program, 2001)

NO: Edward H. Hagen, Michael E. Price, and John Tooby, from *Preliminary Report,* http://www.anth.ucsb.edu/ucsbpreliminaryreport.pdf (Department of Anthropology, University of California Santa Barbara, 2001)

ISSUE SUMMARY

YES: Anthropologist Terence Turner contends that journalist Patrick Tierney's book *Darkness in El Dorado* accurately depicts how anthropologist Napoleon Chagnon's research among the Yanomami Indians caused conflict between groups and how Chagnon's portrayal of the Yanomami as extremely violent aided gold miners trying to take over Yanomami land.

NO: Anthropologists Edward Hagen, Michael Price, and John Tooby counter that Tierney systematically distorts Chagnon's views on Yanomami violence and exaggerates the amount of disruption caused by Chagnon's activities compared to those of others such as missionaries and gold miners.

In September 2000 a startling message flew around the e-mail lists of the world's anthropologists. It was a letter from Cornell University anthropologist Terry Turner and University of Hawaii anthropologist Leslie Sponsel to the president and president-elect of the American Anthropological Association (AAA), with copies to a few other officers, warning them of the imminent publication of a book that they said would "affect the American Anthropological profession as a whole in the eyes of the public, and arouse intense indignation and calls for action among members of the Association." The book in question, which they had read in galley proofs, was

Patrick Tierney's *Darkness in El Dorado: How Scientists and Journalists Devastated the Amazon* (W.W. Norton and Company, 2000). The letter summarized some of Tierney's charges that medical researcher James Neel, anthropologist Napoleon Chagnon, and others seriously harmed the Yanomami Indians of Venezuela, even causing a measles epidemic that killed hundreds.

The leaking of the letter and the subsequent publication of an article by Tierney in *The New Yorker* caused great excitement at the annual meeting of the AAA in San Francisco in mid-November 2000. Discussion climaxed at a panel discussion that filled a double ballroom at the Hilton Hotel with several thousand anthropologists and media representatives from around the world. The panel included Tierney, anthropologist William Irons (representing Chagnon, who declined to attend), and experts on the history of science, epidemiology, and South American Indians. (Neel could not defend himself, as he had died earlier that year.) Numerous members of the audience also spoke. During and after the meeting a consensus developed that Tierney was wrong in his claim that the measles epidemic in 1968 was caused by Neel's and Chagnon's inoculations, since measles vaccines are incapable of causing the actual disease. However, Tierney's accusations that Chagnon had treated the Yanomami in an unethical manner during his research and had distorted his findings were not so easily dismissed. Later, the Executive Board of the AAA established a task force to examine the allegations in Tierney's book. The 300-page Task Force Final Report was completed on May 18, 2002 and is now posted on the AAA Web site.

Why would a book about researchers' treatment of a small Amazonian tribe have caused such an uproar? The reason is that, due to the enormous sales of Chagnon's book *The Yanomamö* (now in its fifth edition) and the prizewinning films he made with Timothy Asch, the Yanomami (as most scholars spell their name) are probably the world's best-known tribal people and Chagnon one of the most famous ethnographers since Margaret Mead. Chagnon's use of his Yanomami data to support his sociobiological explanation of human behavior has also had influence outside anthropology (for example, in evolutionary psychology). The idea that the most aggressive men win the most wives and have the most children, thus passing their aggressive genes on to future generations more abundantly than the peaceful genes of their nonaggressive brethren, is a cornerstone of the popular view that humans are innately violent (see Issue 2). Thus, Tierney's attack on Chagnon's credibility sent shock waves through the scholarly community.

In this selection, Turner argues that Tierney is correct in claiming that Chagnon failed to object when gold miners used his portrayal of the Yanomami as violent to hinder the establishment of a Yanomami reserve in Brazil, that Chagnon manipulated his demographic data to support his hypothesis that more violent Yanomami men have more wives and children than less violent ones, and that his fieldwork practices caused conflict between Yanomami groups. Hagen, Price, and Tooby counter that Tierney deliberately misrepresents evidence in claiming that Chagnon violated Yanomami taboos in his fieldwork and that he manipulated his data to support his claim that killers have more offspring than nonkillers.

Terence Turner

 **YES**

The Yanomami and the Ethics of Anthropological Practice

Controversy over the mistreatment of the Yanomami, an indigenous people of Venezuela and northern Brazil, by scientific researchers and anthropologists had smoldered for over a decade before it burst into flame [in 2001] with the publication of Patrick Tierney's *Darkness in El Dorado*. The controversy over the issues raised in the book, and more broadly over what has been done to the Yanomami by anthropologists and other researchers, confronts the discipline of anthropology, as represented by it professional society, the American Anthropological Association, and several universities and learned societies with which some of the principals in the case were connected, with ethically fraught issues. How these issues are dealt may well set significant precedents for the ethical and scientific standards of the institutions and professions involved, particularly in regard to the responsibilities of professional associations for the conduct of their members, and of researchers in the field for their human subjects....

My work as head of the AAA Special Commission to Investigate the Situation of the Brazilian Yanomami in 1990–91 was the original reason for my involvement in Yanomami affairs. Together with subsequent work with NGOs and anthropologists engaged in the struggle to support and defend the Yanomami, it remains the basis of my appraisal of much of Tierney's account of Chagnon's activities among the Yanomami, including his attacks on Yanomami-support NGOs and Yanomami leaders. I was appointed to head the Special AAA Commission on the Brazilian Yanomami by the then President of the AAA, Annette Weiner, on the basis of my work as an activist with Brazilian indigenous groups and indigenous support NGOs and my personal acquaintance, based on long-standing cooperation, with many actors and groups involved in the Yanomami struggle. My mission was to report back to the President and Executive Board of the Association on what if any action the Association should take on behalf of the Yanomami of Brazil. The context of this unusual appointment was the desperate, and at the time apparently losing battle to save the huge Yanomami Reserve. After a ten year struggle led by the Brazilian NGO, the CCPY (Committee to Create a Yanomami Park), the area had been studied, surveyed and tentatively demarcated by an official Brazilian governmental team, only to be invaded by 40,000 illegal gold miners in 1988....

My investigation of the situation created by the multiple Yanomami crises of 1988 to 1991 for the AAA involved me in new or renewed contacts with Brazilian NGO workers, indigenous rights activists, medical doctors and health workers from governmental and private agencies, personnel of FUNAI, missionaries, progressive journalists, lawyers, politicians, and anthropologists (including officers of the Brazilian Anthropological Association, ABA). These encounters and consultations, together with further contacts and collaborations on subsequent visits to Brazil, comprise the basis of my published responses to Chagnon's unfounded calumnies against NGOs, Missions and the Yanomami leader Davi Kopenawa at the time of the gold miners' invasions and the campaign to dissolve the Yanomami Reserve from 1988 to 1991, his untruthful statements on the responsibility of the Salesians and the Yanomami themselves for the massacre at Haximu in December 1993, and his renewed diatribes against Davi Kopenawa at the 1994 AAA Meetings and on more recent occasions. They are also the basis of my evaluation of Tierney's account of the same events in his book, which I find substantially correct....

The great majority of contemporary researchers who have worked with the Yanomami, or who have studied the effects of Chagnon's representations of the Yanomami in both Brazil and Venezuela, have critically challenged many of Chagnon's ethnographic and theoretical claims, his methods and actions in the field, and a number of his statements in popular media....

The interdependence of ethical and empirical issues is unavoidable in dealing with Chagnon's work, in which factual claims of Yanomami aggressiveness and the link between killing and reproductive success are adduced, explicitly or implicitly, as "scientific" evidence for the sorts of statements he has made in the media that have been decried on ethical grounds. The issue becomes even more complex when one confronts the criticisms of Chagnon's data and analysis summarized and extended by Tierney. These criticisms, notably in Tierney's Chapter 10 that deals with Chagnon's 1988 article in *Science,* seriously imply the manipulation and withholding of data to support unsound but theoretically and ideologically desired conclusions....

I will organize my discussion under five general headings [excerpt: from two are included here], designating general types of ethically problematic behavior, comprising representative instances from Tierney's text that seem to me to be sufficiently well documented and analyzed, and/or attested from other sources, to be considered "well founded"....

I. Statements and Silences by Chagnon Damaging to the Yanomami

I.A. Statements About "Fierceness" or Violent Aggressiveness as a Dominant Feature of Yanomami Society, and Silences (Failure to Speak Out Against Misuses of These Statements Damaging to the Yanomami)

Chagnon stood by virtually without demur during the drive to dismantle the Brazilian Yanomami reserve in 1988–92, while politicians, military leaders and journalists allied with mining interests employed his portrayal of the

Yanomami as ferocious savages involved in chronic warfare over women, to justify the dismemberment of Yanomami territory. Their argument ran that Yanomami communities needed for their own safety to be isolated from one another by "corridors" of open land, which would incidentally be accessible to gold miners. Chagnon's refusal to disown this use of his work in Brazilian media, where it might have had some effect, became understood by both sides in the struggle over the Yanomami reserve from 1988 to 1992 as a statement by omission in support of the miners and their political allies. This had a serious enough impact that the Brazilian Anthropological Association formally appealed to the American Anthropological Association in 1989 demanding that the U.S. Association investigate the ethics of its member's tacit support of those who were exploiting his statements. The American Association failed to take action, and this failure has come back to haunt it....

The issue, as the Brazilian Association's new statement forcefully put it, is not simply that third parties exploited Chagnon's statements and silences for their own purposes. Anthropological researchers, its statement acknowledges, have an obligation to speak the truth about their research findings, and cannot control the uses to which others may put their findings. They do, however, have an ethical responsibility to speak out against the misuse of their findings by third parties, especially when such misuse directly damages the people referred to and most especially when these people were the subjects of the anthropologist's research....

I.B. Repeated and Untruthful Attacks on NGOs, Anthropological Activists and Yanomami Leaders

I.B.1. Attacks on NGOs, Anthropological Activists

... Tierney ... accurately reports Chagnon's shocking charge "that the very people who posed as defenders of the Indians were actually destroying them". This was Chagnon's allegation, which he repeated in the *Times Literary Supplement* and the *New York Times,* that the medical clinics and outreach programs instituted by missionaries and NGOs were not actually helping but rather "killing" the Indians ("killing by kindness", in his words. Although primarily directed against the Salesians in Venezuela, this allegation was phrased so as implicitly to include missions and secular NGOs in Brazil. He further asserted that the Salesian missionaries, as well as unnamed Protestant missionaries at Mucajaí, were promoting warfare among Yanomami villages by giving or selling shotguns to the Indians on their mission stations. Yanomami leaders like Davi Kopenawa, he claimed, were not authentic leaders but "pawns" or "parrots", mindlessly repeating what their NGO and missionary manipulators told them to say....

I.B.3. Chagnon's Attacks on Yanomami Leaders: (1) Davi Kopenawa

Chagnon has publicly charged on several occasions, beginning in the late 1980's and early 1990's, that the Brazilian Yanomami leader Davi Kopenawa was a mere "parrot" of NGOs, mouthing lines he was fed by the do-gooder organizations that supposedly kept him as a useful symbol for self-serving fund-raising campaigns (again, he never cited specific statements or texts). Davi Kopenawa was a major asset in these struggles, as virtually the only Yanomami leader capable of speaking out for Yanomami interests in the Brazilian and international political arenas, who at the same time commanded genuine support among the Yanomami of his own and other communities. Kopenawa was and remains the most important spokesman for the Brazilian Yanomami: he is a dynamic, effective, and independent person and leader. Chagnon's gratuitous and untruthful attacks damaged (or were clearly intended to damage) him. Chagnon is still at it: A CNN TV crew that interviewed Chagnon in November 2000 was startled to hear him call Kopenawa "a cigar store Indian")....

I.C. Ethnographic Misrepresentation as an Ethical Issue

Tierney analyzes a number of Chagnon's texts and statements that appear to involve possible manipulations of statistical data to support theoretical conclusions that would otherwise not follow, and the use of the same kinds of manipulations to implicate political enemies in causing the deaths of (or, in Chagnon's blunter term, "killing") Yanomami. Cases of the first kind may be considered to constitute a grey area between incorrect statistical analysis and deliberate manipulation. There seems little doubt, however, about the ethics of the much graver charges in the second category....

Chagnon's article, "Life Histories, Blood revenge, and warfare in a tribal population", published in *Science* in 1988, has been taken by his critics and sociobiological supporters alike as the quintessential formulation of his theoretical claim that violent competition (fierceness) among males is driven by competition for sexual access to females, and that success in this competition, as measured by killing other men, therefore leads to increased reproductive success. Sociobiologists seized upon the Yanomami, as represented by Chagnon, as living examples of the evolutionary past of the race: the most direct links between the human present and the supposed primate heritage of Alpha male-centered harems and dominance hierarchies. . . . Tierney correctly points out that this notoriety, and the central misconception on which it was based, was overtly cultivated by Chagnon in public statements such as his presidential address to the Human Behavior and Evolutionary Society:

> I demonstrated that Yanomamo men in my 25 year study who had partici-
> pated in the killing of other men had approximately three times as many
> children and more than two times as many wives as men their own ages
> who had not.

As Tierney also correctly says, this statement is thoroughly false....

Tierney, relying partly on Lizot, somewhat more on Albert and most heavily on Ferguson, and contributing some findings of his own, provides a reasonably accurate summary of the criticisms of Chagnon's analysis. He reviews three fundamental criticisms of Chagnon's statistical manipulation of his data. Firstly, Chagnon's statistical comparison of the number of wives and children of "killers" (defined as "unokai", on the basis of their having undergone the ritual of purification for those who have participated in the killing of a person, *unokaimou*) to those of non-killers has been criticized as skewed by his inclusion of a large number of young men between 20–25 and 25–30 as members of the statistically relevant population. Very few Yanomami men of this age had killed anyone and almost none had wives or children. The result was to inflate the relative advantage of the killers, almost all of whom were older men, some over 30 and most over 40. When killers were compared with men of their own age-bracket, "the reproductive success of killers was not nearly as impressive—ranging between 40 to 67 percent, a fraction of the 208 percent advantage that Chagnon had broadcast to the press". In other words, age was a factor that accounted for much of the variation, and Chagnon had not taken it properly into account.

Another variable Chagnon left out of account, according to critics like Ferguson and Albert, was headman status (and the additional, partly overlapping status of shaman). In his 1988 paper, he simply classed all headmen as killers, "*unokai*", but as Tierney says, that is a confusion of categories. Most Yanomami headmen have several wives, because of their status as headmen rather than their status as "killers" ("*unokai*", in Chagnon's translation). Headman status, like age, is thus another variable that must be recognized as accounting for a significant part of the contrast in number of wives and children between men in the killers category and non-killers. Yet another important variable, explicitly excluded by Chagnon in his text, was the death of fathers. For reasons he did not explain, Chagnon excluded the children of dead fathers from his initial analysis. This turns out to have been a strategic point for his whole argument about reproductive success. According to Chagnon and other Yanomami ethnographers, successful killers become themselves the main targets of vengeance raids, and are highly likely to be killed in the midst of their reproductive years. As Brian Ferguson had been the first to point out, if this likelihood of killers to have their reproductive careers cut short were taken into account, the supposed reproductive advantage of killers might actually disappear to become negative. . . .

Tierney also raises a series of questions about manipulations of statistically strategic bits of data. Two young men in their twenties were listed in Chagnon's 1997 *Yanomamo Interactive* CD on The Ax Fight as having four and five children respectively. This was far more than the other men in their age category, and these two men had been identified as violent participants in the ax fight shown in the CD. Tierney checked Chagnon's original census and found that Mohesiwa was listed as born in 1938 and Ruwamowa in 1939, thus making them 33 and 32, respectively, rather than 24 and 27, as Chagnon now claimed, at the time of filming. Tierney "found no other mistakes in the census transfer. And if these were mistakes, they were statistically perfect ones"— as they seemed to show the greater reproductive success of violent men in contrast to their supposed age-mates in the under-30 categories.

There was also the case of the five young men Chagnon listed as killers in the under 25 age group, all of whom had wives. When challenged by Albert, however, Chagnon removed them to the 30-plus category, remarking that since the Yanomami do not count past three, the estimation of age is necessarily approximate. Their removal substantially altered the statistical predominance of killers as husbands and fathers in their age category. In sum, as Tierney remarks, "Minute manipulations in each age category could easily skew all the results"—and apparently had done so in the cases in question....

Tierney also pointed out that although Chagnon had given the impression in his *Science* article that the three raids he described involved communities that were still living in a relatively traditional way, unaffected by the presence of missionaries and government agents that had led to the decline or suppression of warfare in other areas of Yanomami country, this was not the case. Chagnon had identified the villages in his article only by number, which Lizot had complained made them impossible to match up with any known (named) Yanomami communities. Tierney succeeded in identifying 9 of the 12 villages involved, showing that they were the same ones where he had done most of his fieldwork....

Once identified and connected by Tierney to their known historical contexts, the three raids described in abstract terms in the *Science* article assumed different meanings. Pinning down the actual identities and locations of the villages showed that they were actually situated in an area of heavy contact with Venezuelan society and missionary influence. No longer abstract instances of violent competition for reproductive success, in an indigenous world whose essential patterns of warfare had not yet been affected by alien presences such as missionaries or anthropologists, they now appeared as significantly affected by Chagnon's own presence and activities. Chagnon himself, it transpired, had "filmed, transported, and coordinated" two of the three raiding parties over part of the distance to their targets....

I.C. False Accusations Against Missions and NGO's of "killing" Yanomami or Otherwise Being Responsible for Raising Their Death Rate

In an OpEd column in the New York Times of October 1993, Chagnon claimed that Yanomami were dying at missionary posts with medical facilities at four times the rate obtaining in "remote" villages. This was supposedly based on statistics Chagnon had collected and was the key data he cited in support of his shocking allegation that the Salesian missionaries were "killing the Yanomami with kindness". Tierney notes that this has become "one of the most frequently quoted statements in the Yanomami controversy," but shows that it is actually a misleading effect obtained by switching statistical data between categories of the study. He explains,

> Chagnon divided the villages in three categories of mission contact: "remote", "intermediate", and "maximum". The villages with maximum [mission] contact had a thirty percent *lower* mortality rate than remote groups, while the "intermediate" villages suffered four times as many deaths as the missions. Chagnon's data thus confirmed what all other researchers

have found, but in the NYT Chagnon converted the "intermediate" villages into "missions", which they are not... There is no doubt that the debate about mission mortality has been based on misinformation.

Tierney accurately chronicles Chagnon's attempt to spin the tragic episode of the massacre of twelve Yanomami from the village of Haximu by Brazilian gold miners in July 1993 into a series of spurious charges against the Yanomami from the village of Paapiu for being partly responsible for the massacre and the Salesian missionaries for trying to cover it up. The "cover up", in Chagnon's version, chiefly consisted in a campaign by the missionaries to block his "investigation" of the massacre, in order to prevent him from discovering and disclosing their role in "killing the Yanomami by kindness" at their mission stations (see preceding section). This was tantamount to accusing the Salesians of being accessories after the fact to mass murder.

Chagnon claimed he had the right to investigate the murders as a member of a Venezuelan Presidential Commission on Yanomami affairs. With his ally Brewer-Carias, Chagnon had in fact been appointed to a commission to supervise the projected Yanomami Biosphere Reserve by the transitional President who succeeded Carlos Andres-Perez after the latter's impeachment. This commission, however, lacked any specific investigative powers relevant to the massacre. An unprecedented national outcry, with massive street demonstrations and protests against Brewer's and Chagnon's appointments, specifically including their declared intention to conduct an investigation of the massacre, followed the announcement of these appointments. This historically unprecedented wave of opposition led the President to appoint a different commission specifically to investigate the massacre. The intent was clearly to remove Chagnon and Brewer from any connection with the Haximu investigation, and it was so understood by the Venezuelan media and public, although the President did not get around to formally dissolving the Brewer-Chagnon commission until later.... Chagnon, accompanied by Brewer, nevertheless attempted to go to Haximu to "investigate", regardless of the fact that the new Presidential investigating commission was already en route to the spot, and they lacked the necessary authorization to go to the area, let alone to conduct an investigation. When they landed at the village airstrip, two miles from the massacre site, they were summarily ordered to leave by the judge who headed the legitimate investigative commission. She gave Brewer and Chagnon a choice: get out of Haximu immediately or face arrest. The air force pilot who had flown them to the spot sided with the judge. He flew Chagnon straight to Caracas, confiscated his notes and told him to get out of Venezuela within twenty-four hours. Chagnon did so....

Another of Chagnon's attempts to implicate missionaries in fomenting Yanomami killings by distributing shotguns was his attack, in the fourth edition of his book, on the Protestant Missionaries of the Evangelical Mission of Amazonia, supposedly stationed at Mucajaí. Tierney shows that this account is a fictional pastiche, combining aspects of the geography, personnel and history of the distant, and long-abandoned, mission station of Surucucu with those of Mucajaí, and adding elements of fantasy and distorted and displaced versions of actual actions. Indians lugging a washing machine over the mountain by the mission station at Surucucu becomes a single Missionary carrying a refrigerator on his back over a non-existent mountain at Mucajaí. The refusal of missionaries at Surucucu to sell shotguns to the Indians, and their abandonment of the mission post there rather than be obliged to do so, becomes the provision of shotguns by the Mucajaí missionaries to the Yanomami, their guilt supposedly redoubled by their subsequent refusal to inquire if the guns they had provided had been those used in an attack on a "remote" village (Chagnon suggests that if they found out that the guns they had provided had been the ones used, they would have to confiscate them, which would have made the Yanomami forsake the mission. As Tierney reports, everyone with any knowledge of these events, including the missionaries in question and others familiar with the different posts and mission families Chagnon had conflated, denounces Chagnon's account as fictional....

II. Field Methods Disruptive of Yanomami Society

Drawing heavily on the writings of Brian Ferguson and his own data, Tierney documents charges that Chagnon's methods of obtaining the names of dead relatives, by exploiting enmities between factions and hostile communities, and above all by giving massive amounts of steel goods as presents, destabilized Yanomami communities and inter-communal relations, giving rise to conflicts, raids and wars. He also documents that Chagnon took a limited part in raids by transporting raiding parties in his motor launch. The issues here centrally involve the scale of operations and the time-pressure under which Chagnon was obliged to collect his pedigree data. Whether working for James Neel or on his own, his commitment to surveying the maximum possible numbers of villages in relatively minimal periods of time precluded normal anthropological methods of building rapport and finding culturally appropriate ways of obtaining culturally taboo information that have been used successfully by other anthropologists who have worked among the Yanomami. This forced him to resort to bullying and intimidation, including shooting off firearms and performing shamanic rituals of magical child-killing. It also led him to resort to bribery on a massive scale, using huge amounts of steel tools, pots, etc. These hoards of otherwise rare and highly valued items became foci of conflict between rival factions and villages, which on a number of documented occasions led to raids and wars in which people were killed.

As his work continued over the years, Chagnon, rather than modifying his modus operandi to diminish its destabilizing effects, continued to raise the ante, becoming a player in the regional system of conflicts and the struggle for dominance that were set off in part by quarrels over the wealth he brought with him. There began to be wars between "Chagnon's" village, containing Yanomami dependent on him for steel goods, and villages associated with other sources of goods, such as the anthropologist Lizot, and the independent Yanomami cooperative SUYAO. All of this, Tierney, Ferguson, Albert, and others have argued, represented a massive disruption of Yanomami social peace consequent upon Chagnon's field methods. If so, it may be considered to constitute a violation of clause III.A.2 of the AAA Code of Ethics: "Anthropological researchers must do everything in their power to ensure that their research does not harm the safety, dignity, or privacy of the people with whom they work ...".

The sheer scale of Chagnon's operations thus came to constitute a sui generis factor with ethical effects and implications not anticipated by the existing AAA Code of Ethics. Over a period of thirty years, according to anthropologist Brian Ferguson and others familiar with the political and historical aspects of his research, Chagnon has used methods to extract culturally sensitive data and biological specimens from Yanomami that have involved the violation of Yanomami cultural norms and caused dissension, and occasionally conflict, between communities and between factions of the same community. These conflicts, according to Ferguson, seconded by Tierney, have sometimes led to the breakup of communities and to inter-village raiding. Chagnon's tactics reportedly included giving large amounts of steel tools, the most esteemed presents, to certain villages or factions, thus inevitably destabilizing relations with non-recipients groups. The[se] also included, by his own account, deliberately lying to a village or faction that he had obtained the taboo names of their dead relatives from another village or faction, thus arousing anger and resentment that he could exploit to get the village or faction in question to give up the names of the deceased ancestors of the other group. After Chagnon got his data and departed, the villagers were left with bitter resentments that could aggravate existing tensions and provoke open conflicts. Chagnon seems also to have employed bullying and intimidation, brandishing weapons and shooting off firearms to make the Yanomami (who are usually the opposite of "fierce" in relations with non-Yanomami such as Venezuelans and Euro-North Americans) willing to give him information, if only to get rid of him.

The effectiveness of these tactics owed much to Chagnon's dramatic exploitation of the great discrepancy between his resources of wealth and power and those of the Yanomami as leverage to extract information, without regard to the ways this disrupted the social relations, stability and political peace of the communities of the people among whom he worked. The main authority for these allegations are the writings and public statements of Chagnon himself. One does not need to be a "left wing academic" or an "anti-science culturologist" to agree that these tactics raise questions of research ethics....

IV.B. What Is to Be Done?

I believe that we as anthropologists owe it to the Yanomami, and to ourselves, to speak the truth publicly about what has been done to the Yanomami. In this sense, the role of the Association and its Task Force may be compared to that of truth commissions in places like South Africa or Guatemala: not to punish individuals, but to make principled public statements about what has been done, by whom, and in what ways the actions and statements in question may have violated the collective ethical standards of the profession....

Anthropology as a discipline and as a profession can learn valuable lessons from analyzing what went wrong in Neel's and Chagnon's work, and why. I have suggested that a common thread connecting the ethical problems of both researchers is that concern with large-scale data collection under high time pressure, exacerbated in some cases by the institutional pressures of big scientific research projects, led both to make inadequate allowance for ethical and cultural standards, and in some cases, the social and physical well-being of the individual persons and communities comprising their subject populations. For anthropology, the lesson is that the pursuit of large amounts of quantitative data in abstraction from the cultural and social forms of life of the local people may become an end in itself that leads researchers to lose sight of or ignore the social standards and needs of the people they study. Such data, no matter how scientifically valuable, must never be pursued to the point of disruption of local social relations and cultural standards, or allowed to take priority over the well being of persons and communities....

**Edward H. Hagen,
Michael E. Price, and John Tooby**

Preliminary Report

Introduction

As we will begin to show in this report, *Darkness in El Dorado* is essentially a work of fiction. Its author, Patrick Tierney, has very selectively quoted hundreds of sources in order to, first, caricature anthropologist Napoleon Chagnon's work on the Yanomamö, and second, to discredit what he claims is "Chagnon's ethnographic image of the ferocious Yanomami" by instead portraying them as meek, peaceful, helpless, and, ultimately, victims of Chagnon himself. Tierney's creative use of primary sources in this venture begins almost immediately. After a brief introductory chapter, Tierney wastes little time attempting to undermine Chagnon's portrayal of Yanomamö males as relatively healthy and frequently engaged in war:

> Before going into the jungle, I had read and admired The Fierce People. So it was surprising to see that the Yanomami—so terrifying and "burly" in Chagnon's text—were, in fact, among the tiniest, scrawniest people in the world. Adults averaged four feet seven inches in height, and children had among the lowest weight-height ratios on the planet.

References are supposed to support, not refute, the claims one is making. Tierney's reference above cites a relatively short paper by Rebecca Holmes on Yanomamö health. Although the paper does confirm the widely known fact that Yanomamö are short, it does not support one of Tierney's major themes: that Chagnon has exaggerated the frequency of Yanomamö warfare. What Tierney fails to mention here or anywhere else in his book is what Holmes says in her paper about Yanomamö war:

> Raids resulting in serious wounds and death occur *several times a year* in spite of missionary pressure to restrict warfare. About 20 warriors from Parima A, a two-day walk through the jungle from Parima B, raided one of the settlements in Parima B during our fieldwork. There were no injuries, although a study of the nurse's recent medical records indicates that these raids not uncommonly result in wounds from poison arrows. (Holmes 1985, p. 249; emphasis added).

Tierney cites Holmes' paper four times but he fails to mention her evidence on war and violence on any of these occasions, evidence which is directly relevant to one of the major themes of his book. This failure is obviously deliberate....

Preliminary Evaluation of Chapter 3

Naming the Dead

Tierney, in Chapter 3 (The Napoleonic Wars) and elsewhere in his book, fingers Chagnon's method of obtaining accurate genealogies as a source of conflict between individuals and villages, and, more generally, as an affront to Yanomamö dignity (Chagnon's recent statement on this issue can be found in Appendix XIV). What we will show below is that Tierney's account is substantially undermined by the very sources he cites.

First, however, it may be useful to note that most societies, including the US, have a 'name taboo.' In the US, for example, it is not wrong to mention one person's first name or nickname to another person who does not know it, but it is often considered rude to *use* the nickname or first name of someone if you do not know them well. For example, even if Judith Smith's friends call her 'Judy', she might be offended if a stranger used that name instead of 'Judith' or Ms. Smith. How many news articles on *Darkness* have referred to 'Pat' or even 'Patrick' instead of 'Patrick Tierney' or 'Mr. Tierney'? None. In professional contexts, it is also rude to use someone's first name instead of their title and last name (e.g., Dr. Smith). In court rooms, we do not even use the judge's name, but instead address him or her as 'your honor' even though it is perfectly OK to know the judge's name, or ask someone what his or her name is. So, Americans have a rather elaborate name taboo.

The Yanomamö 'name taboo' is quite similar to the American 'name taboo.' Names are *not* 'scared [*sic*] secrets' (almost everyone knows them, in fact), but their *use* in particular social contexts is considered rude and insulting, just as, for Americans, *knowing* someone's first name or nickname is not insulting or wrong, but the *use* of nicknames and first names is rude and insulting in certain social contexts. (For the Yanomamö, the improper use of names is much more insulting than for Americans, however.) Here is Chagnon explaining the name taboo:

> The taboo is maintained even for the living, for one mark of prestige is the courtesy others show you by not using your name publicly. This is particularly true for men, who are much more competitive for status than women in this culture, and it is fascinating to watch boys grow into young men, demanding to be called either by a kinship term in public, or by a teknonymous reference such as 'brother of Himotoma' (see Glossary). The more effective they are at getting others to avoid using their names, the more public acknowledgment there is that they are of high esteem and social standing. Helena Valero, a Brazilian woman who was captured as a child by a Yanomamö raiding party, was married for many years to a Yanomamö headman before she discovered what his name was. The sanctions behind the taboo are more complex than just this, for they involve a combination of fear, respect, admiration, political deference, and honor.

The Yanomamö were understandably concerned that if the stranger in their midst (Chagnon) learned their names, he might *use* them disrespectfully. Chagnon *never* did this. Chagnon *always* addressed individuals in the proper manner, and he never intentionally used names disrespectfully (nor does Tierney present any evidence that Chagnon used names disrespectfully). Chagnon always used the Yanomamö equivalent of 'Judith' when that was appropriate, 'Ms. Smith' when that was appropriate, and 'Your Honor' when that was appropriate. Because he was struggling with a foreign culture, Chagnon occasionally but *unintentionally* offended individuals. Unlike academics, the Yanomamö are forgiving; they knew his missteps were accidental, and took no lasting offence.

Chagnon also found that it was easier to obtain a person's name from non-kin or enemies. In the US, Judith Smith's friends might be reluctant to reveal Judith's nickname to a stranger—not because *knowing* the nickname is taboo, but because its improper *use* might offend their friend—but people who were not close friends of Judith's would feel no such reluctance, nor would they violate any taboo by revealing the nickname. The same applies to the Yanomamö—asking non-kin and enemies about names is *not* taboo (remember, these names are widely known, and there is no taboo against outsiders knowing these names).

Contrary to Tierney's claims, Chagnon did *not* play enemies or villages off one another to obtain names. Notice that in Tierney's account of Chagnon's method, these claims have no supporting citations:

> Chagnon found himself in a difficult predicament, having to collect genealogical trees going back several generations. This was frustrating for him because the Yanomami do not speak personal names out loud. And the names of the dead are the most taboo subject in their culture.
> "To name the dead, among the Yanomami, is a grave insult, a motive of division, fights, and wars," wrote the Salesian Juan Finkers, who has lived among the Yanomami villages on the Mavaca River for twenty-five years.
> Chagnon found out that the Yanomami "were unable to understand why a complete stranger should want to possess such knowledge [of personal names] unless it were for harmful magical purposes." So Chagnon had to parcel out "gifts" in exchange for these names. [Anthropologists have 'to parcel out gifts' for most interviews with most informants on most topics. Giving gifts in exchange for extensive genealogical information is common practice in anthropology] One Yanomami man threatened to kill Chagnon when he mentioned a relative who had recently died. Others lied to him and set him back five months with phony genealogies [both these events are discussed in detail by Chagnon]. But he kept doggedly pursuing his goal.
> Finally, he invented a system, as ingenious as it was divisive [no citation], to get around the name taboo [Chagnon was not trying to 'get around the name taboo,' a claim that makes no sense ('getting around the name taboo' would entail *using* names disrespectfully—something he never did, nor had any desire to do). Chagnon was trying, not only get information necessary to his research, but also to integrate himself into Yanomamö society by learning what was common knowledge: everyone's name, including those of ancestors]. Within groups, he sought out "informants who might be considered 'aberrant' or 'abnormal,' outcasts in their

own society," people he could bribe and isolate more easily. These pariahs resented other members of society, so they more willingly betrayed sacred secrets [names are not 'sacred secrets'—they are public knowledge] at others' expense and for their own profit. [son-in-laws doing bride service—who are therefore not living with their kin—are a common example of what Tierney terms 'pariahs'] He resorted to "tactics such as 'bribing' children when their elders were not around, or capitalizing on animosities between individuals." [using children as informants is, again, common practice among anthropologists—usually because they have the patience for the all the tedious questions that anthropologists ask]

Chagnon was most successful at gathering data, however, when he started playing one village off against another. "I began traveling to other villages to check the genealogies, picking villages that were on strained terms with the people about whom I wanted information. I would then return to my base camp and check with local informants the accuracy of the new information. If the informants became angry when I mentioned the new names I acquired from the unfriendly group, I was almost certain that the information was accurate." [see below for the material that Tierney has omitted from this quote]

When one group became angry on hearing that Chagnon had gotten their names, he covered for his real informants but gave the name of another village nearby as the source of betrayal [no citation]. It showed the kind of dilemmas Chagnon's work posed. In spite of the ugly scenes he both witnessed and created, Chagnon concluded, "There is, in fact, no better way to get an accurate, reliable start on genealogy than to collect it from the enemies."

His divide-and-conquer information gathering exacerbated individual animosities [no citation], sparking mutual accusations of betrayal [no citation]. Nevertheless, Chagnon had become a prized political asset of the group with whom he was living, the Bisaasi-teri.

As usual, Tierney deliberately omits critical evidence that readers need to fairly evaluate his accusations and insinuations. With the exception of the quote from the Salesian missionary Juan Finkers, all of the cited information in the above quote comes from Chagnon's publications.

Tierney also conveniently fails to mention that Kaobawa, a Yanomamö headman, *demanded* that Chagnon learn the truth, even though he knew that would involve Chagnon learning the names of his dead kinsmen:

[Kaobawa's] knowledge of details was almost encyclopedic, his memory almost photographic. More than that, he was enthusiastic about making sure I learned the truth, and he encouraged me, indeed, *demanded* that I learn all details I might otherwise have ignored.... With the information provided by Kaobawa, and Rerebawa [another informant], I made enormous gains in understanding village interrelationships based on common ancestors and political histories and became lifelong friends with both. And both men knew that I had to learn about his recently deceased kin from the other one. It was one of those quiet understandings we all had but none of us could mention.

This information is in Chagnon's popular monograph, *Yanomamö* (which Tierney cites numerous times).

When Chagnon began his fieldwork with a Yanomamö village in the sixties, the Yanomamö did not know why Chagnon wanted to know their names, and were understandably quite reluctant to reveal this information to an outsider who might use it disrespectfully. Chagnon recounts the humorous and ingenious tactics the villagers used to deceive him about their real names during his initial stint in the field, and his own equally ingenious method of penetrating this deception by getting the information from other Yanomamö in enemy villages (see Appendix XIII for the monograph excerpt). Indeed, this is one of the major flaws in Tierney's account: he conveniently fails to mention that the methods that Chagnon discusses are those he used during the first six months or so of his fieldwork, before the Yanomamö had come to trust that Chagnon was not going to use the information disrespectfully. That Chagnon made strenuous attempts to avoid offending anyone while collecting names is clear from sentences that immediately follow those Tierney chooses to cite (material in bold not cited by Tierney):

> I began traveling to other villages to check the genealogies, picking villages that were on strained terms with the people about whom I wanted information. I would then return to my base camp and check with local informants the accuracy of the new information. If the informants became angry when I mentioned the new names I acquired from the unfriendly group, I was almost certain that the information was accurate. **For this kind of checking I had to use informants whose genealogies I knew rather well: they had to be distantly enough related to the dead person that they would not go into a rage when I mentioned the name, but not so remotely related that they would be uncertain of the accuracy of the information. Thus, I had to make a list of names that I dared not use in the presence of each and every informant. Despite the precautions, I occasionally hit a name that put the informant into a rage, such as that of a dead brother or sister that other informants had not reported. This always terminated the day's work with that informant, for he would be too touchy to continue any further, and I would be reluctant to take a chance on a accidentally discovering another dead kinsman so soon after the first.**
>
> **These were always unpleasant experiences, and occasionally dangerous ones, depending on the temperament of the informant.**

Chagnon stresses his efforts to avoid mentioning the names of the dead to close kin in all five editions of his monograph, yet Tierney *deliberately* fails to mention this....

However history may judge Chagnon's method of obtaining accurate genealogies (Native North Americans rely heavily on accurate genealogies in laying claim to valuable government benefits, etc.) it is important to properly represent what he did. Tierney instead deliberately omits key evidence that would allow the reader to evaluate his claims and improperly characterizes names as "sacred secrets" of the Yanomamö as a group; instead, their public *use* reflects the status and respect accorded to particular individuals. Using the same sources cited by Tierney, it is clear that Chagnon never used names disrespectfully, and soon came to be trusted on this matter by the Yanomamö....

Detailed Evaluation of Chapter 10:
To Murder and to Multiply

Brief Introduction

Chapter 10 of *Darkness in El Dorado* by Patrick Tierney is an extended attack on a well-known 1988 paper published by Chagnon in *Science* entitled "Life Histories, Blood Revenge, and Warfare in a Tribal Population." In this paper, Chagnon argues that warfare among the Yanomamö is characterized by blood revenge: an attack on one group by another prompts a retaliatory attack, which itself prompts retaliation, *ad infinitum.* In other words, Yanomamö war is quite similar to the patterns of conflict we see in the Balkans, the Middle East, Africa—anywhere ethnic groups come into armed conflict. In order to understand this pattern among the Yanomamö (and thus, perhaps, everywhere else), Chagnon presents data which suggest that successful Yanomamö warriors (unokai—men who have killed) are rewarded for their bravery and success. Among the Yanomamö, these rewards take the form of wives. Chagnon showed that unokai have more wives, and consequently more offspring, than non-unokai. Chagnon argued that if, over evolutionary time, cultural success lead [sic] to reproductive success, individuals would be selected to strive for cultural success. He further argued that cultural success is often achieved by engaging in successful military actions against enemies. Perhaps, then, the cycles of violence suffered by countless groups worldwide are driven, in part, by men who seek status and prestige by successfully attacking enemies.

This entire thesis has been assailed by Chagnon's critics, and Tierney hopes to bury it by demonstrating that Chagnon's research was shoddy, dishonest, and contradicted by other studies. In fact, whether or not Chagnon's theory is correct, *many* studies have demonstrated that, in small-scale societies, cultural success does lead to reproductive success, that cultural success is frequently associated with military success, and conflicts are often caused by conflicts over women. Tierney reviews almost none of these studies, and when he does, he omits key evidence that supports Chagnon's thesis.

Before we begin our analysis of Tierney's efforts in this chapter, we note that people often misconstrue Chagnon's work to mean that the Yanomamö are exceptionally violent, unlike other groups. Nothing could be further from the truth. In fact, we now know that most non-state societies have (or had) high rates of violence compared to state societies. Chagnon was one of the first to document in detail the profound impact of intergroup violence on a non-state society....

Chagnon has also famously claimed that Yanomamö wars often start with conflicts over women. Tierney implies or states several times that this is either unimportant, "secondary," or a fabrication of Chagnon's. For example:

> Yet the popular image of the Yanomami waging war for women persisted. Chagnon deftly *created it* by repeatedly claiming that men went on raids, captured women, and raped them at will afterward.

If Chagnon had created this image, then there should be no independent reports of Yanomamö raiding for women, and there should especially be no such reports predating Chagnon's. There are, however, many accounts of Yanomamö raiding for women that predate Chagnon's, accounts that place more emphasis on wife-capture than Chagnon does (Chagnon has stated several times that it is often not the principle [sic] motivation for a raid)....

Selective Omission of Data Which Support Chagnon's Findings

Claim   Tierney argues against Chagnon's claim that warriorship and reproductive success are correlated in tribal societies, citing a study of the Waorani:

> Among the Waorani of the Ecuadorian Amazon, a tribe with the world's highest known rate of attrition of war, every known male has killed at least once. But warriors who killed more than twice were more than twice as likely to be killed themselves—and their wives were killed at three times the rate of other, more peaceful men. Most prolific killers lost their wives and had to remarry—which made it look as if they had more wives if they survived.

Misrepresentation   Here, Tierney omits important information which supports the validity of Chagnon's result. Tierney refers to a recent ethnography of the Waorani in which the authors actually went out and collected the data to test Chagnon's model. The problem was, since all Waorani males had participated in a killing, they could not separate killers from non-killers. Instead they categorized men based on how many killings they had participated in: 1–5, 6–10, and 11+. Then they compared the numbers of wives and offspring among men in each of these categories. They found that killers of 1–5 people averaged 1.35 wives and 4.37 offspring, killers of 6–10 people averaged 2.00 wives and 6.08 offspring, and killers of 11+ people averaged 2.25 wives and 8.25 offspring. Thus, these data are highly consistent with those of Chagnon. The Robarcheks have essentially replicated Chagnon's finding, although they have a different interpretation of this result. They go on to present data showing that more prolific killers are more likely to get killed themselves and to lose a wife to violence; the latter are the only data that Tierney chooses to report. Tierney thus omits what is both the crux of the Robarcheks' study, and also the most useful element for evaluating the reliability of Chagnon's result: the successful replication of that result. . . .

Insinuates That Chagnon Dishonestly Confounded Unokais and Headmen

Claim   Tierney insinuates that Chagnon dishonestly includes headmen, in addition to unokais, in his sample and that the presence of headmen somehow skewed his results:

> "In his *Science* piece all headmen were also included as "killers," a confusion of categories; when the headmen were factored out, the study's statistical significance in one of its major age categories collapsed, Chagnon admitted. He would not say which category it was.... Again, Chagnon maintained a tenacious silence in the face of public challenge, this time by the anthropologist Brian Ferguson."

Misrepresentation   Chagnon does indeed include headmen in his sample of unokais, but only because these headmen are unokai, as Chagnon states clearly: "All headmen in this study are unokai." Tierney seems to suggest that Chagnon includes some headmen that he knows not to be unokai. Brian Ferguson, in *American Ethnologist,* did challenge Chagnon's inclusion of headmen in his study, saying that since headmen usually have more wives and children, and since all headmen in the study were unokai, the inclusion of headmen might increase the correlation between unokainess and reproductive success. Ferguson's point is actually misguided: the fact that all headmen were unokai is highly consistent with Chagnon's theory that in tribal societies "cultural success leads to biological success," i.e. good warriorship leads to high social status, which in turn leads to high reproductive success, and it is absurd to suggest that the presence of unokai headmen somehow contradicts a theory which it in fact strongly supports. Nevertheless, in a piece entitled "Response to Ferguson" which immediately followed Ferguson's challenge in the same issue of *American Ethnologist,* Chagnon agreed to reanalyze the data with headmen removed. Even with headmen removed, unokais (compared to non-unokais) had significantly more offspring in all four age categories, and more wives in three of four age categories ($ps < .05$). In one age category (ages 31–40), the difference between unokai and non-unokai wives was just barely not significant ($p = .07$). The statistical "collapse" to which Tierney refers is apparently the fact that $p = .07$ rather than $<.05$ for the 31–40 category, an extremely minor discrepancy misleadingly referred to as a "collapse." And there was no "tenacious silence" by Chagnon with regard to which age category was affected by the removal of headmen: Chagnon states clearly in his *American Ethnologist* piece that the category is "31–40." Tierney is clearly aware of this article (he cites it and it appears in his bibliography), so it is odd that he seems to overlook it here. . . .

Misrepresents Chagnon's Explanation for Unokai Reproductive Success

Claim   Tierney suggests that Chagnon claims that the link between killing and reproductive success is due solely to the fact that Yanomamö killers are more successful in abducting women in raids. Tierney notes that this link is "tenuous" because only a "low" number of women are actually abducted in raids:

> Nor was there anything but the most tenuous connection between killing, raiding, and the capture of women. The number of women captured in the warfare of the Yanomami is low, despite their reputation. . . . Yet the popular image of the Yanomami waging war for women persisted. Chagnon deftly created it by repeatedly claiming that men went on raids, captured women, and raped them at will afterwards.

Misrepresentation   In fact, Chagnon has stated repeatedly that when he says the Yanomamö "fight over women," he does not mean that they usually initiate raids for the purpose of abducting women. He simply means that most conflicts begin as some kind of sexual dispute, and he makes this clear in the target article: "most fights begin over sexual issues: infidelity and suspicion of infidelity, attempts to seduce another man's wife, sexual jealousy, forcible appropriation of women from visiting groups, failure to give a promised girl in marriage, and (rarely) rape." On the same page he is clear that most wars are perpetuated by revenge, not the desire to abduct women: "The most common explanation given for raids (warfare) is revenge for a previous killing, and the most common explanation for the initial cause of the fighting is 'women'." In his famous ethnography—cited extensively by Tierney—Chagnon says "although few raids are initiated solely with the intention of capturing women, this is always a desired side benefit" and "Generally, however, the desire to abduct women does not lead to the initiation of hostilities between groups that have no history of mutual raiding in the past." Tierney completely ignores that Chagnon downplays the significance of abduction as a motivation to raid and then claims that Chagnon "deftly created" the image of the Yanomamö waging war in order to abduct women.

Further, by concentrating exclusively on abduction as the only explanation for the high reproductive success of unokais, Tierney ignores what Chagnon claims might be "the most promising avenue of investigation to account for the high reproductive success of unokais," the fact that "cultural success leads to biological success." Chagnon explains that unokais, because of their prowess and willingness to take risks in military matters, are regarded as more valuable allies than non-unokais: "in short, military achievements are valued and associated with high esteem." This high status of unokais makes them more attractive as mates. In a published response to criticism about the target article, Chagnon goes into even greater detail about how unokai status makes men more attractive as mates.

Why Has Tierney Been So Dishonest?

To conclude our preliminary report, we ask the obvious question, "Why has Tierney been so dishonest?" The short answer is, we don't know. We offer the following two speculations [one included here]—but we must stress that these are only speculations, speculations we ourselves find less than satisfying....

The field of anthropology has been riven for at least the last two decades by a debate between 'scientifically oriented' anthropologists and 'humanistically oriented' anthropologists. The former tend to believe that there is an objective human reality and that scientific methods will help us discover it. The latter tend to believe that realities are relative, and socially or culturally constructed, and they are often extremely skeptical and critical of Western science. The debate between these two camps has frequently been so bitter that it has caused prominent anthropology departments, like Stanford's, to split in two (http://www.stanford.edu/group/anthro). The debate is not confined to anthropology. It is widespread in the humanities and social sciences, and has come to be known as the Science Wars.

Tierney clearly hoped to successfully indict two of the most famous scientists to work with indigenous people in the Amazon, Chagnon and Neel, with serious crimes and breaches of ethics, and thus strike a blow against scientific, and particularly evolutionary, anthropology. For students and others, we provide our perspective on this issue, and how it may account, in part, for Tierney's dishonesty.

There are three fundamental aspects of Chagnon's career that place him at ground zero in the debate between 'scientific' anthropologists and 'humanistic' anthropologists. First, Chagnon has been a staunch and vocal proponent and practitioner of scientific anthropology, one whose books and films are widely assigned in anthropology courses around the world. Second, and even more galling to 'humanistically' oriented anthropologists (and disconcerting to many 'scientific' anthropologists as well) is Chagnon's use of sociobiological theory. Sociobiology is a set of theories and general principles about animal social behavior that derive from Darwin's theory of evolution by natural selection. Although biologists were excited by the sociobiological theories that appeared in the 1960's and 1970's, there was an immediate outcry by some biologists (e.g., Stephen J. Gould) and many social scientists when E. O. Wilson suggested that sociobiology might be useful for understanding *human* social behavior. It was 'obvious' to both sides in the sociobiology debate that the other side was motivated entirely by politics. In the ensuing war of words between supporters and critics of sociobiology, the field became stigmatized. Few social scientists are willing to use the theory, and even the many biologists employing sociobiology in their study of non-human animals avoid mentioning the word 'sociobiology.' Despite this, sociobiology is a standard part of the theoretical toolkit used by biologists in virtually every biology department in the world. It is, without doubt, the theory most widely used to study and understand the social behavior of all (non-human) living things. The world's most prestigious scientific journals, Science and Nature, routinely publish research articles using sociobiology, and hundreds of research articles using sociobiology are published every year in major biology journals. Applying sociobiology to humans, however, remains strictly taboo. Chagnon has openly violated this taboo by interpreting his data in light of sociobiological theories.

Finally, Chagnon has focused his career on one of the most contentious issues in anthropology: violence and aggression in small-scale, 'primitive' societies. Critiquing Western culture has been a popular topic in anthropology since the 1920's. (In fact, a widely used cultural anthropology text is titled *Anthropology as Cultural Critique*.) In order to critique Western culture, anthropologists often feel they must find non-Western cultures that do things better. Because violence and aggression in Western societies are well deserving of critique, anthropologists hoped to discover societies with little aggression or violence that could serve as examples of a better way of living. Chagnon, by contrast, argues that violence and aggression are common in most non-Western societies—even small-scale societies like the Yanomamö—and that violence and aggression are probably part of human nature. This has infuriated the many anthropologists who prefer practicing anthropology as cultural critique. The favorite alternative to Chagnon's interpretation of Yanomamö war is that of Brian Ferguson. Ferguson, unsurprisingly, blames Yanomamö war on the influence of Western culture.

By taking aim at Chagnon, Tierney has charged into the middle of this debate on the side of the humanists against the scientists, particularly against the tiny minority who apply Darwinian theory to people. The subtitle of his book is "How Scientists and Journalists Devastated the Amazon." The very first words in the book, in the frontpiece, are from Daniel Dennett: "It is important to recognize that Darwinism has always had an unfortunate power to attract the most unwelcome enthusiasts—demagogues and psychopaths and misanthropes and other abusers of Darwin's dangerous idea." (Although Tierney doesn't mention it, Dennett is actually a strong advocate of Darwinian approaches to social science, and has written in defense of Chagnon.) And much of the book is a muddled attempt to attack Chagnon's sociobiological approach to Yanomamö warfare. Tierney constantly inserts comments like "Chagnon picked up where Social Darwinists left off" (Ch. 2), and he is even willing to make unsupported accusations of murder: "the incredible faith the sociobiologists had in their theories was admirable. Like the old Marxist missionaries, these zealots of biological determinism sacrificed everything—including the lives of their subjects—to spread their gospel." (Ch. 2).

Maybe Tierney thought that if he could destroy Chagnon, arch-enemy of many humanistic anthropologists and culture critics, he would be a hero in the Science Wars. And maybe he really thought a victory in the Science Wars would help the Amazon and its peoples. But the Amazon is not being devastated by scientists. Or journalists. Or sociobiologists. It is being devastated by logging, mining, road building, and slash-and-burn farming by the region's burgeoning population. Character assassination will do precisely nothing to change this.

POSTSCRIPT

Did Napoleon Chagnon and Other Researchers Adversley Affect the Yanomami Indians of Venezuela?

Turner agrees with journalist Patrick Tierney that Chagnon callously refused to disavow the image he created of the Yanomami as violent when gold miners and their supporters used that image against them. He also blames Chagnon for manipulating his data to contend that Yanomami are genetically programmed to be violent, due to violent males having more children than nonviolent ones, and for actually causing violence by his gift giving and violations of taboos. Hagen, Price, and Tooby retort that Tierney systematically selects and distorts his evidence to portray Chagnon in the worst possible light, and they argue that the amount of harm Chagnon did to the Yanomami pales compared to that caused by missionaries, gold miners, and other intruders into their territory.

This controversy exposed a deep rift in the anthropological community. The rift has been variously defined as between those who see anthropology as a science and those who consider it a humanistic discipline, between sociobiologists and cultural determinists, and, at the basest level, between scholars who personally like or dislike Neel and Chagnon. The battle lines are sharply drawn, and few anthropologists have remained neutral. The antagonists are pulling no punches in their charges and countercharges.

The El Dorado Task Force of the American Anthropological Association (AAA), which investigated Tierney's accusations, concluded, among other things, that Neel and his associates should be praised, not condemned, for vaccinating Yanomami against measles, an action that "unquestionably ... saved many lives" (see the Final Report on the AAA Web site at http://www.aaanet.org). However, it criticized Chagnon on ethical and professional grounds for working with a group of wealthy and corrupt Venezuelans to gain access to the Yanomami in 1990, despite having been denied a research permit by the Venezuelan government. It also criticized him for misrepresenting the Yanomami as the "fierce people," a view used by others to justify violence against them, and for not correcting that image or supporting their human rights. Not surprisingly, the report has been criticized by Chagnon's supporters as too harsh and by his enemies as too lenient. To further confuse the issue, in the spring of 2005 the members of the AAA voted to repudiate the task force's report.

This controversy has generated a huge literature in a short time, the speed being due in large part to the widespread use of the Internet. The literature includes articles and book reviews in newspapers, popular magazines, and scholarly newsletters and journals; radio programs; and numerous documents and opinions posted on Web sites. The most comprehensive and balanced guide to sources is the Web site of Douglas Hume, a graduate student at the University of Connecticut (http://members.aol.com/archeodog/darkness_in_el_dorado/index.htm). It includes a comprehensive bibliography of materials published from September 2000 to the present and links to relevant Web sites and documents. The Web site for Public Anthropology (http://www.publicanthropology.org) contains papers from a round table discussion among several scholars with varying points of view. The Department of Anthropology at the University of California at Santa Barbara Web site (http://www.anth.ucsb.edu/chagnon.html) provides a number of documents and statements supporting Chagnon. The paperback edition of Tierney's book contains an eleven-page postscript responding to his critics. Other printed publications include the *Current Anthropology* Forum entitled "Reflections on Darkness in El Dorado," which presents comments by six scholars (*Current Anthropology*, vol. 42, no. 2, pp. 265–76, 2001). A relevant earlier source is Leslie Sponsel's article "Yanomami: An Arena of Conflict and Aggression in the Amazon" (*Aggressive Behavior*, vol. 24, no. 2, pp. 97–122, 1998).

ISSUE 17

Should Anthropologists and Linguists Be Concerned About Losing Endangered Languages?

YES: Ken Hale, from "On Endangered Languages," *Language* (March 1992)

NO: Peter Ladefoged, from "Another View of Endangered Languages," *Language* (December 1992)

ISSUE SUMMARY

YES: Linguist Ken Hale contends that the loss of endangered languages represents a major tragedy for humanity, because each language that goes extinct reduces the world's linguistic diversity. The pace of extinctions has increased over the past century, mostly because government policies routinely encourage language loss. While linguists have a responsibility for recording and documenting endangered languages, they also have a role to play in influencing government policies that can encourage retention of these minority languages.

NO: Linguist Peter Ladefoged accepts the fact that endangered languages are disappearing, but feels that the position taken by Ken Hale and his colleagues is unacceptably paternalistic. He contends that while it is a good thing to study linguistic diversity, the people who speak endangered languages have just as much right to participate in their nation's affairs as anyone else, even if it means their children will learn the metropolitan language, not the endangered language.

Approximately 6,000 languages are spoken around the world. Some—such as English, French, German, Spanish, Russian, Hindi, Mandarin, Indonesian, and Tagalog—are spoken by millions of people, but about half of the world's languages are spoken by very small numbers of people in remote places with difficult environments. Many of these languages have fewer than 100 speakers.

Linguist Michael Krauss has estimated that 3,000 languages will become extinct by the end of the twenty-first century. Linguists and linguistic anthropologists have come to refer to these as "endangered languages," comparing them to natural species that are at the brink of extinction.

Languages can become extinct in a number of ways. Whole communities of Native Americans perished from introduced diseases for which they had no resistance, and their languages disappeared with them. In many more cases, Native children were sent to boarding schools where speaking their native language was forbidden and its use punished. Later, these young people were no longer fluent in their native language and did not teach it to their children. After a generation or so, these languages have come close to extinction.

Today, most communities around the world where endangered languages are spoken are not themselves dying out. They may even have large numbers of young people, but rather than use their parents' mother tongue, which feels backward and unsophisticated, they prefer to use the national language or some other important language used in commerce, in schools, or in films and music. In some cases, young people use a neighboring language that seems exciting and sophisticated. In such cases, it is not so much that the societies are dying out, but the young people are attracted to languages that have a higher status politically, economically, or socially.

Linguists like Ken Hale and Peter Ladefoged have spent more than 30 years studying obscure languages in remote corners of the world. In this issue, they acknowledge that the loss of another language means that linguists in the future will have less linguistic diversity to study. Where they differ from one another is whether linguists have any right to interfere with the linguistic preferences of the youth in these communities.

Hale argues that when people lose their language, they lose part of their cultural heritage. He thinks that linguists and anthropologists should encourage the revival of endangered languages. The youth are often attracted to the language and culture expressed in the dominant community's popular culture. For him, scholars should confront government policies that encourage young people in rural and undeveloped areas to abandon their native languages.

Ladefoged acknowledges that people lose some of their cultural heritage when they lose their language, but he argues that the attitudes of the speakers of endangered languages usually vary. He feels that scholars who are trying to convince them to continue to teach their children and actively use their language in daily life may be working against the interests of the people. In many cases, tribal people are excluded from the mainstream society because they use a different language. How can it be right to urge them not to participate in the mainstream society, with its jobs and consumer goods?

In these selections, consider who has the responsibility for maintaining these endangered languages. Does any researcher have the right to tell people what language to speak? Do indigenous people have a duty to preserve their languages? Does language really play a key role in cultural identity, as many anthropologists have argued?

Ken Hale

Endangered Languages

On Endangered Languages and the Safeguarding of Diversity

Like most people who have done linguistic field work for thirty years or so, I have worked on languages which are now extinct, eight of them in my case, and I have studied, and continue to study, many languages which are seriously imperiled. My experience is far from unusual, and the testimony of field workers alone would amply illustrate the extent of language loss in the world of the present era.

It is reasonable, I suppose, to ask what difference it makes. On the one hand, one might say, language loss has been a reality throughout history; and on the other, the loss of a language is of no great moment either for science or for human intellectual life.

I think, personally, that these ideas are wrong and that language loss is a serious matter. Or, more accurately, it is part of a process which is itself very serious.

From what I have been able to learn, ... language loss in the modern period is of a different character, in its extent and in its implications [from the past]. It is part of a much larger process of LOSS OF CULTURAL AND INTEL-LECTUAL DIVERSITY in which politically dominant languages and cultures simply overwhelm indigenous local languages and cultures, placing them in a condition which can only be described as embattled. The process is not unrelated to the simultaneous loss of diversity in the zoological and botanical worlds. An ecological analogy is not altogether inappropriate. We understand to some extent the dangers inherent in the loss of biological diversity on this earth. It is correct to ask, I think, whether there are also dangers inherent in the loss of linguistic diversity.

This and other aspects of language endangerment in these times are addressed [here].

We have not attempted here to be truly representative either geographically or topically. Instead, we attempt to represent as forcefully as we can TWO facets of the situation of language endangerment—namely, (1) the reality of language loss and decline as a condition of the modern world and (2) the response to language imperilment on the part of various entities, e.g., above all, the communities directly affected by language loss. Our examples come from North and Central America.

From *Language,* vol. 68, no. 1, March 1992, pp. excerpts from 1–3, 35–38, 40–41. Copyright © 1992 by Linguistic Society of America. Reprinted by permission. References omitted.

MICHAEL KRAUSS was given the daunting task of preparing the first essay, a report on the realities of language loss for the world as a whole. This is our sole attempt to present a global perspective on the matter. Although, as Krauss notes, it is impossible now to be completely accurate in assessing the language situation in the world, it is clear that language extinction has reached an extraordinary level in recent times and that the outlook for an impressive percentage of the world's surviving languages is very poor.

These indications are certainly not heartening. But it is important, we feel, to counterpoise these realities with another, more encouraging reality—that of the great energy, courage, good sense, and optimism which many endangered language communities and allied support organizations are bringing to the formidable challenge of ensuring in this era a position of strength and dignity for their linguistic and cultural wealth....

A local response to perceived language endangerment is exemplified... in the essay by LUCILLE WATAHOMIGIE and AKIRA YAMAMOTO, which describes the Hualapai Bilingual/Bicultural Education Program, of Peach Springs, Arizona, recognized as one of the very best in the country. The essay goes on to describe the manner in which this local community program played a central role in the development of regional and national movements affecting Native American languages and their speakers—specifically, the creation of the American Indian Languages Development Institute and the formulation and passage of the Native American Languages Act.

It happens occasionally that a responsible government, responding to the legitimate demands of its indigenous and ethnic populations, accepts as a proper part of its program the establishment of instruments and institutions designed to promote the development and use of the local languages under its authority....

[Finally], I present an example of the kind of material that we can expect to lose with the loss of a language. I have chosen an example involving language and the expression of intellectual life, to emphasize the fact that the loss of a language is part of the more general loss being suffered by the world, the loss of diversity in all things.

Language Endangerment and the Human Value of Linguistic Diversity

Linguists typically celebrate the tension that plays between two realities of human linguistic knowledge, universality and diversity. But linguistic diversity is not something whose future can be taken for granted. Many local languages and cultures find themselves in great peril in this era, a fact well documented elsewhere in this collection.

In the following paragraphs I will be concerned with the idea that linguistic diversity is important to human intellectual life—not only in the context of scientific linguistic inquiry, but also in relation to the class of human activities belonging to the realms of culture and art.

From the perspective of linguistic science, arguments for safeguarding the world's linguistic diversity require no special discussion in this journal. Suppose English were the only language available as a basis for the study of general human grammatical competence. We know enough about the latter to be able to say now that we could learn a great deal about it from English alone. But we also know enough about linguistic diversity to know that we would miss an enormous amount.

If English were the only language, we could learn a lot about the fundamental principles of grammar, but we could only guess at the nature of that which can vary, except to the extent that this is evident from the varieties of English itself. And this would amount to missing an important point of human linguistic competence. By itself, English would supply a mere hint of the complexity of the system of principles and parameters....

The notion that the world's linguistic diversity is a precious resource does not derive solely from linguistic science, of course. Language is much more than grammar. The term 'language' embraces a wide range of human competences and capacities, and it is not clear that it makes sense to think of it as a single entity.

Of supreme significance in relation to linguistic diversity, and to local languages in particular, is the simple truth that language—in the general, multifaceted sense—embodies the intellectual wealth of the people who use it. A language and the intellectual productions of its speakers are often inseparable, in fact. Some forms of verbal art—verse, song, or chant—depend crucially on morphological and phonological, even syntactic, properties of the language in which it is formed. In such cases the art could not exist without the language, quite literally. Even where the dependency is not so organic as this, an intellectual tradition may be so thoroughly a part of a people's linguistic ethnography as to be, in effect, inseparable from the language.

In this circumstance, there is a certain tragedy for the human purpose. The loss of local languages, and of the cultural systems that they express, has meant irretrievable loss of diverse and interesting intellectual wealth, the priceless products of human mental industry. The process of language loss is ongoing. Many linguistic field workers have had, and will continue to have, the experience of bearing witness to the loss, for all time, of a language and of the cultural products which the language served to express for the intellectual nourishment of its speakers.

In the remainder of this essay, I would like to describe one such product of a people's intellectual work. This is a tradition whose decline and virtual disappearance I witnessed in the course of field work in Australia. It was the treasure of a small group of Australian Aboriginal people, the Lardil, living on Mornington Island in North Queensland.

While working on the syntax and lexicon of Lardil in 1960, I heard of the existence of an auxiliary language, called Damin, which some initiated men in the community could still use. Most men could not, since the mission administrating Mornington Island during the early decades of this century had forbidden the practice of initiation many years earlier, and it was in the context of initiation that Damin was learned. Only men initiated before the mission was established had had the opportunity to learn Damin, and only a few of those men were still living in 1960.

I was not able to work on Damin until 1967. An anthropologist working with the Lardil people sent me a tape of Damin while I was working in another community farther south. When I heard the tape, I knew that Damin was something very special, so I arranged to visit Mornington Island again. The feature of Damin that first caught my attention was its phonology. It departs drastically from the phonology of Lardil, and it has sounds in it which do not exist in any other Australian language. For example, it has click consonants, otherwise found only in Africa—in the Khoisan languages, for example, and in the Nguni languages of the Bantu family, languages with no historical connection to Lardil. The use of clicks in Damin developed locally. Damin has the appearance of an invented language, and it is attributed, in fact, to a legendary figure named Kalthad (Yellow Trevally). If it was invented, then it is a clever invention, indeed, because it is almost unheard of for an invented language to depart radically from the phonological constraints of the ordinary language of the inventor. The impression that Damin is an invention is strengthened by the fact that it not only has sounds absent elsewhere in Australia, but it also has sounds found nowhere else in the world—as true phonological segments, that is. These include an ingressive voiceless lateral and a labia-velar lingual ejective.

Although its sound system is spectacular, the extraordinary genius of Damin is to be found in its lexicon. In its original purpose, Damin was an 'auxiliary language', in the sense that it was used in place of Lardil when this was necessary for ritual reasons. An idea of its nature can be gained from a consideration of how it was learned and used. According to the accounts of surviving Demiinkurlda, or 'Damin-possessors', as they were called, Damin was learned by novices in the advanced phase of men's initiation. Men who went through this stage were called Warama, and in theory only Warama learned Damin. In practice, however, since it was used in public, many people who were not Warama, both men and women, had passive knowledge of it. Its purpose, apart from the intellectual pleasure it gave, was to serve as a vehicle of communication between Warama and all individuals involved in their initiation. The use of ordinary Lardil with these people was forbidden, until they had been repaid the ritual debt owed to them by the Warama as a result of initiation. Damin is a lexicon, not an entire language. The rule in using Damin correctly is this: each lexical item of Lardil must be replaced by a Damin item, the inflectional morphology and syntax of Lardil remains intact....

While inflectional and derivational morphology is the same for Lardil and Damin, the lexicon is totally different. Thus, each noun, verb, or pronoun in the Lardil of 1 matches a distinct item in Damin. It is the nature of this replacement lexicon which is extraordinary. It is constructed in such a way that, in principle, it can be learned in one day. In practice, it is said, learning Daniin took place over a longer period, though one could, in fact, learn it in a day. The lexicon can be learned in one day, yet, in combination with Lardil syntax and morphology, it can be used to express virtually any idea. How can a lexicon be SMALL enough to learn in one day and, at the same time, be

RICH enough to express all ideas? A moment's reflection on this question can only inspire admiration, in my judgment.

The answer, of course, is abstractness. The Damin lexicon cannot be rich in the usual sense of having large numbers of lexical items denoting concepts of great specificity (like the ordinary Lardil or English vocabulary, for example). Rather, the richness of Damin is of a different sort, the opposite of this in fact. Damin lexical items are abstract names for logically cohesive families of concepts. The richness of Damin resides in the semantic breadth of its lexical items, permitting a small inventory (less than 200 items) to accommodate the same range of concepts as does the much larger ordinary vocabulary (of unknown size)....

The Damin lexicon must achieve a balance between abstraction and expressive power, since it must satisfy two essentially contradictory requirements. It must be such that it can be learned quickly and, at the same time, it must be such that it can be used, in cooperation with Lardil inflectional morphology and syntax, to express any idea which Lardil itself can be used to express. It cannot be TOO abstract, therefore.

The Damin kinship terminology exemplifies this point well. The system has five terms.... This amounts to a massive reduction from the Lardil kinship terminology, which, like most Australian systems, is very large. There is a mystery in the reduction, though, since the logic of the classificatory kinship system would lead one to expect an even number, say four. But while this would be appropriately abstract, it would require merger of one of the most important kinship distinctions in Lardil society, that between second-cross cousins ... the class that includes the preferred marriage partners, and first-cross cousins ..., the class of alternant marriage partners. The Damin terminology strikes the optimal balance between abstraction and expressive power.

It is clear from what little we know of Damin that it involves a sophisticated semantic analysis of the lexical resources of Lardil. The system of abstractions lays bare aspects of lexical semantic structure to a degree which, quite possibly, is not achieved by any other system of analysis that attempts to accommodate an ENTIRE vocabulary.

The last fluent user of Damin passed away several years ago. The destruction of this intellectual treasure was carried out, for the most part, by people who were not aware of its existence, coming as they did from a culture in which wealth is physical and visible. Damin was not visible for them, and as far as they were concerned, the Lardil people had no wealth, apart from their land.

We cannot say that the Damin tradition is utterly lost to the Lardil people. However, it is all but gone, since revival of [it] would be from recorded sources; and if revival were to be attempted, a NEW Damin tradition would be initiated, necessarily, since the cultural context of the original tradition is irrecoverable—there are no survivors of that period. The development of a new Damin tradition is not a bad thing, of course; in fact it would be an exciting thing. But the old Damin tradition is effectively lost. And the destruction of this tradition must be ranked as a disaster, comparable to the destruction of any human treasure.

It is perhaps of little use simply to bemoan the loss of a treasure. The example of Damin is offered as an instance of the nature of things that have been lost and of what can be lost if linguistic and cultural diversity disappears. On the other hand, the safeguarding of linguistic and cultural diversity does not guarantee the perpetuation of existing traditions of intellectual endeavor, of course. In fact, a living tradition implies change. And it is precisely the development of new traditions which is most consonant with the human purpose. And it is precisely where local languages are viable that new traditions develop. Thus, for example, in the Southwest of the United States, beside the continuing traditions of sung verse, a new tradition of poetry is developing, in Papago, Pima, Yaqui, Navajo, and Hualapai, for example, in the context of the growing use of the written form of these languages (encouraged by such institutions as AILDI, described elsewhere in this collection).

If the foregoing discussion is at all reasonable, then certain things follow. While it is good and commendable to record and document fading traditions, and in some cases this is absolutely necessary to avert total loss of cultural wealth, the greater goal must be that of safeguarding diversity in the world of people. For that is the circumstance in which diverse and interesting intellectual traditions can grow. Consider again the case of Damin. We have a small record of that auxiliary language, enough to appreciate its worth. But we have no idea what it would have become, how it would have changed, or, most important, what kind of role it might have played in Lardil intellectual life in this or the next decade. It might have disappeared, of course. That would have been their business. But it might have led to something even greater. We will never know, since the necessary condition has not existed—namely, an environment safe for cultural diversity which would have permitted the Lardil people to learn and use Damin into the next century.

NO

Peter Ladefoged

Another View of Endangered Languages

Language seldom publishes opinion pieces, such as that of Hale, Krauss, Watahomigie, Yamamoto, Craig, Jeanne, & England 1992 on endangered languages. I have nothing but praise for the work that these linguists do. But language preservation and maintenance is a multifaceted topic on which different opinions are possible. The views expressed in these papers are contrary to those held by many responsible linguists, and would not be appropriate in some of the African countries in which I have worked in the last few years. Tanzania, for example, is a country which is striving for unity, and the spreading of Swahili is regarded as a major force in this endeavor. Tribalism is seen as a threat to the development of the nation, and it would not be acting responsibly to do anything which might seem, at least superficially, to aid in its preservation.

Hale et al. (1992) write from the perspective of linguists who have worked in particular cultures; but the attitudes of the speakers of the languages that they describe are far from universal. As they indicate, in many communities the language is regarded as sacred—literally God-given. Linguists working in such communities should obviously respect the opinions of the speakers, and honor their wishes. The speakers are giving access to something that is sacred to them, and it should be treasured accordingly. But not everyone holds this view. The half a dozen speakers of Angami (Tibeto-Burman) with whom I worked earlier this year had a different attitude. They regarded it as an intellectually valid pursuit for me to take an interest in their language. Admittedly, they were all high school or college educated students who had a similar intellectual interest in my language. They might therefore be regarded as part of an elite, with views that were only those of the elite. But I do not think this is so. The profane, as opposed to sacred, view of language is widely shared, even among those who are certainly not part of the socio-economically elite. Many of the people with whom I have worked in undeveloped parts of India and Africa regard being a language consultant as just another job, and a reasonably high status one at that. They have no problem with satisfying my intellectual curiosity. They in no way regard their work as prostituting something that is holy. Instead they are pleased with the honored status of being teachers. Furthermore, it pays better than alternative occupations, such as picking tea or digging yams, and it is much less hard work.

From *Language,* vol. 68, no. 4, December 1992, pp. 809–811. Copyright © 1992 by Linguistic Society of America. Reprinted by permission. Some references omitted.

Even among those for whom language is a vital part of the sacred way of life, the attitude towards linguists is not always that outlined in Hale et al. 1992. The Toda, speakers of a Dravidian language in the Nilgiri Hills of Southern India, have a series of songs which are an important part of their religious life. They eagerly welcome linguists who wish to assist them in recording their language. They also realize that with less than 1,000 speakers they are unlikely to remain a distinct entity. Many of the younger people want to honor their ancestors, but also to be part of a modern India. They have accepted that, in their view, the cost of doing this is giving up the use of their language in their daily life. Surely, this is a view to which they are entitled, and it would not be the action of a responsible linguist to persuade them to do otherwise. In the circumstances of my fieldwork it would also have been somewhat hypocritical. I was working with an Indian colleague who has decided to forego the use of his and his wife's native language in their own home, so that their child could be brought up as a native language speaker of English. This choice, and any choices that the Toda might make, are clearly their prerogatives.

So now let me challenge directly the assumption of these papers that different languages, and even different cultures, always ought to be preserved. It is paternalistic of linguists to assume that they know what is best for the community. One can be a responsible linguist and yet regard the loss of a particular language, or even a whole group of languages, as far from a 'catastrophic destruction' (Hale et al. 1992:7). Statements such as 'just as the extinction of any animal species diminishes our world, so does the extinction of any language' (Hale et al. 1992:8) are appeals to our emotions, not to our reason. The case for studying endangered languages is very strong on linguistic grounds. It is often enormously strong on humanitarian grounds as well. But it would be self-serving of linguists to pretend that this is always the case. We must be wary of arguments based on political considerations. Of course I am no more in favor of genocide or repression of minorities than I am of people dying of tuberculosis or starving through ignorance. We should always be sensitive to the concerns of the people whose language we are studying. But we should not assume that we know what is best for them.

We may also note that human societies are not like animal species. The world is remarkably resilient in the preservation of diversity; different cultures are always dying while new ones arise. They may not be based on ethnicity or language, but the differences remain. Societies will always produce subgroups as varied as computer nerds, valley girls, and drug pushers, who think and behave in different ways. In the popular view the world is becoming more homogeneous, but that may be because we are not seeing the new differences that are arising. Consider two groups of Bushmen, the Zhu|oãsi and the !Xóõ, who speak mutually unintelligible languages belonging to different subgroups of the Khoisan family, but otherwise behave in very similar ways. Are these two groups more culturally diverse than Appalachian coalminers, Iowa farmers, and Beverly Hills lawyers? As a linguist, I am of course saddened by the vast amount of linguistic and cultural knowledge that is disappearing, and I am delighted that the National Science Foundation has sponsored our UCLA research, in which we try to record for posterity the phonetic structures of some of the languages that will not be around much longer. But it is not for me to assess the virtues of programs for language preservation versus those of competitive programs for tuberculosis eradication, which may also need government funds.

In this changing world, the task of the linguist is to layout the facts concerning a given linguistic situation. The approach that I would advocate is exemplified in our study of language use and teaching in Uganda. With the full coöperation of the then (more or less) duly elected government (this was immediately before the time of Idi Amin), we assembled data on the linguistic situation. We tried to determine the linguistic similarities and mutual intelligibility of some of the major languages spoken in Uganda (about 16 Bantu, 5 Western Nilotic, 4 Eastern Nilotic, 2 Central Sudanic, and 4 non-Ugandan). We found that about 39% of the people could hold a conversation in Luganda (the largest single language), 35% in Swahili, and 21% in English. We noted that Radio Uganda put out programs in 16 Ugandan languages (some of them mutually intelligible), plus Swahili and English, and that there were literacy campaigns in 20 languages. Six Ugandan languages were used in schools. We summarized all our data so that the government could assess the linguistic situation. We did not try to determine the costs of making changes or of maintaining the *status quo*, in either monetary or human terms. It would have been presumptuous of us to weigh the loss of a language against the burdens facing Uganda. We tried to behave like responsible linguists with professional detachment.

Last summer I was working on Dahalo, a rapidly dying Cushitic language, spoken by a few hundred people in a rural district of Kenya. I asked one of our consultants whether his teen-aged sons spoke Dahalo. 'No,' he said. 'They can still hear it, but they cannot speak it. They speak only Swahili.' He was smiling when he said it, and did not seem to regret it. He was proud that his sons had been to school, and knew things that he did not. Who am I to say that he was wrong?

Reference

Hale, Ken; Michael Krauss; Lucille J. Watahomigie; Akira Y. Yamamoto; Colette Craig; Laverne Masayesva Jeanne; and Nora C. England. 1992. Endangered languages. Lg. 68.1–42.

POSTSCRIPT

Should Anthropologists and Linguists Be Concerned About Losing Endangered Languages?

Both of these linguists have spent their careers studying obscure languages, many of which have few surviving speakers and which are considered endangered languages. Neither wants to encourage any of these languages to go extinct, yet they take very different approaches to the question of whether linguists and linguistic anthropologists should be concerned about languages dying out.

Ken Hale argues that the extinction of languages is very similar to the loss of natural species of animals, because it robs humanity of part of its natural diversity. Each language offers us a better sense about what is linguistically possible for human beings. Hale argues that in recent decades language loss is largely due to government policies that make it desirable for indigenous people to abandon their languages in favor of important national or regional ones. The key measure of language endangerment is the number of children who speak the vernacular language, because if children do not speak the language it is unlikely that the language will be passed on to their descendants. For these younger people, popular culture has a compelling attraction. There can be little doubt that popular culture attracts adolescents to view the national or regional language associated with music, videos, films, and the like as exciting, while their parent's vernacular seems old fashioned out of step with modern times.

Peter Ladefoged agrees with Hale about the general attractiveness of modern life, employment, and popular culture. He acknowledges that it may be sad for linguists to see the object of their studies disappear as children and adolescents learn national or regional languages rather than their traditional vernacular. But he contends that no matter how unpleasant it may be for linguists, scholars have an obligation to recognize that people in most communities around the world want jobs, consumer goods, and participation in modern national life. It is paternalistic for researchers to attempt to decide for their subjects and informants whether they can participate in modern life.

Over the last decade or so, studying what communities that speak endangered languages are doing has become a topic of great interest for social researchers. Nancy Dorian's book *Language Death* (University of Pennsylvania Press, 1980) was one of the earliest; her paper "A Response to Ladefoged's Other View of Endangered Languages" (*Language* 69(3):575–579, 1993) supports Hale's point of view. Other informative texts would include Robert H. Robins and Eugenius M. Uhlenbeck's edited collection *Endangered Language* (Berg, 1991) and Lenore A. Grenoble and Lindsay J. Whaley's edited volume *Endangered Languages: Language Loss and Community Response* (Cambridge University Press, 1998).

ISSUE 18

Should Anthropologists Work to Eliminate the Practice of Female Circumcision?

YES: Merrilee H. Salmon, from "Ethical Considerations in Anthropology and Archaeology, or Relativism and Justice for All," *Journal of Anthropological Research* (Spring 1997)

NO: Elliott P. Skinner, from "Female Circumcision in Africa: The Dialectics of Equality," in Richard R. Randolph, David M. Schneider, and May N. Diaz, eds., *Dialectics and Gender: Anthropological Approaches* (Westview Press, 1988)

ISSUE SUMMARY

YES: Professor of the history and philosophy of science Merrilee H. Salmon argues that clitoridectomy (female genital mutilation) violates the rights of the women on whom it is performed. She asserts that this operation is a way for men to control women and keep them unequal.

NO: Professor of anthropology Elliott P. Skinner accuses feminists who want to abolish clitoridectomy of being ethnocentric. He states that African women themselves want to participate in the practice, which functions like male initiation, transforming girls into adult women.

For more than a century anthropologists have seen cultural relativism as an essential antidote to ethnocentrism, a perspective that evaluates and judges the practices of other peoples according to the standards and sensitivities of one's own culture. This issue raises questions about the boundaries and limits of the anthropologist's cultural relativism. By evaluating cultural practices in a culture's own terms, anthropologists have long defended cultural diversity and the general principle that dominant cultures should not force members of weaker cultures to abandon traditional customs and practices, simply because practices appear peculiar, bizarre, or wrong to those in power. But today the world is increasingly integrated, and a number of international organizations have emerged whose purpose is to defend a single universal vision of human rights. Few anthropologists would object in principle to the notion that human rights should be defended for all people, but universal moral codes also challenge the rights of cultural groups to be different.

In this issue two scholars debate whether or not anthropologist sshould interfere with the cultural practice, found in many parts of Africa and the Middle East, of clitoridectomy and infibulation, variously called female circumcision or female genital mutilation. The practice is typically part of female initiation ceremonies and takes different forms in different ethnic groups, varying from relatively minor surgery to the clitoris (clitoridectomy) to the complete surgical removal of the clitoris and much of the woman's external sexual organs, after which the vagina is sewn up, leaving only a small opening (infibulation).

Merrilee H. Salmon refers to this practice as female genital mutilation and argues that it is fundamentally wrong, a violation of a woman's human rights. She contends that the practice is part of a male-centered power structure, which allows men to control women. Although Salmon acknowledges that women often control the ritual and even the surgery, the practice of female circumcision nevertheless supports male dominance within the community. In her view this cultural practice is an immoral one, and anthropological calls for moral relativism in this case are fundamentally ill-founded.

Elliott P. Skinner counters that female circumcision is only found in African societies where male circumcision is also practiced. Both practices involve mutilation of the genitals and are the means of transforming male and female children into adult men and women, respectively. Skinner maintains that not only are the female rituals entirely in the hands of other women, but that the practices empower women within a society where men might otherwise dominate them. Feminists who argue that this practice is an example of male power over women, in his view, have got it wrong. Calls for the abolition of female circumcision began with Western missionaries who found the practice repugnant. He states that Africans supported female circumcision as a form of resistance to white domination, and in Skinner's view current calls from Western people for the abolition of this practice is another example of Western domination of African societies.

At issue here are several key questions: Is female circumcision morally repugnant? Should anthropologists defend it or work to stop it? How should anthropologists deal with such practices when they see them occurring in their village communities where they work?

Although this issue seems very narrowly focused on a particular traditional custom in only one part of the world, it has important general implications for cultural relativism and universal human rights. Should anthropologists defend cultural practices simply because they are traditional? Do anthropologists have a responsibility to help end practices that they find morally abhorrent? If so, whose moral notions should be followed? Is moral relativism fundamentally flawed, as Salmon asserts?

Merrilee H. Salmon  **YES**

Ethical Considerations in Anthropology and Archaeology, or Relativism and Justice for All

Cultural Relativism and Ethical Relativism

Respect for the beliefs, practices, and values of other cultures, no matter how different from one's own, is a hallmark of anthropological wisdom. Franz Boas, the father of American academic anthropology, rejected invidious comparisons between European "high culture" and indigenous American languages, myths, art forms, and religions. Boas, dismissing absolute scales of cultural development such as those proposed by Condorcet and L. H. Morgan, insisted on studying the culture of each group in the context of its own historical development. Boas's work forms the historical basis for the anthropological doctrine known as *cultural relativism*.

Many anthropologists regard *ethical relativism* as an easy corollary of cultural relativism. I show that this view is incorrect. Cultural relativism does not entail ethical relativism; an anthropologist can consistently embrace cultural relativism while rejecting ethical relativism. As most anthropologists understand it, ethical relativism identifies the concepts of good and evil, or right and wrong, with what a particular culture approves or disapproves. Because ethical standards arise within particular cultures and vary from culture to culture, ethical relativists deny any extracultural standard of moral judgments. According to them, moral judgments of good or bad are possible only within a given culture, because such judgments refer only to compliance or noncompliance with that culture's norms.

The fact that a belief arises within a cultural context, however, does not imply that it can have no other basis. Although moral beliefs, like all other beliefs, arise within a given cultural setting, some of those beliefs may transcend the cultures in which they arise. Condemnation of murder and recognition of obligations to help others who are in extreme need, for example, are common to many cultures. Moreover, societies that differ in derivative moral judgments about marriage between close relatives frequently agree about more fundamental moral judgments, such as the immorality of incest. This modicum of moral consensus has encouraged some critics to try to refute ethical relativism by identifying a set of universally acceptable moral principles.

Whether universal agreement exists on any specific basic moral judgment is partly an empirical matter and partly dependent on how such terms as "murder," "cruelty," and "incest" are defined. Colin Turnbull's (1962) admittedly controversial studies suggest that the Ik do not embrace the most likely candidates for fundamental moral principles, on any reasonable definition of such principles. In Turnbull's account, the Ik provide a striking counterexample to general views that cruelty to children, for example, is universally condemned. Even if Turnbull's account is rejected, the search for moral principles that are both reasonably specific and universally acceptable is problematic.

The lack of agreement about principles, however, is not sufficient to demonstrate the truth of ethical relativism. What a culture regards as right or wrong conduct depends to some degree on both the members' factual beliefs about the state of the world and their beliefs about the likely consequences of their conduct. The absence of any universally accepted standards would support ethical relativism only if cultures that shared all the same factual beliefs and agreed about the consequences of particular behavior nevertheless disagreed in their ethical judgments. This situation has not been demonstrated. In fact, many apparent differences in ethical matters are resolved by bringing forth pertinent facts about the conditions under which moral choices are made. Even Turnbull (1962) goes to considerable trouble to show that severe hardship and deprivation of material resources in Ik society have altered their perceptions of reality. Whereas lack of universally accepted moral principles does not prove ethical relativism, however, neither would the universal acceptance of some specific moral principles disprove ethical relativism. The agreement could be accidental instead of arising from some feature of the human condition. Berlin and Kay's (1969) refutation of the relativism of color classification was convincing only because they were able to demonstrate the physiological—and thus cross-cultural—basis for color classification.

Ethical relativism apparently accords with anthropologists' determination to reject ethnocentrism and maintain a nonjudgmental stance towards alien cultural practices. Nevertheless, both anthropologists and philosophers have noted a serious problem with relativistic ethics: it seems to rule out condemning even such obviously immoral acts as genocide so long as they do not conflict with prevailing cultural norms. Ethical theories about what constitutes right and wrong behavior are severely tested when they go against our deepest moral intuition in this manner; in such cases one naturally questions the theory rather than giving up the intuition. H. Russell Bernard (1988:117), for example, says that

> cultural and ethical relativism is an excellent antidote for overdeveloped ethnocentrism. But cultural relativism is a poor philosophy to live by, or on which to make judgments about whether to participate in particular research projects. Can you imagine any anthropologist today defending the human rights violations of Nazi Germany as just another expression of the richness of culture?

Bernard's use of "is" in the first sentence shows that he does not distinguish cultural from ethical relativism. If he had done so, his point would be less confusing. *Cultural* relativism, in Boas's sense of trying to understand and evaluate the practices of other cultures in their own historical context, is a good antidote for ethnocentrism. Identifying the practices of any culture as the ultimate moral standard for that culture, however, is a different matter and rightly raises problems for a reflective anthropologist. Bernard in mentioning Nazi Germany has offered the standard counterexample to the claim that morality recognizes no extracultural authority.

Despite its fatal flaw, however, ethical relativism still enjoys wide acceptance among practicing anthropologists. Ethical relativism, for example, played a role in testimony by a French ethnologist in the trial of Bintou Fofana Diarra for complicity in the genital mutilation of her infant daughter. As reported in the *New York Times* (Weil-Curiel 1993), the unnamed ethnologist testified that "Africans should not be punished [for genital mutilation of infant girls] because they act under social pressure." The principle implicit in this statement—that one should not be punished for acts done under social pressure—is uncomfortably similar to the defense offered by Nazi war criminals.

A second problem with making cultural standards the final arbiter of morality is that this practice presumes a uniformity in cultures that current research denies, even for small, isolated, and tightly knit societies, or it gives a privileged moral position to powerful subgroups within the society. In the latter case, for example, the power to set cultural norms may belong to a minority whose control of valuable resources enables it to force others to follow its standards. Conversely, the power to set norms may accrue to those who are members of the majority, while significant minorities have no voice. In either case, one can only refer to the norms of "the culture" by ignoring ethical disagreement within the culture.

Some anthropologists believe that relativism is the only ethical stance that is compatible with a scientific investigation of other cultures. A scientific anthropologist presumably formulates "neutral" descriptions of the culture, reporting such quantifiable information as the frequency of occurrence of behaviors and perhaps the observed attitudes (approval, disapproval) of members of the society, while refraining from judging the culture or interfering with it in any way. Whether such detachment is required to maintain scientific integrity and whether such detachment is even possible are points raised by D'Andrade (1995) and Scheper-Hughes (1995). D'Andrade (1995:399) points to the alleged subjectivity of ethical judgments and contrasts these with the objectivity of scientific judgments. Scheper-Hughes (1995), however, objects to a scientific detachment that would prevent anthropologists from taking an active role in alleviating suffering among their research subjects. This debate is somewhat at cross-purposes because D'Andrade's main concern seems to be with an epistemic relativism that claims that such notions as knowledge and truth have no extracultural basis.... Scheper-Hughes, in contrast, is worried about the behavioral implications of a relativist ethics that takes the existing social arrangements in a culture as the ultimate moral authority.

The strict separation of science and values, a cherished principle of logical positivism, is increasingly difficult to defend in the face of ethical problems raised by scientific advances in many fields. In particular, current biomedical techniques for genetic engineering and research on human embryos raise important problems that tend to blur lines between scientific and value judgments. Bernard (1988) notes that when resources are limited, the very choice of anthropological research topics is value laden. The possibility of an ethically neutral or completely value-free science of human behavior now seems to many scientists both unattainable and undesirable, but recognition of the interrelationships between science and values need not prevent the limited type of objectivity that D'Andrade argues is possible for anthropological research.

Anthropologists may continue to avow ethical relativism despite its difficulties because they have not articulated an alternative ethical theory that is consistent with their distaste for ethnocentrism and their respect for cultural diversity. Nevertheless, maintaining a consistent form of ethical relativism is highly problematic in the present research climate. Facing the loss of valuable anthropological and archaeological resources, anthropologists have reexamined traditional relationships with their subjects, their colleagues, and the general public. To resolve problems and achieve clarity, they are currently debating and revising professional ethical standards. Despite the traditional commitment of anthropologists to relativism, the ethical principles that underlie their professional codes are not relativistic. The codes refer to their duties and responsibilities, and—by implication at least—to the corresponding rights of their research subjects, colleagues, and the general public. The conflict, often unacknowledged, between the avowed relativism of anthropologists and their sincere concern with justice and rights can lead to confusion and ineffectiveness in achieving the important goals of preserving anthropological resources and protecting cultural minorities....

An Anthropological Example—Female Genital Mutilation

The arguments of feminist anthropologists for altering discriminatory practices of other cultures similarly compromise a commitment to ethical relativism. In some cultures, all females are subjected to genital mutilation. In its severe form, this involves cutting away most or all of the external sex organs (euphemistically called "circumcision") and sewing or sealing (infibulating) the vagina so as to leave only a pinhole opening for urination and menstruation. The practice affects an estimated ninety-five million or more women in at least twenty-five countries, mostly, but not all, in Africa (Lightfoot-Klein 1989). Within the cultures that practice genital mutilation, little disagreement exists about its value, though different groups offer various justifications for the practice. Most, but not all, of the countries that engage in the practice are predominantly Muslim, but it is absent in many other Muslim countries. The operation typically is performed on girls from six to nine years old but also on younger girls and infants. Sometimes when a bride is an "outsider," she is infibulated just before she marries into a group that follows the custom.

Anthropologists have attempted to document, understand, and explain this practice, which, aside from its harshness, strikes most Westerners as extremely bizarre. Why do they do it? What possible benefit do they see from it? How could it be so widespread? In contrast to most accounts in the contemporary press which dismiss the practice simply as a way of oppressing women, anthropologists' explanations are appropriately complex. They refer to the cult of virginity, the cultural association between female purity and the society's honor, and the antiquity of the tradition—Herodotus, writing in the fifth century B.C., obliquely refers to its practice in Egypt, and some mummies show evidence of infibulation. Anthropologists also cite the symbolic role female circumcision plays in distinguishing the Arab-Muslim African societies that practice it from their culturally distinct neighbors.

In places such as the Sudan, where the practice is nearly universal, anthropologists discuss genital mutilation in the context of social practices that involve other forms of mutilation practiced upon both males and females, such as tribal scarring of the face and piercing of body parts. Anthropologists also emphasize the cultural value of enduring pain without complaint. Economic explanations are also proposed. Midwives who perform the operations are sustained by the fees not only from the original circumcision and infibulation but also from treatment of the inevitable medical problems that result. Other explanations are psychological, such as those that refer to the attitudes of older women who say that they have gone through the experience and therefore do not see why the younger ones should be spared.

Besides offering their own historical and cultural explanations, anthropologists report the explanations of the people who engage in the practice. These include such claims as we have always done it, our religion requires it, no one will marry an uncircumcised woman, it makes us clean, it makes us more beautiful, it improves health, it limits the sex drive, it is good for fertility, and—referring to reinfibulation after childbirth—it deters a husband from seeking additional wives.

Some—relatively few—women and men in such societies do question the practice or its supposed benefits, particularly if they have been exposed to modern Western culture. But when asked why they nevertheless have their daughters circumcised, they refer to tradition, or say that their female relatives insisted, or insist that no one would marry the girl unless she were circumcised. Most explanations of female genital mutilation come from women, since few men can be persuaded to discuss the issue, claiming for the most part that it is women's business. Jomo Kenyatta, the revered former leader of Kenya and member of the Kikuyu tribe, who earned a Ph.D. in anthropology under [Bronislaw] Malinowski, however, said, "No proper Kikuyu would dream of marrying a girl who has not been circumcised" (Kenyatta 1938, quoted in Lightfoot-Klein 1989:71).

Women in cultures that practice genital mutilation claim that it is done for the benefit of the men, but women alone are responsible for arranging and performing the operations. Even the question of the acceptability of bridal candidates is largely under control of the women since arranged marriages are the rule, with the groom's mother having a prominent voice. (Recently a young woman from Togo sought and was granted asylum in the United States to avoid genital mutilation. The woman became endangered, however, only after her father had died. Her guardianship then passed to her aunt, who attempted to commit the woman to an arranged marriage.) Thus the practice is unusual inasmuch as it is intended to control women, it affects them almost universally, and they suffer the greatest harm from it; but they manage and control it almost exclusively.

The presence in European cities of sizable African communities that maintain the practice—despite local laws that prohibit it—has brought female genital mutilation to the attention both of the courts and of feminists who see it as "butchery intended to control women" (Weil-Curiel 1993). Anthropologists who claim to be relativists face the ethical dilemma of whether their responsibility ends with describing the practice and placing it in a cultural context, whether they are obligated to protect the practice from outside interference, or whether they should help to end the practice. Relativism might suggest that they have a further responsibility to protect, or at least not interfere with, this culturally sanctioned practice. At the same time, as relativists, they must also consider their responsibility to cooperate with members of their own culture who are trying to end the practice on the grounds that human rights are being violated.

Although relativistic anthropologists are reluctant to try to alter the values of other cultures, many think it appropriate to try to correct mistaken factual beliefs when this would benefit the welfare of members of the culture. Value judgments that are based on mistaken factual beliefs may be revised without undermining the values themselves. Clearly some beliefs of cultures that practice genital mutilation are factually mistaken. Contrary to those who say the practice is beneficial to sanitation or health, mutilation causes severe medical damage in many cases. The operation can cause immediate infection, excessive bleeding, and even death. Delayed common effects of the operation are infections of the urinary tract, menstrual problems, painful intercourse, reduction in fertility, and complications in childbirth. Nor does the Muslim religion command infibulation, as some believe. The practice does not guarantee virginity, since reinfibulation, which simulates the virginal state, is widely practiced. Because sex drive is more a matter of endocrinology than external organs, the claim that infibulation limits sex drive is likewise questionable.

Insofar as genital mutilation is motivated by sanitary or medical considerations, therefore, knowledge of the facts would tend to undermine the practice without reducing the cultural commitment to the values of purity, fertility, or health. Insofar as genital mutilation is motivated by other factors, such as maintenance of cultural distinctiveness and increasing the ability to endure pain, its medical harm could be alleviated by practicing less severe forms of circumcision without infibulation and by performing the operation only in a sterile clinical setting.

Such a medical solution, while it would save lives and preserve health, does not address the ethical question, raised by feminists, of the right to control one's body and whether or to what extent this right is inalienable. Since genital mutilation is usually performed on children, an important issue is whether parents have the right to harm the child in this way. Parents and guardians cannot violate *inalienable* rights of their children even for some supposed benefit. Parents may, however, subject children to some kinds of discipline, as well as to dangerous and sometimes painful medical treatment, when it is for the good of the child. Erroneous views about the supposed benefits of genital mutilation, of course, cannot justify harming the child.

Unlike mistaken claims about the medical benefits of mutilation, other claims are apparently correct. Marriage within the culture as things now stand may not be an option for an uncircumcised woman. Moreover, for females in that culture, marriage is a prerequisite for obtaining any other rights. So being able to marry is a clear benefit and may outweigh the harm of circumcision from the point of view of the girl. (According to principles of justice, the benefit that justifies a harm must accrue to the individual who undergoes the harm, not merely to her extended family. Thus, loss of a bride price for the family would not, without further argument, justify the harm to the child.) Feminist anthropologists, as well as others who are concerned with human rights, want to take both educational and legal means to end the practice of genital mutilation. Their attitude, however, is not consistent with a commitment to ethical relativism....

Individual Rights and the Common Good

... In looking at the question of genital mutilation, the following pertinent questions arise. How fundamental is the right not to have one's body altered? At what age does the girl have the right to decide for herself whether to undergo a mutilation? Young girls in the Sudan who are not circumcised by their eighth year usually ask to have it done. Should we disregard these requests because the children are mere dupes of the culture? If they are, can they ever reach an age of consent? Many Western cultures practice ear piercing on infant girls, and many others accede to the wishes of six or eight year olds to have their ears pierced. Circumcision of male infants is common. Bodily mutilations are as much a part of cultural identity for some cultures as distinctive styles of clothing. Some mutilations we regard as attractive, some as beneficial to health, some as harmless, some as aesthetically offensive, others as brutal. Severe genital mutilation surely falls into the brutal category. Moreover, its rationale is empirically flawed, and because its harms disproportionately affect females, it raises serious questions about violating rights. In cases such as this, anthropological understanding of the practice can legitimately be used to aid attempts to eradicate or modify it for the benefit of the members of the culture where it is practiced. Those who disagree should at least argue for the practice on stronger grounds than the value of cultural diversity....

Anthropologists who work in cultures that withhold fundamental human rights from women, children, or any other subgroup face difficult choices about taking any *action* to restore rights. Some anthropologists would say that their decision to work in such cultures obligates them to alleviate the problem. Others hold that their role as anthropologists is to observe cultural phenomena and record and analyze them as accurately as possible, but not to try to alter conditions. In either case, the anthropologist has a minimal obligation to report the observed and analyzed state of affairs in normal anthropological outlets for publication. Anthropologists do not betray secrets or violate confidences when they describe a custom that is almost universally practiced in the culture. By calling attention to an unjust practice, however, anthropologists at least implicitly invite groups devoted to the protection of rights to take action. By presenting the offensive practice in its full cultural context, which may involve revealing its latent functions in addition to its manifest or stated functions, anthropologists also provide valuable information about how to control or prevent the practice.

After the anthropologist acts to present information in an appropriate way to a suitable audience, his or her responsibility to try to alleviate the injustice seems to me neither greater nor less than that of any person who is in a position to help the victims of an unjust practice. Even if no further action is taken, I think that the anthropologist who refuses to recognize that the value of cultural diversity is morally subordinate to that of protecting rights is on shaky moral ground. The anthropologist who retreats into ethical relativism in such situations, as did the ethnologist at the trial of Bintou Fofana Diana, does not demonstrate tolerance by appealing to social pressures in another culture but instead risks being committed to the same morally untenable position as the "Nazi defense."

Conclusion

I have reiterated some criticisms of ethical relativism, a position which once seemed to offer anthropologists a way to profess tolerance and avoid criticizing the morality of some practices of other cultures. My arguments try to show not so much that ethical relativism is "false" but that its consequences conflict with our deepest held moral intuitions and that it cannot be held consistently while embracing those intuitions. I have tried to show also that anthropologists need not forego tolerance if they abandon relativism in favor of a morality based on principles of justice and fairness. The concern with justice that guides anthropologists' codes of professional conduct can provide the starting point for a more sophisticated analysis of rights, which can be used to analyze cultural practices. (The philosophical literature on rights is vast, but a useful entry for anthropologists is available in Baker 1994.) Ethical judgments of another culture's practices, especially when based on deep understanding of their life, customs, and tradition, are indicative neither of ethnocentrism nor of intolerance. Instead, they show respect for the basic anthroplogical belief in "the psychic unity of humans" and a commitment to justice and fairness for all.

References

Baker, J., ed., 1994, Group Rights, Toronto: University of Toronto Press.

Berlin, B., and P. Kay, 1969, Basic Color Terms: Their Universality and Evolution. Berkeley and Los Angeles: University of California Press.

Bernard, H. R., 1998, Research Methods in Cultural Anthropology. Newbury Park, N.J.: Sage Publications.

D'Andrade, R., 1995, Moral Models in Anthropology. Current Anthropology 36(3):399–408.

Kenyatta, J., 1938, Facing Mount Kenya. London: Secker and Warburg.

Lightfoot-Klein, H., 1989, Prisoners of Ritual: An Odyssey into Female Genital Circumcision in Africa. Binghampton, N.Y.: Haworth Press.

Scheper-Hughes, N., 1995, The Primacy of the Ethical. Current Anthropology 36(3):409–20.

Turnbull, C., 1962, The Forest People. New York: Simon and Schuster.

Weil-Curiel, L., 1993, Mutilation of Girls' Genitals: Ethnic Gulf in French Court. New York Times, November 23.

Elliott P. Skinner

Female Circumcision in Africa: The Dialectics of Equality

Culture and society must, of course, always take account of human bi-ology, but they do so in complex ways. The distinctive characteristics of culture is that it transcends nature; but this does not mean that it has left it behind—rather, it has turned it upside down.

— Robert F. Murphy (1977)

Female circumcision or clitoridectomy, called by the Mossi, the *Bongo*, is [a] not too subtle mechanism of Mossi women to challenge the superiority of men. This was the thought that flashed through my mind, as I watched with amazement, the quiet pride of the women and girls performing the rituals of the graduation ceremonies of their own Bongo. Here were women doing things that they usually never did, and more importantly, should not have been doing. They had procured the drums from men and, much to my surprise and their amusement, were beating them. Where had they learned? Oh yes! They must have practiced these rhythms while pounding millet and sorghum in their mortars. Inexplicable was the source of their knowledge of the songs and dances of the Bongo which were allegedly the sole province of males, but which they performed equally well. True, I had learned both the dances and songs of the Bongo during my numerous visits to the circumcision lodge, but these female graduates did them better than I ever did. Surely some Delilah had tricked a Samson who had then revealed the secrets of arrogant men. During the Bongo ceremony, Mossi women were showing to the men publicly, that they knew male secrets, and moreover, these were not important after all....

The subject of male circumcision and female clitoridectomy and infibulation in African societies has been the source of great speculation and controversy, primarily because it involves the "fundamental ontological differences between the sexes—conditions of simple *being*—based in the first instance on anatomical distinctions" and what flows from these. Questions raised have been: 1. Are these operations cruel? 2. Do they have anything to do with sex? 3. Do they reveal anything about the relative merits of various cultures' sexual sensibilities? and 4. Do male and female versions of the operations differ with

From Elliott P. Skinner, "Female Circumcision in Africa: The Dialectics of Equality," in Richard R. Randolph, David M. Schneider, and May N. Diaz, eds., *Dialectics and Gender: Anthropological Approaches* (Westview Press, 1988). Copyright © 1988 by Elliott P. Skinner. Notes and some references omitted.

regard to the answers to questions 1 and 2? Some anthropologists and some non-anthropologists have already strong views on these questions.

Fran P. Hosken discussing "Genital Mutilation in Africa," severely criticized those "Anthropologists (mostly men) who have studied African traditions have done no service to women by utterly disregarding women's health while they attribute 'cultural values' to such damaging traditions as excision and infibulation." Considering these practices "deleterious to health and indeed dangerous," Hosken lamented that many African groups "subject their female children to genital mutilation for a multitude of 'reasons,' many of which conflict and all of which are based on total ignorance concerning reproduction." She wondered aloud whether it was really in the interest of such populations "that such damaging myths are perpetuated under the cloak of silence and are praised as 'culture' in the literature? I think not. The time has come to face the facts." (Hoskin 1976:6) Hosken is tired of, and angry about those "explanations" of men and of what she calls "brain-washed women" who attribute clitoridectomy "to the fear of female sexuality," and the need to "prevent adultery." (Ibid.)

Simon D. Messing, an applied anthropologist, feels that he and his colleagues "cannot evade the issue of such a serious and widespread problem as genital mutilation of females, if they are concerned with public health ... they should not leave the burden of this task entirely on the shoulders of radical feminists—and the latter in turn should welcome our cooperation." (Messing 1980:296)

Neither the radical feminists nor the anthropologists have considered the possibility that in the frequent dialectics that we find in social life, female circumcision might well be one of the numerous ways in which women challenge the vaunted superiority of men....

Given the contemporary controversy surrounding "female" circumcision (really an interesting misnomer), it is generally ignored that circumcision is predominantly a "male" ritual. Many well-known ancient peoples, such as the Hebrews (who probably adopted this ritual in ancient Egypt as they borrowed other interesting aspects of that culture) limited circumcision to males. The same thing is true for many African populations. As far as I can ascertain, there is not a single African society in which female circumcision exists without its male counterpart. The reasons for this are as intriguing as they are germane to this article....

Initiation ceremonies preparatory to marriage, sexual relations, and the creation of families, are widespread in African societies, but are not necessarily linked to either circumcision or clitoridectomy.... Characteristic of this *rite de passage* is the customary withdrawal of the initiates from the world of people; their education into the knowledge and lore of their societies; and their subjection to a great deal of physical pain and other hardships....

The Mossi initiated and subjected their pre-pubescent youth to both circumcision and clitoridectomy. In the Manga-Nobere districts of Burkina Faso (formerly Upper Volta) in southern Mossi country, every three or four years, during December, the coldest part of the year, and depending upon the food supply, the Mossi opened the "Bongo" or the initiation ceremony for boys, in a secluded area in the woods. Here were gathered about twenty to thirty boys, age seven or eight to twelve years old, from the surrounding villages and their helpers. Known as Bankousse, these youths built a camp called the *Keogo*, placing barriers on the paths leading to it so as to warn off uncircumcised children and women. The mothers of the boys brought food daily to the barrier, but did not cross it.

The Mossi considered circumcision to be a simple surgical act which was only incidental to the Bongo—a veritable initiation to life involving a great many hardships. Almost immediately after arriving at the Keogo the boys were circumcised by the head of the camp, known as the *Nane* who used a sharp razor for the operation. As in other parts of Africa, the initiates were not expected to cry, and their wounds were cared for by the Nane. Then came the important post operation period called *komtogo* or "bitter water" by the Bankousse because of the pain involved. Despite the cold nights, they had use of only a small fire and were not permitted to use any covers. Every morning they were forced to bathe in a cold pool, and when they returned, they had lessons to learn involving history, nature study, and life.

The Bongo had its own mystery language whose words turned out on analysis to be synonyms for ordinary More (the language of the Mossi) with the prefix "na." The camp had its own rules on which rank was based, not on those on the outside, but on the order in which the youths were circumcised. What the Nane attempted to do was to forge a link between the boys in opposition to himself, who acted like a veritable ogre. Walking about the camp with a long stick, he whipped the youngsters into line, threw sand in the food brought by the women, and made the Bankousse dance and sing until they were exhausted.

Graduation ceremonies of the Bongo involved going into the woods, cutting grass for the horses of the chiefs, and wood for their fires. Then on the appointed day, the mothers brought new clothes for their sons, hoping that none of them had died during the ordeal of the Bongo. Then on the appointed day the graduates dressed in their new clothing marched through the market place, and visited the chief. Then they engaged in dancing and singing at a public place just outside the market place.

As usual in almost all parts of Africa, the Mossi women were in complete charge of their Bongo from which they excluded all men. Their *Keogo* was not in the woods, but was in the compound of a woman who lived by herself. But as usual for males, I could find out nothing about the nature of the excision that took place. I did hear the drumming and singing that took place there all night until the wee hours of the morning, and did observe the young girls going backward and forward to their homes. Invariably they carried a tufted staff, said to have been given to them by their prospective husbands. The women would say nothing about the symbolism involved, considering the information specific to women alone. The most that they would say about what went on in the female Bongo was that the males have their secrets and so did the women.

Like the graduation exercises of the male Bankousse, the female ritual was a village-wide affair, but strictly within the province of the women. Market days before, the relatives and prospective husbands of the graduates, shopped for the clothes and headties, and makeup for them. Then on the day of the exercise, the young girls went to the home of the female Nane and accompanied by their mothers and sisters who were beating drums and singing, went to the village square where the Bankousse danced and sang the traditional airs of the Bongo. From time to time, male relatives and husbands would detach themselves from the line of spectators and approach the dancers, giving them presents of money. To all intents and purposes, the female Bongo was structurally and functionally quite similar to that of the males. This ceremony demonstrated to all that the Mossi women were just as capable as the men in performing an initiation ceremony whose function was to transform girls into women, as the male version transformed boys into men. Moreover, they had more effectively kept men from knowing their secrets than did the males, whose secrets they had obviously shared....

What is important about the puberty rituals in African societies, whether they involved painful initiation, and whether they involved genital mutilation with recognizable pain, are the emic and etic features involved. The Africans do have their own views of their rituals even though others have ignored these views and insist upon their own interpretations. This is perhaps par for human beings involving as it does relative power. There is no doubt that had they the requisite power, Africans would insist that the world accept their interpretation of their own rituals, as well as their views of the rituals of others. Anthropologists would do well to keep this in mind.

The Mossi are not much given to speculating on the imponderables of social life, or the world in general, judging such ratiocinations quixotic. To them the Bongo for men and for women have the same meaning and serve the same function for both men and women: preparation for marriage and rearing families. Indicative of this equality is that the two genders control their own initiation rituals, even though women have to borrow drums from the males. When badgered about the sexual features involved in genital mutilation, an admittedly chauvinist Mossi male might suggest that since females are inferior to males they are not permitted to touch the male organ during sexual congress, and that clitoridectomy makes sexual congress easier. This may be as good a rationalization as any other, but flies in the face of the anxiety of Mossi men over the conduct of their wives, and their stated axiom: "Women are so important that if a man receives as a wife, either a blind woman or a leper, he should close his eyes, close his mouth, and close his ears, and keep her."

The equally male chauvinist Dogon explicitly associate both circumcision and clitoridectomy with elaborate myths concerning creation and cosmology. Both operations are said to have been instituted as punishments and are indicative of the incomplete state of human beings resulting from the primordial crime of a godling. There is the removal of the opposite sex complement with which all human beings were originally intended to be equipped. Thus for the Dogon there is complementarity in the operation. Mary Daly criticizes the Dogon for what she considered an emic patriarchal obfuscation of the true purposes of the operation, namely the intimidation and humiliation of women. What she conveniently ignores is the fact that the Dogon forbid men to have intercourse with their wives against their will and that the sexual responses of wives are in large part conditioned by the treatment they generally receive from their husbands (Daly 1978).

Somewhat like the Dogon, both the Egyptians and the Northern Sudanese stress the complementarity of circumcision and clitoridectomy. Referring specifically to the Sudanese, [Janice] Boddy asserted that

> Through their own operation, performed at roughly the same age as when girls are circumcised (sic) (between five and ten years), boys become less like women: while the female reproductive organs are covered, that of the male is uncovered, or, as one Sudanese author states, of a child's sex ... by removing physical characteristics deemed appropriate to his or her opposite: the clitoris and other external genitalia, in the case of females, the prepuce of the penis, in the case of males. This last is emphasized by a custom now lapsed in Hofriyat wherein one of the newly circumcised boys' grandmothers would wear his foreskin as a ring on the day of the operation (Boddy 1982:687–8).

Paying special attention to the widespread African emic notion of complementarity in the rituals of circumcision and clitoridectomy, Boddy insists that

> By removing their external genitalia, women are not so much preventing their own sexual pleasure (though obviously this is an effect) as enhancing their femininity. Circumcision as a symbolic act brings sharply into focus the fertility potential of women by dramatically de-emphasizing their inherent sexuality. By insisting on circumcision for their daughters, women assert their social indispensibility, an importance that is not as the sexual partners of their husbands, nor in this highly segregated, male-authoritative society, as their servants, sexual or otherwise, but as the mothers of men. *The ultimate social goal of a woman is to become, with her husband, the cofounder of a lineage section. As a respected haboba she is "listened to," she may be sent on the* hadj *(pilgrimage to Mecca) by her husbands or her sons, and her name is remembered in village genealogies for several generations* (italics supplied) (*Ibid.*:687).

Although Boddy had her own etic views of female genital mutilation among the Sudanese, her ethnographic data support the etic argument of this paper, namely that in this instance of the dialectics of social life, clitoridectomy rather than a ritual performed by women, to demean their already low status in many African societies, is a declaration of equality. What is interesting is that there are few, if any, cases in the ethnographic record where African women (as contrasted to the normally sexist African men) see this ritual as reducing their status. Feminists may consider the African women who defend this practice as "brain-washed," but should be aware that many African women, as well as men, take the same jaundiced view of many rituals of Western Christendom. True, some contemporary African women object to clitoridectomy, but few had dared to confront their mothers and grandmothers over the issue for fear of being taken for "black" white women. The implication here is that these women have failed to assert that cultural equality for which Africans have fought long and hard.

What is important about the controversy about clitoridectomy in Africa is that African women were never part of it. The issue grew out of a Judeo-Christian concern over human sexuality, involved Christian missionaries in Africa, and was used by African men in their struggle for cultural autonomy from Europeans, and ultimately for political independence....

Missionary opposition to clitoridectomy among the Kikuyu was very much linked to their opposition to all aspects of African culture that could frustrate their attempts to impose Western Christendom. We are told that

> The missionaries recognized the significance of the initiatory rites, of which circumcision was the outward physical symbol, and they were appalled at what they saw in them. The physical operation they considered brutal and unhygenic and in the case of girls a barbaric mutilation with permanent ill-effects. *But the atmosphere in which the ceremonies were carried out seemed to them even more evil, with what they took to be the sexual linnuendo of the dances and songs, the licentiousness of the old men and women and the gloating cruelty of the operators and their attendants. They taught against the practices and prayed that the people might forego them altogether* (Italics added) (Murray–Brown 1972:50–51).

... What had started out as an issue over clitoridectomy, and a practice which many African Christians were prepared to change, became a cause c´el'ebre over the issue of African cultural and political freedom. Much to the alarm of the colonial government, it became known locally in October 1919 that "John [Jomo] Kenyatta" who had gone to Britain to protest settler colonialism, had been to Moscow and was "in close touch with Communists and Communist Organizations." Songs praising Kenyatta and ridiculing the governor were outlawed as seditious, creating anger among anti-mission Kikuyu....

The problem now was that clitoridectomy had become inextricably linked to the Kikuyu desire for equality in their homeland. The missionaries were insisting that Kenyatta "should tell his people to obey government officers, Kikuyu chiefs, and missions in control of schools...."

Kenyatta's subsequent defense of clitoridectomy as an operation in which the operator had "the dexterity of a Harley Street surgeon ... with a stroke she cuts off the tip of the clitoris ... the girl hardly feels any pain" (Jomo Kenyatta 1962) is only understandable in light of the role that clitoridectomy had played in the drive of the Kikuyu to achieve equality for their institutions in the face of Europe's arrogance. Like Bob Murphy, Kenyatta was very aware of the dialectics of social life. For him colonial tutelage was oppressive and alien. He wrote:

> In our opinion, the African can only advance to a 'higher level' if he is free to express himself, to organize economically, politically, socially, and to take part in the government of his own country. In this way he will be able to develop his creative mind, initiative, and personality, which hitherto have been hindered by the multiplicity of incomprehensible laws and ordinances (*Ibid.*:192).

What the conflict over clitoridectomy did was to bring to "an abrupt close the paternalistic phase of missionary activity; henceforth the emphasis would be on the growth of native churches. The high noon of imperialism ... [and the attempt] to extend white dominion over all of East Africa, was over." (*Ibid.*:151)

Kenyatta has been pilloried by many female scholars and feminists, for defending a practice (which he was prepared to see abolished), in the greater interest of political equality for Africans. Few noted, as did Harriet Lyons, that Kenyatta had suggested, perhaps as an after thought, that clitoridectomy may have been practiced to prevent masturbation, a practice condemned in both Kikuyu boys and girls, and that his major emphasis was "largely on social structure." (1981:510) Moreover, he was fully prepared to use education to abolish it. A more intemperate view of Kenyatta's action is that of Fran Hosken who declared that

> An international feminist observer cannot help but wonder why the male African leadership does not speak out about the mutilation of women, a custom that was reinforced by Kenyatta in Kenya and is also supported by the independence movement under his leadership.... It clearly affects the status of women in political affairs (Hosken 1976:6).

Understandably, there are some African feminists who agree with Hosken. Nevertheless, it should be noted that "the resistance of African feminists to anti-clitoridectomy agitation—evident at the United Nations World Conference on women held in Copenhagen in 1980" accords fully with the demand of Kenyatta for African cultural autonomy. Like him, these women realize that African practices must be brought into line with those characteristics of the emerging global civilization. What they insist upon is respect, and the end of European arrogance.

The problem with blaming Kenyatta and other African men for clitoridectomy misses the important point that African women have always been in control of this ritual (until now when male doctors may perform it in modern hospitals), and probably used it, to declare their equality with men. Faced with discrimination for not possessing those characteristics with which dominant social strata have linked their dominance, African women, like other women, and subordinate groups, have striven to acquire the traits viewed as valuable. These practices vary cross-culturally in time and space, and can be as different as Japanese females surgically operating on their eyes to approximate those of American males during the occupation of their country; to certain American females bobbing their noses; other Americans bleaching or darkening their skins; and still others dressing like males, and creating female counterparts of such organizations as Masonic lodges, veteran groups, and institutions of higher learning. In many of these cases, the males or dominant groups whose characteristics were being imitated, were not aware of the attempts to achieve equality with them, or to win their favor. That they were responsible for the behavior in the first place may well have been true, but a dialectician like Robert Murphy, whose eyes were probably opened by his wife, Yolanda, would smile at the irony of it all.

References

Boddy, Janice, 1982. "Womb as oasis: the symbolic context of Pharaonic circumcision in rural Northern Sudan," *American Ethnology*, 9: 682–698.

Daly, Mary, 1978. *Gyn/Ecology: The Metaethics of Radical Feminism*, Boston: Beacon Press.

Hosken, Fran P., 1976. "Genital Mutilation of Women in Africa." *Munger Africana Library Notes*, #36, October, p. 6.

Kenyatta, Jomo, 1962. *Facing Mount Kenya*, New York, Vintage Brooks.

Lyons, Harriet, 1981. "Anthropologists, moralities, and relativities: the problem of genital mutilations." *Canadian Review of Sociology and Anthropology,* 18: 499–518.

Messing, Simon D., 1980. "The Problem of 'Operations Based on Custom' in Applied Anthropology: The Challenge of the Hosken Report on Genital and Sexual Mutilations of Females." *Human Organizations*, Vol. 39, No. 3, p. 296.

Murphy, Robert F., 1977. "Man's Culture and Woman's Nature," *Annals of the New York Academy of Sciences.* Vol. 293, 15–24.

Murray-Brown, Jeremy, 1980. *Kenyatta.* London, George Allen & Unwin Ltd.

POSTSCRIPT

Should Anthropologists Work to Eliminate the Practice of Female Circumcision?

The issue of female circumcision raises important questions about whether or not there are limits to cultural relativism. Critics of cultural relativism have often pointed to the Nazi atrocities during the Second World War as examples of immoral practices that can be understood in culturally relative terms but should not be condoned. Cultural relativists in such cases counter that unlike male or female circumcision in Africa, genocide was never morally acceptable in German society.

At issue here is whether or not an unhealthy practice should be suppressed because it is unhealthy. If anthropologists work to abolish female circumcision, should they also work to prohibit use of alcohol, tobacco, and recreational drugs in our own society because such products are unhealthy? Are there limits beyond which cultural relativism has no power? If anthropologists and international organizations are right to stop female circumcision, would they also be justified in working to abolish male circumcision in Jewish and Muslim communities on the same grounds?

Without dealing directly with issues of cultural and moral relativism, Skinner argues that anthropologists should take seriously the concerns of both African men and women, the majority of whom want to continue to practice clitoridectomy and resent Western attempts to suppress the practice. For another view from a similar perspective, see Eric Winkel's essay "A Muslim Perspective on Female Circumcision," *Women & Health* (vol. 23, 1995).

Many books and articles urge abolition of female circumcision, which most refer to as female genital mutilation. A lengthy bibliography can be found at http://www.fgmnetwork.org/reference/biblio.html. A typical example is Anke van der Kwaak's "Female Circumcision and Gender Identity: A Questionable Alliance?" *Social Science and Medicine* (vol. 35, 1992).

For anthropological discussions of female circumcision and cultural relativism, see Harriet Lyons's "Anthropologists, Moralities, and Relativities: The Problem of Genital Mutilations," *Canadian Review of Sociology and Anthropology* (vol. 18, 1981) (which influenced Skinner), Carole Nagengast's "Women, Minorities, and Indigenous Peoples: Universalism and Cultural Relativity," *Journal of Anthropological Research* (vol. 53, 1997), and Ellen Gruenbaum's *The Female Circumcision Controversy: An Anthropological Perspective* (University of Pennsylvania Press, 2001).

For a discussion of issues dealing with cultural relativism and anthropological ethics, see *Ethics and the Profession of Anthropology,* Carolyn Fluehr-Lobban, ed. (University of Pennsylvania Press, 1991).

Contributors to This Volume

EDITORS

ROBERT L. WELSCH is a visiting professor of anthropology at Dartmouth College and adjunct curator of anthropology at The Field Museum in Chicago. He received a B.A. in anthropology from Northwestern University in 1972, an M.A. in anthropology from the University of Washington in 1976, and a Ph.D. from the same department in 1982. He has conducted field research among the Ningerum people of Papua New Guinea, the Mandar people of South Sulawesi, Indonesia, and the diverse peoples of the Sepik Coast of Papua New Guinea. He is the author of *An American Anthropologist in Melanesia* (University of Hawaii Press, 1998) and coeditor, with Michael O'Hanlon, of *Hunting the Gatherers: Ethnographic Collectors, Agents, and Agency in Melanesia* (Berghahn Publishers, 2000).

KIRK M. ENDICOTT is a professor of anthropology at Dartmouth College. He received a B.A. in anthropology from Reed College in 1965, a Ph.D. in anthropology from Harvard University in 1974, and a D.Phil. in social anthropology from the University of Oxford in 1976. He has repeatedly conducted field research among the Batek people of Malaysia. He is the author of *An Analysis of Malay Magic* (Clarendon Press, 1970) and *Batek Negrito Religion: The World-view and Rituals of a Hunting and Gathering People of Peninsular Malaysia* (Clarendon Press, 1979), and is coauthor, with Robert K. Dentan, Alberto G. Gomez, and M. Barry Hooker, of *Malaysia and the "Original People": A Case Study of the Impact of Development on Indigenous Peoples* (Allyn and Bacon, 1997).

STAFF

Larry Loeppke   Managing Editor
Jill Peter   Senior Developmental Editor
Nichole Altman   Developmental Editor
Lori Church   Permissions Coordinator
Beth Kundert   Production Manager
Jane Mohr   Project Manager
Kari Voss   Lead Typesetter
Luke David   eContent Coordinator

AUTHORS

LILA ABU-LUGHOD is a professor of anthropology and Middle Eastern studies at Harvard University. She has conducted research in Egypt about gender roles and modern media, and is the author of many books and journal articles, including *Veiled Sentiments: Honor and Poetry in a Bedouin Society* (University of California Press, 1986) and *Dramas of Nationhood: The Politics of Television in Egypt* (University of Chicago Press, 2005).

CHRISTOPH BRUMANN is an anthropologist at the University of Cologne, who has conducted research in Japan. He is the author of many journal articles on the anthropology of religion and theoretical topics in anthropology.

ROBERT L. CARNEIRO is a cultural anthropologist and a curator of anthropology at the American Museum of Natural History in New York. He has conducted field research in Brazil, Peru, and Venezuela, focusing on cultural evolution and political evolution. He is the author of many books and articles, including *Evolutionism in Cultural Anthropology: A Critical History* (Westview, 2003).

NAPOLEON A. CHAGNON is a professor emeritus of anthropology at the University of California at Santa Barbara. He is best known for his extended research over many years among the Yanomami Indians of Venezuela, about whom he has produced several ethnographic films and written many books, including *Yanomamö*, 5th ed. (Harcourt Brace, 1997).

JAMES CLIFFORD is a professor of the history of consciousness at the University of California at Santa Cruz. He has written many books and articles about postmodern anthropology, including *Routes: Travel and Translation in the Late Twentieth Century* (Harvard University Press, 1997).

VEENA DAS is a professor of anthropology at Johns Hopkins University. Her research has focused on issues of violence and suffering, especially in the Indian subcontinent. She has published many books, including *Critical Events: An Anthropological Perspective on Contemporary India* (Oxford University Press, 1995) and *Remaking a World: Violence, Suffering, and Recovery* (University of California Press, 2001), which she edited.

JAMES R. DENBOW is an associate professor of anthropology at the University of Texas at Austin. He has conducted field research in southern Africa and was curator of archaeology at The National Museum of Botswana. He has published many journal articles on southern Africa and Kalahari topics.

DENIS DUTTON is associate professor of art theory in the School of Fine Arts at the University of Canterbury at Christchurch, New Zealand. He is a specialist on aesthetics and tribal art and is the author of *The Forger's Art: Forgery and the Philosophy of Art* (University of California Press, 1983).

R. BRIAN FERGUSON is a professor of anthropology at Rutgers Univeristy. He has conducted field research in Puerto Rico and among the Yanomami in South America. He is author of many books and journal articles, including *Yanomami Warfare: A Political History* (School of American Research Press, 1995).

DEREK FREEMAN (1916–2001) was an emeritus professor of anthropology at the Research School of Pacific and Asian Studies at the Australian National University. He conducted field research among the Iban of Borneo and the Samoans of Western Samoa. He is the author of many books and articles, including *The Fateful Hoaxing of Margaret Mead* (Penguin, 1999).

ERIKA FRIEDL is a professor of anthropology at Western Michigan University. She is a specialist on the lives of women and children in Iran. She is the author of many books and articles, including *Children of Deh Koh: Young Life in an Iranian Village* (Syracuse University Press, 1997).

CLIFFORD GEERTZ is a professor at the Institute for Advanced Study in Princeton, New Jersey. He has conducted field research in Indonesia and Morocco. He is the author of many books, including *The Interpretation of Cultures: Selected Essays* (Basic Books, 1973) and *Works and Lives: The Anthropologist as Author* (Stanford University Press, 1988).

STEVEN GOLDBERG is a professor of sociology at City University of New York. He has written many books and journal articles, including *Why Men Rule: A Theory of Male Dominance* (Open Court, 1993).

EDWARD H. HAGEN is an anthropologist in the Institute for Theoretical Biology at Humboldt University in Berlin. His research has focused on evolutionary approaches to depression. He has published several articles about biosocial science and sociobiology.

ROBERT A. HAHN is an epidemiologist with the Centers for Disease Control and Prevention and an adjunct professor of anthropology at Emory University. He has published many articles and books on various topics in medical anthropology, including *Anthropology in Public Health: Bridging Differences in Culture and Society* (Oxford University Press, 1999).

KEN HALE (1934–2001) was an emeritus professor of linguistics at Massachusetts Institute of Technology. He has studied languages from most parts of the world and is the author of many books and articles, including *The Green Book of Language Revitalization Practice* (Academic, 2001), which he coedited with Leanne Hinton.

ELLEN RHOADS HOLMES has conducted field research in Samoa. She is coauthor, with her husband Lowell D. Holmes, of *Samoan Village: Then and Now* (Harcourt Brace, 1992) and *Other Cultures, Elder Years: An Introduction to Cultural Gerontology* (Sage, 1995).

LOWELL D. HOLMES is an emeritus professor of anthropology at Wichita State University. He has conducted field research in Samoa and in contemporary America. He is the author of many articles and books, including *Quest for the Real Samoa* (Bergin & Garvey, 1986).

SUDHIR KAKAR is widely known as the father of Indian psychoanalysis and has practiced for many years in New Delhi. He has been a visiting professor of psychology at the University of Chicago and is currently a senior fellow at the Center for the Study of World Religions at Harvard University. His books include *The Colors of Violence: Cultural Identities, Religion and Conflict* (University of Chicago Press, 1996).

ROGER M. KEESING (1935–1993) was a professor of anthropology at McGill University. He is best known for his research among the Kwaio people of Malaita in the Solomon Islands and published four books and many articles about them, including *Custom and Confrontation: The Kwaio Struggle for Cultural Autonomy* (University of Chicago Press, 1992).

PETER LADEFOGED is a professor of linguistics at the University of California at Los Angeles who specializes in the sound systems of the world's language. He has studied the sound systems of endangered languages around the world, and is author of many books and articles including *Vowels and Consonants: An Introduction to the Sounds of Languages* (Blackwell, 2004) and *The Sounds of the World's Languages* (Blackwell, 1996).

FREDERICK (FRITZ) P. LAMPE is the Lutheran chaplin at Syracuse University, where he is also affiliated with the department of anthropology. He spent four years as a Lutheran missionary and chaplin at the University of Technology (Unitech) in Lae, Papua New Guinea.

RICHARD B. LEE is a professor of anthropology and chair of the African Studies Programme at the University of Toronto. He is best known for his research among the San peoples of the Kalahari Desert. He is senior editor of *The Cambridge Encyclopedia of Hunters and Gatherers* (Cambridge University Press, 1999).

MARIA LEPOWSKY is a professor of anthropology at the University of Wisconsin. She has conducted field research in Papua, New Guinea and is the author of *Fruit of the Motherland: Gender in an Egalitarian Society* (Columbia University Press, 1993).

BETTY JEAN LIFTON is a therapist, freelance writer, and adoption rights advocate who has published widely on adoption in the United States. Her books include *Twice Born: Memoirs of an Adopted Daughter* (St. Martin's Press, 1998).

ROGER IVAR LOHMANN is a professor of anthropology at Trent University, Oshawa, Ontario. He conducted research concerning the anthropology of religion among the Asabano of Papua New Guinea. He was editor of *Dream Travelers: Sleep Experiences and Culture in the Western Pacific* (Palgrave Macmillan, 2003).

JOHN H. McWHORTER is a professor of linguistics at the University of California at Berkeley. His research has focused on creole and pidgin languages as well as dialect variations in North America. He is the author of many books, including *Doing Our Own Thing: The Degradation of Language and Music and Why We Should, Like, Care* (Gotham, 2003) and *Defining Creole* (Oxford University Press, 2005).

JUDITH MODELL is a professor of anthropology, history, and art at Carnegie Mellon University in Pittsburgh, Pennsylvania. Best known for her research on adoption, she has written many articles and books, including *A Sealed and Secret Kinship: Policies and Practices in American Adoption* (Berghahn Books, 2001).

ANTHONY OBERSCHALL is professor of sociology at the University of North Carolina at Chapel Hill. He has written many books and articles dealing with social conflict, including *Social Movements: Ideologies, Interests, and Identities* (Transaction Books, 1993).

PARVIN PAIDAR works in international development and is currently with UNIFEM in Afghanistan. Her research has focused on gender and social development in developing countries, especially on feminism and Islam in Iran. She is the author of *Women and the Political Process in Twentieth Century Iran* (Cambridge University Press, 1997).

MICHAEL E. PRICE is an anthropologist and postdoctoral fellow at the University of Indiana, formerly a graduate student at the University of California at Santa Barbara. He has published several articles about biosocial science and sociobiology.

FRANCIS ROBINSON is a professor of history at the University of London. His research has concentrated on Muslim history in the Indian subcontinent. He has published many books, including *Islam and Muslim History in South Asia* (Oxford University Press, 2000).

MERRILEE H. SALMON is a professor of the history and philosophy of science at the University of Pittsburgh. Her recent research concerns the philosophy of anthropology. She is the author of many books and articles, including *Philosophy and Archaeology* (Academic, 1982).

ELLIOTT P. SKINNER is an emeritus professor of anthropology at Columbia University. He has conducted fieldwork in Burkina Faso (Upper Volta), where he formerly served as United States ambassador. He is the author of many books and articles, including *The Mossi of Burkina Faso* (Waveland, 1990).

ERNIE SMITH is a professor of linguistics at the California State University at Fullerton. He was an early supporter of ebonics and has been a consultant to the Oakland School District's program on Standard English Proficiency. He has written many essays and articles about ebonics.

SANGUN SUWANLERT was a physician and psychiatrist at Srithunya Hospital in Nondhaburi, Thailand. His research has focused on the use of psychotropic drugs and other psychological phenomena in Thailand, about which he has published several articles in English.

JOHN TERRELL is curator of oceanic archaeology and ethnology at The Field Museum in Chicago. He has conducted extensive field research in Papua, New Guinea as well as in New Zealand, Tonga, Samoa, and Fiji. He has written numerous articles and books, including (with John P. Hart) *Darwin and Archaeology: A Handbook of Key Concepts* (Bergin and Garvey, 2002).

JOHN TOOBY is a professor of anthropology at the University of California at Santa Barbara (UCSB) and codirector of UCSB's Center for Evolutionary Psychology. He is a specialist on the evolution of hominid behavior and cognition. He is coeditor of *The Adapted Mind: Evolutionary Psychology and the Generation of Culture* (Oxford University Press, 1992).

HAUNANI-KAY TRASK is a professor of Hawaiian studies at the University of Hawai'i at Manoa. She is a well-known Native Hawaiian activist with Ka Lahui Hawai'i, one of several organizations advocating Native Hawaiian sovereignty. She is the author of *From a Native Daughter: Colonialism and Sovereignty in Hawai'i*, rev. ed. (University of Hawai'i Press, 1999).

TERENCE TURNER is a professor of anthropology at Cornell University. He is best known for his research among the Kayapo of the Amazon. His current research focuses on, among other topics, ethics and human rights. He has published many articles and book chapters about the Kayapo.

EDWIN N. WILMSEN is a research fellow at the University of Texas at Austin. He has conducted research in Botswana and is the author of *Land Filled With Flies: A Political Economy of the Kalahari* (University of Chicago Press, 1989).

Index

Papua New Guinea, natural-supernatural distinction in, 139–45
parents, birth, desire of adopted children to find, 150–66
pastoralists, hunter-gatherers as, 109–27
patriarchy, 179–83
perfection, in Islam, 260–62, 265
Peter Pan, 150
phii pob, 274–83
politics: and contemporary Pacific cultures, 78–79; and warfare: in Yanomami society, 229–30, 329–31; in Yugoslavia, 243–52
polygyny, in Yanomami society, 227–28
Polynesian culture, 77
Popper, Karl, 27, 38
post-modernism, and anthropology, 14–22
Post-Modernism and the Social Sciences (Rosenau), 17
poststructuralism, 314–17
power: gender and, 171–83; in Iran, 188–207; religion as, 204–5; resistance as, 199–202; work as, 202–4
Powers, Marla, 142
practice, in anthropology, 51
Pratt, Mary Louise, 51–52
prestige, conflict and, 217–20
Price, Michael E., on effects of research on Yanomami, 334–44
primordialist view, of ethnicity, 243

R
refusal, as tool of power, for women in Iran, 201–2
relativism, cultural and ethical, 361–77
religion: natural-supernatural distinction in, 131–45; as power, in Iran, 204–5
reproduction, in evolutionary theory, 212
reproductive effort, 213–16, 214
reproductive fitness, warfare and violence of Yanomami as effort to maximize, 212–31, 339–42
research, ethics of, 324–44
resistance, as power, in Iran, 199–202
rights, of individuals, versus the common good, 367–68
Robinson, Francis: critique of, 264–69; on Islam and Muslim history in South Asia, 257–63
Rockefeller Wing, of Metropolitan Museum, 304, 305
Roggeveen, Jacob, 43
Rose, Ronald, 42
Rosenau, Pauline, 17
Ryle, Gilbert, 5–6

S
Sahlins, Marshall, 58, 64–65
saint worship, in Islam, 259
Saler, Benson, 133

Salmon, Merrilee H., on cultural and ethical relativism, 361–69
Samoa, Margaret Mead's fieldwork in, 27–45
Samoa mo Samoa (Davidson), 31
San, as pastoralists, 109–27
Scandinavian nations, gender equality in, 181
science, humanism and, 14–17
scientific knowledge, 27–28
secrecy, adoption and, 150–51, 153
segregation, in Iranian schools, 206
self: concept of, in adopted children, 153, 155–56; and other, in anthropology, 49
Serbs, ethnic violence and, 243–52
sexual behavior, of Samoans, 33–34, 40–41
sexually egalitarian societies, 171–83
Shalako ceremony, 307
Shamatari, 223, 224, 228
Shi'i, and feminism, 189, 190–91
Sikh militancy, 237–41
Skinner, Elliott P., on female circumcision, 370–77
Smith, Andrew, 124
Smith, Dorothy, 53
Smith, Ernie, on Black English and Ebonics, 92–97
Smith, Jonathan Z., 144
Smith, Wilfred Cantwell, 266
Social Organization of Manu'a, 33
societies, sexually egalitarian, 171–83
sociobiology, application to humans, 343–44
Solomon Islands, contemporary native peoples in, 72
Solow, Robert, 12
somatic effort, 213, 214
South Asia, Islam and Muslim history in, 257–63
Spier, Leslie, 30
spirit beings, 134–35, 136–37
spirit possession: in India, 236; in Thailand, 274–83
Sranan language, 100–101
Steichen, Edward, 308–9
Stepan, Alfred, 244
Stephen, Michele, 134, 136, 137
Stevenson, Robert Louis, 31, 43
Strong, Isobel, 31–32
subversion, as tool of power, for women in Iran, 201
Sudanese people, and female circumcision, 374
suicide, as strategy of resistance, 199
supernatural-natural distinction, 131–45
superstructure, of Yanomami society, 230–31
survival, in evolutionary theory, 212
Suwanlert, Sangun, on spirit possession in Thailand, 274–83
Sweden, gender equality in, 181
symbolic system, culture as, 9–10
syndromes, culture-bound, 284–94

T
technology, introduction to Yanomami society, 224–25